MINDFUL LEADERS

A SELF-COACHING GUIDE & TOOLKIT

Laura Delizonna, PhD
&
Ted Anstedt, CEO

Copyright © 2015 by Laura Delizonna and Ted Anstedt.

All rights reserved. Printed in the United States of America. Except as permitted under the United States copyright Act of 1976, no part of this publication may be reproduced or distributed in any form or by any means, or stored in a database or retrieval system, without prior written permission of the authors. Requests for permission should be directed to Dr. Laura Delizonna: laura@choosinghappiness.com.

ISBN—13: 978-1511763288

ISBN—10: 1511763280

Dedication

I dedicate this book
to my father, who taught me to dream big dreams, and
to my mother, who taught me to have the audacity to actually go after them.
- Laura

I dedicate this book to Suzanne, the light of my life, who has collaborated with me on many a book, and who continues to be my greatest source of happiness.
- Ted

Acknowledgments

We deeply appreciate the contributions from our stellar teaching and research team:
Bernie Wong, Tiffany Chhay. and Andy Hyunh. Bernie, your leadership is exceptional.
A special thanks to Tiffany and Bernie for their contributions to this book.

Your efforts improve this workbook,
your enthusiasm adds spark to the process,
and your support elevates all of us.

Thank you!

We would also like to say thank you to the thousands of Stanford students and Silicon Valley professionals who have shared their stories and experiences about how they apply mindfulness, positive psychology, and the *Self-Coaching for Happiness® Process* to enhance their lives and careers.

Your stories of personal and professional transformation
continue to inspire us all.

TABLE OF CONTENTS

Prologue ix

INTRODUCTION: MINDFULNESS AND MINDFUL LEADERSHIP 1
    What is Mindfulness?
    What is Mindful Leadership?
    Some Qualities of Mindful Leaders
    Case Study: Observing Mindful Leadership—George C. Marshall, Secretary of State
        Exercise: Mindful Leadership Case Study Questions
        Mindful Leadership Self-Assessment
        Observing Mindful Leadership Worksheet & Tracking Log

PART ONE: THRIVING IN THE WORKPLACE

MINDFUL LEADERS HELP EMPLOYEES THRIVE 28
    Positive Psychology and Leadership
    ZAPPOS: A Company Built on PERMA
    The Business Case for Happiness in the Workplace

WHY DOES HAPPINESS CAUSE SUCCESS? 35
    Broaden and Build Effect of Positive Emotions
    Research—Positive Emotion in the Workplace
    Choice: The Key to Thriving
    Mindfulness Expands the Freedom to Choose
        Choices Worksheet & Tracking Log

NEUROSCIENCE AND MINDFUL LEADERSHIP 45
    The Triune Brain
    Increasing Mindful Leadership—High Road & Low Road Strategies
    The Middle Road—The Wise Mind of a Mindful Leader

MEDITATION—A LOW ROAD METHOD TO REWIRE THE BRAIN 48
    What is Meditation?
    Benefits of Meditation
    Research—Meditation, Neural Plasticity, and Wellbeing
    Meditation to Rewire Neural Circuitry
        Three Breaths Meditation Guide & Tracking Log

THE SCIENCE OF BECOMING AN EXPERT 59
    Self-Coaching Process—Assess, Plan, Practice, Track
    Additional Readings and Websites

Coaching Guidelines 65

PART TWO: LEARNING THE SKILLS OF MINDFUL LEADERSHIP

AWARENESS IN THE MOMENT

Introduction: Awareness in the Moment 71
    Case Study: Observing Mindful Leadership—John Wood, Room to Read
        Exercise: Mindful Leadership Case Study Questions

***Skill 1:* SHOW UP** 77
    Tune in to the Present
        Exercise: Mindful of a Moment
    Savor: Pause, Expand, Absorb
        Mindful of A Moment Worksheet & Tracking Log

Skill 2: LISTEN MINDFULLY..83
    Three Levels of Listening—Internal, Focused, Global
    Check Your Listening Style
    Signs of Mindless Listening
    How to Listen Mindfully
        Mindful Listening Worksheet & Tracking Log

Coaching Guidelines..93

POSITIVITY AND POSSIBILITY

Introduction: Positivity & Possibility..97
    Case Study: Observing Mindful Leadership—Howard Schultz, Starbucks
        Exercise: Mindful Leadership Case Study Questions

***Skill 3:* SHIFT TO POSITIVITY AND POSSIBILITY**..105
    Shift Your Focus
    The 3W's Technique
        3W's Worksheet & Tracking Log
    Positivity Meditation
        Positivity Meditation & Tracking Log

***Skill 4:* CREATE OPTIMISM**..115
    Why is Optimism Beneficial?
    Research on Optimism in the Workplace
    Fixed Mindsets—Roots of Pessimism
    Growth Mindsets—Roots of Optimism
    How to Create Optimism: Cultivate a Growth Mindset
    Best Possible Future Self
        Best Possible Future Self Journaling Worksheet
        How Can I Worksheet & Tracking Log
    Ideal Situation Meditation
        Ideal Situation Meditation & Tracking Log

Coaching Guidelines..129

POSITIVE RELATIONSHIPS

Introduction: Positive Relationships..133
    Case Study: Observing Mindful Leadership—Jeff Weiner, LinkedIn
        Exercise: Mindful Leadership Case Study Questions
    Relationship Positivity Ratio (5 to 1)
    Research—Positive Relationships in the Workplace

***Skill 5:* CULTIVATE EMPATHY**..142
    Consider Another's Individuality
    Consider Vulnerabilities
    Research on Empathy
        Empathy Worksheet & Tracking Log
    Just Like Me Meditation
        Just Like Me Meditation & Tracking Log

***Skill 6:* DEEP DIVE CONVERSATIONS**..157
    Craft Deep Dive Conversations
    Craft Win-Win Solutions
        Deep Dive Conversations Worksheet & Tracking Log
    Gift of Relationship Meditation
        Gift of Relationship Meditation Guide & Tracking Log

***Skill 7:* IDENTIFY CONFLICT ESCALATORS**..163
    Conflict Escalators—The Four Horsemen
        Conflict Escalators Worksheet & Tracking Log

Skill 8: **POSITIVE CONFLICT**..169
    The Key to Crafting Positive Conflict
    First, Do Your Homework
    How to Craft Positive Conflict
        Positive Conflict Worksheet & Tracking Log
    Being Kindness Meditation
        Being Kindness Meditation & Tracking Log

Coaching Guidelines..183

AUTHENTICITY & INTEGRITY

Introduction: Authenticity & Integrity..187
    Case Study: Observing Mindful Leadership—John Mackey, Whole Foods
        Exercise: Mindful Leadership Case Study Questions
    Finding Flow
        Exercise: A Flow Experience

Skill 9: **LEVERAGE STRENGTHS**...197
    A Strengths Perspective
    How to Leverage Your Strengths
        Personal Mentor Journaling Worksheet
        Personal Best Leadership Experience Journaling Worksheet
        Identify Core Strengths & Tracking Log
    Use Strengths in New Ways
        Use Strengths in New Ways Worksheet & Tracking Log
    Leverage Others' Strengths
        Leverage Others' Strengths & Tracking Log
    Moment of Strength Visualization
        Moment of Strength Visualization & Tracking Log

Skill 10: **ALIGN ACTIONS WITH VALUES**..225
    Do What Matters to You
    Research—Values in Action
        Values Assessment Worksheet
        Values Alignment Worksheet & Tracking Log
    Life Reflection Visualization
        Life Reflection Visualization & Tracking Log
    Values Journaling
        Values Journaling Worksheet

Skill 11: **ALIGN ACTIONS WITH PRIORITIES**..239
    How to Align Activities and Priorities: Life Buckets
        Life Buckets Worksheet
        Priorities Reality Check Tracking Log

Coaching Guidelines..245

MANAGE STRESS & ENERGY

Introduction: Manage Stress & Energy..249
    Case Study: Observing Mindful Leadership—Arianna Huffington, Huffington Post Media Group
        Exercise: Mindful Leadership Case Study Questions
    Information Processing Chain & Stress
    Research on Stress in the Workplace

Skill 12: **CHALLENGE THOUGHTS**..258
    Benefits of Challenging Thoughts
    Overcoming Mindlessness & Unconscious Bias
    How to Challenge Thoughts: The 3 C's Technique

3C'S Worksheet & Tracking Log
Neutralize Thoughts—An Alternate Strategy to Challenging
Leaves on a Stream Meditation
Leaves on a Stream Meditation & Tracking Log

Skill 13: IDENTIFY EMOTIONAL TRIGGERS 273
Emotional Equations
Examples—Anxiety, Anger, Sadness
Triggers & Reactions Chart
Emotional Triggers Worksheet & Tracking Log
Take a S.E.A.T. to Overcome Emotional Hijacking
Take a S.E.A.T Meditation & Tracking Log

Skill 14: MANAGE ENERGY 287
Build New Lifestyle Habits
Sleep Adequately
Sleep Tracking Log Tracking Log
Body Scan Meditation
Body Scan Meditation & Tracking Log
Eat Mindfully
Eat Mindfully Tracking Log
Move—Exercise Daily
Exercise Regularly Tracking Log
Meditate Daily
Meditate Daily Tracking Log

Coaching Guidelines 305

RESILIENCE

Introduction: Resilience 309
Case Study: Observing Mindful Leadership—Dr. Rhonda Cornum, Director of CSFP
Exercise: Mindful Leadership Case Study Questions

Skill 15: LET GO OF PERFECT 317
Pitfalls of Perfectionism
Roots of Perfectionism
How to Let Go of Perfect: Cultivate Satisfaction
Let Go of Perfect Worksheet & Tracking Log

Skill 16: TELL HERO STORIES 323
Hero Story Model: The Hero's Journey
How to Tell a Hero Story
Hero Story Worksheet & Heroic Acts Tracking Log
Resilience Meditation
Resilience Meditation & Tracking Log

Skill 17: SELF-COMPASSION 337
Three Components of Self-Compassion
Research on Self-Compassion
Guided Self Compassion Meditations
Four Steps to Self-Compassion
Self-Compassion Worksheet & Tracking Log
Self-Compassion Meditation
Self-Compassion Meditation & Tracking Log

Coaching Guidelines 351
Self-Assessment: Mindful Leadership

STANFORD SERIES: Positive Psychology and the Keys to Sustainable Happiness 355

PROLOGUE

For 15 years I have been training people from the boardroom to the classroom to attain greater happiness and success. This professional work, however, was born from my own desire to thrive. My quest began early one morning, twenty-five years ago.

I had dropped out of University of Southern California to go soul-searching. Atop Mount Sinai where Moses is said to have seen the Burning Bush, I watched the sun rise. Gazing over a sea of golden mountain peaks, sunrays bursting into the pink sky, I had an epiphany. In my mind's eye, I saw myself trudging through life as if carrying a backpack full of rocks. A voice inside me said, "You are supposed to be dancing through life."

As tears streamed down my face, I made a vow: I would find my way to happiness, and when I arrived, I would teach what I had learned to others. I sealed my decision with a stack of stones and descended from the mountain. My journey began.

I studied under the world's best scholars. My mentors included top scientists at Stanford, Harvard, and Boston University. I listened to whomever had a nugget of wisdom, which included many unlikely geniuses—a French carpenter, Buddhist monks, a quirky suburban housewife, taxi drivers, Maasai warriors, Silicon Valley business titans, an old cowboy at a campfire, and countless other seekers.

What I discovered was a greater truth: Happiness is a choice. It emerges from our choices in what we focus on and act upon. We choose happiness when we turn toward the positive and possible—when we choose gratitude over greed, kindness over criticism, humor over hostility, faith over fear, or service over selfishness. No matter what we face, our challenge is to find the magic or the mystery of life. Flat tires, soft heartbreaks, and bruised knees still happen. Integral to the journey, they invite us to live wholeheartedly, define who we are, and rediscover love.

After earning a PhD and specializing in positive psychology, I began creating this happiness program. I distilled my personal insights and applied cutting edge research from neuroscience, positive psychology, and mindfulness. While teaching at Stanford, I had the incredible fortune to meet Ted Anstedt. For the past six years he and I have partnered in the service of our shared vision. We aim to positively impact society. This collaboration has tremendous synergy due to our passion, complementary skill sets, and diverse professional experiences. We design and deliver programs that empower individuals and organizations to reach extraordinary heights.

This program represents the current state of our understanding of how people thrive. We are motivated by the belief that when enough people live their best life, humanity will hit a tipping point. The result will be an unimaginable transformation in the world.

May you thrive,
Laura Delizonna

Other books in the
Positive Psychology and the Keys to Happiness series:

Thrive: Self-Coaching for Happiness ® and Success

Enhancing Emotional Intelligence: Mindfulness-Based Strategies for Success & Happiness

Mindful: Science-Based Strategies to Thrive at Work and in Life

Please visit the website for more information:

ChoosingHappiness.com

INTRODUCTION

MINDFULNESS & MINDFUL LEADERSHIP

Mindfulness is a state of being fully present, aware of oneself and other people, and sensitive to one's reactions to stressful situations.

Leaders who are mindful tend to be more effective in understanding and relating to others, and motivating them toward shared goals.

Hence, they become more effective in leadership roles.

~ William F. George

INTRODUCTION

MINDFULNESS & MINDFUL LEADERSHIP

We create our experiences.
~ Ellen Langer, Harvard Professor

Mindful Leadership is about being aware in your everyday life and in your work. It is being more self-aware of what you are thinking, feeling and doing; more observant of what is going on around you; more focused on the positive and possible; more intentional about your emotions, feelings, thoughts, and behaviors; more observant of your impact on others; and more thoughtful about your relationship strategies.

Mindful Leadership enhances your ability to observe and shift the self-limiting mindsets and behaviors that can undermine personal and organizational effectiveness. Mindful Leadership increases optimal functioning through enhanced levels of presence, clarity, perspective, agility, and control.

The purpose of the *Mindful Leaders Self-Coaching Guide and Toolkit* is to assist you to develop and expand your skills as a mindful leader—to be more self-aware and agile in the moment, to increase your positivity and your possibility thinking, to be more capable in building effective relationships, to act with authenticity and integrity, to better manage your energy and stress, and to build resilience in yourself and others.

Our goal is to contribute to the development of mindful change makers who are better able to thrive in their personal and professional lives and who are effective, lead with compassion, and serve the greater good.

WHAT IS MINDFULNESS?

While mindfulness as a work related skill is growing in popularity, its definitions differ significantly. There is no universal definition of mindfulness. Our conceptualization of mindfulness blends traditional views and modern research perspectives.

We define mindfulness as an active mental state that emerges when one is open and receptive in the present moment, engaging in direct observation, and taking multiple perspectives.

MINDFULNESS
Mindfulness is an active mental state that emerges from:
1. Being open and receptive.
2. Direct Observation.
3. Taking multiple perspectives.

This "Langerian" definition of mindfulness is primarily based on Ellen Langer's conceptualization of mindfulness. Ellen Langer is a social psychologist at Harvard University who has studied mindfulness for over 40 years. She was the first tenured female professor at Harvard and has published many research articles in prestigious scientific journals and five books. She defines mindfulness as a state characterized by openness to new information, noticing new perspectives, and revising mindsets. Curiosity is a way to conceptualize this active mental state.

Mindful thinking refers to the ability to be curious and notice new things, take different perspectives in a situation, be objective, and consider multiple points-of-view.

1. Being Open and Receptive. Being open and receptive is the habit of tuning in and paying attention to what is happening in the present moment.

- Being present and aware in the moment.
- Noticing new information or aspects of a situation.
- Paying attention to changes.
- Being willing to consider alternatives.

2. Direct Observation. Direct observation is the habit of observing what is actually going on without bias or adding anything. It is simply noticing what is happening and collecting raw data like a good scientist. It is initially non-judgmental. That can come later. The goal of direct observation is to first see the situation as it is.

- Observing thoughts, emotions, behaviors, and the situation.
- Observing without bias, mental preconceptions, or other distorting mind frames.
- Observing and noticing from multiple points-of-view.
- Being non-judgmental.

3. Taking Multiple Perspectives. Taking multiple perspectives is the habit of seeing things from multiple points of view. It includes nurturing our natural curiosity, cultivating flexible mindsets, observing things from different angles, noticing different points of view, revising according to data collected.

- Considering from multiple points of view.
- Noticing new aspects of a situation.
- Considering micro and macro analyses; past, present, and future perspectives.
- Learning and growing
- Changing one's mind and conclusions
- Finding alternatives and hidden opportunities.
- Developing more complex understandings.
- Forming tentative rather than foregone conclusions.
- Being more intentional about one's feelings, thoughts, and behaviors.

Jon Kabat-Zinn Model Of Mindfulness. Jon Kabat-Zinn, Professor of Medicine at University of Massachusetts, has popularized a similar definition of mindfulness. He is credited as bringing the concept and practice of mindfulness to the medical world and beyond with his program called *Mindfulness-Based Stress Reduction*. This program has been highly researched, showing the strongest positive impact on reducing chronic pain and anxiety. His definition has roots in Buddhist philosophy. He defines mindfulness as a state that is characterized by:

- In the present moment
- Paying attention on purpose
- Non-judgmental

Our approach blends traditional (Kabat-Zinn) and modern (Langerian) views of mindfulness. These definitions are not contradictory. To eliminate confusion between the Kabat-Zinn and Langerian definitions, note the similarities:

LANGERIAN MINDFULNESS	KABAT-ZINN MINDFULNESS
1. Being Open and Receptive	1. In the present moment
2. Direct Observation	2. Paying attention on purpose
3. Taking multiple perspectives	3. Non-judgmental

The essence of mindfulness is flexibility and presence. Flexibility is a hallmark of optimal functioning. It leads to creativity, deep understanding, and ultimately to wisdom. Flexible thinking, compared to rigid thinking, increases possibilities because alternatives are considered. Increasing the range of interpretations for events may lead to more options for coping strategies and expand the repertoire of possible responses.

Change alone is unchanging. – Heraclitus

Change is a characteristic of every living environment. It is common, however, to approach situations as if they were unchanging. Ellen Langer posits that this occurs because individuals mistake the stability of their mindsets with stability in the environment. A static approach often leads to errors in judgment and ineffective actions, because it is more likely to be inconsistent with the realities of a given situation.

Prominent psychologists such as Ellen Langer as well as Carol Dweck at Stanford University demonstrate how rigid mindsets limit ability to succeed, undermine relationships, decrease confidence and ability to reach goals, create negative self-perceptions, and ultimately diminish happiness and well-being. When people are closed to the possibility that situations can be understood in a number of ways, they become more vulnerable to self-imposed limitations. Rigidity in thinking narrows the range of information that is processed, which diminishes the ability to exert control over circumstances. The way to avoid rigid mindsets is to cultivate the habit of noticing new aspects of situations, which produces mindful thinking.

This workbook focuses on cultivating mindfulness as a way of being, and as a powerful tool to use in daily life and an essential ability for effective leaders. We all have the natural ability to live in this state but few do. It takes practice.

Is Mindfulness A Trait, A State, Or Practice? Many people including professionals in the field confuse definitions of mindfulness, misusing the term and lacking precision in its use. The term mindfulness can refer to any of the following three domains:

(1) *A Practice*—techniques such as mindfulness meditation.

(2) *A State*—temporary psychological state.

(3) *A Trait*—a way of being.

In the popular media, the term mindfulness commonly refers to a technique, especially mindfulness meditation, or a state as in Jon Kabat-Zinn's definition.

The term "being mindful" commonly is used (and misused) in popular media and in yoga and meditation communities. For example, in yoga class the instructor might say, "Be mindful of your breath." or if you forget where you put your keys, you might say, "I wasn't being mindful and lost my keys." Typically, when people say this they are referring to the present-oriented focus or noticing. This present-oriented paying attention is only one of the three elements of our scientific definition of mindfulness.

Mindlessness. Initially, Langer studied the opposite of mindfulness, which is mindlessness. This line of research examined how we tend to get locked into mindsets and fail to revise them. Instead, we follow them like actors following a script.

Langer defines mindlessness as a state of mind characterized by rigid mindsets or lack of awareness in the present moment. After decades of research on mindlessness and mindfulness, Langer emphasizes that we have a tendency to "look but not see". When mindless, we stop noticing, learning, and asking questions. Her research suggests that mindlessness is the cause of problems, unhappiness, failures, accidents, and even poor health.

Often we lose curiosity with the familiar and predictable. This is natural because minds are designed to get easily accustomed to circumstances where change is slow or subtle. The problem, however, is that change is always happening whether we realize it or not. Without noticing changes, we fall under the illusion that there is nothing more to learn or gain; that we know all there is to know in a situation. When this happens the quality of our attention changes. We tune out. We become mindless. This is why Self-Awareness is a difficult competency to master. We can never be fully mindful of ourselves across domains in every moment and from every perspective. Thus, total self-awareness is impossible.

WHAT IS MINDFUL LEADERSHIP?

A Leader is someone inspires, guides, and empowers others in the service of a common goal or value. Whether you lead by example, supervise one person, manage a small team, or are an executive of a multi-national enterprise, you can be a leader. Everyone can be a leader to someone, and everyone can develop the ability to be aware and shift the self-limiting mindsets and behaviors that undermine personal and organizational effectiveness.

Mindful Leaders are mindful thinkers who take a leadership role. A Mindful Leader is someone who inspires, guides, and empowers others, and serves a greater good. Mindful Leaders are self-aware of what they are thinking, feeling and doing; more observant of what is going on around them; more focused on the positive and possible; more intentional about their emotions, feelings, thoughts, and behaviors; more observant of their impact on others; and more thoughtful about their relationship strategies.

MINDFUL LEADERSHIP

Mindful Leadership is about being aware in your everyday life and in your work.

It is being aware of what you are thinking, feeling and doing;

observant of what is going on around you;

focused on the positive and possible;

intentional about your emotions, feelings, thoughts, and behaviors;

observant of your impact on others;

and thoughtful about your relationship strategies.

Why Mindful Leadership? An estimated 60-80% of employees in the American workforce are actively disengaged or neutral, according to Gallup Surveys. Stress costs U.S. companies an estimated $300 billion per year. We can do better than that. Something is wrong with how we approach work and design the workplace. It is time to do something about it.

We need leaders who think about work differently—leaders who are grounded in reality and agile in response, prioritize building effective relationships, promote sustainable performance, and drive long-term business results. We need leaders who pay attention to what matters most and skillfully inspire, guide, and support employees to bring their best to work. We need mindful leaders. Mindful leaders are powerful leaders. They lead from the inside out—with self-awareness, positivity, authenticity, compassion, vision, and wisdom.

The Objective Of This Workbook. This workbook aims to provide you with a process and toolkit to unlock your potential to be a mindful leader. Mindfulness is a state of optimal functioning—characterized by clarity, presence, flexibility, and control. We all have the natural ability to live in this state but few do. It takes practice.

Whether you lead by example, manage a small team, or are an executive of a multi-national enterprise, this workbook provides tools to cultivate mindful leadership. These practical techniques are based on a modern view of mindfulness, including practices with and without meditation. They are developed from decades of research on mindfulness at Harvard University, as well as from the fields of positive psychology, neuroscience, organizational development, and sports psychology.

This workbook provides simple, straightforward tools for learning essential practices of mindful leadership, and will help you to:

- Step out of conditioned behaviors, unconscious biases, and reactivity.
- Improve decision-making and judgment.
- Maintain focus and clarity in the midst of high stakes challenges.
- See the bigger perspective.
- Direct positive conflict and orient others toward solutions.

According to Annie McKee and colleagues' research, in order to succeed at work people need:

- A sense that they can bring their whole person to work.
- A concrete vision for the organization linked to meaning with their day-to-day work duties.
- Good relationships in the work setting.

A mindful leader can create these conditions. They actively craft an environment where employees feel purpose-driven, connected to their colleagues, and secure enough to address their challenges and aspirations.

SOME QUALITIES OF MINDFUL LEADERS

The qualities of mindful leaders that we cover in this workbook relate to awareness, possibility thinking, positive relationships, authenticity and integrity, stress and energy management, and resilience.

SOME QUALITIES OF MINDFUL LEADERS

AWARENESS IN THE MOMENT
1. Show Up
2. Listen Mindfully

POSITIVITY & POSSIBILITY
3. Shift to Positivity & Possibility
4. Create Optimism

POSITIVE RELATIONSHIPS
5. Cultivate Empathy
6. Deep Dive Conversations
7. Identify Conflict Escalators
8. Positive Conflict

AUTHENTICITY & INTEGRITY
9. Leverage Strengths
10. Align Action with Values
11. Align Action with Priorities

MANAGE STRESS & ENERGY
12. Challenge Thoughts
13. Identify Emotional Triggers
14. Manage Energy

RESILIENCE
15. Let Go of Perfect
16. Tell Hero Stories
17. Self-Compassion

---

1. Awareness in the Moment. Mindful Leaders are self-aware of what they are thinking, feeling, and doing, and are aware of what is going on around them. They tune in to the present, to themselves, to their surroundings, and to others. They listen mindfully for information and for emotions and practice global listening. They focus first on determining what is real, before attempting to alter reality.

Self-Awareness refers to a range of abilities, including being able to detect and describe one's cognitive, affective, and physical states; recognizing broader patterns of functioning and responding; knowing sources of meaning, priorities, and values; and recognizing self-perceptions, viewpoints, strengths, and limitations. Self-Awareness emerges when we are mindful of ourselves across domains and on a moment-to-moment basis. It is the fundamental building block of emotional intelligence. It is a very difficult skill set to master, and we all have blind spots in our self-awareness.

2. Positive and Optimistic. Mindful Leaders are more focused on the positive and the possible than on the negative and impossible. They remain aware of the failures, the risks, the dangers, the realities, and the downsides, but they practice the discipline of thinking in terms of the positives, the opportunities, the probabilities, the options, and the alternatives. Mindful Leaders are aware of the power of positivity to broaden and build positive potential, to encourage novel thoughts and actions, and to inspire productivity and creativity in themselves and others.

Mindful Leaders pause to notice, consider, feel, and expand the positive circumstances and experiences they have. The habit of shifting to the good includes tuning in to the present, savoring moment-to-moment experiences, listening mindfully, appreciating positive daily situations, directing attention to what one wants to go well, having gratitude for the meaningful and positive circumstances in life, and reflecting on experiences and gifts in life.

3. Positive Relationships. Mindful Leaders are aware of the power and importance of positive relationships, put conscious time and effort into the development of positive networks, and cultivate empathy, deep dive conversations, and win-win solutions with others. They recognize that some positive conflict can be productive, but go out of their way to avoid negative conflict escalators that thwart communication and cooperation. They take charge of their emotions and responses and work hard to build community and engagement.

Mindful Leaders build connection and synergy for productivity and teamwork. Building positive relationships involves establishing positive emotional bonds and engaging in wise mind interactions. Feeling connected is a fundamental human need and a necessity in our modern, interdependent societies. Having connection sets the stage for friendship, collaboration, and bonding. In times of conflict, it engenders trust, understanding, mutual support, and respect. Expressing positive regard, communicating that we are "on the same team," and working toward a mutually beneficial outcome are some techniques used by Mindful Leaders for creating more positive relationships.

4. Authenticity and Integrity. Mindful Leaders are often respected for their authenticity and integrity. Their authenticity is reflected in the truthfulness of their intentions, behaviors, and commitments. Their integrity is reflected in their honesty, their strong moral principles, and their ability to live by those principles. Mindful Leaders are clear on their values and their priorities and make decisions and take actions based upon these values. They are aware of their strengths and look for ways to leverage their strengths in the pursuit of their goals and in the service of others.

Mindful leaders inspire others to act in the service of a common goal by reaching into their hearts, by tuning into their purpose, meaning, and reasons why their vision is of highest importance. They communicate this passion to others and touch them so deeply that the leader's reason for action then becomes the reason for others. The leaders' purpose, meaning, reasons and vision becomes their followers'.

5. Manage Stress & Energy. Mindful Leaders manage their energy and stress in order to maintain high levels of physical, mental, and emotional well-being. They challenge their thoughts to stay in touch with reality, they identify their emotions and emotional triggers and manage their responses, and they consciously monitor and manage their energy.

Mindful Leaders not only manage their own stress effectively to maintain peak mental and physical performance, they also monitor the stress levels of their colleagues and team members and help to create an environment that reduces stress and encourages high levels of energy and creativity. The goal is to waste as little energy as possible on reactivity and worry, and to direct emotional and physical energy toward goals, values, relationships, and tasks.

6. Resilience. Mindful leaders work to develop resilience—the capacity to recover from difficulties and adversity. They focus on the heroic rather than the debilitating aspects adversity; they let go of perfectionism and shortcomings and focus on the possible and potential; and they practice compassion and self-compassion.

Mindful Leaders develop resilience in themselves and others. Life's infernos leave some people buried in the ashes while others emerge flourishing. The secret is in how one responds. Hardships inevitably arise, so part of being prepared for them is building resilience before they happen. This serves like an emotional bank account that can be drawn upon during the hard times.

Essentially, resilience is having the capacity to acknowledge the difficulty and refocus on the positive and possible. This shift of perspective is profound and paves the way for recovering from adversity, for growth, and ultimately, for developing confidence in one's ability to manage the challenges that will inevitably arise. The goal of resilience is to thrive.

CASE STUDY: OBSERVING MINDFUL LEADERSHIP

GEORGE C. MARSHALL

5-Star General, Supreme Commander of the Armed Forces,
Secretary of State, Secretary of Defense
Winner of the Noble Peace Prize

Let's consider what the qualities of a mindful leader might look like in action at the highest levels of leadership and international diplomacy. We begin on December 10, 1953, and a man is awarded the *Noble Peace Prize*, an award that is given to someone who has "done the most or the best work for fraternity between nations." But this is no ordinary man or ordinary peacemaker. He is a warrior, a soldier, and a leader who commands other men in battle.

Why would a military man be awarded a peace prize?

The answer is an interesting one. The man is George C. Marshall, professional soldier, five-star general, Supreme Commander in WWII, and leader of over 10 million Americans in the ground and air forces from 1939 to 1945. He is also George C. Marshall, Secretary of State and architect of the European Recovery Act, known by posterity as the "Marshall Plan."

- Without Marshall's leadership as supreme commander in organizing America for war, and in managing both the European and Pacific Theaters, totalitarian powers might have ruled our planet.

- Without Marshall's efforts as Secretary of State and through the Marshal Plan to provide an economic plan and resources to restore economic prosperity and peace to the destroyed cities of both friends and former enemies, then the poverty, the despair, and the continued violence would have made our victory hollow and possibly led to another war.

George C. Marshall was a leader who achieved results on a large scale.

- Most leaders would be proud to have a career which included rising to the highest rank in the army, becoming the first five-star general in the history of America, commanding all the forces in nine theaters of war in WWII with men like Eisenhower and McArthur reporting directly to him, and for being honored as *Man of the Year* on the cover of Time in 1943 for his war time contributions.

- However, in his "retirement years" Marshall served as the president's Special Envoy and Ambassador to China, as the Secretary of State, as the Secretary of Defense, as the President of the Red Cross, and was once again honored as *Man of the Year* on the cover of Time in 1947, this time for his peace-time contributions. A few years later, he received the *Noble Peace Prize*, the only professional soldier to ever receive this honor.

Throughout his career, George Marshall demonstrated many of the qualities of mindful leadership, and we can learn much from his example about mindful leadership practiced on a global scale.

---

1. Awareness in the Moment. *Mindful Leaders are self-aware of what they are thinking, feeling, and doing, and are aware of what is going on around them. They tune in to the present, to themselves, to their surroundings, and to others. They listen mindfully for information and for emotions and practice global listening. They focus first on determining what is real, before attempting to alter reality.*

Marshall was known for being aware of what was going on with himself, the people and the situations around him. He was a realist and was respected for his ability to honestly assess situations and people.

Early in his career, Marshal demonstrated his life-long ability to tune in to the present. In World War I, he recognized the appalling state of unpreparedness, and, at the risk of his career, was candid in reporting it to his superiors. Instead of resulting in his dismissal, his focus on reality, as well as his passion, insight, and candor resulted in his promotion to Chief of Operations.

Marshall was a mindful listener. As Assistant to General John J. Pershing in WW I, he tuned in to the complexities of the personalities of the leaders of the American, French, and Italian forces. He practiced global listening and was able to understand the interpersonal dynamics as well as the facts of the complex situation.

He was put in charge of coordinating the first major American battles, and he was instrumental in the planning, coordination, and implementation of two back-to-back offensives—the Saint-Mihiel salient offensive and the far greater Meuse-Argonne Offensive. His challenge included removing 220,000 French and Italian soldiers and their equipment from the front lines, and simultaneously moving in some 600,000 U.S. and French troops, their supplies, and their equipment on the same constricted roads, all in total secrecy. The success of this offensive contributed to the defeat of The German Army on the Western Front, and contributed to the reputation of Marshall as a brilliant tactician.

Marshall could use his global listening insights to help others grasp the bigger picture. Before World War II, he once again was aware of the appalling state of unpreparedness of the U.S., and was not only candid in reporting it to his superiors, but appeared many times before an isolationist Congress to deliver his unpopular message. Because of his clear grasp of reality, he was not only able to help convince Congress to implement the first peace-time draft in history, but was able to get them to extend the one year commitment of the one million draftees in 1941, just months before the surprise attack on Pearl Harbor.

Marshall required others to focus on the reality of the present. He required his subordinates to be aware not just of successes, but of the realities of how success is accomplished. He often used his influence as well as his talents as a teacher to insure that officers studied the first six months of a war when there is chaos and confusions, when arms and men are lacking, and when there is little direction or strategy, instead of the closing phases when supplies, troops, and plans are plentiful.

He encouraged his leaders to be aware of their strengths and weakness, to think for themselves, and to keep their plans simple and grounded in reality.

---

2. Positive and Optimistic. *Mindful Leaders are more focused on the positive and the possible than on the negative and impossible. They remain aware of the failures, the risks, the dangers, the realities, and the downsides, but they practice the discipline of thinking in terms of the positives, the opportunities, the probabilities, the options, and the alternatives. Mindful Leaders are aware of the power of positivity to broaden and build positive potential, to encourage novel thoughts and actions, and to inspire productivity and creativity in themselves and others.*

Marshall was known for being both a realist and an optimist. He was respected for his ability to honestly assess the downsides of situations and the weaknesses of the people around him, as well as for seeing the upsides and the strengths, and for finding solutions to overwhelming problems. Because of his access to top-secret information in both WWI and WWII, Marshall was perhaps more aware of the realities, the risks, the downsides, and the impossibilities than any man in the country. But, he consistently looked for the upside, the options, and the possibilities, and then more often than not, figured out a way to turn the impossible into the possible.

Marshall could look at the impossible and see the possibilities. He took over as Chief of Staff on the same day that Hitler invaded Poland. Hitler had been preparing for all-out war for over a decade, and the U.S. was woefully unprepared. As Chief of Staff and the chief military advisor to President Franklin D. Roosevelt, Marshall started with a seemingly impossible task.

Marshall focused not on the impossibilities, but on the question: *How can I* achieve what needs to be done? In a few years he built the US Armed Forces from less than 175,000 in 1939 to over 8,500,000 by the end of the war. His optimism and incredible organization skill helped expand a small, homeland defense force—smaller than Bulgaria's—into the mightiest army ever assembled.

Marshall knew the power of positivity and optimism for the men under his command and placed a great emphasis on morale. With a civilian army, he knew morale was of the utmost importance and knew that the men would need all the encouragement they could get. He said, *"Morale wins the victory because it provides courage and hope, confidence and loyalty."*

Marshall was so aware of the power of positivity that he would remove a general if they were not positive. In the new army, in which millions of citizens were temporary soldiers, he knew that respect for leadership, rather than fear, was the best motivator.

Like many mindful leaders in Silicon Valley today, Marshall was aware of the power of a positive environment on morale. In mid-1941 he convinced Congress to grant him a contingency fund of $25 million to be used to circumvent the army's cumbersome financial procedures in morale-related expenditures.

As Chief of Staff, he made numerous visits to his troops and made lists of items that needed correction. He was aware that little things make a difference and shortages of shoes, blankets, hospital supplies, and laundry facilities were targeted for immediate action. He established Post Exchanges to keep up with the troops overseas. He directed that hot Thanksgiving turkey dinners be supplied to all troops even in the front lines.

Marshall knew the power of reinforcing positive results with positive rewards. In WW I, Marshall saw the power of immediate feedback and recognition on morale. He insisted that the value of medals and battlefield promotions lay in prompt recognition as a model of leadership and valor for all to see. He changed the military policy of delaying awards to one of immediate recognition.

During WW II, he pressured a reluctant President to add various new awards for soldiers, which included the Good Conduct Medal, the Bronze Star, the infantryman's badges, and the theater ribbons. Marshall hated war and felt the war was a terrible thing, but he was realistic about its existence, and focused on acknowledging the positive results achieved by the men whose heroic actions were called upon to win the victories.

---

3. Positive Relationships. *Mindful Leaders are aware of the power and importance of positive relationships, put conscious time and effort into the development of positive networks, and cultivate empathy, deep dive conversations, and win-win solutions with others. They recognize that some positive conflict can be productive, but go out of their way to avoid negative conflict escalators that thwart communication and cooperation. They take charge of their emotions and responses and work hard to build community and engagement.*

Marshall had a reputation for being a shrewd judge of character and capability, for being candid and fair in his relations with others, and for being loyal. He was known for his high standards, self-control, fairness, exceptional patriotism, and profound humility—traits that instilled tremendous loyalty in others.

Marshall built an enormous network of positive relationships. As Assistant Commandant of the Infantry School at Fort Benning, he personally trained over 150 future generals including Bradley, Ridgeway, Patton, Stillwell, and others. He trained hundreds more that became field grade officers. They became known as "Marshall Men." He nurtured these relationships and kept a careful record of those officers he considered to be most capable, and called on many of them during WWII.

Marshall respected the power of positive conflict and speaking truth to power. When Marshall first met President Roosevelt, he attended a meeting with a number of FDR's close advisors. The president outlined a plan for building floods of airplanes to fight the war in Europe. FDR then asked everyone in the room if they agreed. Everyone said yes, except Marshall. FDR turned to Marshall and said, "George, don't you agree?"

To the shock of FDR and everyone in the room, Marshall said, "No, Mr. President, I don't." Marshall went on to systematically point out all of the logistical problems with the plan—problems the President had not considered. After the meeting the people in attendance said goodbye to Marshall thinking his days in Washington were numbered. However, FDR, recognized Marshall valuable insights and his integrity, and Marshall soon became one of FDR's most trusted advisors.

4. Authenticity and Integrity. Mindful Leaders are often respected for their authenticity and integrity. Their authenticity is reflected in the truthfulness of their intentions, behaviors, and commitments. Their integrity is reflected in their honesty, their strong moral principles, and their ability to live by those principles. Mindful Leaders are clear on their values and their priorities and make decisions and take actions based upon these values. They are aware of their strengths and look for ways to leverage their strengths in the pursuit of their goals and in the service of others.

Marshall was known and respected for his authenticity. His intention was to serve his country, his commitment was to the people and actions that would best serve his country, and his behavior consistently demonstrated his intention and commitment. On December 3, 1942, on the occasion of Marshall's birthday, Henry L. Stinson, Secretary of War said of Marshall, "You are one of the most selfless public officials that I have ever met."

Marshall was also known and respected for his integrity. Not only was he highly respected by the Armed Services, by the people of the United States, by the heads of the Western European powers, and by the president of the United States, but he was also respected by an extremely politicized Congress.

Under President Franklin Roosevelt, Marshall's integrity often carried more weight with Congress than the power of the presidency. He appeared forty-eight times before various House and Senate committees between the summer of 1939 and the autumn of 1941. Whereas proposals from the President were often criticized as manipulative and partisan, almost anything suggested or supported by Marshall came to be seen as in the national interest.

Secretary of the Treasury, Henry Morgenthau, once advised President Roosevelt: "Let General Marshall, and only General Marshall, do all the testifying in connection with the Bill you are about to send up for additional appropriations for the Army."

Under President Harry Truman, Marshall's integrity once again often carried more weight with Congress than that of the President. Marshall had only one day of retirement from the Army, before President Harry Truman asked him to come back to work for his country. Both men shared the same philosophy of public service. Truman wrote: "The objective is the thing, not personal aggrandizement," which was consistent with Marshall's own philosophy of public service. For Truman, Marshall was " a tower of strength and common sense," and he also lent Truman's democratic administration a quantity of prestige, particularly with a Republican congress.

Once, when an aide suggested that the multibillion-dollar *European Recovery Act* be named after the President, Truman wisely said that Congress would never accept anything less than the "Marshall Plan."

House Speaker Sam Rayburn once explained why General Marshall had so much influence and respect from Congress.

"When General Marshall takes the witness stand to testify, we forget whether we are Republicans or Democrats. We know we are in the presence of a man who is telling the truth about the problem he is discussing."

5. Manage Energy & Stress. *Mindful Leaders manage their energy and stress in order to maintain high levels of physical, mental, and emotional well-being. They challenge their thoughts to stay in touch with reality, they identify their emotions and emotional triggers and manage their responses, and they consciously monitor and manage their energy.*

Marshall learned early in his career the importance of physical, mental, and emotional stamina. When working in the Philippines in 1913, overwork and stress brought him to the edge of a nervous breakdown. He said, "I woke to the fact that I was working myself to death." He vowed that from that time on he would "relax as completely as I could, and manage in a pleasurable fashion."

Marshall set rigid emotional and physical standards for himself. He told his wife, "I cannot afford the luxury of sentiment—that is for others. I cannot allow myself to get angry for it is too exhausting. My brain must remain clear at all times."

Marshall also set rigid physical and emotional standards for others. When Marshall faced the difficult task of forcing the retirement of hundreds of officers who had advanced through the outdated seniority system between the wars, one of the major standards that he used was their physical, mental, and emotional energy.

Marshall said, "Leadership in the field depends on strong physical stamina, the ability to withstand hardship and lack of sleep, yet have enough energy to command and dominate men on the battlefield."

Marshall made it a point to teach others to manage their stress and energy. He often advised important subordinates who were overworking to manage their stress and energy more intentionally because "your physical collapse would make you useless to your country and to me."

Marshall made a point of renewing his energy through exercise, relaxation, time in nature, and time with his wife. He rode horses and played tennis on a regular basis. He would take walks with his wife, spend time in nature, and during the stressful war years would often meet his wife with a picnic basket at the end of the day and go rowing on the Potomac River.

---

6. Resilience. *Mindful leaders work to develop resilience—the capacity to recover from difficulties and adversity. They focus on the heroic rather than the debilitating aspects of adversity; they let go of perfectionism and shortcomings and focus on the possible and potential; and they practice compassion and self-compassion.*

Marshall learned the importance of resilience early in his life. He was a poor student and his father thought of him as a failure. He wanted to go to Virginia Military Institute, but his father did not think he was up to the difficult military and academic standards. Marshall was discouraged, but managed to convince his mother that he was up to the challenge. Marshall went on to VMI and graduated as First Captain, the highest military honor at VMI.

Marshall was an expert at turning adversity into opportunity. When he was serving in the Philippines, he broke his ankle, which confined him to quarters and severely restricted his ability to lead in the field. However, Marshall turned this adversity into an opportunity. He used his convalescence time to help the local Inspector General clear up the paperwork of the demobilized Army. Marshall later recalled, "I became quite an expert on papers. It helped me a great deal in later years."

Marshall set very high standards for himself, but he learned how to let go of perfectionism. In the mid 1930's, Marshall was discouraged with his slow progress of promotion in the Army and came very close to resigning his commission. However, he refocused on the possible and potential, and within a few short years of rapid promotion over the heads of many of his contemporaries, he became the first 5-star general in the Army.

Marshall knew how to practice the art of self-compassion. In spite of his enormous success, he sometimes became the focal point of public criticism. The most disgraceful instance happened during the post-war era of McCarthyism. Joseph R. McCarthy, Republican Senator from the state of Wisconsin, made a name for himself by fueling cold war tensions and fears of the threat of communism. He went so far as to accuse Marshall of being a traitor to his country and being a communist sympathizer. This initially caused Marshall a great deal of personal pain, but he practiced self-compassion, and refused to dignify McCarthy's attacks with a defense of any kind. Marshall continued to do his job, serve his country, and soon regained his full stature as an American hero and patriot. It was McCarthy who went down in American history as the demagogue and fraud.

A MINDFUL LEADER OPERATING ON A WORLD STAGE IN WAR AND PEACE

Winston Churchill wrote a tribute to George C. Marshall will sums up the amazing scope of his leadership:

"During my long and close association with successive American administration, there are few men whose qualities of mind and character have impressed me so deeply. He was a great American, wise in war, understanding in counsel, resolute in action.

In peace he was the architect who planned the restoration of the battered European economy. He always fought victoriously against defeatism, discouragement and disillusion. Succeeding generations must not forget his achievements and his example."

Historians often compare George C. Marshall to George Washington. They both commanded American Armies that started out poorly prepared but ended up with victory. They both resigned from their military duties after the end of hostilities, and both were called back to serve their countries in even more important service. Both were brilliant leaders in war and peace, and both served their country with unselfish patriotism. Both were mindful leaders.

Footnote: The information on George C. Marshall and quotes used in this case study can be found in the following sources:
• *George C. Marshall Soldier-Statesman of the American Century* by Mark A. Stoler. Twayne Publishers, 1989.
• *General of the Army George C. Marshall The George Washington of the 20th Century* by LTC David Saltman, AUS (Ret), Officer Review/December 1995.
• Forest C. Pogue's Four Volume Biography of George C. Marshall.
• *George Marshall: Soldier and Statesman* Video, George C. Marshall Foundation, 2013.
• YouTube. *Soldier and Statesman* (Part 2)
• Special thanks to Marshall scholar, Suzanne Oldfield, for helping us to navigate through the source material, and providing many insights into the mindful leadership of George C. Marshall.

EXERCISE: MINDFUL LEADERSHIP CASE STUDY QUESTIONS

One of the ways to build a better understanding of the skills of mindful leadership is through role models who demonstrate the skills of mindful leadership in their actions. In the *Observing Mindful Leadership Case Studies*, we examine the accomplishments, the actions, the statements, and sometimes the thoughts and emotions of well-known leaders. The cases can help us to see a diversity of mindful leaders operating in many different types of environments, and help us to see how different leaders and different personalities practice the skills of mindful leadership. Use the following questions to help you to better understand this mindful leader.

---

1. AWARENESS IN THE MOMENT. Mindful Leaders are self-aware of what they are thinking, feeling, and doing, and are aware of what is going on around them. They tune in to the present, to themselves, to their surroundings, and to others. They listen mindfully for information and for emotions and practice global listening. They focus first on determining what is real, before attempting to alter reality.

What can you observe from the writings, statements, and actions of the leader in this case study that demonstrate the skills of awareness in the moment?

_____
_____
_____
_____
_____
_____
_____
_____
_____

2. POSITIVITY & POSSIBILITY. Mindful Leaders are more focused on the positive and the possible than on the negative and impossible. They remain aware of the failures, the risks, the dangers, the realities, and the downsides, but they practice the discipline of thinking in terms of the positives, the opportunities, the probabilities, the options, and the alternatives. Mindful Leaders are aware of the power of positivity to broaden and build positive potential, to encourage novel thoughts and actions, and to inspire productivity and creativity in themselves and others.

What can you observe from the writings, statements, and actions of the leader in this case study that demonstrate the skills of positivity and possibility?

_____
_____
_____
_____
_____
_____
_____
_____

3. POSITIVE RELATIONSHIPS. Mindful Leaders are aware of the power and importance of positive relationships, put conscious time and effort into the development of positive networks, and cultivate empathy, deep dive conversations, and win-win solutions with others. They recognize that some positive conflict can be productive, but go out of their way to avoid negative conflict escalators that thwart communication and cooperation. They take charge of their emotions and responses and work hard to build community and engagement.

What can you observe from the writings, statements, and actions of the leader in this case study that demonstrate the skills of positive relationships?

_____

_____

_____

_____

4. AUTHENTICITY & INTEGRITY. Mindful Leaders are often respected for their authenticity and integrity. Their authenticity is reflected in the truthfulness of their intentions, behaviors, and commitments. Their integrity is reflected in their honesty, their strong moral principles, and their ability to live by those principles. Mindful Leaders are clear on their values and their priorities and make decisions and take actions based upon these values. They are aware of their strengths and look for ways to leverage their strengths in the pursuit of their goals and in the service of others.

What can you observe from the writings, statements, and actions of the leader in this case study that demonstrate the skills of authenticity and integrity?

_____

_____

_____

_____

5. MANAGE STRESS & ENERGY. Mindful Leaders manage their energy and stress in order to maintain high levels of physical, mental, and emotional well-being. They challenge their thoughts to stay in touch with reality, they identify their emotions and emotional triggers and manage their responses, and they consciously monitor and manage their energy.

What can you observe from the writings, statements, and actions of the leader in this case study that demonstrate the skills of manage stress and energy?

_____

_____

_____

_____

6. RESILIENCE. Mindful leaders work to develop resilience—the capacity to recover from difficulties and adversity. They focus on the heroic rather than the debilitating aspects adversity; they let go of perfectionism and shortcomings and focus on the possible and potential; and they practice compassion and self-compassion.

What can you observe from the writings, statements, and actions of the leader in this case study that demonstrate the skills of resilience?

_____

_____

_____

_____

MINDFUL LEADERSHIP SELF-ASSESSMENT

NAME: _____ DATE: _____

Mindful Leadership is about being aware in your everyday life and in your work. It is being more self-aware of what you are thinking, feeling and doing; more observant of what is going on around you; more focused on the positive and possible; more intentional about your emotions, feelings, thoughts, and behaviors; more observant of your impact on others; and more thoughtful about your relationship strategies. This informal self-assessment tool is designed to assist you to become more familiar with the qualities of mindful leadership. It can also provide you with a way to measure your progress in developing the qualities of mindful leadership.

Instructions: Below is a collection of statements about your everyday use of mindful leadership skills. Using the 1-7 scale below, please indicate how frequently or infrequently you currently use the skill. Please answer according to what your are really doing rather than what you think you should be doing. This will help you get a more accurate current assessment. Please treat each item separately from every other item.

RATING SCALE

1	2	3	4	5	6	7
Never	Almost Never	Very Infrequently	Somewhat Infrequently	Somewhat Frequently	Very Frequently	Almost Always

AWARENESS IN THE MOMENT

#	Statement	Rating
1.	I am self-aware of what I am thinking, feeling, and doing.	1 2 3 4 5 6 7
2.	I am aware of what is going on around me.	1 2 3 4 5 6 7
3.	I tune in to the present, and can eliminate mental chatter.	1 2 3 4 5 6 7
4.	I tune in to others without being distracted.	1 2 3 4 5 6 7
5.	I take time to savor the moment and my experiences.	1 2 3 4 5 6 7
6.	I listen for information and for emotions.	1 2 3 4 5 6 7
7.	I practice global listening.	1 2 3 4 5 6 7
6.	I find out what are the real facts before I make judgments.	1 2 3 4 5 6 7

POSITIVITY & POSSIBILITY

#	Statement	Rating
7.	I focus more on the positive than on the negative.	1 2 3 4 5 6 7
8.	I focus on the possible rather than the impossible.	1 2 3 4 5 6 7
9.	I look for risks, dangers, and downsides, but practice the discipline of thinking in terms of the probabilities, options, and opportunities.	1 2 3 4 5 6 7
10.	I use positivity and positive emotions to broaden and build my awareness and to encourage novel thoughts and actions.	1 2 3 4 5 6 7
11.	I challenge my fears and stimulate productive planning by asking myself: HOW can I?	1 2 3 4 5 6 7

POSITIVE RELATIONSHIPS

#	Statement	Rating
12.	I am aware of the power and importance of positive relationships.	1 2 3 4 5 6 7
13.	I endeavor to make personal and professional connections with others.	1 2 3 4 5 6 7
14.	I put conscious time and effort into development of positive networks.	1 2 3 4 5 6 7
15.	I cultivate my ability to understand the feelings of another.	1 2 3 4 5 6 7

#		Rating
16.	I engage in deep conversations with others.	1 2 3 4 5 6 7
17.	I look for ways to craft win-win solutions with others.	1 2 3 4 5 6 7
18.	I strive to avoid negative conflict escalators (criticism, defensiveness, stonewalling, contempt) that thwart communication and cooperation.	1 2 3 4 5 6 7
19.	I attempt to direct disagreement and conflict toward positive outcomes that build on the insights gained from the conflict.	1 2 3 4 5 6 7

AUTHENTICITY & INTEGRITY

#		Rating
20.	My behaviors are consistent with my intentions and my commitments.	1 2 3 4 5 6 7
21.	I have strong moral principles and I live by those principles.	1 2 3 4 5 6 7
22.	I am clear on my values and my behaviors are consistent with my values.	1 2 3 4 5 6 7
23.	I am clear on my priorities and my behaviors are consistent with my priorities.	1 2 3 4 5 6 7
24.	I am aware of my strengths and weaknesses.	1 2 3 4 5 6 7
25.	I deliberately organize my work to leverage my strengths.	1 2 3 4 5 6 7
26.	I am aware of the strengths and weaknesses of my associates and team members.	1 2 3 4 5 6 7
27.	I deliberately look for ways to leverage the strengths of my associates and team members.	1 2 3 4 5 6 7

MANAGE STRESS & ENERGY

#		Rating
28.	I purposely manage my stress and energy in order to maintain high levels of physical, mental, and emotional well-being.	1 2 3 4 5 6 7
29.	I consciously monitor and manage my stress.	1 2 3 4 5 6 7
30.	I consciously monitor and manage my energy.	1 2 3 4 5 6 7
31.	I use healthy techniques to manage my stress and use them every day.	1 2 3 4 5 6 7
32.	I challenge my thoughts to stay in touch with reality and reduce stress.	1 2 3 4 5 6 7
33.	I Identify my emotions and emotional triggers, and intentionally manage my responses.	1 2 3 4 5 6 7

RESILIENCE

#		Rating
34.	I let go of perfectionism and cultivate satisfaction.	1 2 3 4 5 6 7
35.	I focus on positives and potential rather than shortcomings and failures.	1 2 3 4 5 6 7
36.	I focus on the heroic aspects of dealing with the adversities and setbacks in my life.	1 2 3 4 5 6 7
37.	I practice compassion for others.	1 2 3 4 5 6 7
38.	I practice self-compassion for myself.	1 2 3 4 5 6 7

OBSERVING MINDFUL LEADERSHIP WORKSHEET

A Mindful Leader is someone who inspires, guides, and empowers others, and serves a greater good. Mindful Leaders are self-aware of what they are thinking, feeling and doing; more observant of what is going on around them; more focused on the positive and possible; more intentional about their emotions, feelings, thoughts, and behaviors; more observant of their impact on others; and more thoughtful about their relationship strategies. Mindful Leaders have the ability to confront and shift the self-limiting mindsets and behaviors that undermine personal and organizational effectiveness.

The purpose of this worksheet is to help you to build your awareness of mindful leadership by observing examples of mindful leadership in life and in work. Look for examples in your self and in others. Observe how mindful leadership impacts your productivity and your relationships with your colleagues. Think about the benefits of mindful leadership for a business, its employees, its leaders, its customers, and its shareholders. Jot down your thoughts.

SOME QUALITIES OF MINDFUL LEADERS		
AWARENESS IN THE PRESENT 1. Show Up 2. Listen Mindfully	**POSITIVE RELATIONSHIPS** 5. Cultivate Empathy 6. Deep Dive Conversations 7. Identify Conflict Escalators 8. Positive Conflict	**MANAGE STRESS & ENERGY** 12. Challenge Thoughts 13. Identify Emotional Triggers 14. Manage Energy
POSITIVITY & POSSIBILITY 3. Shift to Positivity & Possibility 4. Create Optimism	**AUTHENTICITY & INTEGRITY** 9. Leverage Strengths 10. Align Action with Values 11. Align Action with Priorities	**RESILIENCE** 15. Let Go of Perfect 16. Tell Hero Stories 17. Self-Compassion

OBSERVING MINDFUL LEADERSHIP IN ACTION

1. A FAMOUS MINDFUL LEADER. Think of a high-profile mindful leader that you admire in the business community. What are some of the qualities that you recognize as mindful leadership?

_____
_____
_____
_____
_____
_____
_____

2. A MINDFUL LEADER IN YOU WORKPLACE. Think of a mindful leader that you admire in your workplace. What are some of the qualities that you recognize as mindful leadership?

_____
_____
_____
_____
_____
_____
_____

3. YOUR MINDFUL LEADERSHIP. Think about your own thoughts, feelings, and behaviors in your workplace. What are some of the qualities that you recognize as mindful leadership?

_____
_____
_____
_____
_____
_____
_____
_____

4. BENEFITS OF MINDFUL LEADERSHIP. What are some benefits of mindful leadership that you have seen or could imagine?

_____
_____
_____
_____
_____
_____
_____
_____

5. THRIVING IN THE WORKPLACE. How can a mindful leader contribute to creating a thriving workplace? What are some examples, how have you seen this, or how do you imagine this could happen?

_____
_____
_____
_____
_____
_____

6. OBSTACLES. What are some common obstacles mindful leaders face when aiming to create a thriving workplace?

_____
_____
_____
_____
_____
_____
_____

OBSERVING MINDFUL LEADERSHIP TRACKING LOG

The purpose of this *Tracking Log* is to help you to build your awareness of mindful leadership by observing examples of mindful leadership in life and in work. For the next seven days look for examples of mindful leadership in your self and in others. Observe how mindful leadership impacts your productivity and your relationships with your colleagues. Observe the impact of mindful leadership on your workplace, other members of your team, your supervisors, your customers. Record at least one example each day.

SOME QUALITIES OF MINDFUL LEADERS		
AWARENESS IN THE PRESENT 1. Show Up 2. Listen Mindfully	**POSITIVE RELATIONSHIPS** 5. Cultivate Empathy 6. Deep Dive Conversations 7. Identify Conflict Escalators 8. Positive Conflict	**MANAGE STRESS & ENERGY** 12. Challenge Thoughts 13. Identify Emotional Triggers 14. Manage Energy
POSITIVITY & POSSIBILITY 3. Shift to Positivity & Possibility 4. Create Optimism	**AUTHENTICITY & INTEGRITY** 9. Leverage Strengths 10. Align Action with Values 11. Align Action with Priorities	**RESILIENCE** 15. Let Go of Perfect 16. Tell Hero Stories 17. Self-Compassion

DAY	**APPLICATION** What example of mindful leadership did I observe?	**IMPACT** What was the impact on me, others, or the situation?
Day 1		
Day 2		
Day 3		
Day 4		

OBSERVING MINDFUL LEADERSHIP TRACKING LOG

DAY	APPLICATION What example of mindful leadership did I observe?	IMPACT What was the impact on me, others, or my situation?
Day 5		
Day 6		
Day 7		

INSIGHTS—What patterns or benefits emerged?

_____
_____
_____
_____
_____

PART ONE

THRIVING IN THE WORKPLACE

*My mission in life is not merely to survive,
but to thrive; and to do so with some passion, some
compassion, some humor, and some style.*

~ Maya Angelou

THRIVING IN THE WORKPLACE

*Rethink Your Success Mindset: Times are getting tougher.
We need tougher mindsets to ensure that we go beyond survive to thrive.*
~ Tony Dovale

Thrive means to prosper, to flourish, to grow or develop well or vigorously. The idea of thriving in the workplace is one that has great appeal since most of us spend a good portion of our waking hours at work. In her book entitled, *Thrive: The Third Metric to Redefining Success and Creating a Live of Well-Being, Wisdom, and Wonder,* Arianna Huffington contends that our notion of success in life and business should not be limited to money and power. She asserts that business needs a third metric of success, one that goes beyond the two metrics of money and power. The metric that she suggests is thriving which consists of well-being, wisdom, wonder, and giving.

There is a growing body of research and evidence that indicates that this third metric can pay huge dividends to individuals and organizations in the form of increased productivity, profitability, employee and customer satisfaction, and happiness.

THRIVING IN THE WORKPLACE PREVIEW

MINDFUL LEADERS HELP EMPLOYEES THRIVE
    Positive Psychology and Leadership
    ZAPPOS: A Company Built on PERMA
    The Business Case for Happiness in the Workplace
    Research on Mindfulness and Its Benefits

WHY DOES HAPPINESS CAUSE SUCCESS?
    Broaden and Build Effect of Positive Emotions
    Research—Positive Emotion in the Workplace
    Choice: The Key to Thriving
    Mindfulness Expands the Freedom to Choose
        Choices Worksheet & Tracking Log

NEUROSCIENCE AND MINDFUL LEADERSHIP
    The Triune Brain
    Increasing Mindful Leadership—High Road & Low Road Strategies
    The Middle Road—The Wise Mind of a Mindful Leader

MEDITATION—A LOW ROAD METHOD TO REWIRE THE BRAIN
    What is Meditation?
    Benefits of Meditation
    Research—Meditation, Neural Plasticity, and Wellbeing
    Meditation to Rewire Neural Circuitry
        Three Breaths Meditation Guide & Tracking Log
    Additional Readings and Websites

THE SCIENCE OF BECOMING AN EXPERT
    Self-Coaching Process—Assess, Plan, Practice, Track
    Additional Readings and Websites

Coaching Guidelines

MINDFUL LEADERS HELP EMPLOYEES THRIVE

Thriving can be defined as living to one's potential. It is an emergent state that occurs when one is firing on all cylinders. Research has identified five realms of life that are essential for thriving. Martin Seligman created the acronym PERMA to summarize these five life realms necessary for thriving:

- **P**ositive Emotion
- **E**ngagement
- **R**elationships
- **M**eaning
- **A**ccomplishment

POSITIVE PSYCHOLOGY AND LEADERSHIP

Build what's right rather than just fix what's wrong.

The aim of psychology for many years was relieving misery and eliminating the immobilizing conditions of life. In 1998, Mihalyi Cziksentmihalyi and Martin Seligman chartered a new course to emphasize well-being over and above the absence of pathology. As president of the American Psychological Association (APA), Seligman urged psychologists to expand their perspective in this way.

Positive psychology is the scientific study of mental styles, attitudes, emotional processes, behaviors, and other factors that lead to *thriving*. It is a new academic discipline that applies the scientific method to understand the causes of and conditions for happiness and success. It has gained tremendous respect (attracting researchers and funding) and has significantly impacted traditional psychology. These concepts and practices are being applied to increase the well-being of individuals, communities, organizations, and nations.

In the world of business, two branches of positive psychology are focused on positive organizational scholarship and positive organizational behavior. Organizational positive psychology concentrates on discovering and developing positive-psychological abilities that improve job performance. Just as organizations invest economic capital and human capital, individuals need to invest in their psychological capital—a positive mindset that can impact attitudes toward work and the outcomes achieved. Psychological capital is comprised of self-efficacy, optimism, hope, and resiliency.

- *Self-Efficacy*—One's confidence in one's ability to achieve a specific goal in a specific situation.
- *Optimism*—A generally positive view of work and one's potential for success.
- *Hope*—A belief in the ability to persevere towards goals and find the methods or paths to reach them.
- *Resiliency*—The ability to bounce back in the face of adversity or failure.

Psychological Capital. Research studies have established a strong relationship between psychological capital and a number of desired workplace outcomes including job satisfaction, organizational commitment, and psychological well-being. Psychological capital has shown to be negatively correlated with negative organizational behaviors like cynicism, anxiety, stress, and the intention to turnover. Psychological capital appears to be a "state like" quality and is open to change. It can be developed and strengthened through behavioral techniques as well as through workplace attributes such as leadership style, role design, performance feedback, etc.

ZAPPOS: A COMPANY BUILT UPON PERMA

Zappos, is a company that has consciously built happiness into its strategy. Nick Swinmurn, a Bay Area entrepreneur, founded Zappos—an adaptation of the Spanish word for shoes, "zapatos." Nick founded the company in 1999 after unsuccessfully trying to find a specific pair of shoes in several stores. Although he lacked specific experience in retail or the shoe industry, he believed that the Internet could address this supply problem by removing the physical constraints of shoe stores.

During the same time period, Tony Hsieh (pronounced "Shay") and Alfred Lin sold their Internet ad-banner business, *Link Exchange*, to Microsoft for $265 million, just three years after graduating from Harvard. In 1999, Hsieh and Lin founded a venture capital fund called *Venture Frogs*. Hsieh originally served as an investor and advisor to Zappos and then joined the company in 2000, serving as the co-CEO with Swinmurn. Lin later joined as COO/CFO. Swinmurn was intent on building the next Internet retailing powerhouse and satisfying customers' needs faster and more simply than ever before. Hsieh, on the other hand, was not focused solely on profits. He wanted to create a new universe, a company that was different from any other company he had known. His focus was on culture and employee happiness. Recalling his outlook on the new position, Hsieh explained, "It was about: What kind of company can we create where we all want to be there, including me? How can we create such a great environment, where employees get so much out of it that they would do it for free?" What Hsieh did not know at the time was that he would move beyond a focus on creating enjoyment and fulfillment for employees towards delivering happiness to both customers and the greater public.

Zappos Core Values. Tony Hsieh and his employees created a set of core values that provide the foundation for their culture, brand, and business strategies:
1. Deliver WOW Through Service
2. Embrace and Drive Change
3. Create Fun and a Little Weirdness
4. Be Adventurous, Creative, and Open-Minded
5. Pursue Growth and Learning
6. Build Open and Honest Relationships with Communication
7. Build a Positive Team and Family Spirit
8. Do More with Less
9. Be Passionate and Determined
10. Be Humble

We can learn a good deal about happiness at work by analyzing what Zappos has done to build happiness into its strategy.

THE BUSINESS CASE FOR HAPPINESS IN THE WORKPLACE

Sustainable Happiness. In this program, the term "happiness" refers to *sustainable happiness*. This type of happiness is deeper, more pervasive, and constant than a fleeting happiness characterized by positive emotions, although positive emotions are important and can have a cumulative effect on the attainment of sustainable happiness.

Sustainable happiness refers to having a general sense of contentment in life. It consists of positive emotion, meaning, overall satisfaction, and a positive view of one's life. It stems from engaging activities, good relationships, and skillful response to life's challenges and opportunities. It results from living life well. It cannot be grasped for—rather, it is a sense that emerges from living in a manner that cultivates positivity and meaning.

Happiness in the workplace. Happiness in the workplace contributes to productivity and profitability. Research on happiness in the workplace indicates that happiness is the antecedent to achievement and success rather than the other way around. It appears that optimism and happiness often provide the energy that drives accomplishment. This discovery has been supported by more than 200 scientific studies and research on 275,000 people worldwide.

As we review the research, we will discover some of the reasons *why* happiness is important and *how* it is produced in the workplace:

WHY?—What Is the Business Case for Happiness in the Workplace?
- Increase Wellness, Performance, Productivity, & Profitability
- Decrease Stress, Burnout, Disengagement

HOW?—What Are the Practices Used to Increase Personal & Team Happiness?
- Enhance Positive Emotion (*Personal Positivity Ratio*)
- Create Positive Relationships (*Relationship Positivity Ratio*)
- Heighten Engagement (*Finding Flow*)
- Reduce Stress and Manage Energy *(Keep Your Cool and Cultivate Resiliency)*

Levels of Unhappiness. Unfortunately, the level of happiness is not as high as it might be in many companies. In 2010, the Washington Post published the results of a survey commissioned by the Conference Board, a research firm funded by 2,000 corporations from around the world. The survey was entitled *"I Can't Get No...Job Satisfaction, That Is."* It pointed out that U.S. job satisfaction was at its lowest level in two decades. A recent survey by ComPsychCorp, a provider of employee assistance programs, found that 74% of 791 surveyed workers had become more worried about their job stresses and workloads in 2010.

Right Management, a subsidiary of the staffing firm Manpower Group, released a survey indicating that only 19% of 411 workers in the United States and Canada were satisfied with their jobs. The majority—nearly two-thirds—expressed that they were not happy at work. Other studies report similar results: A recent joint job happiness survey from Yahoo Finance and PARADE magazine found that almost 60 percent of 26,000 workers in the United States were so unhappy with their current jobs that they would prefer to choose a new career.

The Employee Benefits Conference statistics reported in US News & World Report indicate that 68% of customers stop patronizing a place of business because of a negative attitude or indifference among employees. Managers who are not addressing the happiness of employees may indirectly be causing their business to lose customers.

EMPLOYEE HAPPINESS

A study by Jessica Pryce-Jones, outlined in the book, *Happiness at Work: Maximizing Your Psychological Capital for Success* (2010), makes a strong business case for employee happiness:

1. Are More Productive. Happier employees are 47% more productive every week that those who are less happy. That is equivalent to working more than an extra day a week.

2. Embrace Challenges & Goals. Happier employees embrace 18% more challenges and 33% more goals than unhappy employees.

3. Feel Better About Themselves. Happier employees experience a sense of:

Contribution	23% more
Conviction	31% more
Better Fit with Culture	38% more
Commitment	40% more
Confidence	40% more
Believe Achieving Potential	40% more
Pride and Trust	33% more
Recognition	50% more

4. Experience Greater Respect.

> Happier employees report that they experience 31% more respect from their bosses.
> Happier employees report that they experience 28% more respect from their colleagues.

5. Have Increased Engagement & Job Satisfaction.

> The happiest employees are 108% more engaged than their least happy coworkers.
> The happiest employees have 82% more job satisfaction.

6. Have Higher Motivation. People who are most happy are 50% more motivated than people who are least happy at work.

7. Have Higher Efficiency, Effectiveness, and Self-Belief.

> People who are happier are 25% more effective and efficient than the least happy.
> People who are happier have 25% more self-belief than the least happy.

8. Have Higher Energy. The happiest people at work have 180% more energy than their least happy coworkers. This has a powerful effect on what they do as well as the relationships that they have with others.

9. Take Reduced Sick Leave. People who are happiest at work take 42% less sick leave than those who are the least happy.

RESEARCH ON MINDFULNESS AND ITS BENEFITS

Since 2005, we have designed programs to develop higher levels of mindfulness. Mindfulness enables optimal functioning, because it results in presence, clarity, perspective, agility, and control. Langer's research demonstrates that mindfulness drives effectiveness across life domains. Mindfulness is the root of health, happiness, satisfying relationships, and success. Mindfulness is trainable and has a multitude of benefits in an organization, including but not limited to, stellar performance, outstanding leadership, and an increase in overall happiness. Research demonstrates that mindful people enjoy many advantages in wellbeing, vitality, and success. Mindfulness is especially relevant in our fast-paced era with increased demands on attention, productivity, innovation, and energy.

WORKPLACE MINDFULNESS PROGRAMS

Aetna's "Mindfulness at Work" Program. Since 2010, Aetna has offered "Mindfulness at Work," a stress-management program developed with *eMindful*, to its employees. A total of 6,000 Aetna employees have participated in the "Mindfulness at Work" program. The program draws core principles from mindfulness meditation practices to teach brief, 5- to 15-minute practices that target work-related stress and work-life balance. A research study was conducted on 96 employees evaluating the effectiveness of the program. Results demonstrated that employees not only expressed reduced levels of stress but were shown to have improved heart-rate measurements as well—a mind and body shift. Those who participated in the program in-person and through a virtual online classroom showed similar benefits.

Intel's "Awake@Intel" Program. In 2012, Intel began rolling out a 9-week mindfulness program to its employees in California and Oregon. Two years later, it made this same program available to over 100,000 employees across 63 countries. The program, called Awake@Intel, uses a train-the-trainer model to teach employees several mindfulness practices including quieting the mind, setting intentions, emotional intelligence, the role of vulnerability on innovation, and the idea of collective mindfulness. Employees who participate in the program have been shown to express a reduction in stress levels and feelings of being overwhelmed as well as an increase in overall happiness and well-being. Additionally, many employees report the feeling that they have new ideas and insights at work, greater mental clarity, creativity, and focus, greater engagement to their work, and an improvement in the quality of their work relationships.

MINDFULNESS AND EMOTIONAL INTELLIGENCE

Mindfulness applied to different realms of experience allows the conditions from which emotional intelligence naturally emerges. This is important because decades of research show that emotional intelligence is a core skill set that underlies success and wellbeing. At the heart of emotional intelligence is choosing what aspect of experience to attend to. Mindfulness practices help us build this muscle. As Philippe Goldin, researcher at University of California at Davis, says, mindfulness fosters the capacity to volitionally redirect attention. Regardless of the situation, when in a mindful state, attention can be turned to the most important aspects of a situation.

RESEARCH—MINDFULNESS AT WORK

Below are abstracts from a selection of scientific studies published in major peer reviewed journals.

Meditation Improves Performance, Job Satisfaction, and Wellbeing. In a recent study, the effect of meditation on work-related wellbeing and job performance was evaluated. Researchers found that managers who participated in an 8-week meditation awareness training left with greater levels of job satisfaction and employer-related job performance as well as lower levels of work-related stress and psychological distress. The training included themes like compassion, perspective-taking, patience, generosity, and perspective-taking. Shonin posits that these elements can play a beneficial role to wellbeing and performance at work by improving employees' attention and focus, response to stressors, and aligning oneself to organizational goals. Shonin, E., Van Gordon, W., Dunn, T. J., Singh, N. N., & Griffiths, M. D. (2014). Meditation awareness training (MAT) for work-related wellbeing and job performance: A randomized controlled trial. *International Journal of Mental Health and Addiction*, 12, 806–823.

Meditation Improves Confidence and Alignment with Organizational Goals. In this 2014 study, Shonin interviewed 10 managers who participated an 8-week meditation awareness training shown to improve work-related wellbeing and job performance in order to gain a deeper insight into the mechanisms behind these benefits. From these interviews rose several themes. Participants in the training experienced a change in attitudes toward work; specifically, that work was less of a separate part of their lives, but an important place where they can learn and grow. Many felt that they were also better able to navigate and interact with work-related stressors and situations, which fostered a sense of confidence around decision-making. They also felt that they were better able to identify with corporate strategy and organizational goals. Participants also reported improved job performance and greater wellbeing at work. Moving forward, many felt a responsibility to continue their own growth at work as a result of these perceived benefits. Shonin, E. & Van Gordon, W. (2014). Managers' experience of meditation awareness training. *Mindfulness*.

Mindfulness Correlated to Work Engagement and Wellbeing. A 2015 study by Malinowski and Lim found that mindfulness, wellbeing, and work engagement were all positively correlated. Therefore, if an individual is more mindful, than he or she was more likely to also experience greater levels of wellbeing and work engagement. The study also found that the mindfulness component of non-reactivity had the greatest impact on an employee's level of wellbeing, because it equipped them with the ability to remain calm in the face of adversity. Malinowski, P. & Lim, H.J. (2015). Mindfulness at work: Positive affect, hope, and optimism mediate the relationship between dispositional mindfulness, work engagement, and wellbeing. *Mindfulness*.

Mindfulness as a Protective Factor Against Frustration. Mindfulness plays a powerful and direct role in protecting against work ill-being. The association between work environment and the experience of frustration at work was moderated by mindfulness. When mindfulness was higher, there was a less strong relationship between work environment and levels of frustration experience. Schultz, P.P., Ryan, R.M., Niemiec, C.P., Legate, N., Williams, G.C. (2014). Mindfulness, work climate, and psychological need satisfaction in employee wellbeing. *Mindfulness*, 1-15.

RESEARCH ON MINDFUL THINKING

Studies suggest that the ability to generate alternative interpretations leads to creating opportunities, generating solutions, improved performance, and coping with potential stressors in health.

Mindful Thinking Decreases Damaging Effect of Social Comparisons. Laura Delizonna and Ellen Langer conducted a study to test the effect of mindful thinking on creativity and social comparisons. Social comparisons have been established as diminishing performance, happiness, and satisfaction. Individuals were less apt to be negatively impacted by social comparisons after they practiced generating alternative appraisals of seemingly negative events (e.g., "You forgot your mother's birthday."). The individuals Participants who considered hypothetical negative events from alternative positive perspectives were more able to resist negative self-evaluations in a subsequent creativity task. In contrast, negative self-evaluations were typical of the participants who did not engage in the mindful thinking condition. Delizonna & Langer, (2005). The Mindlessness of Social Comparisons.

Mindful Attention Improves Heart Rate Control. Laura Delizonna and Ellen Langer conducted a study to test the effect of mindfulness on one's ability to control heart rate, a seemingly involuntary bodily process. Our experiment tested our hypothesis that mindful attention to change regarding heart rate (HR) would result in greater control over HR. Experimental groups monitored the changing or stable nature of HR, respectively. All participants' HR slowed during the decrease phase. Participants whose attention was directed to the stable nature of HR performed the worst on the increase phase of the HR control task. These results suggest that mindfulness, instantiated here as perspective taking (i.e. attention to fluctuation), is a means to breaking mindsets, and ultimately, increasing control. Delizonna, L. & Langer, E. (2009). The Effect of Mindfulness on Heart Rate Control. *Journal of Adult Development*.

Simple Changes in Semantics Improve Creativity. Langer and Piper (1987) showed that individuals who were presented with objects that were described with unconditional language (e.g., "This is a dog's toy.") generated fewer novel uses for the object compared to individuals who received conditional descriptions (e.g., "This could be a dog's toy.").

Mindful Consideration improves Learning. Mindfulness researchers have also explored the impact of conditional versus unconditional presentation of "facts" during learning phases (Langer, Hatem, Joss, & Howell, 1989). For example, elementary students were more able to apply information spontaneously and creatively when taught using "could be," "may be," and "it would seem that," compared to unconditional language.

Flexibility in Thinking Improves Coping. In an early study (Langer, Janis, & Wolfer, 1975), surgical patients were encouraged to consider alternatives to their expectation that hospitalization would be a completely negative experience. The patients who were asked to consider how hospitalization could be a positive event for them recovered faster compared to the patients who were given the typical preparatory information about the surgery. Those who generated alternative interpretations had decreased hospital stays, fewer requests for pain medication, and appeared less distressed.

Flexibility in Thinking Is Linked to Longevity. In a long-term study, individuals practiced thinking mindfully by working on a cognitive flexibility type task or practicing reasoning from alternative perspectives (Alexander et al., 1989). These individuals lived longer and had higher levels of perceived control than the individuals who practiced relaxation strategies or had no treatment.

Flexibility in Thinking Improves Coping with Stress. Studies of personality dimensions and individuals' reactions to life stressors support the idea that cognitive flexibility relates to coping. Studies of Linville's (1985; 1987) concept of self-complexity suggest that people whose self-constructs include a greater number of alternative approaches are buffered from stressful life events. It seems that these people generally cope better than those with limited self-constructs.

Flexibility in Thinking Improves Coping with Pain. People differ in their appraisals (Hassinger, Semenchuk, & O'Brien, 1999) and the meaning they associate with stressors (Cioffi, 1991). Such interpretations can influence the subjective experience of the stressor. Cioffi (1993) explains that by noticing the subtle distinctions between physical sensations, individuals are better able to tolerate pain. Cioffi (1993) suggests that monitoring the distinctions in bodily sensations improves coping with an aversive stimulus. Monitoring is believed to increase the number of possible cognitive interpretations of such a stimulus. The possibility of alternative interpretations, Cioffi (1993) hypothesizes, enhances people's ability to change their subjective experience of the sensations.

WHY DOES HAPPINESS CAUSE SUCCESS?

A large body of research shows that happiness actually causes success. The relationship is both correlational and causal. Positivity builds upon itself to create an upward spiral of growth and enjoyment. Psychologists refer to these benefits as the Broaden and Build Theory of Positive Emotions, established by Barbara Fredrickson at University of North Carolina, Chapel Hill. This research shows that positive emotions don't just feel good, they also are good for us.

THE BROADEN AND BUILD EFFECT OF POSITIVE EMOTIONS

Positive emotions *broaden* our vision and help us to *build* resources and grow as individuals. Positive emotions help us thrive. These "approach" emotions motivate us through pleasant feelings to get more of something or to do it again. They feel rewarding, satisfying, or pleasurable. They also encourage others to come along and join us.

Like the sail on a sailboat, positive emotions drive us toward our objectives, hopes, dreams, and goals. They are the fuel behind aspirations.

Positive emotions:
- Help us see new possibilities
- Enhance creativity
- Make us feel more secure and help us take moderate risk
- Enhance connections to others
- Help us bounce back from setbacks
- Attract others and make others seem attractive
- Increase generosity, interest, and cooperation with others

Simply by sailing in a new direction you could enlarge the world.
-Allen Curnow

Research suggests that people with more positive emotions enjoy many benefits over their more negative peers:

Work. Happy workers enjoy multiple advantages over less happy colleagues. Multiple studies have shown that happy people are more satisfied with their jobs (e.g., Connolly & Viswesvara, 2000). Employees who tend to experience more positive emotions had jobs that had more autonomy, meaning, and variety (Staw, Sutton, & Pelled, 1994), which would be considered by most to be highly desirable jobs. Happy people receive higher ratings from supervisors, and work performance is more highly related to overall well-being than a worker's satisfaction with her or his job (Cropanzano & Wright, 1999). In addition to work performance, income seems to be related to happiness. In an examination of 286 scientific studies, Pinquart and Sorensen (2000) found that income was more related to happiness and life satisfaction than it was to education.

Resilience. Research suggests that happy individuals are more creative, helpful, charitable, and self-confident. They have better self-control and show greater self-regulatory and coping abilities. Happy people are not simply lucky or exempt from misfortune; they do notice and feel distress. The difference is that they are *resilient*: they quickly recover, create possibilities, and flourish. Happy people are not free from problems—they overcome them.

Health. Happy people report better health and fewer unpleasant physical symptoms (Kehn, 1995; Lyubomirsky et al. in press). Positive feelings have been shown to relate to quality of life in cancer patients over the course of their illnesses (Collins, Hanson, Mulhern, & Padberg, 1992). The number of days of work missed because of health problems was also related to happiness in a large Russian study (Graham et al., in press).

Relationships. Married people have been shown to be happier than those who are single, divorced, or widowed (Diener et al., 1999). Happy individuals have more fulfilling marriages and are more satisfied with their marriages (Headey et al., 1991). Research indicates that happiness leads to being married rather than the reverse. Several longitudinal studies show that happy people are more likely to get married (e.g., Lucas et al, 2003; Marks & Fleming, 1999). Chronic happiness is also related to the actual number of friends or companions people report they can rely on (Baldassare, Rosenfield, & Rook, 1984).

Social Contribution. Happy people do more good and cause fewer problems than unhappy people. Happy people are more altruistic and compassionate. People who score higher on measures of general positive emotions over time report a tendency to act in a pro-social or cooperative manner, such as helping others or enjoying sharing with others (Rigby & Slee, 1993). Happy people probably create less financial burden in society because they tend to have fewer physical and mental problems. They are the givers and often the producers and leaders in society. They exemplify Mahatma Gandhi's suggestion, "Be the change you want to see in the world"—and they do tend to manifest positive change in the world. It is infectious both for the happy person and for those around her or him.

RESEARCH—POSITIVE EMOTIONS IN THE WORKPLACE

Affect and Creativity at Work. Research suggests that positive emotion is closely linked to the degree of creativity in employees. Using both quantitative and qualitative longitudinal data from the daily diaries of 222 employees in seven companies, they examined the nature, form, and temporal dynamics of the affect-creativity relationship. The researchers found that positive emotion in employees relates to creativity in organizations and that the relationship is linear. Positive affect is an antecedent of creative thought with incubation periods of up to two days. Positive emotion is also a consequence of creativity, as well as a concomitant of the creative process. Amabile, T., Barsade, S., Mueller, J. & Staw, B. (2005) Affect and creativity at work. *Administrative Science Quarterly,* 50 (2005), 367-403.

The Benefits of Frequent Positive Affect: Does Happiness Lead to Success? Numerous studies show that happy individuals are successful across multiple life domains, including marriage, friendship, income, work performance, and health. In particular, a study by Lyumbomirsky, King, and Diener (cited below) supports a conceptual model suggesting that the happiness-success link exists not only because success makes people happy, but also because positive affect engenders success. Three classes of evidence—cross-sectional, longitudinal, and experimental—are documented to test this model. Relevant studies are described and their effect sizes combined meta-analytically. The results reveal that happiness is associated with and precedes numerous successful outcomes, as well as behaviors paralleling success. Furthermore, the evidence suggests that positive affect—the hallmark of well-being—may be the cause of many of the desirable characteristics, resources, and successes correlated with happiness. Lyubomirsky, S., King, L., and Diener, E. (2005). The benefits of frequent positive affect: Does happiness lead to success? *Psychological Bulletin,* 131, 803-855.

Employee Positive Emotion and Favorable Outcomes at the Workplace. This paper by Staw, Sutton and Pelled (cited below) draws on psychology, sociology and organizational behavior principles to present a conceptual framework of the link between positive emotion and favorable outcomes at work. They propose that feeling and expressing positive emotions on the job have a favorable impact on:

(1) employees independent of their relationships with others (e.g., greater persistence)

(2) reactions of others to employees (e.g., "halo," or overgeneralization to other desirable traits)

(3) reactions of employees to others (e.g., helping others)

These three sets of intervening processes are proposed, in turn, to lead to work achievement, job enrichment, and a higher-quality social context. A partial test of this framework is made in an 18-month study of 272 employees.

Results indicate that positive emotion on the job at time 1 is associated with evidence of work achievement (more favorable supervisor evaluations and higher pay) and a supportive social context (more support from supervisors and coworkers) at time 2. But positive emotion at time 1 is not significantly associated with job enrichment at time 2. Staw, B. M., Sutton, R. I., & Pelled, L. H. (1994). Employee positive emotion and favorable outcomes at the workplace. *Organization Science*, 5(1), 51-71.

Salesperson and Mood at Work: Implications for Helping Customers. This article by George (cited below) focuses on the importance of salesperson helping behavior directed at customers and concentrates on understanding how salespeople can be managed so that they seek to help satisfy each customer's relatively unique needs and desires. The extent to which salespeople experience positive moods at work is proposed to be an important determinant of how helpful they are to customers and the quality of service they provide. Positive moods at work may be fostered by promoting a sense of competence, achievement, and meaning in the workplace, providing rewards and recognition, keeping work group or team size relatively small, and *modeling of a positive mood by the leader.* George, J.M. (1998). Salesperson and mood at work: Implications for helping customers. *Journal of Personal Selling and Sales Management,* 17, 23-30.

Doing Well and Doing Good: The Relationship Between Leadership Practices That Facilitate a Positive Emotional Climate and Organizational Performance. Researchers investigated the relationship between leadership practices that facilitate a positive emotional climate (the "PEC practices") and organizational outcomes.

A panel study was conducted among 229 entrepreneurs and small business owners operating in Greater Vancouver, British Columbia, Canada. In the first wave of the study, the authors collected data regarding the PEC practices. The data on outcome variables (revenue, strategic growth, and outcome growth) were collected in the second wave 18 months later. Regression analyses showed that the PEC practices were positively related to the outcome measures, providing support for the hypotheses in the study. This study provides valuable insights about the role of emotional factors in organizational-level outcomes, a relatively unexplored area in emotion research. Ozcelik, H., Langton, N., & Aldrich, H. (2008). Doing well and doing good: The relationship between leadership practices that facilitate a positive emotional climate and organizational performance. *Journal of Managerial Psychology*, 23, 186-203.

The Role of Positive Psychology in Enhancing Satisfaction, Motivation, and Productivity in the Workplace. This study by Martin (cited below) adapts a model of motivation to develop the Occupational Motivation and Engagement Wheel. It includes a discussion of workplace resilience, authoritarian versus authoritative leadership/management styles, motivating workplace climates, personal bests, staff morale, flow in work, the value individuals attach to tasks and outcomes, and the centrality of relationships in the performance context. The article concludes with a multi-level "broaden and build" framework for enhancing satisfaction, motivation, and productivity in the workplace. Martin, A.J. (2005) The role of positive psychology in enhancing satisfaction, motivation and productivity in the workplace. *Journal of Organizational Behavioral Management*, 24, 111-131.

CHOICE—THE KEY TO THRIVING

Thanks to advances in neuroscience and psychology, we know more than ever about the causes of happiness. Yet less than 30 percent of people say they are deeply happy. Some doubt they have the capacity to change their happiness level.

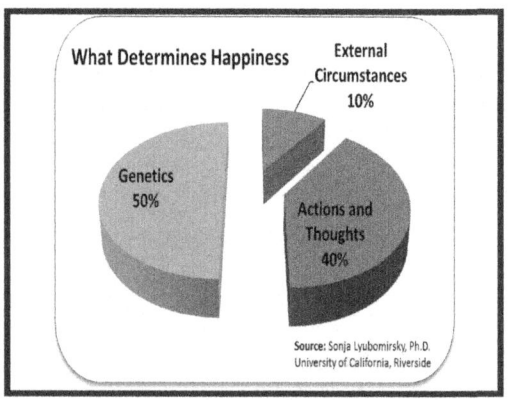

Genetics. Research does suggest that some people were born with brains hardwired for happiness. Happiness levels are inherited. In the pie chart of happiness, genetics contribute about 50%. This figure is an estimate based on twin studies of wellbeing across the lifespan.

External Circumstances. What you do and what you have do not weigh heavily in the happiness equation. The problem is that most look outside themselves for happiness. Life circumstances account for only 10% in the pie chart of happiness. In one study, the responses of lottery winners were compared to those who had not won. After a short time period, there were no significant differences in their levels of reported happiness. The same researcher also interviewed accident victims who had become quadriplegic or paraplegic and found that they did not experience any significant difference in their happiness levels two years after their accident.

Even finding the love of your life will not significantly change your happiness level. Married people are happier than singles, but only by a few percentage points. Newlyweds get a slight boost in happiness, but shortly they return to their pre-marriage baselines. Although happy people have closer relationships, the relationship probably does not cause their happiness. Instead, happy people seem to attract others and create close relationships.

The "Hedonic Treadmill". Humans have an exquisite ability to get used to, or "habituate" to circumstances. This in addition to our "Drive to Thrive" easily creates an exhaustive pursuit of something more and something better. Pleasurable experiences do give a short-lived boost to happiness. Initially, we will feel better driving that convertible BMW, moving into a new house, or donning a flashy diamond ring. Soon, however, the initial high wears off, and we tend to seek an upgrade.

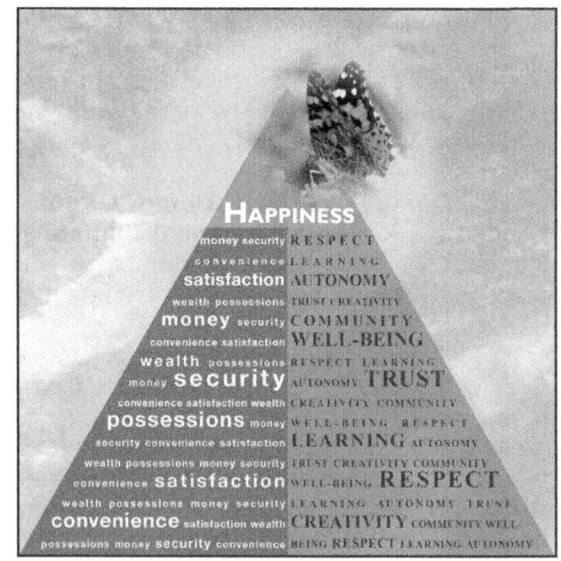

With 247 commercial messages hitting the average American every day, it can be hard to resist buying into the idea that acquiring goods, services, and social status will increase happiness. After comfort needs are met, however, material possessions do not contribute significantly to an increase in happiness.

Actions and Thoughts. Lyubomirsky's research indicates that 40% of our happiness is dictated by our actions and thoughts. Clearly, a huge amount of happiness is in our direct control.

Does Money Increase Happiness? Money is a strong motivator and we spend much of our life trying to get more. Naturally, this begs the question if it is worth all that sacrifice. How much time and sacrifice goes toward making money? Does it pay off? The research is seemingly conflicting on the topic of money. Some studies show its benefits, while others warn of its pitfalls. Money has the potential to increase happiness but it also has the potential to decrease happiness.

When one looks at the big picture, there are some general conclusions that can be drawn from the research findings. The answer is similar to any other life circumstance: There are opportunities to increase happiness, but ultimately it depends on you.

How you think about your money and what you do with it makes all the difference.

If you compare yourself to richer peers, derive your worth from it, allow it to be a source of stress and anxiety, or distract you from meaningful and engaging activities then it will probably decrease your happiness. If you use money to increase meaningful and engaging activities, savor the benefits and luxuries it affords, or allow it to increase your gratitude, then it will probably increase your happiness. After basic means are met, money cannot buy happiness, but it does bring opportunities that can help you cultivate happiness.

In an article for *Scientific American*, Lyubomirsky writes, "We are not looking at the problem in the right way. The truth is that money's pitfalls can be overcome with a little effort and forethought. Happiness is a choice. We can choose to become never-satisfied janitors of our possessions, or we can use our money in ways that improve our worlds and, as a bonus, supply us with genuine and lasting well-being." She adds a quote from a famous Lexus advertisement: *"Whoever said money can't buy happiness isn't spending it right."*

Wealth Is Related to Less Savoring. Researchers found that wealthier individuals were less able to savor. Quoidbach, J., Dunn, E., Petrides, K., & Mikolajczak, M. (2010). Money giveth, money taketh away: The dual effect of wealth on happiness. *Psychological Science,* 21(6), 759-763.

Big-money lottery winners were unable to enjoy life's simple pleasures as well as a control group of non-lottery winners. Brickman, P., Coates, D., & Janoff-Bulman, R., (1978). Lottery winners and accident victims: Is happiness relative? *Journal of Personality and Social Psychology,* 36(8), 917-927.

MINDFULNESS EXPANDS THE ABILITY TO CHOOSE

"Between a stimulus and a response is a space. In that space we can choose our response.
In our response lies our growth and our freedom."
Viktor Frankl

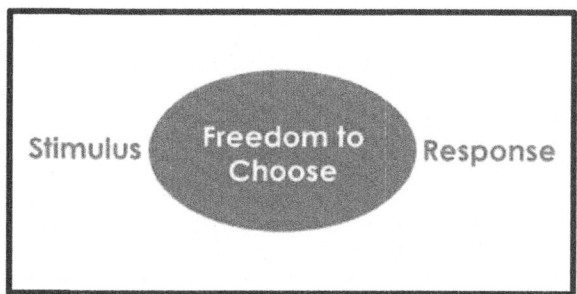

Every moment presents us with an awesome opportunity: We have the freedom to choose our response. No matter what circumstances we face, our response is ours to choose. In that way, happiness is a choice to be made in each and every situation. It is choosing the type of response that is likely to increase the positive and to decrease the negative in life.

How we respond to situations, not the situations in themselves, largely determines how happy people are. Whether or not you get that job, take that vacation, or even get married will not ensure happiness. Happiness depends upon what you do with those situations. For example, having an optimistic attitude, gratitude for the good things in life, and perseverance typically lead to higher levels of happiness. Sometimes choosing responses that are likely to increase happiness in situations is easy; other times it requires incredible fortitude and courage. It may not always be an obvious choice.

A growing body of research explains why external circumstances alone do not determine one's level of happiness and well-being. Unequivocally, our perceptions and responses to circumstances cause increases or decreases in happiness levels. This happens in two ways:

- Our perceptions and responses improve how we *feel* about obstacles and opportunities.
- Our perceptions and responses improve how we *deal* with obstacles and opportunities.

For example, happy people are better able to maintain a bright outlook even amid seemingly dismal circumstances. They are more apt to consider roadblocks as opportunities for switching directions, mistakes as useful feedback for modifying strategies, and challenges as motivators for greater learning. Instead of getting stuck, happy people tend to invent solutions.

CHOICES WORKSHEET

Mindful leadership depends upon choosing to respond to things differently. That requires intention and choice. The choice begins like an invisible fork in the road where you either decide to move toward mindful choice or get derailed by the challenges of work and relationships. It may not always be an obvious or easy choice.

Choice assumes a certain conscious awareness of what contributes to mindful leadership and what detracts from our mindfulness. Mindfulness can have a very personal meaning to each of us and can be caused by very different factors. Let's begin by considering what considering mindfulness means and how it shows up in daily life. The purpose of this worksheet is to provide you with an opportunity to look closely at your concept and causes of mindfulness.

BROADEN AND BUILD EFFECT OF POSITIVE EMOTIONS

1. EXAMPLES OF THE BROADENING EFFECT OF POSITIVE EMOTIONS. How have I seen the broadening effect of positive emotions at work?
- Help us see new possibilities
- Enhance creativity
- Make us feel more secure and help us take moderate risk

_____
_____
_____
_____
_____
_____

2. EXAMPLES OF THE BUILDING EFFECT OF POSITIVE EMOTIONS AT WORK. What does happiness look like in my life at work? To what extent do I experience the following effects:
- Enhance connections to others
- Help us bounce back from setbacks
- Attract others and make others seem attractive
- Increase generosity, interest, and cooperation with others
- Increase energy or motivation

_____
_____
_____
_____
_____
_____
_____

CHOICES THAT I HAVE MADE

1. CHOICES I MADE THAT LED TO THE BROADENING EFFECT OF POSITIVE EMOTIONS. What did I do that created an upward spiral of positive emotions?
- Help us see new possibilities
- Enhance creativity
- Make us feel more secure and help us take moderate risk

_____
_____
_____
_____
_____
_____
_____
_____
_____
_____

2. CHOICES I MADE THAT LED TO THE BUILDING EFFECT OF POSITIVE EMOTIONS AT WORK. What does happiness look like in my life at work?
- Enhance connections to others
- Help us bounce back from setbacks
- Attract others and make others seem attractive
- Increase generosity, interest, and cooperation with others
- Increase energy or motivation

_____
_____
_____
_____
_____
_____
_____
_____
_____
_____

CHOICES TRACKING LOG

DAY	CAUSES When did I feel positivity or energized? What caused this uplift? When did I feel negativity or de-energized? What caused this disruption?	EMOTIONS What were the associated emotions and bodily sensations?	INFLUENCE How did my choices, actions, attitude, or reactions play a role in my experience of positivity or negativity in this situation?
Day 1			
Day 2			
Day 3			
Day 4			

CHOICES TRACKING LOG

DAY	CAUSES When did I feel positivity or energized? What caused this uplift? When did I feel negativity or de-energized? What caused this disruption?	EMOTIONS What were the associated emotions and/or bodily sensations?	INFLUENCE How did my choices, actions, attitude, or reactions play a role in my experience of positivity or negativity in this situation?
Day 5			
Day 6			
Day 7			

INSIGHTS - What benefits or patterns emerged?

_____
_____
_____
_____
_____

NEUROSCIENCE & MINDFUL LEADERSHIP

The brain is fundamentally a lazy piece of meat. It doesn't want to waste any energy.
—Gregory Burns, Neuroscientist

Neuroscientists refer to a general model for the brain regions that shape emotional response. Although it is an oversimplification to say that a specific brain region is responsible for complex phenomena such as an emotional response, it is helpful for non-neuroscientists to use basic models. The major regions of the brain are sometimes referred to as the "Triune Brain", including the Reptilian complex, the Limbic system, and the Neo-cortex. Below describes these regions' gross functions.

Reptilian Complex. This primitive part of the brain is located at the base of the brain and the top of the spinal cord. It controls bodily functions and instinctive survival responses.

Limbic System. The hippocampus and the amygdala evolved after the brainstem. Emotional, survival-linked responses to visual and other inputs are stored in this region. The amygdala is known for catalyzing impulsive action and overpowering slower thought processing and considered reactions. This is the source of "emotional hijackings."

Neo-cortex. This large, well-developed, top region of the brain comprises the center of our thinking, memory, and reasoning functions.

TRIUNE BRAIN

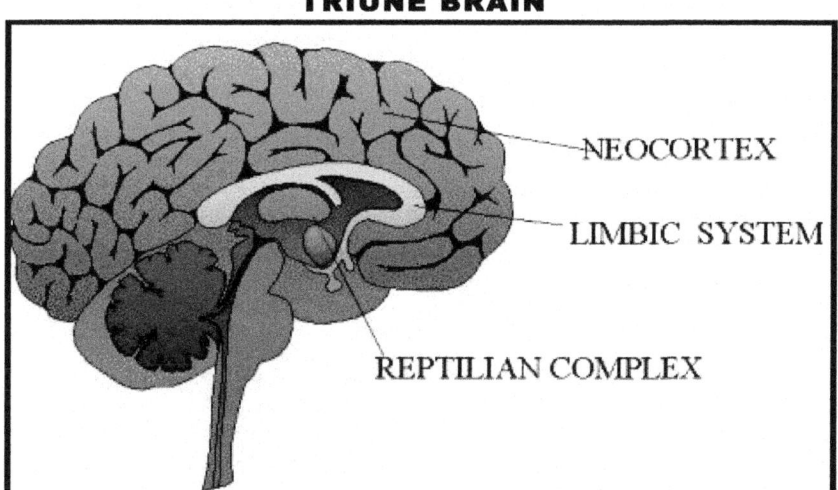

As Daniel Goleman states, "The brain is an elegant machine for survival and has been shaped by what works in survival." Our most primitive emotions evolved first as powerful survival mechanisms. Our higher-order cognitive functions evolved much later. Due to the course of evolution, our *emotions* and our *thinking* are situated in *separate areas* of the brain.

Role of the Amygdala. The amygdala is primarily responsible for our ability to "act fast, think later." This almond-shaped mass of gray matter resides bilaterally in the anterior portion of the temporal lobe and specializes in threat and fear. The amygdala operates on a hairpin trigger, sounding the alarm bells to recruit other areas of the brain to ignite the fight-or-flight system. The amygdala floods the body with hormones designed to activate systems involved in the protective fight-or-flight response. The tense muscles, increased blood pressure and respiration rates, and shunting of blood away from the gut to the muscular system (among others) are part of this exquisitely synchronized cascade of reactions.

Role of the Cortex. As information slowly makes its way to the cortex, the cortex perceives the difference between the stick and the snake. It finally says, *"It's only a stick."* Once the discriminating cortex has determined that there is no call for panic, it sends a message to the amygdala, quieting the fear response.

INCREASING MINDFUL LEADERSHIP—HIGH ROAD & LOW ROAD STRATEGIES

We designed this program with two types of strategies that can be used to build the skills of emotional intelligence. These map onto the Triune Brain regions.

In his book *Social Intelligence,* Daniel Goleman refers to the brain processes as falling into two general types of circuitry, which he calls the *High and Low Roads.* Although this oversimplifies the complex circuitry of the brain, his metaphor is helpful for understanding at a gross level how the brain operates at emotional and logical levels. The *Low Road* represents our automatic response system. The *High Road* represents our voluntary response system.

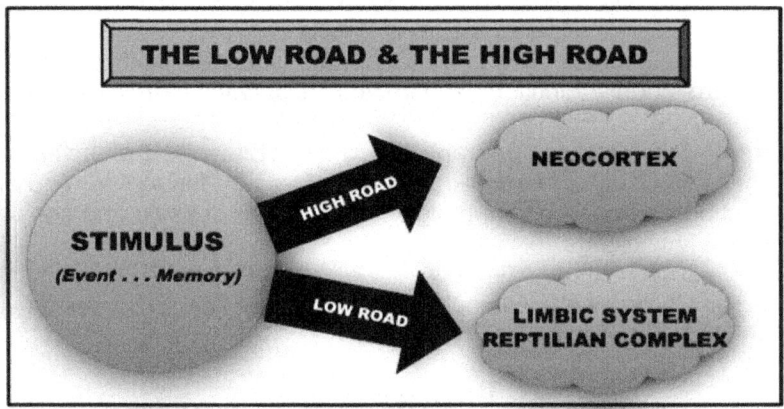

Together, these high-road and low-road practices can increase overall mindfulness, effectiveness, and well-being.

High Road. These strategies employ analytical and cognitive reasoning to consciously take different perspectives and challenge existing mindsets to arrive at a different or more complex understanding. This can be thought of as activating the neocortex functions.

High Road (Cognitive Practices). The cognitive practices will help you increase your mindful thinking.

The High Road represents the conscious response system. It operates more slowly than the automatic response system and with voluntary control. It requires effort and conscious intent. High Road circuitry activates when automatic process are interrupted by novelty, unexpected events, a mistake, or a threat, among other stimuli. Consciously engaging with thoughts and concepts also occurs within this system. High-level and abstract thinking, such as problem solving, considering ideas, reflecting and other types of cogitation, occurs here. This system includes the anterior cingulate cortex, lateral prefrontal cortex, posterior parietal cortex, and hippocampus, among others.

Low Road. These strategies are more experiential. They build muscle memory to create habits at the nonverbal or subconscious level and recondition emotional, mental, and behavioral reactions. These experiential techniques activate the emotional and memory centers, attempting to recondition and build new associations between stimuli and response. The Low Road relates to the automatic response system. It operates automatically at high speeds and outside of awareness.

Low Road (Nonverbal Practices). The nonverbal practices will help you reprogram your mind.

The Low Road is the "default" mode of the brain. Countless automatic brain processes perform crucial functions below our awareness. Structures comprising these regions are the amygdala, basal ganglia, lateral temporal cortex, ventromedial prefrontal cortex, and dorsal anterior cingulate cortex.

The Low and High Road systems often work concurrently. For example, as you read this, you are engaging High Road functions to direct attention and reflect on the meaning and implications of this content. At the same time, numerous Low Road functions perform the countless supporting functions of recognizing patterns, decoding syntax, and so on. Goleman speculates that there may be no purely High Road mental functions, but there are many purely low road functions.

High Road processing can override the automatic processing at the Low Road level. This capacity allows for conscious choice and is occurring when we manage emotions, thoughts, and behavior.

Example: Fear on the Low Road and High Road. Fear is among the evolutionary oldest and most primitive emotions. Two parallel routes process fear. Low-level processing is prioritized due to its quick, automatic circuitry that helps us stay safe.

Imagine you are on a nature hike, and suddenly at the corner of your eye, your brain perceives a thin black curvy object. Instinctively, you freeze, your heart rate and respiration spike, and your eyes widen, fixated on the object. All of this happens in milliseconds, outside of conscious processing. You then realize it is a stick. Heart and respiration rates slow, and you continue walking. What happened? We have evolved to fear snakes and our automatic, or Low Road system, is vigilant and reactive to threats.

THE MIDDLE ROAD—THE WISE MIND OF A MINDFUL LEADER

Marsha Linehan, a leading researcher in the development of innovative and effective psychotherapy interventions, developed a metaphor for effective thinking and action. Her metaphor maps onto Goleman's High and Low Road model.

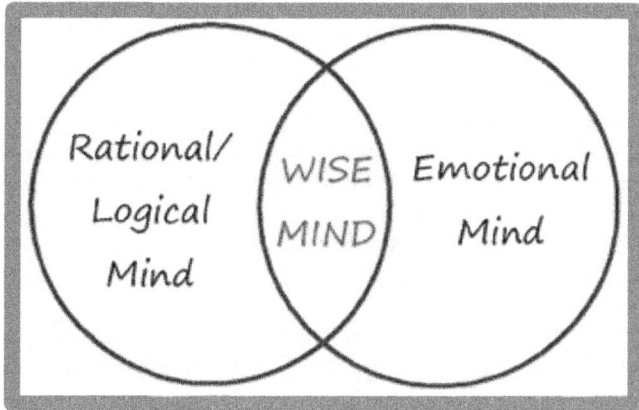

The emotional mind processes stimuli based on feeling, not logical reasoning. This "mind" helps us know what feels good or bad to us, what we like and don't like. This is similar to the hot, Low Road system where emotions and impulses reside.

The logical mind processes stimuli based on logical reasoning. This "mind" helps us consider the past and future, determine cause and effect, and develop working models of the world. This relates to the cool, High Road system where high-level abstract and rational thinking resides.

The wise mind represents the combination of the rich information provided by the emotional mind and logical mind. The wise mind can help you to employ more effective thoughts and engage in more effective actions. The cognitive exercises and meditations in this workbook are designed to further develop your ability to access the wise mind, drawing from the best of the emotional mind and the logical mind. This, we refer to as the Middle Road—sourcing the intelligence of the emotional mind and logical mind. This is where emotional intelligence resides—utilizing both analytical, logical thinking and emotional information.

MEDITATION: A LOW ROAD METHOD TO REWIRE THE BRAIN

Meditation refers to a family of mental training practices that are designed to familiarize the practitioner with specific types of mental processes.
-Brefczynski-Lewis, 2007

WHAT IS MEDITATION?

Meditation is a practice that can operate at the Low Road level and can rewire the neural circuitry. Meditation is simply directing attention with intention and then intending to sustain that attention. The meditations presented here are simply structured visualizations and exercises for focusing attention to sensations and other internal experiences. There is nothing mystical or religious about meditation. Many people associate meditation with religion, but this is simply because focusing inward in the form of contemplative practices has been used in many religions including Christianity (prayer), Eastern Religions (e.g., Zen meditation, Buddhism, Hinduism), Judaism, tribal religions, and more.

BENEFITS OF MEDITATION

Meditation is a fundamental aspect of this mindful leadership program due to a growing body of research findings. Research has shown that meditations increase happiness, well-being, decrease loneliness and anxiety, and improve health. Strikingly, meditation can change the neural circuitry in the brain.

Mindful awareness of internal experience has scientific support as a means to reduce stress, improve attention, boost the immune system, reduce emotional reactivity, and promote a general sense of health and well-being. Researchers' interest in mindfulness practice has steadily increased as studies continue to reveal its beneficial effects. Current research is examining how the brain responds to mindfulness practice and the benefits reaped for relationships, and physical and mental health. A burgeoning amount of research reveals that mindful awareness enhances many aspects of well-being.

A number of studies have related meditation practice to positive changes to the brain. One of the best-known studies in 2005, led by Sara Lazar, indicated that meditation experience is associated with increased cortical thickness.

Richard Davidson, a neuroscientist at the University of Wisconsin, has worked with the Dalai Lama and other experienced meditators on meditation and its effects on the brain. His results suggest that meditation practice causes different levels of activity in brain regions associated with such qualities as anxiety, depression, anger, fear, attention, and the ability of the body to heal itself. These changes in function may be caused by changes in the physical structure of the brain.

RESEARCH—MEDITATION, NEUROPLASTICITY, & WELLBEING

Below are abstracts from a selection of research studies on meditation. These studies have been conducted in respected research institutions and are published in peer reviewed scientific journals.

Mind Wandering Diminishes Happiness. Where we place our attention has a huge impact on our happiness, more so than what we're actually *doing*. According to a recent Harvard study, "A Wandering Mind is an Unhappy Mind", our minds are wandering approximately 47% of the time. Importantly, when considering predictors of happiness, what people were thinking about was a better predictor than what they were actually doing. Researchers explain that when our minds are wandering, there is a tendency for the "negativity bias" to kick in, and we tend to worry about the past or future rather than living in the moment. Killingsworth, M. A., & Gilbert, D. T. (2010). A Wandering Mind Is an Unhappy Mind. *Science.*

Rewire the Brain. A number of studies have indicated that meditation helps to rewire the brain. A recent study at Yale University, for example, indicates that the brains of experienced meditators may actually work differently that the brains of non-meditators. The study provides evidence that meditation changes the way that the brain works and could give meditators an advantage when it comes to dealing with life issues and stress.

Neurons that fire together wire together.

Brain Changes with Mindful Awareness. Mindful awareness practices are associated with physiological changes in the brain. After 2 months of participation in a mindfulness meditation-training program, participants showed changes in brain and immune functioning. The brain changes were in areas associated with positive emotions. Davidson, et al. (2003). Changes in brain function with mindfulness meditation.

A recent study involving long-term mindfulness meditators showed increases in theta band activity and coherence in frontal areas of the brain during deep meditative states. Increase in theta activity in this region suggests an increase in attentional processing and working memory operations. This increase was accompanied by deactivation in theta activity in parietal-occipital areas signifying a reduction in the processing associated with self, space, and time. Baijal, S. & Srinivasan, N. (2010). Theta activity and meditative states: Spectral changes during concentrative meditation. *Cognitive Processing*, 11(1), 31-38.

Thirty-minutes of meditation for 8 weeks changes the brain. A recent study shows that practicing thirty minutes of mindfulness meditation a day for eight weeks can improve the brain. This study shows that areas of the brain involved in memory, sense of self, empathy, stress, and emotion regulation all showed increases in density of gray-matter after the trial period. The study also found a decrease in gray-matter in the amygdala pointing to a decreasing stress and anxiety. Holzel, B., Carmody, J., Vangel, M., Congleton, C., Yerramsetti, S., Gard, T., Lazar, S. (2011, January) Mindfulness practice leads to increases in regional brain gray matter density. *Psychiatry Research Neuroimaging.* 191(1). 36-43.

Meditation Improves Cognitive Functioning. Mindfulness meditation was compared to a control condition (listening to an audio of The Hobbit) for effects on self-report measures and a visuo-spatial task. After each of the four 20-minute sessions of meditation training, participants indicated reduced fatigue and anxiety as well as significantly improved visuo-spatial processing, working memory, and executive function. Zeidan, F., Johnson, S. K., Diamond, B. J., David, Z., & Goolkasian, P. (2010). Mindfulness meditation improves cognition: Evidence of brief mental training. Consciousness and Cognition

The attentional component of mindfulness has been associated with better task performance and fewer cognitive failures. (e.g. forgetting, distraction, blunders, etc.) . Dane, E. (2010). Reconsidering the trade-off between expertise and flexibility: A cognitive entrenchment perspective. *Academy of Management Review*, 35, 579–603.

Meditation Reduced Fatigue and Increased Job Satisfaction. Employees who practiced mindfulness meditation reported less emotional exhaustion and greater job satisfaction after the practice compared to employees who did not practice mindfulness meditation. Hulsheger, U. R., Alberts, H. J., Feinholdt, A., & Lang, J. W. (2012). Benefits of Mindfulness at Work: The Role of Mindfulness in Emotion Regulation, Emotional Exhaustion, and Job Satisfaction. *Journal of Applied Psychology.*

Brain and Immune Function Changes. For an 8-week period, 25 employees were trained in a well-known mindfulness meditation program (MBSR) and data were collected on brain changes using an EEG. There were 16 control subjects who were not given the program and EEG data was also recorded. At the end of the 8 weeks, both groups were given the influenza vaccine. Results show an increase in left-sided anterior brain activation (pattern associated with positive affect) in the meditators, as well as a significant increase in antibody titers compared with the control group. Most importantly, the magnitude of left-sided activation predicted the magnitude of antibody titer found in the bodies of meditators. These findings demonstrate that meditation can change brain and immune function in a positive way. Davidson, R J. (2003). Alterations in brain and immune function produced by mindfulness meditation. *Psychosomatic medicine*, 65(4), 564-570.

Psychological Functioning. A study of long-term meditators and non-meditators showed that long-term meditators have higher levels of psychological functioning. Long-term meditators showed decreased rumination, lower avoidance of emotion, and increases in adaptive functioning and emotional regulation. Lykins, E. L. B., & Baer, R. A. (2009). Psychological functioning in a sample of long-term practitioners of mindfulness meditation. *Journal of Cognitive Psychotherapy*, 23(3), 226-241.

Decreased stress, improved immune response. Many studies have shown that months or years of intensive meditation training can improve attention. However, in this study, after only 5 days of mind-body meditation training for 20 minutes, meditators showed significantly better attention and control of stress compared to the control group who received relaxation training. More specifically, meditators showed greater improvement in conflict scores on the Attention Network Test, lower anxiety, depression, anger, and fatigue, and higher vigor on the Profile of Mood States scale, significant decrease in cortisol and increase in immunoreactivity. Tang, Y., et al. (2007). Short-term meditation training improves attention and self-regulation. PNAS,104(43), 17152-17156.

Meditation and Health. This review examined the link between meditative practices and whether or not there is a long lasting impact on physical health. Meditation induces psychological changes, which further results in improvements to one's immune and cardiovascular health. The mind-body interaction is strongly linked and can be changed through meditative practices. Kok, B.E., Waugh, C.E., & Fredrickson, B.L. (2013). Meditation and health: The search for mechanisms of action. *Social and Personality Psychology Compass, 7(1),* 27-39.

Meditation and Healing. In an early study by Jon Kabat-Zinn, the data revealed that mindfulness can greatly accelerate the healing of psoriasis, a skin condition. All participants were given the usual PUVA or UVB treatments, but for half of them, listened to recordings of John Kabat-Zinn's guided meditation during the treatment. Those listening to guided meditation instructions while receiving usual treatment had a significantly accelerated rate of skin clearing.

Improve Concentration and Ability to Cope with Stressors. Research suggests that meditation increases awareness, improves concentration, and provides meditators with a better ability to deal with the cognitive and emotional stresses of contemporary life. Dr. Judson Brewer, the medical director of the Yale Therapeutic Neuroscience Clinic, conducted a study during which experienced meditators and people with no meditation experience practiced three basic meditation techniques—*concentration, loving-kindness,* and *choice-less awareness.* fMRI (functional magnetic resonance imaging) was used to observe the participants' brain activity when they were practicing the meditative techniques and when they were asked to not think of anything in particular. The experienced meditators had decreased activity in an area of the brain call the "default mode network," a region that is usually at work when the mind wanders. Even when the meditators were not meditating, this area of the brain was much calmer than that of the inexperienced meditators. When the "default mode" networks of the experienced meditators were active, so too were the brain regions that are associated with self-monitoring and cognitive control.

Researchers concluded that one of the things that meditation and basic mindfulness appear to be doing is to quiet down this "default mode" region of the brain, which is the self-monitoring region. Brewer suggests that this may indicate the neurological basis for the many benefits reported by meditators. It is worth noting that a psychological hallmark of many forms of mental illness—anxiety, depression, post-traumatic stress disorder, and schizophrenia—is a fixation on one's own negative thoughts. A series of studies have linked these disorders with over-activity or faulty neurological wiring in the "default mode" network.

Meditation Relieves Negative Emotions. Fred Luthans and colleagues examined randomized clinical trials to determine the effectiveness of mindfulness meditation in improving psychological stress. They found that mindfulness meditation had a moderate positive impact on anxiety, depression, and pain and underscore the importance of further studies to explore how meditation may improve the positive aspects of mental health. Luthans, F., Avolio, B. J., Avey, J. B., & Norman, S. M. (2007). Positive psychological capital: Measurement and relationship with performance and satisfaction. Personnel Psychology, 60(3), 541-572.

Mindfulness and Positivity. A mindfulness-based stress reduction study explored whether healthy college-students could decrease psychological distress through a 6-week adapted mindfulness-based stress reduction (MBSR) intervention. Compared to the control group, study participants self-reported a significant reduction in psychological distress and a marked increase in mindful awareness by beginning mindfulness practices, suggesting that MBSR can bring a wide range of positive benefits in a relatively short time. Canby, N. K., Cameron, I. M., Calhoun, A. T., & Buchanan, G. M. (2014). A Brief Mindfulness Intervention for Healthy College Students and Its Effects on Psychological Distress, Self-Control, Meta-Mood, and Subjective Vitality. *Mindfulness*, 1-11.

Greater empathy. A study researching experienced meditators found that seasoned practitioners have greater levels of empathy. The study showed that mindfulness meditators had stronger activation in temporal parietal junctures when exposed to the sound of suffering indicating a higher empathic response. Lutz, A., Brefczynski-Lewis, J., Johnstone T., Davidson,RJ. (2008, March) Regulation of the neural circuitry of emotion by compassion meditation: effects on meditative expertise. 26;3(3).

Reduced Social Anxiety. In a study using Mindfulness Based Stress Reduction (MBSR), a cognitive therapy program utilizing principles of mindfulness, people with social anxiety disorder completed therapy in order to determine its effects on emotion reactivity and regulation on negative self-beliefs. Fourteen patients underwent MRI scans while completing 3 tasks: reacting to negative self-beliefs, emotion regulation using breath-focused attention, and emotion regulation using distraction-focused attention. Results for people who completed MBSR showed: improved self-esteem, as well as depression and anxiety symptoms; decreased negative emotion experience; reduced amygdala activity (amygdala is the fear center of the brain); and increased activity in brain areas involved in attention. Goldin, P R.; Gross JJ. (2010). Effects of mindfulness-based stress reduction (MBSR) on emotion regulation in social anxiety disorder. *Emotion*, 10(1), 83-91.

For information on fMRI studies on mindfulness meditation:

• Gollub Neuroimaging Lab projects or the recently studies on Tibetan meditation practices at the University of Wisconsin.

• Harvard Medical School Neuroimaging Lab, www.mgh.harvard.edu/depts/neuroimaging/gollublab

• Health Emotions Research Institute, Scientifically Determining How Emotions Influence Health, University of Wisconsin, www.healthemotions.org

• Erisman, S. M. & Roemer, L. (2010). A preliminary investigation of the effects of experimentally induced mindfulness on emotional responding to film clips. *Emotion*, 10(1), 72-82.

- Epel, E. (2009). Can meditation slow rate of cellular aging? Cognitive stress, mindfulness, and telomeres. Longevity, regeneration, and optimal health: Integrating Eastern & Western perspectives, 34-53.
- Birnie, K., Garland, S. N. and Carlson, L. E. (2010), Psychological benefits for cancer patients and their partners participating in mindfulness-based stress reduction (MBSR). *Psycho-Oncology*, 19: 1004–1009. doi: 10.1002/pon.1651
- Evans, D. Baer, R. Segerstrom, S. (2009, September) The effects of mindfulness and self-consciousness on persistence. *Personality and Individual Differences*, 47(4), 379-382.

Other Meditation Sources. There are many online sources for meditations. Recordings of the meditations in this book are at ChoosingHappiness.com. Several additional sources are listed below.

- ChoosingHappiness.com. Go to the Shop webpage for guided meditations.
- UCLA Mindful Awareness Research Center (marc.ucla.edu)
- The Guided Meditation Site (www.the-guided-meditation-site.com)
- Insight Meditation Society (www.dharma.org)
- Guided Meditation (www.healthjourneys.com)

RESEARCH ON MEDITATION AND TELOMERE ACTIVITY

Understanding the malleable determinants of cellular aging is critical to understanding human longevity. Telomeres may provide a pathway for exploring this question. Telomeres are the protective caps at the ends of chromosomes. The length of telomeres offers insight into mitotic cell and possibly organismal longevity. Telomere length has now been linked to chronic stress exposure and depression. Telomerase activity is a predictor of long-term cellular viability, which decreases with chronic psychological distress.

Buddhist traditions claim that meditation decreases psychological distress and promotes well-being, but previously it had not been established that this happens in a measurable way or if it does, how meditation does this. Telomeres provide one source of evidence for this relationship.

Perceived Control and Negativity Linked to Meditation and Telomerase Activity. In the first study to link meditation and positive psychological change with telomerase activity, researchers investigated the effects of a 3-month meditation retreat on telomerase activity and two major contributors to the experience of stress: Perceived Control (associated with decreased stress) and Neuroticism (associated with increased subjective distress). In addition, they investigated whether two qualities developed by meditative practice, increased Mindfulness and Purpose in Life, accounted for retreat-related changes in the two stress-related variables and in telomerase activity. The data suggested that increases in perceived control and decreases in negative affectivity contributed to an increase in telomerase activity, with implications for telomere length and immune cell longevity. Further, Purpose in Life was influenced by meditative practice and directly affects both perceived control and negative emotionality, affecting telomerase activity directly as well as indirectly. Jacobs, T.L., et Al. (2011). Intensive meditation training, immune cell telomerase activity, and psychological mediators. Psychoneuroendocrinology.

Meditation Affects Telomere Length By Decreasing Stress. In this study, researchers investigated the question: *How might cellular aging be modulated by psychological functioning?* They considered two psychological processes or states that are in opposition to one another–threat cognition and mindfulness–and their effects on cellular aging. Psychological stress cognitions, particularly appraisals of threat and ruminative thoughts, can lead to prolonged states of reactivity. In contrast, mindfulness meditation techniques appear to shift cognitive appraisals from threat to challenge, decrease ruminative thought, and reduce stress arousal.

Mindfulness may also directly increase positive arousal states. They reviewed data linking telomere length to cognitive stress and stress arousal and present new data linking cognitive appraisal to telomere length. Given the pattern of associations revealed so far, they concluded that some forms of meditation may have salutary effects on telomere length by reducing cognitive stress and stress arousal and increasing positive states of mind and hormonal factors that may promote telomere maintenance. Aspects of this model are currently being tested in ongoing trials of mindfulness meditation. Epel, E., Daubenmier, J., Moskowitz, J. T., Folkman, S., & Blackburn, E. (2009). Can Meditation Slow Rate of Cellular Aging? Cognitive Stress, Mindfulness, and Telomeres. Annals of the New York Academy of Sciences.

Meditation Improves Telomerase Activity in Family Care Givers. This pilot study found that brief daily meditation practices by family dementia caregivers can lead to improved mental and cognitive functioning, and lower levels of depressive symptoms. This improvement was accompanied by an increase in telomerase activity suggesting improvement in stress-induced cellular aging. Thirty-nine family dementia caregivers were randomized to practicing Kirtan Kriya or listening to relaxation music for 12 minutes per day for eight weeks. The severity of depressive symptoms, mental and cognitive functioning were assessed at baseline and follow-up. Telomerase activity in peripheral blood mononuclear cells was examined pre- and post-intervention. Lavretsky, H., et Al. (2012). A pilot study of yogic meditation for family dementia caregivers with depressive symptoms: effects on mental health, cognition, and telomerase activity. International Journal of Geriatric Psychiatry.

Loving-Kindness Meditation Associated with Telomere Length in Women. Researchers examined relative telomere length in a group of individuals experienced in Loving-Kindness Meditation, a practice derived from the Buddhist tradition, which utilizes a focus on unselfish kindness and warmth towards all people, and control participants who had done no meditation. Fifteen Loving-Kindness practitioners and 22 control participants. Among women, the Loving-Kindness practitioners had significantly longer telomeres than controls, which remained significant even after controlling for past depression. Although limited by small sample size, these results offer the intriguing possibility that Loving-Kindness practice, especially in women, might alter telomere length, a biomarker associated with longevity. Hoge, E.A., et Al. (2013). Loving-Kindness Meditation practice associated with longer telomeres in women. Brain, Behavior, and Immunity.

Meta-Analysis of Mindfulness Meditation and Telomeres. The enzyme telomerase, through its influence on telomere length, is associated with health and mortality. Four pioneering randomized control trials, including a total of 190 participants, provided information on the effect of mindfulness meditation on telomerase. A meta-analysis study indicated that mindfulness meditation leads to increased telomerase activity in peripheral blood mononuclear cells. These results suggest the need for further large-scale trials investigating optimal implementation of mindfulness meditation to facilitate telomerase functioning.
Schutte, N.S. & Malouff, J.M. (2014). A meta-analytic review of the effects of mindfulness meditation on telomerase activity. Psychoneuroendocrinology.

Mindfulness Meditation Affects Telomerase Activity in Women With Breast Cancer. Meditation Mindfulness-based stress reduction (MBSR) reduces symptoms of depression, anxiety, and fear of recurrence among breast cancer survivors. Breast cancer patients (142 women) with Stages 0–III cancer who had completed adjuvant treatment with radiation and/or chemotherapy at least 2 weeks prior to enrollment and within 2 years of completion of treatment with lumpectomy and/or mastectomy were randomly assigned to either a 6-week MBSR or a usual care. These results provide preliminary evidence that MBSR increases telomerase activity in peripheral blood mononuclear cells from BC patients and have implications for understanding how MBSR may extend cell longevity at the cellular level. Lengacher, C.A., et Al. (2014). Influence of Mindfulness-Based Stress Reduction (MBSR) on Telomerase Activity in Women With Breast Cancer. Biological Research For Nursing.

Mindfulness Meditation decreases distress and influence cortisol levels. Group psychosocial interventions including mindfulness-based cancer recovery and supportive-expressive group therapy can help breast cancer survivors decrease distress and influence cortisol levels. Although telomere length has been associated with breast cancer prognosis, the impact of these two interventions on telomere length had not been studied prior to this study.

Experimental participants either engaged in training in mindfulness meditation and gentle Hatha yoga or supportive-expressive group therapy focused on emotional expression and group support. The control group received usual care, which did not include group work. Both of the groups in receiving psychosocial interventions providing stress reduction and emotional support resulted in maintenance of telomere length whereas it was found to decrease for participants receiving usual care. Carlson, L., et Al. (2014). Mindfulness-Based Cancer Recovery (MBCR) and Supportive Expressive Therapy (SET) Maintain Telomere Length (TL) and Cortisol Slopes Relative to Control in Distressed Breast Cancer Survivors. The Journal of Alternative and Complementary Medicine.

THREE BREATHS MEDITATION

One of the simplest and most effective meditations that you can use is simply taking a few conscious breaths. It is quick, easy, and powerful. We stop, breathe, observe, and connect with inner and outer experience.

This basic Low Road technique increases awareness of the body and gets the attention away from thought so that calmness and clarity can potentially arise. This technique can be used at any point during the day and incorporated into other practices.

During all the meditations, try to let go of expectations about how the practice is supposed to feel or what is supposed to happen. Your job is to do two things. First, observe sensations in your body with a nonjudgmental, explorative manner. Second, each time your mind wanders, turn your attention back to sensations in your body.

INSTRUCTIONS
(1 minute)

1. FOCUS INWARD: Breathe and Center

- **Center**—Close your eyes and turn your attention inward.
- **Anchor in Your Breath**—Feel your breath fill and release your body. Breathe deeply with a slower exhale and natural inhale. Place your hand on your abdomen to feel your diaphragm rise and fall.

2. DIRECT ATTENTION: Three Breaths

- *First Breath:* **Feel Your Breath**—Feel the air flowing in and out of your chest, down into your lungs and diaphragm. Feel your chest rising and falling. We have some 20,000 breaths per day. Notice these breaths in this moment. Breath is one of the constants in life. From the moment life begins to the moment life ends there is breath.

- *Second Breath:* **Feel Your Body**—Notice the sensations in your body.

- *Third Breath:* **Connect with Calm, Joy or Centeredness**—Experiment with summoning a momentary sense of calm, joy, or simply feeling centered in your body and mind.

3. REFLECT ON INSIGHTS: Reflect

- Reflect on the insights or benefits you gained during this meditation.

4. MAINTAIN INNER AWARENESS: Soft Gaze and Stay with Awareness

- Slowly open your eyes and keep your gaze soft, directed downward, settling on a neutral object.
- Stay with the awareness you gained during the meditation.

THREE BREATHS MEDITATION WORKSHEET

After you have completed the meditation, jot down observations about what you experienced, observed, thought, or felt during your meditation.

1. FOCUS INWARD.

To what extent were you able to focus inward and turn your attention away from what was going on around you?

_____
_____

To what extent were you able to center yourself in this time and place?

_____
_____

To what extent did you turn your attention back to the meditation when thoughts came into your mind?

_____
_____

2. DIRECT ATTENTION.

What was it like to feel the sensations in your breath anchor point?

_____
_____

What was it like to feel the sensations in your body?

_____
_____

What was it like to attempt to summon feelings of calm, joy, or centeredness?

_____
_____

3. INSIGHTS AND BENEFITS. What insights or benefits did you gain from this meditation?

_____
_____

How might you use or modify this meditation to increase your ability to thrive?

_____
_____
_____
_____

THREE BREATHS TRACKING LOG

DAY	APPLICATION How did I use Three Breaths meditation? When and where?	IMPACT What was the impact of this meditation on me, others, and/or my situation?
Day 1		
Day 2		
Day 3		
Day 4		

THREE BREATHS TRACKING LOG

DAY	APPLICATION How did I use Three Breaths meditation? When and where?	IMPACT What was the impact of this meditation on me, others, and/or my situation?
Day 5		
Day 6		
Day 7		

INSIGHTS - What benefits or patterns emerged?

_____
_____
_____
_____
_____
_____

THE SCIENCE OF BECOMING AN EXPERT

Research suggests that there is a formula for becoming an expert in any domain. It requires training, deliberate practice, and feedback. With these three ingredients, skill level in just about any domain will improve. We apply this model to help you become an expert in Mindful Leadership.

Sports Psychology. Applied sport psychology investigates and works with the psychological aspects of performance. The goal of applied sports psychology is to optimize performance and enjoyment through the use of psychological skills, which is a parallel objective of this program. Just like coaches for Olympian athletes or professional sports teams, we, too, use a coaching approach to improve performance. Coaches use a systematic process, which assists the individual to become more aware of their thoughts, actions, and emotions that influence their performance.

Modern Psychology. In this program, we pull upon findings from high-performance sports psychology as well as in Cognitive Behavioral Therapy (CBT) and Acceptance and Commitment Therapy (ACT), which are cutting edge empirically-supported psychotherapy approaches. CBT is a form of modern psychotherapy that emphasizes the role of thinking in how we feel and what we do. In recent years, it has gained extreme popularity because of the rapid and powerful results.

SELF-COACHING PROCESS & TOOLKIT

The Self-Coaching Process is a systematic process to build expertise. For each skill, *assess* your current level of expertise or need, *plan* how you will apply the skill, *practice* the application of the skill and concepts, *track* your practice and impact, and *reassess* skill level and need.

SELF-COACHING PROCESS

1. ASSESS
2. PLAN
3. PRACTICE
4. TRACK

The toolkit refers to the worksheets, guides, and tracking logs that accompany each skill in this workbook. These tools equip you to be your own coach when you apply them in this Self-Coaching Model.

STEP 1. ASSESS—Assess current mastery level. Assess the need and benefits of practicing this particular skill. Identify reasons why this particular skill will improve your Target Area and positivity ratio. Assess your current mastery level of the skill. Use one of the on-line assessment tools if one is available for the skill. The Coaching Worksheet will also help you assess your need and benefits of using the skill.

Assessments—Questionnaires that assess your current skill level and provide data on progress.

Many of the *Assessments* are questionnaires to help you to assess your current standing with the skill, and to help you to track your progress. The research on the psychometrics of positive psychology is producing a growing number of *assessment tools* that can be used to measure various components of happiness. You may want to access these tools as you continue to coach yourself.

The assessment tools are one of many ways a systematic approach can be employed to develop a greater understanding our own levels of skills. Many of the assessment questionnaires can be found online, and a number of them can be found at Dr. Seligman's website at www.authenticehappiness.org.

Worksheets—The coaching worksheets also are designed to help you to assess your skill or a situation, as well as to plan strategies.

STEP 2. PLAN—Identify your goal. Create a plan. Create an action plan to apply the strategies to an area of your life, and to build new habits of thought and action. For each skill, you have the opportunity to take an *assessment* if one is available, complete a *coaching worksheet* on a situation of your own, practice a *meditation* reinforcing the skill using a *meditation guide*, and track your application of the skill over a seven-day period using a *tracking log*. You can build all of these resources into your action plan. To create an action plan, understand how a technique can help you improve your Target Area and build greater mastery of a skill. Next, consider how you can apply it to your own situations.

Coaching Worksheets—Tools for learning and creating an action plan for practicing the techniques. In the handbook, we emphasize the development of the habits and skills. The readings, lectures, exercises, and meditations help us to understand the concepts, principles and research. In order to actually change our habitual ways of responding, we need to do some "reprogramming" of our thinking patterns.

Mental Programs. Cognitive psychology often uses the computer metaphor to help us to understand what is going on in our mind and how it effects our emotions and our behavior. If we use the computer metaphor in discussing happiness, emotional and social intelligence, we can think of certain "destructive habits" as "programs," programs that typically make us unhappy.

Reprogramming. Continuing with the metaphor, we might say that learning new habits of thinking and behaving, which may make us happier, is achieved by "reprogramming" our mind. For the handbook, we have developed a set of easy-to-use tools to assist us in our reprogramming efforts. Each module in the handbook has exercises that introduce you to worksheets that help you to apply the skills. The worksheets are designed to provide you with a very focused set of activities to assist you to apply the concepts.

Practice. If we shift from the computer metaphor to a sports analogy, we know that we learn to become more proficient in a sport by practicing it systematically on a daily basis. This is similarly true of cooking, playing the piano, ballroom dancing, etc. There are procedures or steps to follow, and the more we practice them, the more proficient we become. Learning the skills can be enhanced with the worksheets, which help us to focus on the behaviors and thought processes that we need to practice during the week.

STEP 3. PRACTICE—Practice high- and low-road exercises. The application of these tools will help you to build the habit patterns connected with the skill. For that one skill that you have selected, complete any assessments for the skill, and fill out the coaching worksheet for the skill. During the following seven days, apply the skill daily, and record your use of the skill and its impact on you in the Tracking Log. Do the meditation connected with the skill on a regular basis during the seven days. Use both the High Road techniques and the Low Road techniques to practice the skill.

Tracking Logs—Habit forming tools to guide your efforts as you practice the techniques for seven days.

The logs encourage you to use the skill on a daily basis and track your use of a particular skill over a period of seven days. They also encourage you to record the impact of the skill on your feelings and thoughts. They provide you with a well organized and specific method of daily journaling.

Meditation Guides—Low Road techniques to build the skill at the emotional or nonverbal level.

Meditation Guides are learning tools to help you more directly practice the skill at the nonverbal level. They are designed to be used with the guided meditations. This low road approach can often help us to get more directly to unhelpful thoughts and emotions and can help to more rapidly rewire our mental and emotional patterns.

STEP 4. TRACK—What did you do? What impact did it have? *Tracking Logs* provide a place to note the impact of the skill on your experience. Tracking Logs help you become more aware of behaviors and patterns in yourself. They are a source of feedback so you can modify a technique to make it more effective.

ADDITIONAL RESOURCES

OTHER MINDFULNESS-BASED PROGRAMS

In the last ten years there has been an upwelling of mindfulness-based emotional intelligence and positive intelligence programs. The leading expert is Robert Weissberg at the Center for Academic and Social and Emotional Learning. Their social and emotional intelligence programs have been well-researched and are highly respected. Since adding mindfulness practices to their programs, they state they have seen even greater benefits. The *MindUp Curriculum* created by the actor Goldie Hawn's The Hawn Foundation has demonstrated strong advantages for children learning this mindfulness-based emotional intelligence program.

Search Inside Yourself, an emotional intelligence program developed at Google, is based in mindfulness practice. This program has been taught to thousands of Googlers around the world. Its mission is to train enlightened leaders worldwide in order to create the conditions for world peace. In the service of this mission, since 2013, this program has been delivered in major companies outside of Google. We provided Chade-Meng Tan, the mastermind behind the program, with an earlier version of this *Enhancing Emotional Intelligence* workbook when he was developing Search Inside Yourself and writing his book of the same name. Laura Delizonna is a lead trainer for Search Inside Yourself.

Daniel Goleman, who popularized emotional intelligence and recently released his latest book entitled *Focus*, describes mindfulness as a foundational skill that enables emotional intelligence to emerge. Annie McKee, co-author of *Resonant Leadership and Primal Leadership*, also emphasizes the importance of mindfulness in emotional intelligence. She calls mindfulness an essential factor in resonant, or highly effective, prosocial leadership.

RESEARCH—OTHER MINDFULNESS-BASED PROGRAMS

Mindfulness Education (ME) program. ME facilitates the development of social and emotional competence and positive emotions. Students engaged in mindful attention training three times a day. A total of 246 pre- and early adolescent students in the 4th to 7th grades (six ME program classrooms and six comparison wait-list control classrooms) completed pretest and posttest self-report measures assessing optimism, general and school self-concept, and positive and negative affect. Teachers rated pre- and early adolescents on dimensions of classroom social and emotional competence. Results revealed that pre- and early adolescents who participated in the ME program, compared to those who did not, showed significant increases in optimism from pretest to posttest. Similarly, improvements on dimensions of teacher-rated classroom social competent behaviors were found. Schonert-Reichl & Stewart-Lawlor (2010). The Effects of Mindfulness-Based Education Program on Pre- and Early Adolescents' Well-Being and Social and Emotional Competence, Mindfulness(1) 137-151.

MindUP Curriculum. Kimberly Schonert-Reichl at University of British Columbia evaluated the effectiveness of MindUP™ on students in grades 4 and 5, based on evidence centered on neuroendocrine regulation, executive functions and self and peer reports of pro-social behaviors.

Improved Optimism and Self- Concept:
    82% of children reported having a more positive outlook
    81% of children learned to make themselves happy
    58% of children tried to help others more often

Healthy Neuroendocrine Regulation:
    Measurement of salivary cortisol revealed MindUP™ children maintained a healthy, regulated diurnal pattern.

Increased Executive Function:
    Children demonstrated faster reaction times while performing tests such as Dr. Diamond's "Flanker Fish" trials. The correlates to heightened self-regulatory ability.

Positive Teacher Response:
   100% reported that MindUP™ positively influenced classroom culture and that students were significantly more attentive.

Academic Achievement:
   15% of students improved their math achievement scores

Schonert-Reichl, K. A. and Lawlor, M. (2010). The Effects of a Mindfulness- Based Education Program on Pre- and Early Adolescents' Well-Being and Social and Emotional Competence. Mindfulness and

Schonert- Reichl, K. A., Oberle, E., Lawlor, M. S., Abbott, D., Thomson, D., Oberlander, T., & Diamond, A. (2011). Enhancing cognitive and social- emotional competence through a simple-to- administer school program.

ADDITIONAL BOOKS

There are many books related to emotional intelligence written by top research psychologists. A few are listed below:

Damasio, Antonio. *Descartes' Error: Emotion, Reason, and the Human Brain.* 2005.

Ekman, Paul. *Emotions Revealed, Recognizing Faces and Feelings to Improve Communication and Emotional Life.* 2007.

Ekman, Paul, and Dali Lama. *Emotional Awareness: Overcoming the Obstacles to Psychological Balance and Compassion.* 2008.

Elias, Maurice (Editor), and Arnold, Harriett (Editor). *The Educator's Guide to Emotional Intelligence and Academic Achievement: Social-Emotional Learning in the Classroom.* 2006.

Goleman, Daniel. *Focus.* 2014.

Goleman, Daniel. *Emotional Intelligence, Why It Can Matter More Than IQ.* 1996.

Goleman, Daniel, Boyatzis, Richard. *Primal Leadership: Learning to Lead with Emotional Intelligence.* 2004.

Goleman, Daniel. *Social Intelligence, The New Science of Human Relationships.* 2006.

Hughes, Marcia. *Emotional Intelligence In Action: Training and Coaching Activities for Leaders and Managers.* 2005.

LeDoux, Joseph. *The Emotional Brain: The Mysterious Underpinnings of Emotional Life.* 1998.

Nelson, Darwin B., and Low, Gary R. *Emotional Intelligence: Achieving Academic and Career Excellence in College and in Life.* 2010.

Pink, Daniel. *A Whole New Mind: Why Right-Brainers Will Rule the Future.* 2006.

INTERNET RESOURCES

Choosing Happiness, Dr. Laura Delizonna, www.choosinghappiness.com

Authentic Happiness, University of Pennsylvania, http://www.authentichappiness.sas.upenn.edu

Center for Positive Organizational Scholarship, Stephen M. Ross School of Business, University of Michigan, www.bus.umich.edu/Positive/

Laboratory for Affective Neuroscience, http://psyphz.psych.wisc.edu/

Emotional Intelligence Information, http://www.unh.edu/emotional_intelligence/

Foundation for Education in Emotional Literacy, http://www.eq.org/

Consortium for Research on Emotional Intelligence in Organizations, http://www.eiconsortium.org/

Daniel Goleman, http://danielgoleman.info/

Professor Sonja Lyubomirsky, UC Riverside, www.faculty.ucr.edu/~sonja

Pew Research Center, Are We Happy Yet?, http://pewresearch.org/pubs/301/are-we-happy-yet,

Positive Emotion and Psychophysiology Lab, University of North Carolina, Chapel Hill, www.unc.edu.peplab

Positive Psychology Center, University of Pennsylvania, www.ppc.sas.upenn.edu

Reflective Learning, www.reflectivelearning.com

University of Pennsylvania, Positive Psychology News Daily, www.pos-psych.com

Values in Action VIA Strengths, Values in Action Institute, www.viastrengths.org

COACHING GUIDELINES

Use the self-coaching process and coaching tools to create long-term change. For maximum effectiveness, focus on one skill at a time. For each skill, take an *assessment* if one is available, complete a *coaching worksheet*, practice high road and low road techniques, and track your application of the skill over a seven day period using a *Tracking Log*.

Select one skill. It is easier to build new habits if you focus on one change at a time. Consider which skill would make the greatest difference in your current life circumstances if you used it more frequently and effectively. Identify reasons why this particular skill would improve your emotional intelligence. Select which skill in this chapter is your priority:

- Mindful Leadership and Its Benefits
- Choice
- Three Breaths

STEP 1. ASSESS. Assess your current mastery level of the skill. Use an online assessment tool if one is available for the skill. The Coaching Worksheet will also help you assess your need and benefits of using the skill.

Assessments—Questionnaires that assess your current skill level and provide data on your progress.

STEP 2. PLAN. To create an action plan, understand how a technique can help you build greater mastery of a skill. Next, consider how you can apply it to your own situations.

Coaching Worksheets—Tools for learning and creating an action plan for practicing the techniques.

- Mindful Leadership and Its Benefits Worksheet
- Choices Worksheet

STEP 3. PRACTICE. During the following seven days, apply the skill daily. Use both High Road techniques and Low Road techniques to practice the skill.

Tracking Logs—Habit forming tools to help guide your efforts as you practice the techniques for seven days.

- Mindful Leadership and Its Benefits Tracking Log
- Choices Tracking Log
- Three Breaths Meditation Tracking Log

Meditation Guides—Low Road techniques to build the skill at the emotional or non-verbal level.

- Three Breaths Meditation

STEP 4. TRACK RESULTS. In addition to structuring your practice of the techniques, *Tracking Logs* provide a place to note the impact of the skill on your experience. Tracking Logs can help you become more aware of behaviors and patterns in yourself. They are a source of feedback so you can modify a technique to make it more effective.

PART TWO

LEARNING THE SKILLS OF MINDFUL LEADERSHIP

What you see determines how you interpret the world, which in turn influences what you expect of the world and how you expect the story of your life to unfold.

~ Sheena Iyengar

AWARENESS IN THE MOMENT

*To live without awareness
is to live as the deaf, blind and dumb
in a world of vibrant light and sound.*

~ Belsebuub

AWARENESS IN THE MOMENT

Let us not look back in anger, nor forward in fear, but around in awareness.
~ James Thurber

Awareness is the ability to perceive, to feel, or to be conscious of events, objects, people, thoughts, emotions, or sensory patterns. Mindful Leaders are self-aware of what they are thinking, feeling, and doing, and are aware of what is going on around them. They tune in to the present, to themselves, to their surroundings, and to others. They listen mindfully for information and for emotions and practice global listening. They focus first on determining what is real, before attempting to alter reality.

Self-Awareness refers to a range of abilities, including being able to detect and describe one's cognitive, affective, and physical states; recognizing broader patterns of functioning and responding; knowing sources of meaning, priorities, and values; and recognizing self-perceptions, viewpoints, strengths, and limitations. Self-Awareness emerges when we are mindful of ourselves across domains and on a moment-to-moment basis. It is the fundamental building block of emotional intelligence. It is a very difficult skill set to master, and we all have blind spots in our self-awareness.

AWARENESS IN THE MOMENT SKILLS PREVIEW

Introduction: Awareness in the Moment
Case Study: Observing Mindful Leadership—John Wood
Exercise: Mindful Leadership Case Study Questions

Skill 1: **SHOW UP**
Tune in to the Present
Exercise: Mindful of a Moment

Savor: Pause, Expand, Absorb
Mindful of A Moment Worksheet & Tracking Log

Skill 2: **LISTEN MINDFULLY**
Three Levels of Listening—Internal, Focused, Global
Check Your Listening Style
Signs of Mindless Listening
How to Listen Mindfully
Mindful Listening Worksheet & Tracking Log

Coaching Guidelines

CASE STUDY: OBSERVING MINDFUL LEADERSHIP

JOHN WOOD
CEO & Founder—Room to Read

World Change Starts with Educated Children ~John Wood

It began with a case of job burnout. John Wood was working hard and making a name for himself as a high-powered executive at Microsoft. He was living the prosperous life of an ex-pat, based out of Sydney and in charge of marketing and business development teams throughout Asia. He was serving as director of business development for the Greater China region and as director of marketing for the Asia-Pacific Region.

But, John needed a vacation, a real vacation far away from the stresses of his 24/7 existence, his cell phone, emails, conference calls, mad dashes for airplanes, and the never ending pressure of making goals and quotas. He happened to pick up a travel brochure with a picture of the snow-capped mountains of the Himalayas on the front. To John it looked peaceful and stress free, and he decided to take a trek through the mountains in Nepal. "I joked that maybe if you went high enough into the Himalayas, you couldn't hear Steve Ballmer screaming at you."

While trekking, at a small lodge on a cold mountain, Wood met a man who turned out to be the "Education Resource Officer" for the schools in the Annapurna Circuit of Nepal. The man invited him to visit a neighboring school and John, In the spirit of friendliness and exploration, went along. After all, John was on vacation and open to life's opportunities.

What John found when he visited the primary school was a place filled with 450 eager, ready-to-learn students, and a library with only four books—a Danielle Steel romance, a thick Umberto Eco novel (in Italian), *The Lonely Planet Guide to Mongolia*, and *Finnegans Wake*. These were back packer leave behinds, but were considered to be so precious that they were kept under lock and key!

John recalls, "My heart sank. How could this be happening in a world with such an abundance of material goods?" John wondered what he could do to help.

"Perhaps sir," said the headmaster, "you will someday come back with books."

This statement haunted John, and he did not wait until he got home to start gathering books. He emailed friends and family from an Internet café in Kathmandu to get things started. A year later John and his father returned to the school with a procession of eight book-bearing donkeys, loaded with 3,000 books. When he came into the village, the villagers were lined up on each side of the road, and little children were spreading flower pedals along the path. The response of the children to the books changed John's life and career path forever. John was aware of the special quality of that moment in his life, and he refers to it as his "epiphany."

"The reaction of the children to those books touched my heart. As they looked at the pictures of African wildlife, and sharks, and the solar system, in my own mind I thought, I'm not going back to my desk to sell software. I'm quitting my job, and dedicating the rest of my life to building hundreds, if not thousands of these rural libraries."

In 1999, John quit his executive position with Microsoft and started *Room to Read*. He began in Nepal, and working with his Co-Founder, Dinesh Shrestha, started working with rural communities to build schools and establish libraries.

John realized that he was taking on an almost impossible task, but instead of looking at the difficulties, he focused on the opportunities. "I challenged my team to think big. I asked them: Why can't we open libraries throughout the world at the same rate that Starbucks is opening new outlets?" Wood took a lesson from the tech world where the founders of companies often announce BHAG's—big, hairy audacious goals.

He thought of Google's mission to "organize the world's information and make it universally accessible and useful;" or Microsoft's pledge to "put a computer on every desk and in every home." John's business was books and literacy, so he decided Room to Read BHAG should be to "reach 10 million children across the developing world with the lifelong gift of education by the end-of-year 2020."

John approached the challenge of educating impoverished children using the tools of business. "When I first started Room to Read, I thought I would be starting from scratch. But, what I realized was that many of the techniques that I used at Microsoft could be applied to this new project—things like thinking big, keeping our overhead low, scaling rapidly."

He likes to say that Room to Read is an organization that "combines the heart of Mother Theresa with the scale-ability of Starbucks." The non-profit is known for its low overhead, transparency, orderly financials, and has received Charity Navigator's highest rating for four stars for eight consecutive years in a row. This is an honor that less than 1% of CN's rated charities can claim.

The core belief of Room to Read is *World Change Starts with Educated Children.* In the first 15 years of its operation, Room to Read has become one of the fastest growing and most effective charities of the past decade. The list of accomplishments is impressive and includes:

- Distributing over 14 million books.
- Building 1,825 schools.
- Establishing 17,366 libraries.
- Training 50,000-plus teachers.
- Benefitting almost 10 million children.

Not only has the charity impacted a large quantity of lives, it has impacted the quality. There are many examples of the programs achieving their stated goals: improving reading skills, and developing the habit of reading among children. In Laos, for example, children at a Room to Read school can read three times faster than children at a control school. In South Africa, 51% of children from supported schools were reading for enjoyment at home compared to 39% from control schools. And children everywhere are seeing new opportunities open up in their lives because they can now read and learn.

John recognizes that positive relationships are one of the major keys to his success. The charity's original list of supporters includes well known Silicon Valley names like Marc Andreessen, Bill Draper, Robin Richards Donohoe, Jeff Skoll and Don Valentine who calls Room to Read "one of the best long-term investments that I have made.

The charity has long-standing relationships and partnerships with companies like *Salesforce*, which houses all of the charity's data free of charge. Software company, *Atlassian*, donates the entire $10 fee for their "starter license" to Room to Read, which has so far amounted to over $4 million.

When asked for his thoughts on Silicon Valley, Wood says one word: "Gratitude." He says he would like to sit down with every early supporter and thank him or her for returning emails, hearing him out, buying in, and for believing. He says that he sees many similarities between tech and philanthropy—working towards a better future, dissatisfaction with the status quo, and a few people seeking to make a large difference.

The Room to Read programs have extremely strong relationships with the local residents. John want positive relationships with the people who have the most influence on the reading success of their children—the parents. Room to Read employs local teams that are personally committed to their own town's educational programs. They know the local customs, speak the language, and understand how to make the programs successful in their community. John says that his favorite part of debuting a new school is meeting he local residents who have invested their own small amounts of money, dug the foundation, or contributed in some other way.

John has a sense of the unfairness of opportunity in the world, something he calls the "lottery of life." He says, "You're born in Scarsdale, you win the right to gain an education. You're born in Bogotá, you're denied that opportunity."

John believes in fairness and has a deep-seated commitment to increase the number of young winners in the lottery of life. "This love of reading, learning, and exploring new worlds so predominates my memory of my youth," he says, "that I simply could not imagine a childhood without books."

John is committed to making a big impact on the big numbers of illiteracy. He points out that nearly 800 million people across the world lack basic literacy—one out of every nine people. One hundred and thirty million youth are out of school and 70% of those are girls. He indicates that if all women in low-income countries had secondary education, there would be 49% fewer child deaths.

Recognizing that educating girls and women is the key to solving some of the world's greatest problems like poverty, hunger, and disease, Room to Read started the *Girls Education Program* in 2001, and thus far over 27,000 girls have been part of the program. The program provides rounded education for a girl, which includes academic support, material support, mentoring, and life skills education-- including everything from financial planning to rights over their bodies.

John also draws on local relationships for local content. There is an enormous need for high quality, age appropriate, children's books in the local language. Wood says, "We responded to this need by setting out to find the JK Rowling of Cambodia, the Dr. Seuss of Nepal, and it's wonderful to see all the creativity we've unleashed." Room to Read has published over 1,000 original titles in 29 local languages and has started a new industry of local authors, illustrators, and editors.

Room to Read will reach its 10 millionth student in 2015, arriving at its almost impossible BHAG goal of 10,000 by 2020 almost five years ahead of schedule. Now that the goal is reached, Wood is not ready to slow down. He suggests that we "look at 10 million not as the culmination of the dream, but as the down payment on the dream. "

In a recent charity annual report, Room to Read's Board Chair, and former Microsoft CFO, Craig Bruya, wrote: "I wonder what our investors would think about adding a zero to our original goal?

Footnote: The information on John Wood and quotes used in this case study can be found in the following sources:
- *Leaving Microsoft to Change the World: An Entrepreneur's Odyssey to Educate the World's Children.* (Haper Collins, 2006)
- *John Wood (activist)* From Wikipedia, the free encyclopedia, en.wikipedia.org/wiki/John_Wood_(activist)4/10/15.
- *Our Story,* Room to Read, www.roomtoread.org/
- *Plot Twist. How a former Microsoft executive changed his storyline and became one of the most innovative and effective philanthropists on the planet.* Story by Amalia McGibbon. Gentry Magazine, March, 2015.
- YouTube. *Room to Read—Leaving Microsoft to Change the World.*

EXERCISE: MINDFUL LEADERSHIP CASE STUDY QUESTIONS

One of the ways to build a better understanding of the skills of mindful leadership is through role models who demonstrate the skills of mindful leadership in their actions. In the *Observing Mindful Leadership Case Studies*, we examine the accomplishments, the actions, the statements, and sometimes the thoughts and emotions of well-known leaders. The cases can help us to see a diversity of mindful leaders operating in many different types of environments, and help us to see how different leaders and different personalities practice the skills of mindful leadership. Use the following questions to help you to better understand this mindful leader.

1. AWARENESS IN THE MOMENT. Mindful Leaders are self-aware of what they are thinking, feeling, and doing, and are aware of what is going on around them. They tune in to the present, to themselves, to their surroundings, and to others. They listen mindfully for information and for emotions and practice global listening. They focus first on determining what is real, before attempting to alter reality.

What can you observe from the writings, statements, and actions of the leader in this case study that demonstrate the skills of awareness in the moment?

_____

_____

_____

_____

_____

_____

_____

_____

_____

_____

2. POSITIVITY & POSSIBILITY. Mindful Leaders are more focused on the positive and the possible than on the negative and impossible. They remain aware of the failures, the risks, the dangers, the realities, and the downsides, but they practice the discipline of thinking in terms of the positives, the opportunities, the probabilities, the options, and the alternatives. Mindful Leaders are aware of the power of positivity to broaden and build positive potential, to encourage novel thoughts and actions, and to inspire productivity and creativity in themselves and others.

What can you observe from the writings, statements, and actions of the leader in this case study that demonstrate the skills of positivity and possibility?

_____

_____

_____

_____

_____

_____

_____

_____

_____

_____

3. POSITIVE RELATIONSHIPS. Mindful Leaders are aware of the power and importance of positive relationships, put conscious time and effort into the development of positive networks, and cultivate empathy, deep dive conversations, and win-win solutions with others. They recognize that some positive conflict can be productive, but go out of their way to avoid negative conflict escalators that thwart communication and cooperation. They take charge of their emotions and responses and work hard to build community and engagement.

What can you observe from the writings, statements, and actions of the leader in this case study that demonstrate the skills of positive relationships?

_____
_____
_____
_____

4. AUTHENTICITY & INTEGRITY. Mindful Leaders are often respected for their authenticity and integrity. Their authenticity is reflected in the truthfulness of their intentions, behaviors, and commitments. Their integrity is reflected in their honesty, their strong moral principles, and their ability to live by those principles. Mindful Leaders are clear on their values and their priorities and make decisions and take actions based upon these values. They are aware of their strengths and look for ways to leverage their strengths in the pursuit of their goals and in the service of others.

What can you observe from the writings, statements, and actions of the leader in this case study that demonstrate the skills of authenticity and integrity?

_____
_____
_____
_____

5. MANAGE STRESS & ENERGY. Mindful Leaders manage their energy and stress in order to maintain high levels of physical, mental, and emotional well-being. They challenge their thoughts to stay in touch with reality, they identify their emotions and emotional triggers and manage their responses, and they consciously monitor and manage their energy.

What can you observe from the writings, statements, and actions of the leader in this case study that demonstrate the skills of manage stress and energy?

_____
_____
_____
_____

6. RESILIENCE. Mindful leaders work to develop resilience—the capacity to recover from difficulties and adversity. They focus on the heroic rather than the debilitating aspects adversity; they let go of perfectionism and shortcomings and focus on the possible and potential; and they practice compassion and self-compassion.

What can you observe from the writings, statements, and actions of the leader in this case study that demonstrate the skills of resilience?

_____
_____
_____
_____

Skill 1. SHOW UP

Often our attention is in the past or future, but rarely in the present moment. We spend much of the time remembering, reflecting, and recalling the past or imagining, forecasting, worrying, or planning for the future. How much time are you actually here and now? Research shows that most of us spend only about half the time in the present moment.

Mind Wandering Diminishes Happiness. Where we place our attention has a huge impact on our happiness, more so than what we're actually *doing*. According to a recent Harvard study, "A Wandering Mind is an Unhappy Mind", our minds are wandering approximately 47% of the time. Importantly, what people were thinking about was a better predictor of happiness levels than what they were actually doing. Researchers explain that when our minds are wandering, there is a tendency for the "negativity bias" to kick in, and we tend to worry about the past or future rather than living in the moment. Even mind wandering on neutral events, however, caused lower happiness levels than being in the present moment. Mind wandering to pleasant events was equal, but not better than, attention on the present. Killingsworth, M. A., & Gilbert, D. T. (2010). A Wandering Mind Is an Unhappy Mind. *Science*.

TUNE IN TO THE PRESENT

The simplest way to increase positivity and to create possibility is to tune into the present moment. We tend to miss our moments because our focus strays to the past, future, or some imagined reality. Effectiveness dramatically diminishes as well. Imagine doing a task while only halfway paying attention. Without realizing it, we often do just that.

The first skill, therefore, is to show up to the present moment. This is surprisingly difficult because we are not there to realize we are not there. By definition, we often do not realize that we are tuned out rather than anchored in the present moment.

EXERCISE: MINDFUL OF THE MOMENT

Slow down your sensory experience to notice all of the subtlety, changes, nuances of a moment. For example, eat just one raisin, listen to one song, or look at one flower with intense curiosity. Focus on the qualities of your sensory experiences.
- Notice the various senses that are involved (taste, smell, hearing, sight, touch).
- Observe your sensory experiences as you mindfully experience.

DESCRIBE. After you have mindfully attended to the experience for a few moments, jot down some words that describe your experience.

_____

_____

INSIGHTS. What are some insights that I got from this experience?

_____

_____

BENEFITS. How might a higher level of presence on a moment-to-moment basis improve my leadership, performance, relationships, health, wellbeing, and overall happiness?

_____

_____

SAVOR: PAUSE, EXPAND, ABSORB

Savoring requires turning your attention to aspects of a situation that are inherently appealing to you. Simply focus and "turn up the volume" on positive experiences, situations or aspects of life. Savoring enhances an already pleasant experience.

Pause to notice, consider, and feel into your positive experiences.

The cliché "stop and smell the roses" is a call to savor. Pausing to take in the sensory experience of a moment heightens enjoyment. By luxuriating in the sensory experience, awareness heightens and positive emotions intensify. Immerse yourself in one of the five senses (taste, smell, sound, sight, or touch). For example, feel the sensory experience of the sweetness of a strawberry, the aroma of fresh-baked bread, the gentle breeze on your skin, the sound of a child's laughter, or the glory of the sky while stuck in traffic. We can also savor an experience, an interaction, an accomplishment, or progress toward a goal. The process is simple, the same no matter the focus of attention, and can profoundly transform experience. When it becomes a habit, this practice can have a powerful impact on happiness and satisfaction.

> **HOW TO SAVOR**
> 1. **Pause**
> 2. **Notice and Expand**
> 3. **Absorb: Take in the Pleasant Experience**

1. PAUSE—Make contact with feelings of a positive experience of a simple pleasure.

The positive experience might be a sight, sound, smell, taste, or touch. It might be a positive experience of a song, a sunrise, a flower, or an exchange with a friend.

2. NOTICE AND EXPAND—Feel the positive sensations and feelings in your body.

Allow the positive feeling to expand and increase in intensity throughout your entire body. Invite this feeling to expand. Perhaps imagine breathing in more of this positive feeling.

3. TAKE IN THE PLEASANT EXPERIENCE—Absorb this positive feeling.

Soak into this positive feeling. Imagine that this positivity is getting absorbed into your memory stores to change you in one small way, increasing your sense of goodness in life.

MINDFUL OF A MOMENT WORKSHEET

When bringing mindful awareness to a pleasant experience it is referred to as savoring. We define savoring as bringing mindful attention to intensify or prolong enjoyment of a pleasant experience. This both is a practice for mindful attention as well as a way to turn positive *events* into memorable *experiences*. The purpose of this worksheet is to plan how you might practice savoring. Consider some experiences that you might savor during the week.

PLAN YOUR PRACTICE

Plan. Ask yourself: *What simple pleasures or progress could I mindfully experience this week?*

IDEAS FOR SAVORING

Sensory Experiences:
- **Taste**—a meal, drink, wine, candy, apple, raisin, etc.
- **Smell**—a flower, ocean, fresh bread, home cooking, etc.
- **Sound**—a song, bird, wind, symphony, voice, laugh, sigh, etc.
- **Sight**—a tree, a flower, a house, a painting, a view, mountain, lake, sunset, etc.
- **Touch**—a hot bath, a sweater, a texture, petting a cat or dog, etc.

Other Daily Experiences:
- **Social connection**—a greeting, smile, laugh, conversation, a synergist team meeting, compassion, etc.
- **Progress**—an accomplishment, reaching a milestone on a project, a synergistic team meeting, etc.
- **Serendipity**—a moment when you had a serendipitous experience
- **Learning or Innovation**—a moment when you realize you have learned something important or cool, are amidst something big happening, cutting edge innovation, etc.

MINDFUL OF A SENSORY EXPERIENCE

Mindfully Taste. What do I plan to savor using my sense of taste? (ex: wine, coffee/tea, chocolate, a meal, etc.)

_____

_____

Mindfully Smell. What do I plan to savor using my sense of smell? (ex: flower, coffee/tea, a meal, etc.)

_____

_____

Mindfully Listen. What do I plan to savor using my sense of hearing? (ex: music, birds, laughing, etc.)

_____

_____

Mindfully See. What do I plan to savor using my sense of sight? (ex: view, art, trees, etc.)

_____

_____

Mindfully Touch. What do I plan to savor using my sense of touch? (ex: warm shower, soft sweater, lotion, petting a cat or dog, etc.)

_____

_____

MINDFUL OF A MOMENT

Social connection—a greeting, smile, laugh, conversation, a synergist team meeting, compassion, etc.
Progress—an accomplishment, reaching a milestone on a project, a synergistic team meeting, etc.
Serendipity—a moment when you had a serendipitous experience
    Learning or Innovation—a moment when you realize you have learned something important or cool, are amidst something big happening, cutting edge innovation, etc.

Social Connection. Which social connection do I plan to be mindful of? (ex: a greeting, smile, laugh, conversation, a synergist team meeting, compassion, etc.)

_____

_____

Progress. How or when could I savor progress? (ex: an accomplishment, reaching a milestone on a project, a synergistic team meeting, etc.)

_____

_____

Serendipity. How or when could I savor when I have a moment of serendipity or similar experience?

_____

_____

Learning or Innovation. How or when could I savor a moment of learning or innovation? (ex: when I have learned something important or cool, am amidst something big happening, doing cutting edge innovation, etc.)

_____

_____

ACTION PLAN

How will I practice being mindful something each day this week?

_____

_____

How will I remember to be mindful?

_____

_____

What are obstacles that might prevent me from practicing mindfulness?

_____

_____

How can I overcome these obstacles?

_____

_____

MINDFUL OF A MOMENT TRACKING LOG

INSTRUCTIONS. Choose something to savor. *Immerse* yourself in your physical and emotional experience of pleasure. Record your experience in the *Tracking Log*.

DAY	APPLICATION How was I mindful in a moment?	IMPACT What was the impact on me, others, or my situation?
Day 1		
Day 2		
Day 3		
Day 4		

MINDFUL OF A MOMENT TRACKING LOG

DAY	APPLICATION How was I mindful in a moment?	IMPACT What was the impact on me, others, or my situation?
Day 5		
Day 6		
Day 7		

INSIGHTS—What patterns or benefits emerged?

_____
_____
_____
_____
_____
_____

Skill 2. LISTEN MINDFULLY

Listening is such a simple act.
It requires us to be present, and that takes practice, but we don't have to do anything else.
We don't have to advise, or coach, or sound wise.
We just have to be willing to sit there and listen.
-Margaret J. Wheatley

Mindfulness is characterized by attending to the moment with awareness, openness, a spirit of receptivity, and non-judging. When we bring this quality of attention to listening, it is commonly referred to as mindful listening. Listening mindfully is being curious and working to understand another's message. The focus is on both the factual and emotional components of the message.

Our version of mindful listening is defined by Harvard Professor Ellen Langer's three elements of mindfulness:

(1) Being open to new information that arises in the present moment.
(2) Non-judgmentally taking multiple perspectives.
(3) Allowing mindsets to be revised based on new information.

When a composer listens to music, he or she hears far more than sound. The composer hears the underlying structure, the interplay of different instruments. The composer hears key changes, recognizes certain musical conventions, as well as unusual or creative additions to the normal patterns of the particular kind of music being played. In the same way, a mindful listener not only hears the words of the other person but also their significance in the context of the larger message. A mindful listener also notices what is not being said, which is often revealing.

Our technique for cultivating this type of attention is based on Lee Glickstein's method that he refers to as "Relational Presence." Relational Presence simply means being available for giving full attention without agenda. It is the pre-condition for connection. It involves being with others without judgment, demands, or expectations. This type of mindful presence improves the capacity to be comfortable with whatever situation arises and to respond in the moment, whether in conflict or sharing joy with another. Lee teaches this way of listening and speaking in a format he refers to as "Speaking Circles."

Sometimes this type of listening is referred to as "active listening," Generally, they refer to the similar practice. Mindful listening techniques generally emphasize the importance of presence, clear mindedness, and non-judgment. Sometimes this includes asking clarifying questions, summarizing the message, and checking for understanding.

Other programs that use mindful listening techniques to build empathy and social skills include but are not limited to: Robert Weissberg's Center for Academic and Social and Emotional Learning, The MindUp Curriculum created by the actor Goldie Hawn's The Hawn Foundation, Search Inside Yourself, and Martin Seligman's positivity-enhancing mindful listening technique he calls Active-Constructive Listening.

BENEFITS

Mindful listening is emphasized in many social intelligence programs, because it is crucial for understanding and managing interactions, relationships, and connection. Lee Glickstein describes a benefit of this method as increasing attunement between the speaker and the listener. Effective leaders do this regularly. Much more information is gained when mindfully listening. Perhaps the greatest benefit, however, is that the feeling of connection between the speaker and the listener improves. Barbara Fredrickson, a leading researcher in positive emotions, emphasizes the importance of this type of attention to create "micro-moments of connection."

MINDLESS LISTENING

Its opposite, mindless listening, is characterized by a quality of attention that is absent, rigid, and governed by mindsets, according to Ellen Langer. In this type of attention as she says, " the lights are on but nobody's home." In an era when attention is under siege, mindless listening seems to become the norm.

In our 21st Century era of distraction, mindful listening is more difficult than ever. Attention is pulled, stretched, and taxed by the constant bombardment of electronic messages. It is common in conversation for the mind to wander, and internal narratives and distracted thoughts to fragment attention. We tend to get caught in our own thoughts, missing emotional signs, verbal cues, and other vital information. Our attention is on our own experience, judging the other, assuming we already know what they will say, or planning a response. This is especially true in a conflict situation.

THREE LEVELS OF LISTENING—INTERNAL, FOCUSED, AND GLOBAL

In her book, *Co-Active Coaching*, Laura Whitworth describes three levels of listening. Mindful listening takes place when listening at Level 2 and Level 3. Mindless listening is characterized by Level 1. In a mindless listener, the focus is on something other than the speaker.

Level 1: Internal Listening. Internal listening is sometimes called "on and off" listening or "distracted" listening. When a person listens at level 1, her attention is on her own experience. She may hear the words of the other person, but she tends to be more aware of her own ideas, feelings, opinions, stories, judgments, and internal chatter. Level 1 listening is characterized by:
- Hearing sounds and words rather than listening.
- Getting only the gist of the conversation.
- Being more interested in talking than listening.
- Nodding and/or saying uh-huh as a cover for disengagement.
- Lack of eye contact.
- Being distracted by things such as mobile phone, email, television, surrounding events, etc.

Level 2: Focused Listening. Focused listening is sometimes called "attentive" listening. When a person listens at level 2, she pays attention to each individual word and phrase and how the other person expresses them. Level 2 listening is characterized by:
- Hearing the words and looking for the meaning.
- Listening for factual content.
- Listening for emotional content.
- Responding by restating, paraphrasing, questioning, and summarizing.

Level 3: Global Listening. Global listening is sometimes called "generous" listening. When a person listens at level 3, he hears the words, tunes into the emotions, and reads the body language, gestures, and tones being used by the other person. Level 3 listening is characterized by:
- Listening without judging.
- Focusing on the present moment.
- Fully processing what is said including factual and emotional content.
- Paying attention to words, tone of voice, and body language.
- Responding by restating, paraphrasing, questioning, and summarizing.

CHECK YOUR LISTENING STYLE

Use the *Listening Style Self-Assessment* to become more aware of your listening style.

MINDFUL LISTENING SURVEY

Instructions: How true are the following statements about you? Please read each statement carefully, and circle the number that corresponds with your level of agreement. Go with your gut response without over-thinking the statements.

Very Strongly Disagree	Strongly Disagree	Mildly Disagree	Neutral	Mildly Agree	Strongly Agree	Very Strongly Agree
1	**2**	**3**	**4**	**5**	**6**	**7**

#	STATEMENT	YOUR RATING
1.	When someone else is talking, I often am preparing my response rather than concentrating on what they are saying.	1 2 3 4 5 6 7
2.	I sometimes finish other people's sentences for them.	1 2 3 4 5 6 7
3.	I get impatient or distracted and start doing other things when I'm bored or annoyed with what another is saying.	1 2 3 4 5 6 7
4.	I interrupt others when they are speaking.	1 2 3 4 5 6 7
5.	I have a hard time looking people in the eye when I am speaking.	1 2 3 4 5 6 7
6.	It is difficult for me to listen without offering my opinion or point-of-view.	1 2 3 4 5 6 7
7.	I find myself changing topics before the person I am talking to is finished with their point.	1 2 3 4 5 6 7

TOTAL SCORE: _____

INTERPRETING YOUR SCORE. If your score was on the higher end, you may especially benefit from practicing mindful listening.

Higher scores *(scores over 35)* indicate that you may be distracted and not really listening well to others. You may find that your attention is on your own experience rather than on the other's experience or message. The words of the other person may be heard, but you may be more aware of your own ideas, feelings, opinions, stories, judgments, and internal chatter.

Midrange scores *(scores 15-34)* indicate that you sometimes engage in mindful listening, but could still improve your ability to listen well.

Low scores *(scores under 14)* indicate that you tend to listen well and focus on the message, speaker, and their spoken and unspoken experience. You are likely to not only hear the content but also tune into the emotions, read the body language, and notice gestures and tones.

SIGNS OF MINDLESS LISTENING

It has been said that communication is a joint game in which the talker and the listener play against the forces of confusion. Mindful listening is important, because communication is difficult even under the best circumstances. When obstacles to mindful listening arise, *mindless* listening is likely to arise. This is characterized by not paying attention to new information, taking narrow or rigid perspectives, judging, and staying in biases or mindsets. Mindless listening compounds difficulty, increasing the probability of mistakes, misunderstanding, hurt feelings, miscommunication, and wasted time and effort.

To reduce impediments to effective communication, watch for signs that you may be more mindless rather than mindful in your listening. The following obstacles or bad habits impede mindful listening and give rise to a mindless listening mode.

Internal Focus. Focusing attention on one's own thoughts, opinions, experiences, or emotions. Often people mean well by listening in this way, especially when they are thinking about how they have had a similar experience or can relate. This prevents mindful listening, however, because the listener is focusing on their own experience, perhaps judging the other from the lens of the listener's experience, assuming they already know what will be said, or planning a response. In conflict, this tends to show up as preparing a reply or thinking some version of "what about me..."

Interruptions. Interrupting the speaker before they finish. The speaker is not allowed to finish thoughts. Interruptions are often interpreted as a lack of respect or interest. Further, the listener who interrupts runs the risk of misinterpreting the message since the speaker was cut short from fully articulating his or her thoughts. People speak at different speeds. A slower speaker may pause frequently to gather thoughts. If another jumps in during their pause, it may feel like interruption to a slower speaker.

Bias. Preconceived ideas or judgments the listener has about the speaker or the message. Biases can distort understanding, acting like a filter that catches some aspects of their message but not others.

Expectations or assumptions about what the other thinks typically result in mindless listening. When holding a belief, we tend to find evidence to confirm it and become blind to contrary evidence. Psychologists refer to this as the Confirmation Bias. This is especially true in a conflict situation. For example, if you believe the other person does not respect you, you are more likely to miss words that express respect and interpret a side-glance or yawn as evidence they are bored with you.

Lack of Focus. Tuning-out, daydreaming, or multi-tasking while a speaker is speaking is a very common poor listening habit. Because the listener is not focused on the speaker, elements of the message will be missed and all of the above habits are likely to strengthen. This is common in our busy, distracted modern culture.

Giving full attention is even more difficult during conflict, because the other's message is inherently hard to hear and distressing. For many, conflict triggers the fight, flight, or freeze reaction. Tuning out is a common attempt to calm the body but this puts us in mindless listening mode.

HOW TO LISTEN MINDFULLY

Listening mindfully generally requires stopping all activity, looking into the speaker's eyes if in person, and allowing the speaker the space to express themselves without interruption. This helps create the conditions through which mindful listening can occur. This is an active process. The conversation can feel quite animated, lively, and balanced. Don't judge what you hear or add meaning to the message initially. Simply observe and experience the speaker and their message. If you become restless or impatient, notice these feelings and allow them, but do not react to them.

HOW TO LISTEN MINDFULLY

1. **Focus.** Give full attention, eye contact, and stop multi-tasking.
2. **Listen without Interrupting.** Speak only when the speaker is finished.
3. **Curiosity.** Notice something new in the message.
4. **Listen Deeply.** Listen for feeling, tone, and intention.

---

1. Focus. Stop multi-tasking and give full attention. The listener simply offers the speaker undivided attention. This is simple yet challenging and surprisingly, uncommon. When one focuses and gets still in mind and body, then mindful listening happens quite effortlessly. This is similar to sleep. If the body is sufficiently tired, the body will naturally fall into sleep without us doing a thing. What tends to get in the way of this process is the mind. When the mind gets busy thinking, worrying, figuring out, regretting, etc., it disrupts the natural sleep process and insomnia ensues.

This is the same with listening. When we get still in our mind and direct focus to the speaker, mindful listening simply happens. However, giving full attention is harder than it seems. Often we think we are giving full attention, but actually we are judging, anticipating our response, thinking about other things, multi-tasking, not looking at the person, and so on.

2. Listen without Interrupting. Speak only when the speaker is finished. When listening mindfully, the listener does not interrupt to provide an opinion, agreement, or a counter viewpoint. Instead, the listener waits until the speaker pauses and then the listener speaks.

Oftentimes, interrupting stems from trying to help the speaker understand better, to offer help, out of excitement, or other well-intended reasons; however, the impact is often the same regardless of the intention. It can send the message that what you have to say is more important than what the speaker is saying. Typically, no one likes to be interrupted.

3. Curiosity. Notice something new in the message. This is the crux of mindful listening. Bring curiosity to the conversation. Rather than assume you know "how it will go," bring a curious, open mind. Allow yourself to be surprised or learn something about the person or situation. When curious, we naturally become more mindful, which is characterized by being open to new information, taking different perspectives, and revising old mindsets. Every conversation can teach us something and impact us in some small way when we bring curiosity to it.

I once met Michael Wallace, one of the original correspondents on the famous American TV show *60 Minutes*. We chatted for a while in a casual, small bookstore on Martha's Vineyard. I asked him what his secret is to interviewing people and his exceptional ability to reveal personal stories. He said, "Everyone has an interesting story—you just have to ask the right questions to pull it out of them." This is a classic demonstration of bringing curiosity to a conversation and, more generally, a high level of mindful listening.

4. Listen Deeply. Consider feelings, intention, or underlying significance (in addition to content). In mindful listening, the listener attends to a deeper level of experience. Slowing down and paying attention enables access to subtle clues about what the speaker is communicating about their emotional and deeper experience.

It can be helpful to intentionally direct attention and take note of the feeling tone of the message, rather than simply the content. It gets really interesting when the speaker's words point to one experience, but the feeling tone conveys an opposite experience. Paying attention at a deeper level also gives access to clues about what matters most to the speaker, what is really important, or significant. This subtle yet critical information often gets lost when not mindfully listening.

MINDFUL LISTENING WORKSHEET

Mindful listening involves getting still in the mind and attention so that we truly hear what the other is saying, what's under their words, what's significant for them, and information about their deeper level of emotional experience. This application gives you an opportunity to practice mindful listening.

SITUATION

Who, Where & When Did I Attempt to Listen Mindfully?

_____
_____
_____

What were some OBSTACLES to mindful listening or SIGNS OF MINDLESS LISTENING that came up? (Interruptions, Criticism, Judgment, Multi-tasking, Preoccupation, Tuning Out)

_____
_____
_____
_____

MINDFUL LISTENING

1. FOCUS. How did I give full attention, stop mullti-tasking, and focus?
Consider intentions, instructions, or reminders you gave yourself. Notice what it looked like, for example, did you give eye contact, stop doing other things, refrain from judgment or rehearsing your response, etc.? What was the impact of listening with full attention?

_____
_____
_____
_____

2. LISTEN WITHOUT INTERRUPTING. To what extent was I able to listen without interrupting? What was the impact of doing this?

_____
_____
_____
_____

3. CUROSITY. What were some new things that I noticed about the message or speaker? What was the impact of listening with curiosity?

_____
_____
_____
_____

4. LISTEN DEEPLY. Which emotions did I pick up on? What was the speaker's intention? What was most significant or important in the speaker's message? What was the impact of listening for feelings, intention, and underlying significance?

_____

_____

_____

_____

5. DEEPER UNDERSTANDING. To what extent did I develop a deeper understanding by listening mindfully? What did I pick up that I might not have otherwise noticed?

_____

_____

_____

_____

_____

6. EMPATHY. What impact did this level of listening have on my level of empathy and sense of connection with the speaker?

_____

_____

_____

_____

_____

7. BENEFIT. How did I benefit from listening mindfully?

_____

_____

_____

_____

8. APPLICATION. How might I improve your ability to listen mindfully during natural conversations to improve understanding and avoid misunderstanding and/or de-escalate conflict situations?

_____

_____

_____

_____

MINDFUL LISTENING TRACKING LOG

DAY	APPLICATION Whom did I mindfully listen to today? How did I do this (i.e., Where was my focus? What was self-talk or reminders I gave myself?)	IMPACT What was the impact of mindful listening on me, others, and/or the situation?
Day 1		
Day 2		
Day 3		
Day 4		

MINDFUL LISTENING TRACKING LOG

DAY	APPLICATION Whom did I mindfully listen to today? How did I do this (i.e., Where was my focus? What was self-talk or reminders I gave myself?)	IMPACT What was the impact of mindful listening on me, others, and/or the situation?
Day 5		
Day 6		
Day 7		

INSIGHTS—What patterns or benefits emerged?

_____
_____
_____
_____
_____

COACHING GUIDELINES

Use the self-coaching process and coaching tools to create long-term change. For maximum effectiveness, focus on one skill at a time. For each skill, take an *assessment* if one is available, complete a *coaching worksheet*, practice high road and low road techniques, and track your application of the skill over a seven day period using a *Tracking Log*.

Select one skill. Consider which skill would make the greatest difference in your current life circumstances if you used it more frequently and effectively. It is easier to build new habits if you focus on one change at a time. Select the *one skill* in this chapter that is your highest priority:

- Show Up
- Mindful Listening

STEP 1. ASSESS. Assess the need and benefits of practicing this particular skill. Assess your current mastery level of the skill. Use one of the on-line assessment tools if one is available for the skill. The Coaching Worksheet will also help you assess your need and benefits of using the skill.

Assessments—Questionnaires that assess your current skill level and provide data on your progress.

STEP 2. PLAN. To create an action plan, understand how a technique can help you build greater mastery of a skill. Next, consider how you can apply it to your own situations.

Coaching Worksheets—Tools for learning and creating an action plan for practicing the techniques.
- Mindful of A Moment Worksheet
- Mindful Listening Worksheet

STEP 3. PRACTICE. During the following seven days, apply the skill daily. Use both the High Road techniques and the Low Road techniques to practice the skill.

Tracking Logs—Habit forming tools to guide your efforts as you practice the techniques for seven days.
- Mindful of A Moment Tracking Log
- Mindful Listening Tracking Log

Meditation Guides—Low Road techniques to build the skill at the emotional or non-verbal level.

STEP 4. TRACK RESULTS. In addition to systematically helping you to practice the techniques, *Tracking Logs* provide a place to note the impact of the skill on your experience. Tracking Logs help you become more aware of behaviors and patterns in yourself. They are a source of feedback so you can modify a technique to make it more effective.

POSITIVITY
&
POSSIBILITY

*I am neither an optimist nor pessimist,
but a possibilist.*
~ Max Lerner

"Most of the things worth doing in the world had been declared impossible before they were done."
~ Louis D. Brandeis

POSITIVITY & POSSIBILITY

*Without leaps of imagination or dreaming, we lose the excitement of possibilities.
Dreaming, after all is a form of planning. ~Gloria Steinem*

Mindful Leaders are more focused on the positive and the possible than on the negative and impossible. They remain aware of the failures, the risks, the dangers, the realities, and the downsides, but they practice the discipline of thinking in terms of the positives, the opportunities, the probabilities, the options, and the alternatives. Mindful Leaders are aware of the power of positivity to broaden and build positive potential, to encourage novel thoughts and actions, and to inspire productivity and creativity in themselves and others.

Mindful Leaders pause to notice, consider, feel, and expand the positive circumstances and experiences they have. The habit of shifting to the good includes tuning in to the present, savoring moment-to-moment experiences, listening mindfully, appreciating positive daily situations, directing attention to what one wants to go well, having gratitude for the meaningful and positive circumstances in life, and reflecting on experiences and gifts in life.

POSITIVITY & POSSIBILITY SKILLS PREVIEW

Introduction: Positivity & Possibility
    Case Study: Observing Mindful Leadership—Howard Schultz
        Exercise: Mindful Leadership Case Study Questions
    The Role of Positive and Negative Emotions

***Skill 3:* SHIFT TO POSITIVITY AND POSSIBILITY**
    Shift Your Focus
    The 3W's Technique
        3W's Worksheet & Tracking Log
    Positivity Meditation
        Positivity Meditation & Tracking Log

***Skill 4:* CREATE OPTIMISM**
    Why is Optimism Beneficial?
    Research on Optimism in the Workplace
    Fixed Mindsets—Roots of Pessimism
    Growth Mindsets—Roots of Optimism
    How to Create Optimism: Cultivate a Growth Mindset
    Best Possible Future Self
    Best Possible Future Self Journaling Worksheet
        How Can I Worksheet & Tracking Log
    Ideal Situation Meditation
        Ideal Situation Meditation & Tracking Log

Coaching Guidelines

CASE STUDY: OBSERVING MINDFUL LEADERSHIP

HOWARD SCHULTZ
Chairman & CEO—Starbucks

To inspire and nurture the human spirit—one person, one cup and one neighborhood at a time.

Howard Schultz was born in Brooklyn, New York, on July 19, 1953, and grew up in the Canarsie Bayview Houses of the New York City Housing Authority. His family was poor, and Schultz filled his time with baseball, football, and basketball, as well as the Boys and Girls club. At Canarsie High School, he excelled at sports and won an athletic scholarship to Northern Michigan University—the first person in his family to go to college.

After working at Xerox Corporation, he went to work for Hammarplast, a Swedish drip coffee maker manufacturer. He rose through the ranks to become Director of Sales, and, in the early 1980, he noticed that a small operation in Seattle, known as the *Starbucks Coffee Tea and Spice Company*, was buying more of his coffee makers than Macy's. Schultz recalls, "Every month, every quarter, these numbers were going up, even though Starbucks just had a few stores. And I said, 'I gotta go to Seattle.'"

The original Starbucks was started by college buddies Jerry Baldwin and Gordon Bowker and their neighbor, Zev Siegl in 1971. The three friends also came up with the company's mermaid logo. There business model was to focus on selling coffee beans and coffee making equipment—not coffee drinks.

Schultz remembers, "When I walked in this store for the first time—I know this sounds really hokey—I knew I was home. I can't explain it. But I knew I was in a special place, and the product kind of spoke to me. I had never had a good cup of coffee. I met the founders of the company, and really heard for the first time the story of great coffee. I just said, "God, this is something I've been looking for my whole professional life."

"We're not in the business of filling bellies, we're in the business of filling souls." ~ Howard Schultz

A year later, in 1982, Schultz was hired as director of retail operations and marketing for Starbucks. The following year, on a buying trip to Milan, Italy, Schultz noticed that coffee bars existed on practically every street. They not only sold great coffee drinks, but they served as meeting places and public squares, they were a part of the sense of community, and there were 200,000 of them in the country. Shultz had an epiphany, and recalls, "I saw something. Not only the romance of coffee, but a sense of community. And the connection that people had to coffee—the place and one another. After a week in Italy, I was so convinced with such unbridled enthusiasm that I couldn't wait to get back to Seattle to talk about the fact that I had seen the future."

The owners of Starbucks did not share Shultz's enthusiasm. Zev Siegl recalls telling Schultz, "Oh no, that's not for us. Throughout the 70's, we served coffee in our store. We even, at one point, had a nice, big espresso machine behind the counter. But we were in the bean business." Schultz persisted and they eventually let Schulz pilot the café concept, but refused to roll it out company-wide, saying they didn't want to get into the restaurant business.

Schultz decided to leave Starbucks in 1985, and despite the lack of the $400,000 needed to open the first store and a wife who was pregnant with their first baby, Schultz looked for ways to made it happen. He shifted his focus from the obstacles and risks, and focused on the dream. By 1986, he raised all the money he needed to open the first store named after the Milanese newspaper, '*Il Giornale*'. Two years later, the original Starbucks management decided to focus on *Peet's Coffee & Tea* and sold its Starbucks retail unit to Schultz and *Il Giornale* for $3.8 million. Schultz renamed *Il Giornale* with the Starbucks name and began building the Starbucks empire. He did not believe in franchising, and required that Starbucks retain ownership of every domestic outlet.

In the years since 1985, Starbucks has grown from its Seattle roots to a worldwide brand and by 2014 had an impressive catalogue of accomplishments:

- 21,000 stores in 66 countries.
- Over 200,000 employees.
- $60 Billion Market Cap.
- Annual Revenue of over $16 billion.
- Serves 60 million customers a day.
- Opens two or three new stores every day.

A Nielsen Scarborough survey in spring 2014 found that nearly 32 million Americans had visited a Starbucks within the last 30 days.

"Not every decision is an economic one." ~ Howard Schultz

Many corporate executives read the news and see the problems—higher medical costs, disengaged workers, unemployed veterans, undereducated work force, higher costs of college, etc. Schultz is a realist, and makes a point of being acutely aware of the problems. But, he then takes the next critical step in positivity and possibility thinking; he shifts his focus to the positive and the possible.

From the beginning, Schultz set out to build a different kind of company—one that brings a sense of humanity and dignity. In the early days, he created two landmark programs that are still an important part of the Starbucks culture.

- Schultz recognized that health care costs have challenged the finances of the average worker and that uninsured medical costs were the number one cause of personal bankruptcy in America. Starbucks offered comprehensive health coverage for eligible full-time and part-time workers. They remain fully committed to health care benefits despite the rising health care costs.

- Schultz recognized that disengagement was epidemic in American business. In addition to an exceptional working environment, he wanted his "partners" to be a real part of the business and share in its financial success. Starbucks offered partners (employees) equity in the company in the form of stock, called *Bean Stock*.

Schultz has continued to focus on the positive and the possible, and has continued to take on problems that others only complain about.

- When the Great Recession hit in 2007-08, Schultz spearheaded efforts to create small business jobs through *Create Jobs for USA*.

- In order to help alleviate the high unemployment rate of US military veterans returning from Iraq and Afghanistan, he launched an initiative to hire of US military veterans and their spouses.

- In order to help make it possible for more Starbucks partners to finish school in spite of the ever increasing costs, and the overwhelming burden of student loans, he created the *Starbucks College Achievement Plan*. Every Starbucks partner can get a free college education through the University of Arizona's on-line program.

- Schultz has been a champion of diversity. In March, 2013, he made headlines for making a statement in support of the legalization of gay marriage. When a shareholder complained that Starbucks had lost sales due to its support for gay marriage, Schultz said to the shareholder: "Not every decision is an economic one. Despite the fact that you recite statistics that are narrow in time, we did provide a 38 percent shareholder return over the last year. I don't know how many things you invest in, but I would suspect not many things, companies, products, investments have returned 38 percent over the last 12 months. Having said that, it is not an economic decision to me. The lens in which we are making that decision is through the lens of our people. We employ over 200,000 people in this company, and we want to embrace diversity. Of all kinds."

In 2007, Howard Schultz was awarded the *FIRST Award for Responsible Capitalism*. The Awards for Responsible Capitalism were initiated by FIRST in 2000 to honor business leaders who have excelled by achieving both commercial success and demonstrating social responsibility. FIRST is a multidisciplinary International Affairs organization. Rupert Goodman, Chairman of FIRST said, "We at FIRST believe that commercial success can be assessed in terms of standard criteria, but that social responsibility involves a greater sense of the needs of the wider community as well as shareholders, a special interest in the well-being of groups in need, care for the areas in which the business operates, environmental initiatives, and support for the arts and culture."

Schultz continues to demonstrate his ability to achieve commercial success. In 2011, he was named Fortune's Businessperson of the year for delivering record financial returns for the company while leading an effort t to spur job creation in the U.S. He consistently makes the Forbes Billionaires list.

He also continues to demonstrate his social responsibility. His efforts have been recognized by such awards as The Rev. Theodore M. Hesburgh Award for business ethics given by Notre Dame University's Mendoza College of Business, and the Botwinick Prize in Business Ethics from Columbia Business School.

His mindful leadership has been acknowledged at a national level and international level. He has been included in Time magazine's *Time 200*, a list of the most influential people in the world, and has recently been featured on the cover of Time with an article entitled, *What Starbucks Knows About America*. He received the first-ever John Wooden Global Leadership Award from UCLA Anderson School of Management.

Howard Schultz is a mindful leader who looks to create an environment in which his employees and his customers can thrive, as well as a company in which his shareholders can receive an above average return on their capital. A succinct summary of Schultz's philosophy of *conscious capitalism* can be found in the Mission Statement of Starbucks reproduced below from their website.

STARBUCKS MISSION STATEMENT

To inspire and nurture the human spirit—one person, one cup and one neighborhood at a time.
Here are the principles of how we live that every day:

- **Our Coffee.** It has always been, and will always be, about quality. We're passionate about ethically sourcing the finest coffee beans, roasting them with great care and improving the lives of people who grow them. We care deeply about all of this; our work is never done.

- **Our Partners.** We're called partners, because it's not just a job, it's our passion. Together, we embrace diversity to create a place where each of us can be ourselves. We always treat each other with respect and dignity. And we hold to that standard.

- **Our Customers.** When we are fully engaged, we connect with, laugh with and uplift the lives of our customers—even if just for a few moments. Sure, it starts with the promise of a perfectly made beverage, but our work goes far beyond that. It's really about human connection.

- **Our Stores.** When our customers feel this sense of belonging, our stores become a haven, a break from the worries outside, a place where you can meet with friends. It's about enjoyment at the speed of life—sometimes slow and savored, sometimes faster. Always full of humanity.

- **Our Neighbourhood.** Every store is part of a community, and we take our responsibility to be good neighbours seriously. We want to be invited in wherever we do business. We can be a force for positive action—bringing together our partners, customers and the community to contribute every day. Now we see that our responsibility—and our potential for good—is even larger. The world is looking to Starbucks to set the new standard, yet again. We will lead.

- **Our Shareholders.** We know that as we deliver in each of these areas, we enjoy the kind of success that rewards our shareholders. We are fully accountable to get each of these elements right so that Starbucks—and everyone it touches—can endure and thrive.

Footnote: The information on Howard Schultz and quotes used in this case study can be found in the following sources:
- *Pour Your Heart Into It: How Starbuck Built a Company One Cup at a Time*. Howard Schultz with Dori Jones Yang, 1997.
- *Onward: How Starbucks Fought for Its Life Without Losing Its Soul*. Howard Schultz with Joanne Gordon, 2011.
- Howard Schultz From Wikipedia, the free encyclopedia, en.wikipedia.org/wiki/Howard_Schultz, 4/10/15.
- Mission Statement / Starbucks Coffee Company, www.starbucks.ph
- *What Starbucks Knows About America* by Rana Foroohar. Time Magazine, 2.16.2015
- YouTube. *Howard Schultz: 6 Habits of Strategic Thinkers* (Inc. Magazine Interview)

EXERCISE: MINDFUL LEADERSHIP CASE STUDY QUESTIONS

One of the ways to build a better understanding of the skills of mindful leadership is through role models who demonstrate the skills of mindful leadership in their actions. In the *Observing Mindful Leadership Case Studies*, we examine the accomplishments, the actions, the statements, and sometimes the thoughts and emotions of well-known leaders. The cases can help us to see a diversity of mindful leaders operating in many different types of environments, and help us to see how different leaders and different personalities practice the skills of mindful leadership. Use the following questions to help you to better understand this mindful leader.

1. AWARENESS IN THE MOMENT. Mindful Leaders are self-aware of what they are thinking, feeling, and doing, and are aware of what is going on around them. They tune in to the present, to themselves, to their surroundings, and to others. They listen mindfully for information and for emotions and practice global listening. They focus first on determining what is real, before attempting to alter reality.

What can you observe from the writings, statements, and actions of the leader in this case study that demonstrate the skills of awareness in the moment?

_____

_____

_____

_____

_____

_____

_____

_____

_____

_____

2. POSITIVITY & POSSIBILITY. Mindful Leaders are more focused on the positive and the possible than on the negative and impossible. They remain aware of the failures, the risks, the dangers, the realities, and the downsides, but they practice the discipline of thinking in terms of the positives, the opportunities, the probabilities, the options, and the alternatives. Mindful Leaders are aware of the power of positivity to broaden and build positive potential, to encourage novel thoughts and actions, and to inspire productivity and creativity in themselves and others.

What can you observe from the writings, statements, and actions of the leader in this case study that demonstrate the skills of positivity and possibility?

_____

_____

_____

_____

_____

_____

_____

_____

_____

3. POSITIVE RELATIONSHIPS. Mindful Leaders are aware of the power and importance of positive relationships, put conscious time and effort into the development of positive networks, and cultivate empathy, deep dive conversations, and win-win solutions with others. They recognize that some positive conflict can be productive, but go out of their way to avoid negative conflict escalators that thwart communication and cooperation. They take charge of their emotions and responses and work hard to build community and engagement.

What can you observe from the writings, statements, and actions of the leader in this case study that demonstrate the skills of positive relationships?

_____

_____

_____

_____

4. AUTHENTICITY & INTEGRITY. Mindful Leaders are often respected for their authenticity and integrity. Their authenticity is reflected in the truthfulness of their intentions, behaviors, and commitments. Their integrity is reflected in their honesty, their strong moral principles, and their ability to live by those principles. Mindful Leaders are clear on their values and their priorities and make decisions and take actions based upon these values. They are aware of their strengths and look for ways to leverage their strengths in the pursuit of their goals and in the service of others.

What can you observe from the writings, statements, and actions of the leader in this case study that demonstrate the skills of authenticity and integrity?

_____

_____

_____

_____

5. MANAGE STRESS & ENERGY. Mindful Leaders manage their energy and stress in order to maintain high levels of physical, mental, and emotional well-being. They challenge their thoughts to stay in touch with reality, they identify their emotions and emotional triggers and manage their responses, and they consciously monitor and manage their energy.

What can you observe from the writings, statements, and actions of the leader in this case study that demonstrate the skills of manage stress and energy?

_____

_____

_____

_____

6. RESILIENCE. Mindful leaders work to develop resilience—the capacity to recover from difficulties and adversity. They focus on the heroic rather than the debilitating aspects adversity; they let go of perfectionism and shortcomings and focus on the possible and potential; and they practice compassion and self-compassion.

What can you observe from the writings, statements, and actions of the leader in this case study that demonstrate the skills of resilience?

_____

_____

_____

THE ROLE OF POSITIVE & NEGATIVE EMOTIONS

Mindful Leaders are aware of the power of positivity to inspire creativity and productivity. Mindful Leaders pause to notice, consider, feel, and expand the positive circumstances and experiences they have. The habit of shifting to the good that exists in your life includes tuning in to the present, savoring moment-to-moment experiences, listening mindfully, appreciating positive daily situations, directing your attention to what you want to go well, having gratitude for the meaningful and positive circumstances in life, and reflecting on experiences and gifts in life.

THE ROLE OF POSITIVE EMOTIONS

Positive emotions help us thrive. These "approach" emotions motivate us through pleasant feelings to get more of something or to do it again. They feel rewarding, satisfying, or pleasurable. They also encourage others to come along and join us. Positive emotions:

- Help us see new possibilities
- Enhance creativity
- Make us feel more secure and help us take moderate risk
- Enhance connections to others
- Help us bounce back from setbacks
- Attract others and make others seem attractive
- Increase generosity, interest, and cooperation with others

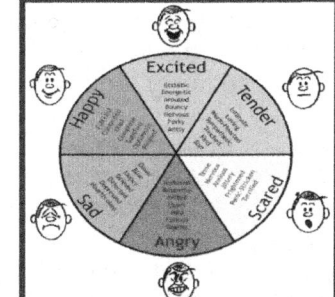

Like the sail on a sailboat, positive emotions drive us toward our objectives, hopes, dreams, and goals. They are the fuel behind aspirations.

THE ROLE OF NEGATIVE EMOTIONS

Negative emotions help us survive. They are designed to ensure safety. Survival as a species has depended upon them. Distressing emotions orient us to avoid aversive circumstances. The classic effect of most negative emotions is some form of the Fight, Flight, or Freeze response. The fight response helps us attack or destroy the threat, the flight response helps us escape from harm, and the freeze response can help us avoid the threat until it passes or otherwise transforms.

Negative emotions motivate through pain or distress to decrease an aversive stimulus or to avoid something that may cause physical harm or mental distress. They focus attention on what's wrong. From an evolutionary perspective, the tendency to feel negative emotions more strongly than positive emotions is highly adaptive. This can be quite beneficial, especially when dealing with a simple threat. A recent study showed that depressed people are better at focusing on simple, concrete problems and solving them. Like the keel on a sailboat, negative emotions help keep us upright during stormy weather.

Negative emotions:
- Help us mobilize for defense or aggression
- Enhance focus on problems
- Make us feel unsafe and inhibit further risk
- Cause us to retreat from others
- Help us reflect on setbacks, losses, and danger
- Repel others and make us feel threatening to them
- Help us conserve resources and focus attention on needs and security
- Protect us from others who may do harm

Primitive Neural Circuitry. In our evolutionary past, the demands on the emotional system were simpler—as a species we wanted to survive, to pass on our genes, and to not get killed. The drive to thrive was secondary to the drive to survive. Now we not only want to survive, but we also want to thrive in a vast number of ways. From our primitive neural circuitry's perspective, we were not designed to pursue a life filled with joy, happiness, and contentment. For a system designed primarily to meet the species' survival needs, this is a lot to ask for. This is why need to put so much effort toward managing our emotional and mental systems.

Amygdala Hijack—Act First, Think Later. When a threat is perceived, brain mobilizes to fight or flee. To do this, slow, higher order thinking shuts down in favor of quick, impulsive reactivity, which is far more useful when facing sudden life threats. This is what we refer to as "amygdala hijacking". In this state, the mind and body go into emotional reactivity, often characterized by impulsivity, highly focused and narrow thinking, and hyperawareness to change. The arousal in the mind and body during an emotional hijack is useful when one must fight off a threat to survival. This primitive reaction limits rational evaluation and response.

Think First, Act Later—The More Effective, Measured Response. Cooling down the amygdala and its emotional circuitry re-engages the higher brain systems like the prefrontal cortex, which is associated with problem-solving, analytical reasoning, perspective taking, and planning. Thus, when emotions spike and overwhelm or distort logical thinking, most of us would benefit from pausing, stepping back from the situation, and managing internal states. This fosters a more thoughtful and intentional response rather than impulsive reaction.

Success in Modern Environments. In the typically safer, more abundant environment that most of us have the privilege of enjoying today in many developed nations, our precautionary system is overly sensitive and overly reactive. In states of heightened negative emotion, creative problem-solving ability actually shuts down. Positive emotions promote moderate risk taking in contrast to negative emotions that promote seeking the shelter of extreme safety. As Rick Hanson states, author of *Buddha's Brain*, our primitive neural circuitry is highly adaptive at keeping us alive long enough to pass on genes, but it is a lousy system for happiness and contentment. The negativity bias is less well-suited for goals such as success, peace, and prosperity. Success, prosperity, and sustainable happiness require cooperation and collaboration rather than independence and zero-sum competition. Thriving is in the domain of positive emotions.

Positivity Provides Balance. The powerful pull of problems and pains explains why we need to bring intentional positivity to life circumstances. Typically, this will result in a more balanced perspective.

Skill 3. SHIFT TO POSITIVITY AND POSSIBILITY

*If you think the grass is greener on the other side of the fence,
it is time to water your lawn.*
–Unknown

SHIFT YOUR FOCUS

The negativity bias is a natural force that pulls focus to negativity and impossibility, even in relatively favorable circumstances.

Negativity Bias. Positive events often go unnoticed. They tend to slip under the radar so fast that they hardly register. The fleeting nature of positive events diminishes their impact and sometimes prevents them from encoding in long-term memory.

Problems and threats, on the other hand, capture and keep our attention until safety is assured. As previously mentioned, being hyper-vigilant to threats has provided tremendous survival advantages. This tendency, however, creates a warped perception of current reality. We see more problems than solutions, and we sense danger, loss, and failure far more intensely than positive experiences. To thrive, we need to offset this tendency.

The counter-force. Shifting attention creates a counter-force to the negativity bias. The happiness boost is reliable and immediate, because it involves taking in the positives that already exist. When shifting toward positivity becomes a habit, happiness levels inch upward. *Pause to notice, consider, and feel into positive experiences.*

THE THREE W'S TECHNIQUE

Even within the same circumstances, it is possible to feel a sense of abundance or of scarcity—it just depends on what we are tuned into. Often positive experiences fly under the radar, failing to register, which can leave us feeling a greater sense of scarcity than is actually necessary. The crucial action is the ability to shift attention.

Focus on what's right rather than what's wrong.

Happiness levels largely hinge on this apbility to shift attention to the positive experiences. People vary dramatically in how much they tune into the good things that happen to them each day, which often contributes to their ability to not "sweat the small stuff." Those who habitually reflect on the positives in daily life benefit tremendously and tend to have higher happiness levels.

Notice the small good things. Life is comprised of a string of moments. Do you notice the small good things that happened on a moment-to-moment basis? For example, did you pause to notice the extra service the waitperson gave you at lunch, praise from a coworker, or perhaps the feeling of relief after completing a difficult project?

Find the positive in negative circumstances. Reflecting on positives is possible even amidst unpleasant circumstances. Finding ways to take in the good during challenging times requires effort, but the benefits can be substantial, including improved creative problem solving and alleviating distress. This is more than simply seeing the world through "rose-colored glasses" or "making lemonade out of lemons." It is finding the positive aspects that may co-exist along with negatives. Too often the human tendency is to lose the good aspects of a situation by only focusing on the disagreeable ones.

> **THE 3 W'S—PAST, FUTURE, & TEAM**
>
> 1. The 3W's Technique—What Went Well?
> 2. Future 3W's—What Do I Want To Go Well?
> 3. Team 3W's—What Went Well For Us?

1. The 3W's Technique—What Went Well? The 3 W's is a technique for recalibrating this radar so that we are scanning for positives, not just for negatives as our natural negativity bias wires us to do. Start by changing the question that you ask yourself. Often we ask "What went wrong?" Instead, ask, "What went well?" Ask yourself,
- "What went well today?"
- "What was my role in creating it?"

The first question trains your mind to scan for what is right, not wrong, in life. You may find that you get more out of positive situations, appreciate events, and find the good even on difficult days. The second question increases self-efficacy. In other words, it helps us feel like we have a role in creating positive events in our lives. This increases our general sense of control over our well-being and our ability to create good experiences in life.

Notice the little things. It is always wonderful to get a raise, win a game, or achieve a major goal, but most of life is comprised of small, seemingly insignificant events. Include the little things in your daily use of this skill. Consider:
- A kind word, gesture, or expression of appreciation, or praise from a colleague.
- A nice email, meeting that went well, conversation, or successful negotiation at work.

2. Future 3w's—What Do I Want To Go Well? When looking toward a goal or even as a way to start the day, you may use this question to direct your efforts and find ways that you can create positivity. Ask yourself,
- "What do I want to go well today?"
- "What could I do to create this outcome?"

RESEARCH—WHAT WENT WELL
In this study, 411 participants completed online questionnaires, follow-up assessments and assigned exercises. The researchers designed 6 exercises, including one placebo:

1. Placebo control exercise: journaling about early memories
2. Gratitude visit
3. Three good things in life
4. You at your best
5. Using signature strengths in a new way
6. Identifying signature strengths

Results show that the "Three Good Things in Life" exercise and the "Using Signature Strengths in a New Way" exercise both increased happiness and decreased depressive symptoms for 6 months. The 'gratitude visit' exercise caused large positive increases in happiness for one month. The remaining exercises, including the placebo, had no significant effects. The 3 W's is based on the Three Good Things exercise. Seligman, M E., Steen, T., Park, N., Peterson, C. (2005). Positive Psychology Progress: Empirical Validation of Interventions. *American Psychologist*, 60(5), 410-421.

3W'S WORKSHEET

This technique can help you create a habit of identifying positives in your day. It will increase your awareness that you do have influence and thus can have the ability to create good experiences.

Use the *Three W's Tracking Log* to track your experience for seven days, and observe the impact of noticing positive events and listing three good things each day. This will help you become more aware of them when they happen, and it will also help you feel more in control of your positive experiences.

3 W'S—WHAT WENT WELL FOR ME TODAY?

1. WHAT WENT WELL (What went well in work relationships, performance, stress management, projects, productivity, etc.)?

_____
_____
_____

My Role. What was my role in creating it?

_____
_____
_____

2. WHAT WENT WELL (What went well in work relationships, performance, stress management, projects, productivity, etc.)?

_____
_____
_____

My Role. What was my role in creating it?

_____
_____
_____

3. WHAT WENT WELL (What went well in work relationships, performance, stress management, projects, productivity, etc.)?

_____
_____
_____

My Role. What was my role in creating it?

_____
_____
_____

FUTURE 3 W'S—WHAT DO I WANT TO GO WELL?

1. WHAT DO I WANT TO GO WELL? (in work relationships, performance, stress management, projects, productivity, etc.)?

_____
_____

My Role. What could I do to create this outcome?

_____
_____

2. WHAT DO I WANT TO GO WELL? (in work relationships, performance, stress management, projects, productivity, etc.)?

_____
_____

My Role. What could I do to create this outcome?

_____
_____

TEAM 3 W'S—WHAT WENT WELL FOR US?

1. WHAT WENT WELL? (in productivity, performance, focus, projects, team work, etc.)

_____
_____

Our Role. What did we do to create this outcome?

_____
_____

2. WHAT WENT WELL? (in productivity, performance, focus, projects, team work, etc.)

_____
_____

Our Role. What did we do to create this outcome?

_____
_____

3W'S TRACKING LOG

DAY	APPLICATION What three things went well today? What was my role in creating these positive experiences?	IMPACT What was the impact of doing the 3 W's on me, others, and the situation?
Day 1	1. 2. 3.	
Day 2	1. 2. 3.	
Day 3	1. 2. 3.	
Day 4	1. 2. 3.	

3W's TRACKING LOG

DAY	APPLICATION What three things went well today? What was my role in creating these positive experiences?	IMPACT What was the impact of doing the 3 W's on me, others, and the situation?
Day 5		
Day 6		
Day 7		

INSIGHTS - What patterns or benefits emerged?

_____
_____
_____
_____

POSITIVITY MEDITATION

The purpose of this meditation is to harvest more from pleasant or rewarding experiences. This low-road technique can change your sense of well-being from the inside out. This practice strengthens the neural circuitry involved in positive feelings.

By replaying a positive experience, the positive emotions have a chance to change your perceptions, memories, and sense of well-being. It also moves the experience from short-term to long-term memory. The memory becomes more prominent and enduring in the memory stores.

Choose a positive experience to replay. It can be any positive experience like a moment when you felt loved, joy, calm and relaxed, or confident. You might experiment with using a positive experience in your Target Area. Relive the experience in your body, holding that pleasant feeling for 15-30 seconds. This will allow the memory to become more consolidated in long-term memory and strengthen the neural pathways associated with pleasant feelings.

INSTRUCTIONS
(1-5 MINUTES)

1. FOCUS INWARD: Breathe and Center

- **Close Your Eyes**—Close your eyes to focus your attention inward.

- **Feel Your Breath**—Focus attention by feeling your breath enter and exit your body. Breathe deep into your abdomen. Place your hand on your abdomen to feel your diaphragm rise and fall. Slowly exhale and naturally inhale.

- **Set Your Intention**—Direct your attention in this time and place, and to the objective of this meditation.

2. DIRECT ATTENTION: Relive a Positive Experience in Your Body

- **Make contact**—Make contact with feelings of a positive experience.

    The positive experience might be in your Target Area but it does not need to be.

    It might be feelings of being cared for, valuable, proud, connection or love, strong, confident, accepted, or optimistic.

    Feel the positive sensations and feelings in your body.

- **Expand the feelings of the positive experience**— Invite the positive feelings to expand and increase in intensity throughout your entire body. Invite these feelings to expand. Imagine breathing in more of these positive feelings.

- **Absorb the positive experience in your memory stores**—Bathe in these positive feelings.

    Savor the good feelings.

    Imagine that this is soaking into your memory stores.

3. REFLECT ON INSIGHTS: Breathe and Reflect

- Come back to your breath.
- Reflect on the insights or benefits you gained during this meditation.

4. MAINTAIN YOUR INNER AWARENESS: Soft Gaze and Stay with It

- Slowly open your eyes and keep your gaze soft, directed downward, and settling on a neutral object.
- Stay with the awareness you had during the meditation.

POSITIVITY MEDITATION WORKSHEET

After you have completed the meditation, jot down any observations about what came up during your meditation. Make note of thoughts you had, feelings you experienced, bodily sensations you felt, and/or detours that you took.

1. FOCUS INWARD: To what extent could you direct attention and turn your mind when it wandered?

_____
_____

2. DIRECT ATTENTION: Feel yourself re-experiencing the situation.

Make contact with a positive experience. What was the experience?

_____
_____
_____

Expand the feeling. Invite the feeling to expand throughout your entire body. What did you feel when you expanded the feeling?

_____
_____
_____

Soak in the positive feelings. Experience the moment in your body. Feel the positive sensations and feelings in your body. What were the feelings?

_____
_____
_____

Absorb the positive experience in your memory stores. What feelings did you have when you invited the experience into your memory stores?

_____
_____
_____

3. REFLECT ON INSIGHTS: What insights or benefits did you gain?

_____
_____
_____
_____
_____
_____

POSITIVITY MEDITATION TRACKING LOG

DAY	APPLICATION What did I meditate on?	IMPACT What was the impact on me, others, and the situation?
Day 1		
Day 2		
Day 3		
Day 4		

POSITIVITY MEDITATION TRACKING LOG

DAY	APPLICATION What did I meditate on?	IMPACT What was the impact on me, others, and the situation?
Day 5		
Day 6		
Day 7		

INSIGHTS - What patterns or benefits emerged?

_____
_____
_____
_____

Skill 4. CREATE OPTIMISM

Whether you think you can or you can't, you're right.
-Henry Ford

Creating optimism involves finding the positives, seeing the opportunities, and creating realistic problem solutions when confronted with challenges and adversity. Optimism is one of the most commonly misunderstood concepts in positive psychology. Optimism is not wishful thinking, blind faith, or persisting in a truly unchangeable situation. Optimism is different from seeing only the bright side of things, or naively hoping for the best, or "Pollyannish thinking." Sugary phrases like "think good thoughts," "don't worry, be happy," or "just let it go" are not optimism—they are distortions or avoidance of reality. Rigid mindsets and unrealistic expectations are not optimism.

Optimism emerges from getting *more* accurate in your appraisal of reality. Only then can you consider what is possible. Optimism is realistic, not idealistic. It results from a logical assessment of what is possible given the circumstances. We refer to having *flexibility in optimism*, because optimism is different from simply focusing on the positive.

WHY IS OPTIMISM BENEFICIAL?

Optimism has beneficial effects across a number of life domains. It positively influences relationships, success, health, and resiliency. Research has shown that optimism results in different coping strategies. A study conducted by George Vaillant at Harvard followed Harvard men for over 30 years. The study found that those who were optimistic during college enjoyed many benefits compared to pessimists throughout their lifetime:

Performance
- More successful
- Perform better
- Take advantage of opportunities
- Persevere
- More motivated

Health
- Live longer
- Superior physical health
- Stronger immune system
- Recover from diseases better
- Better mental health
- Liked by others

Furthermore, one study showed that politicians benefit from optimism as well. In a retrospective study analyzing the speeches of U.S. presidential candidates between 1900-1984, all presidents had higher optimism than their opponent. Optimism has many benefits because it is more than just a way of thinking. It is an approach to life that leads to different actions and responses.

Expectations shape our future. Several lines of research show that expectations shape our future. Self-fulfilling prophecies, confirmation bias, and other tendencies identified by social psychologists show this phenomenon. Our expectations direct attention, distort perception, and influence interpretation. These interpretations create a perspective or understanding, which then shapes reactions and responses such as perseverance and proactive coping.

Optimists use proactive coping strategies. Optimists are more effective at reaching goals because they engage in creative solution finding, persevere, and adapt to real obstacles—the keys to resilience and achievement. When hit with adversity, optimists look to find or create hidden opportunities. They are skillful in the art of possibility. When circumstances are going well, optimists focus on how to facilitate ways that positive outcomes can persist.

In the face of challenge, optimists:
- Engage in creative problem solving
- Are more perseverant
- Seek social support and assistance
- Emphasize positive aspects of stressful situation

Pessimists use passive coping strategies such as avoidance, complaining, and are more prone to give up. Many studies have shown that pessimism underlies depression, feeling hopeless, disappointment, and giving up. Pessimism is associated with focusing on stressful feelings, and with disengagement from the goal with which the stressor was interfering. When the event was construed as uncontrollable, optimists were shown to accept or resign themselves to this, as opposed to denying or avoiding this reality. The film "Life is Beautiful" is a moving depiction of how effective coping strategies can emerge from optimism.

In the face of challenge, pessimists:
- Focus on stressful feelings
- Disengage from the goal
- Resign to status quo

RESEARCH ON OPTIMISM IN THE WORKPLACE

The MetLife Optimism Program. Martin Seligman reports on the MetLife story in his book *Learned Optimism: How to Change Your Mind and Your Life* (cited below). In the late 1980s, turnover was so bad among MetLife salespeople that 50% of them were quitting within the first year. The company was losing $75 million per year in hiring costs alone. Only 20% of the salespeople remained after four years.

Seligman tested levels of optimism in MetLife salespeople. He found that those with the more optimistic styles sold 37% more insurance than the pessimistic ones, and that the most optimistic ones sold 88% more insurance. In addition, he found that agents who were more optimistic were 50% less likely to quit than the pessimists. Based upon Seligman's recommendations, MetLife changed how it hired agents, hiring only the most optimistic ones. Within a few years, MetLife's turnover dropped and its market share increased by 50%.

Seligman, M. E. P. (2006). *Learned optimism: How to change your mind and your life.* New York: Vintage Books.

Optimism related to sales performance. In the Mid-80's, MetLife Insurance was a failing company. 50% of agents were quitting within the first year and only 20% remained after four years. The company was losing $75 million per year in hiring costs. Martin Seligman, UPenn & Peter Schulman, Wharton tested optimism levels of salespeople.

They found:
–More optimistic styles sold 37% more than the pessimistic ones,
–Most optimistic ones sold 88% more.
–More optimistic were 50% less likely to quit.

It was concluded that in this company pessimists had poorer productivity and higher rates of quitting. This had tremendous implications for salesperson selection, training, and organization design.
In response to these findings, the organization changed its hiring policies. MetLife hired only the most optimistic agents. Within two years turnover dropped and market share increased by 50%.

Optimism in managers' ratings of performance. Researchers analyzed managers' ratings of 232 employees (reporting to 41 managers) in 32 Midwestern organizations. Optimism correlated with:
–Managers' ratings of performance
–Employees' perceptions of performance
–Job satisfaction
–Work happiness

Youssef, C. M., & Luthans, F. (2007). Positive Organizational Behavior in the Workplace The Impact of Hope, Optimism, and Resilience. *Journal of Management, 33*(5), 774-800.

RESEARCH ON OPTIMISM AND COPING

Physical and Emotional Well-Being. Research shows that the habitual ways that people explain events have dramatic impact on their well-being. Peterson, Seligman, and Vaillant (1988) conducted a long-term study of styles of explaining negative events. They found that individuals who were pessimistic compared to optimistic in early adulthood were more likely to have poor health 35 years later, regardless of their physical and mental health states at age 25.

Coping with Problems. In a study of control and coping approaches, a positive association was found between optimism and problem-focused coping, seeking of social support and emphasizing positive aspects of the stressful situation (Scheier, Kumari Weintraub, & Carver, 1986). Optimism was also related to acceptance or resignation but only when the event was construed as uncontrollable. Sheier and colleagues report that optimists are more flexible and adaptive when dealing with problems. They state that optimists, as compared with pessimists, more frequently use active coping tactics when confronted with aversive situations and adaptive emotion-focused coping tactics when important life goals are blocked.

Coping with Illness. In a study of cancer patients, even patients who were physically or psychosocially worse off were better adjusted if they had higher perceptions of control (Thompson et al., 1993). In other words, it was more important for patients to believe that they could control their own daily emotional reactions and physical symptoms than to control the course of the disease.

Immune Response. Optimism seems to have physical benefits as well. It is associated with better mood, higher numbers of helper T cells, and higher natural killer cell cytotoxicity (Segerstrom et al., 1998).

Perseverance. Optimists, as compared with pessimists, are more likely to persist in their pursuit of goals when confronted with difficult life situations (Wrosch and Scheier, 2003). Optimists take advantage of the opportunities for development to a greater extent than pessimists do. Optimists might also cope more effectively when goals are blocked. Optimism is a predictor of successful adaptation to stressful encounters. Scheier and colleagues (1986) found that optimists engage in more problem-focused coping, seeking of social support, and emphasizing positive aspects of the stressful situation.

FIXED MINDSETS—ROOTS OF PESSIMISM

Once an event occurs, the mind goes into analytical mode to figure out the reasons behind it. The mind is constantly determining causes and effects. It then lands upon reasons, rational or irrational, behind the occurrence, and these reasons form conclusions. This conclusion hardens into a mindset that informs our actions. This mindset drives optimism or pessimism and their associated actions.

Pessimistic Thinking—Fixed Mindsets. A fixed mindset refers to an assumption that a process is unchangeable. Naturally, this leads to pessimism. The problem is that we tend to overestimate the fixed nature of situations. This diminishes our ability to cope, persevere, and create change for the better. When we conclude that situations, ourselves, or others are unchangeable, we stop looking for possibility and lose opportunities for growth, learning, progress, and ultimately limit change. The problem is that we often prematurely and unconsciously commit to these conclusions.

These mindsets limit us in numerous ways. They prevent active coping, solution finding, perseverance, learning, and often enjoyment and curiosity. Carol Dweck's research shows that when people adopt a fixed mindset about themselves or others, they perform worse, fail to improve, and miss opportunities.

Spot A Fixed Mindset—"Always, Everything, Me". Pessimism emerges when the causes of a negative event are attributed to permanent, pervasive, and personal factors. If unchallenged, causal attributions create a fixed mindset.

1. Permanent attributions (Always). The condition, causes, or obstacles to a goal are permanent, stable or unchangeable. This often takes the form of absolute language like "always" or "never."

2. Pervasive attributions (Everything). The conditions, causes, or obstacles to a goal are global, pervasive, "across the board", or in many circumstances rather than specific to this particular situation. Language that refers to "everything" or "nothing" often signals a pervasive attribution.

3. Personal attributions (Me). Taking failures or limitations *personally*, in that the causes or obstacles are due to inherent limitations, flaws as a human being, or lack of internal capacity. Thinking that "I am flawed" as opposed to "There are flaws in my behavior, plan, or external circumstances" signal problematic personal attributions.

The short hand version of these attributions is "Me, Always, Everything." When something negative happens and the causal attributions fall into these categories, pessimism emerges.

GROWTH MINDSETS—ROOTS OF OPTIMISM

We can't solve problems by using the same kind of thinking we used when we created them.
-Albert Einstein

When people adopt a more flexible way of thinking about themselves and others, they are more resilient, perform better, and are more effective at reaching goals. These are the same benefits we see in optimism. Carol Dweck refers to this style of thinking as a Growth Mindset.

With a Growth Mindset, situations or people are seen as changeable. Problems can be solved with effort, skills can be acquired and strengthened, learning can happen, thereby driving different behavior. This type of mindset is far more flexible. Oriented toward finding hidden opportunities and possibilities for improvement through effort, a growth mindset leads to active coping, solution finding, perseverance, learning, and curiosity. The focus is on process rather than outcome. Growth mindsets tend to result in optimism.

A Growth Mindset Asks, "How Can I?". Optimism is a mental state that emerges when one has a doable plan and reasons to believe that one can successfully execute the plan. It is not a state we can wish ourselves into, but instead is cultivated by directing attention toward reasons why you would likely success. Research establishes that hope, the emotional state that is associated with the cognitive construct optimism, emerges when one has a clear sense of doable plans and a high level of self-efficacy. In other words, we feel hopeful when we have a sensible plan and confidence in our ability to execute that plan. Asking a different question leads to a different answer. When the question is changed from "Can I?" to *"How can I?"* executable steps emerge.

Which question would produce more positive results?

"Can we have a happy, satisfying marriage?" OR *"How can we have a happy, satisfying marriage?"*

"Can I relate better to my teenager?" OR *"How can I relate better with my teenager?"*

"Can I get my landlord to lower rent" OR *"How can I get my landlord to lower the rent?"*

How Can I? When the mind is faced with a question, it automatically launches into discovery mode. "How can I?" directs the mind toward a process-oriented inquiry and solution finding, which increase the probability of success. Furthermore, asking "how" implies that there could be a solution, thereby, introducing openness to possibilities. In short, this simple question focuses the inquiry on potential changeable factors, which lends a growth mindset. As a result, feelings of optimism can naturally emerge.

Can I? This binary question does not serve us as well as asking "How?" The answer to "Can I?" is unknowable. It is fortune telling. Furthermore, this question puts the mind in a mode where it searches for a prediction rather a process, which is a dead end.

RESEARCH ON THE "HOW" QUESTION

Asking, "How Can I?" Improves Performance. Langer and her colleagues' research suggest that perceived control and ability to effectively attain control can be enhanced by focusing on the process rather than outcomes. Outcome orientation results in narrowed thinking that limits performance. In contrast, orienting attention to the process of the task can lead to an improved ability to perceive possibilities and exercise control.

Langer, Johnson, and Botwinick's study (1983) asked people to answer one of two simple questions prior to performing a paper and pencil task. Participants were asked either, "Can you do this task?" or "How would you do this task?" People who were outcome-oriented (Can I do it?) performed much worse than people who were process-oriented (How would I do it?).

HOW TO CREATE OPTIMISM: Cultivate A Growth Mindset

To avoid a troublesome rut, look at where you want to go, not at the rut...
Life's a lot like that.
~ Liz McLoughlin, Dirt Biker

A simple but powerful question that directs the mind toward answers that create optimism is: *If I could reach my goal, how would I do it?* The first step is to challenge limiting, fixed mindsets. The second is to look for possibilities:

1. Challenge Fixed Mindsets: Challenge attributions such as "me, always, everything"

Look for assumptions and interpretations you have of the situation that are Permanent (Always), Pervasive attributions (Everything), Personal attributions (Me).

2. Ask: "HOW Can I?"

Brainstorm multiple pathways. Generate several ideas for pathways toward your goal. Think out-of-the-box, get creative.

Consider ways to empower yourself. An important component of optimism is having the sense that one is capable of executing the plan successfully. Psychologists refer to this as *self-efficacy,* the belief in one's ability to act in a manner that brings a desired outcome. It is believing that you, yourself, that can execute the plan, not just that others can do it, but that you personally can. Self-efficacy is having the sense that you have what it takes and are up for the challenge.

Recall what's worked in the past. Instead of focusing on gaps and inadequacies in a "fix problems" framework, operate from a "do what works" framework. An example of this is a process called "appreciative inquiry." This approach was developed from organizational psychology but is useful in any planning process.

What has been working or has worked in similar situations?
How can we use these approaches in this situation?
What is the best we can be?

Appreciative Inquiry is defined by Dan Baker and Cathy Greenberg in *What Happy Companies Know* as "a business change process that engages employees to find, develop, and spread the most positive aspects of a company throughout the organization." (p. 214). In one field study, appreciative inquiry was conducted on 94 fast-food restaurants of a Fortune 500 restaurant chain. Those who used this approach had 30-32% higher retention rate than the two control groups, as well as an enhanced appreciation of working in that restaurant industry.

Jones, D A. (2000). Appreciative Inquiry: A field experiment focusing on turnover in the fast food industry. Dissertation Abstracts International Section A: Humanities and Social Sciences, 60 (7-A), pp. 2574.

BOOKS ON APPRECIATIVE INQUIRY

What Happy Companies Know by Baker, Greenberg, and Hemingway

Appreciative Inquiry: A positive revolution in change by Cooperrider and Whitney

BEST POSSIBLE FUTURE SELF-JOURNALING WORKSHEET

Your Best Possible Future Self. In the following worksheet you will have a chance to visualize and write about your internal and external goals. Visualizing the achievement of goals is a way to create optimism and uncover the hidden pathways to success. In one study, five months after writing about their best possible selves or trauma, participants experienced decreased illness compared with controls. L. King (2001). *Health Benefits of Writing about Life Goals*.

Instructions: Think about your life in the future. Imagine that everything has gone as well as it possibly could. You have worked hard and succeeded at accomplishing all of your life goals. Think of this as the realization of all of your life dreams. Now, write about what you imagined.

Take some time to visualize and write about your best possible self. These instructions are exactly same as those researchers used in a study that found several benefits immediately after this writing exercise and five months later.

MY BEST POSSIBLE SELF—INTERNAL GOALS ACCOMPLISHED

BEST POSSIBLE FUTURE SELF-JOURNALING WORKSHEET

MY BEST POSSIBLE SELF—EXTERNAL GOALS ACCOMPLISHED

HOW CAN I? WORKSHEET

Optimists are more effective at reaching goals because they engage in creative solution finding, persevere, and adapt to obstacles. The first step is to challenge limiting mindsets and then to look for possibilities.

(1) Challenge Fixed Mindsets (i.e., attributions such as "me, always, everything")

(2) Ask, *"How can I?"*

YOUR SITUATION

An Objective I Feel Pessimistic About. Brief description of the outcome I feel doubtful or pessimistic about. What are my specific objectives?

_____
_____
_____

IDENTIFY FIXED MINDSETS

In what ways am I falling into a Fixed Mindset, thinking that the conditions are unchangeable?

1. Permanent (Always). In what ways do I see the condition, causes, or obstacles as permanent, stable or unchangeable? (e.g., look for always or never self talk)

_____
_____
_____
_____

2. Pervasive (Everything). In what ways do I see the conditions, causes, or obstacles as global, pervasive, "across the board", or in many circumstances rather than specific to this particular situation? (e.g., everything, nothing, "I can never...")

_____
_____
_____
_____

3. Personal (Me). In what ways do I take this personally, in that I see the causes or obstacles as due to my inherent limitations, flaws, weakness or immutable traits of mine. (e.g., "other people can but I just can't...", lack of ability, willpower, etc.)

_____
_____
_____
_____

CULTIVATE A GROWTH MINDSET—ASK: "HOW CAN I?"

A growth mindset approaches conditions as changeable and considers pathways toward a more desirable outcome.

HOW CAN I? How can I take some control over the situation and perhaps exert influence on the outcome of this situation?

_____
_____
_____
_____

What's Worked. What has worked for me in similar situations?

_____
_____
_____
_____

Hidden Opportunities. What are some hidden opportunities that I could find or create?

_____
_____
_____
_____

Support. What or who could help me more effectively reach this objective? (e.g., electronic tools, help from others, advice, coaches)

_____
_____
_____
_____

Release an Unreachable Goal and Pivot to a Reachable Goal. If my original outcome still appears unlikely, what is an alternative goal that is more doable and still serves my greater goal or objective? In regard to this new goal, ask: "How can I?"

_____
_____
_____
_____

One Small Step. What is one small step that I can take today?

_____
_____

IDEAL SITUATION VISUALIZATION

Sonja Lyubomirsky's research has shown that an exercise similar to the one below can increase optimism. This visualization can make your goal seem more familiar and doable. If you can't see it or if you can't imagine yourself in it, then you probably will have difficulty believing and doing what you need to do to bring it to fruition.

Choose a goal that you would like to achieve or a situation that you would like to be different. Consider what you would ideally like to have happen in this situation. This meditation guides you through an exploration of the feelings and sensations that you would experience if this situation actually existed.

INSTRUCTIONS
(4-8 MINUTES)

1. FOCUS INWARD: Breathe and Center

- **Center**—Close your eyes and turn your attention inward.

- **Anchor in Your Breath**—Feel your breath fill and release your body. Breathe deeply with a slower exhale and natural inhale. Place your hand on your abdomen to feel your diaphragm rise and fall. Feel your feet as they rest on the floor. Notice the sensations on the bottom of your feet making contact with the earth. Feel your hands as they rest on your thighs. Open them and notice the sensations and invite them to relax.

- **Set Your Intention**—To direct your attention in this time, place, and to the objective of this meditation.

2. DIRECT ATTENTION: *To Your Ideal Outcome.*

- *Make Contact*—Make contact with what you would ideally like to happen in a situation.

- *Visualize as If*—Visualize what you would see if it existed right now. See it as vividly as possible as if a photograph captured a moment in time. In your mind's eye, see yourself in this picture, what you are doing, where you are, perhaps who is with you.

- *Soak in the Positive Feelings*—Feel the sensations in your body and emotions you would feel in a snapshot of time with this actually existing.

- **Visualize the How**—Present the question to your wise mind: *"How could this happen?" "What would I need to do to make this happen?"* or *"How can we create a win-win solution?"* Even if no insight comes—just hold the question without demanding an answer.

3. REFLECT ON INSIGHTS: Breathe and Reflect
- Come back to your breath.
- Reflect on the insights or benefits you gained during this meditation.

4. MAINTAIN YOUR INNER AWARENESS: Soft Gaze and Stay with It
- Slowly open your eyes and keep your gaze soft, directed downward, and settling on a neutral object.
- Stay with the awareness you gained during the meditation.

IDEAL SITUATION VISUALIZATION WORKSHEET

After you have completed the meditation, jot down any observations about what came up during your meditation. Make note of thoughts you had, feelings you experienced, bodily sensations you felt, and/or detours that you took.

1. FOCUS INWARD: Breathe and Center. Were you able to concentrate inward and turn your attention back to your intention for this exercise?

_____

_____

2. DIRECT ATTENTION: Your Ideal Situation.

Make Contact. What would you ideally like to happen in a situation?

_____

_____

Visualize As If. What did you see as if it existed right now? Did you see it as vividly as if it were a photograph capturing a moment in time? In your mind's eye, what did you see in this picture, what were you doing, where were you, who was with you?

_____

_____

_____

Soak in the positive feelings. What sensations in your body and emotions did you feel in this snapshot of time?

_____

_____

_____

Visualize the How. What happened when you presented the question to your wise mind: *"How could this happen?" "What would I need to do to make this happen?"*

_____

_____

_____

3. REFLECT ON INSIGHTS: Breathe and Reflect. What insights or benefits did you gain in the meditation?

_____

_____

4. Creating Optimism. How might this meditation help you to create optimism?

_____

_____

IDEAL SITUATION VISUALIZATION TRACKING LOG

DAY	APPLICATION What situation did I visualize? What worked well about how I did this visualization?	IMPACT What was the impact on me, others, and the situation?
Day 1		
Day 2		
Day 3		
Day 4		

IDEAL SITUATION VISUALIZATION TRACKING LOG

DAY	APPLICATION What situation did I visualize? What worked well about how I did this visualization?	IMPACT What was the impact on me, others, and the situation?
Day 5		
Day 6		
Day 7		

INSIGHTS – What patterns or benefits emerged?

_____
_____
_____
_____
_____

COACHING GUIDELINES

Use the self-coaching process and coaching tools to create long-term change. For maximum effectiveness, focus on one skill at a time. For each skill, take an *assessment* if one is available, complete a *coaching worksheet*, practice high road and low road techniques, and track your application of the skill over a seven day period using a *Tracking Log*.

Select one skill. Consider which skill would make the greatest difference in your current life circumstances if you used it more frequently and effectively. It is easier to build new habits if you focus on one change at a time. Select the *one skill* in this chapter that is your highest priority:

- Shift to Positivity and Possibility
- Create Optimism

STEP 1. ASSESS. Assess the need and benefits of practicing this particular skill. Assess your current mastery level of the skill. Use one of the on-line assessment tools if one is available for the skill. The Coaching Worksheet will also help you assess your need and benefits of using the skill.

Assessments—Questionnaires that assess your current skill level and provide data on your progress.

STEP 2. PLAN. To create an action plan, understand how a technique can help you build greater mastery of a skill. Next, consider how you can apply it to your own situations.

Coaching Worksheets—Tools for learning and creating an action plan for practicing the techniques.

- 3W's Worksheet
- Best Possible Future Self Journaling Worksheet
- How Can I Worksheet

STEP 3. PRACTICE. During the following seven days, apply the skill daily. Use both the High Road techniques and the Low Road techniques to practice the skill.

Tracking Logs—Habit forming tools to guide your efforts as you practice the techniques for seven days.

- 3W's Tracking Log
- Positivity Meditation Tracking Log
- How Can I Tracking Log
- Ideal Situation Meditation Tracking Log

Meditation Guides—Low Road techniques to build the skill at the emotional or non-verbal level.

- Positivity Meditation
- Ideal Situation Meditation

STEP 4. TRACK RESULTS. In addition to systematically helping you to practice the techniques, *Tracking Logs* provide a place to note the impact of the skill on your experience. Tracking Logs help you become more aware of behaviors and patterns in yourself. They are a source of feedback so you can modify a technique to make it more effective.

POSITIVE RELATIONSHIPS

A relationship is a contract of mutual nurturance. Relationships have to be a rich climate of positivity.

For relationships to be strong, the ideal climate is one teeming with positive interactions.

~ John Gottman

POSITIVE RELATIONSHIPS

In this day and age, it's all about people 360. ~ Jeff Weiner

Mindful Leaders are aware of the power and importance of positive relationships, put conscious time and effort into the development of positive networks, and cultivate empathy, deep dive conversations, and win-win solutions with others. They recognize that some positive conflict can be productive, but go out of their way to avoid negative conflict escalators that thwart communication and cooperation. They take charge of their emotions and responses and work hard to build community and engagement.

Mindful Leaders build connection and synergy for productivity and teamwork. Building positive relationships involves establishing positive emotional bonds and engaging in wise mind interactions. Feeling connected is a fundamental human need and a necessity in our modern, interdependent societies. Having connection sets the stage for friendship, collaboration, and bonding. In times of conflict, it engenders trust, understanding, mutual support, and respect. Expressing positive regard, communicating that we are "on the same team," and working toward a mutually beneficial outcome are some techniques used by Mindful Leaders for creating more positive relationships.

POSITIVE RELATIONSHIPS SKILLS PREVIEW

Introduction: Positive Relationships
- Case Study: Observing Mindful Leadership—Jeff Weiner
    - Exercise: Mindful Leadership Case Study Questions
- Relationship Positivity Ratio (5 to 1)
- Research—Positive Relationships in the Workplace

***Skill 5:* CULTIVATE EMPATHY**
- What is Empathy?
- Benefits and Obstacles
- Consider Another's Individuality
- Consider Vulnerabilities
- Research on Empathy
    - Empathy Worksheet & Tracking Log
- Just Like Me Meditation
    - Just Like Me Meditation & Tracking Log

***Skill 6:* DEEP DIVE CONVERSATIONS**
- Craft Deep Dive Conversations
- Craft Win-Win Solutions
    - Deep Dive Conversations Worksheet & Tracking Log
- Gift of Relationship Meditation
    - Gift of Relationship Meditation Guide & Tracking Log

***Skill 7:* IDENTIFY CONFLICT ESCALATORS**
- Conflict Escalators—The Four Horsemen
    - Conflict Escalators Worksheet & Tracking Log

***Skill 8:* POSITIVE CONFLICT**
- The Key to Crafting Positive Conflict
- First, Do Your Homework
- How to Craft Positive Conflict
    - Positive Conflict Worksheet & Tracking Log
- Being Kindness Meditation
    - Being Kindness Meditation & Tracking Log

Coaching Guidelines

CASE STUDY: OBSERVING MINDFUL LEADERSHIP

JEFF WEINER
CEO—LinkedIn

Connect the world's professionals to make them more productive and successful.

Who is the best CEO in the country? When Glassdoor, a jobs and career community, released it annual report of Highest Rated CEOs for 2014, Jeff Weiner topped the list. The top ten runners up included Alan Mulally, CEO of Ford Motor; Richard Edelman, CEO of Edelman; Paul Jacobs, CEO of Qualcomm; Howard Schultz, CEO of Starbucks; Larry Page, CEO of Google, and Mark Zuckerberg, CEO of Facebook. Pretty heady company for a young CEO who took over the helm at Linkedin in 2009.

Jeff was born in New York City on February 21, 1970. He attended Wharton School of Business, University of Pennsylvania where he got a BS in economics. He went to work for Warner Bros. in 1994 and was Vice President, Online before he became a Founding Partner at Windsor Media in 2000. His mentor at Warner Bros. Terry Semel, convinced Jeff to follow him to Yahoo In 2001 when Semel became CEO of Yahoo. Jeff and served in key leadership roles with the most recent role as Executive Vice President of Yahoo's Network Division managing Yahoo's consumer offerings—Front Page, Mail, Search, and Media products.

Jeff recalls his experience with Yahoo and the problems of operating in a fast paced environment without "a clearly defined mission and core set of values." Jeff helped oversee Yahoo's acquisition of Inktomi and Overture Services, search technologies that put Yahoo in competition with Google, and Jeff in the center of a hotly contested internal debate: Was Yahoo a technology company or a content company? Jeff felt that resources were spread too thinly across too much business and he wanted to focus more. He pushed to acquire YouTube and was overruled. He finally left the company along with many others, but took with him a keen awareness of the need for focus, and the need to build a focused, collaborative team.

In 2008, Jeff did a brief stint as an executive-in-residence at two Silicon Valley venture firms—Greylock Partners and Accel Partners. In December 2008 he moved to LinkedIn. When Weiner joined LinkedIn, it was a fast-growing startup where "scattershot engineering projects were pulling the site in different directions." Reid Hoffman, the co-founder of LinkedIn, who ran the company before hiring Jeff to replace him, says he had built "a collection of very strong people, but not necessarily an effective team." Jeff changed that. He focused on clarity of purpose and building a powerful team.

Since Jeff became CEO of LinkedIn, the company has rapidly expanded its global platform to 19 languages and 26 offices around the world. It has grown its membership base from 33 million to more than 225 million. Jeff took the company public in May, 2011. The LinkedIn stock went from an opening price of 83 to over 230 by the end of 2014.

Jeff has very clear views about the direction and purpose of LinkedIn, and is passionate about communicating it to his team. He says, "One of the most valuable lesson I've learned in business is that managing a hyper-growth company is a little like launching a rock—if your trajectory is off by inches at launch, you can be off by miles out in orbit." He feels that the more specific you can be about who you are and what you stand for as an organization, the more likely you will achieve success. His tools for insuring clarity of direction include the LinkedIn Vision, Mission, Strategy, Values, and Culture.

The **Vision** of LinkedIn is to *create economic opportunity for every member of the global workforce*. Jeff points out that, "One of the greatest challenges in the world today, and I say this without hyperbole, is that the pace of innovation has now accelerated to the point that it is outstripping our ability to train the global workforce to take advantage of the opportunities being created by innovation." He goes on to say, "if you have a workforce that doesn't have economic opportunity or access to economic opportunity, you're going to have a very unstable society."

The ***Mission*** of LinkedIn is *to connect the world's professionals to make them more productive and successful.* He is passionate about the mission and sees it as critical to future global political and social stability. He has focused on making the mission measurable, achievable, and inspirational. For example, he points out that there are roughly 780 million knowledge workers and students in the world. "That's our addressable opportunity, immediately addressable. There are over 3 billion people in the global workforce. Our dream is to create economic opportunity for all of these people."

In discussing how they can achieve this mission, he is specific about LinkedIn products. "There is an incredible sense of the difference we can make with this platform. We know where all the opportunities are and specifically what skills are required to obtain those opportunities. If you have a profile on LinkedIn, we know skills you have. We know your ambitions. We can look at any potential gap and line you up, hopefully, with the source that you can provide you with the skills you need to obtain those opportunities."

The ***Strategy*** of LinkedIn is *to be the professional profile of record; to be the essential source of professional insights; and to work everywhere our members work.*

Jeff knows that people, and positive relationships with those people, is key to implementing the strategy. Jeff notes "The great companies and the great CEOs put talent first. The great students of these companies, folks like Jim Collins, the author of *Good to Great*, tell you that if you had only one priority it should be loading up the bus with talent." He says, "Surround yourself with only the best people you can find. I used to say find the right mentor. Find the right boss. Find somebody who is going to coach you and allow you to make mistakes—to be there for you. But in this day and age, it's all about "people 360." It's your mentor, it's your manager, it's your boss, and it's the people who work for you."

"Just work with the best people your can possibly find. It's not just about talent; you have to define for yourself what makes somebody great for you and why you are going to work well together. The people I most enjoy working with dream big, get stuff done, and know how to have fun."

The ***Culture*** of LinkedIn celebrates *transformation, integrity, collaboration, humor, and results.* The culture places a great deal of emphasis on the power of positive relationships. Jeff works hard to create a spirit of collaboration and fun without ever losing sight of the need for results. He states that he does not want to be surrounded by "yes" men, and encourages his team to stand up and champion their ideas, which of course leads to conflict.

Jeff practices what we call "global listening." Often times, a team member will be emotionally invested in their own idea, will argue passionately for it, and in the end, another idea or direction is chosen. Jeff works to maintain an environment where the best idea wins. He says, "it's not about politics and it's not about maneuvering—it's about aligning yourself, your teams, against what the company is trying to accomplish—that's how you create a winning culture." He points out, "You develop trust over time." He encourages post-mortems, figuring out what went right and what went wrong, and doing course corrections. Rather than punish people for taking the wrong path, the emphasis is placed upon learning from the mistakes made and the wrong paths taken.

Jeff is keenly aware of the importance of the Leader in setting the tone for positive relationships. He says, "The more people you're responsible for, the more your words and the way you communicate those words and your body language and essentially everything you do is taken into consideration by your team. You have to be that much more aware of the way in which you're coming across. And I think the best leaders maintain awareness of their environment and in real time can course correct."

Jeff is very concerned about maintaining the culture as the organization grows in size. He is adamant about considering cultural fit when hiring and on boarding. He says, "Your hiring, it starts with recruiting. I think one of the ways hyper-growth companies go off the rails is that they're growing so quickly, there is so much demand for product, there are so many opportunities ahead of them, that they lower the hiring bar to put people in seats to get the work done. And I think that's the beginning of the end for those companies."

The ***Values*** of Linkedin are the principles that guide the LinkedIn's day-to-day decisions. They include: *Members first; relationships matter; be open; honest and constructive; demand excellence; take* *intelligent risks; act like an owner.*

Jeff is adamant about values. He recalls, "Before going public, I was asked by one of our board members what kind of public company we wanted to be. And I was speechless. I had never been the CEO of a public company." Jeff thought about the question, and at the next board meeting said, "We're going to be the exact same company as a public company as we were as a private company. Same vision, same mission, same strategy, same long-term focus, same culture, same values—all of which have been codified." He went on to say, "If we go public, and something changes, one of two things has happened. Either we weren't ready, or I wasn't the right person to lead this company."

After the meeting the CFO and general counsel pulled Jeff aside and said, "Psst, come here for a sec. You know how you said nothing will change? You realize some things have to change." Jeff said, "What do you mean?" They said, "Well, one of our values is being open, honest, and constructive—and at the all-hands, you're basically transparent with everything. And as a publicly held company, you're not necessarily going to be in the same position." And Jeff said, "Why not." They said, "It's not the way it works—there's risks and so forth and so on." I said, "No, it's not going to change. We're going to play up to who we aspire to be and not play down to the lowest common denominator out of fear of what might happen. As soon as you do that, it's done."

Jeff is passionate about his vision, his mission, and his values, and in the rapidly changing world of technology, he is continually on the look out for new strategic opportunities. He recommends that people always be learning, and realizes that LinkedIn is in a unique position to help people know what they need to learn and what new skills they need to develop. An early lifetime goal of Jeff's was, *reforming the world's educational system*. Jeff recently took a step in achieving that goal.

LinkedIn recently paid $1.5 Billion to acquire *Lynda.com*, an online education company. Building on the premise that in the current market, you won't have the opportunity to get a high skilled job if you don't have the education needed to go along with it, LinkedIn aims to connect people with job opportunities, and Lynda.com aims to connect people with an education needed for those jobs. In following the LinkedIn vision to *create economic opportunity for every member of the global workforce,* this new business model could create more economic opportunity for a member of the global workforce. When you search for a job on LinkedIn, you see the skills required for the job, and then you are directed to a course from Lynda.com that will train you in those skills. Or, a recruiter could search for available candidates based on the courses they've taken.

Jeff Weiner is not standing still. He is continually on the lookout for new possibilities that are compatible with his vision and mission. On the morning of May 19, 2011, Jeff Weiner became the face of technology's new wave of optimism. He rang the bell on the floor of the New York Stock Exchange, and then watched as shares of his company soared above $120, nearly triple the price set by investment bankers. On the day of the IPO, staffers at LinkedIn were given black T-shirts with the company's new stock sticker, LNKD, written across the front. The back of the T-shirts read, NEXT PLAY, the refrain used by Mike Krzyzewski, a mindful leader in his own right, and the basketball coach of Duke University. Coach Krzyzewski is the winningest coach in NCAA history, has superb graduation rates, and a basketball team as close as family. He is one of Jeff's heroes, and he is known for shouting the phrase, "Next Play," every time the ball switches hands and his team heads down the court. Jeff says the phrase on the back of the T-shirt is "to make sure people don't spend too much time celebrating a great outcome or lamenting a poor outcome. That they turn their attention to the next play." This is a worthy motto for a young CEO and a young company who has set out to change the world of relationships.

Footnote: The information on Jeff Weiner and quotes used in this case study can be found in the following sources:
- *LinkedIn's Jeff Weiner on Connecting Talent with Opportunity.* An Interview with the CEO. bcg. Perspectives by the Boston Consulting Group. September 29, 2011.
- *LinkedIn's CEO Jeff Weiner Reveals The Importance of Body Language, Mistakes Made Out of Fear, And One Time He Really Doubted Himself* by Henry Blodget. Business Insider. September 22, 2014.
- *Accelerating Your Career.* SV. The Spin of Silicon Valley. April/May 2016
- *Glassdoor Reveals the Highest Rated CEOs for 2014.* www.glassdoor.com/50-Highest-Rated CEOs.
- *From Vision to Values: The Importance of Defining Your Core* by Jeff Weiner. October 29, 2012. www.linkedin.com
- *Can Jeff Weiner Realize LinkedIn's Full Potential?* By Douglas MacMillan, Bloomberg Business, June 30, 2011.
- YouTube. *A Conversation on Corporate Purpose with LinkedIn CEO Jeff Weiner.* The Aspen Institute

EXERCISE: MINDFUL LEADERSHIP CASE STUDY QUESTIONS

One of the ways to build a better understanding of the skills of mindful leadership is through role models who demonstrate the skills of mindful leadership in their actions. In the *Observing Mindful Leadership Case Studies*, we examine the accomplishments, the actions, the statements, and sometimes the thoughts and emotions of well-known leaders. The cases can help us to see a diversity of mindful leaders operating in many different types of environments, and help us to see how different leaders and different personalities practice the skills of mindful leadership. Use the following questions to help you to better understand this mindful leader.

1. AWARENESS IN THE MOMENT. Mindful Leaders are self-aware of what they are thinking, feeling, and doing, and are aware of what is going on around them. They tune in to the present, to themselves, to their surroundings, and to others. They listen mindfully for information and for emotions and practice global listening. They focus first on determining what is real, before attempting to alter reality.

What can you observe from the writings, statements, and actions of the leader in this case study that demonstrate the skills of awareness in the moment?

_____
_____
_____
_____
_____
_____
_____
_____
_____
_____

2. POSITIVITY & POSSIBILITY. Mindful Leaders are more focused on the positive and the possible than on the negative and impossible. They remain aware of the failures, the risks, the dangers, the realities, and the downsides, but they practice the discipline of thinking in terms of the positives, the opportunities, the probabilities, the options, and the alternatives. Mindful Leaders are aware of the power of positivity to broaden and build positive potential, to encourage novel thoughts and actions, and to inspire productivity and creativity in themselves and others.

What can you observe from the writings, statements, and actions of the leader in this case study that demonstrate the skills of positivity and possibility?

_____
_____
_____
_____
_____
_____
_____
_____
_____
_____

3. POSITIVE RELATIONSHIPS. Mindful Leaders are aware of the power and importance of positive relationships, put conscious time and effort into the development of positive networks, and cultivate empathy, deep dive conversations, and win-win solutions with others. They recognize that some positive conflict can be productive, but go out of their way to avoid negative conflict escalators that thwart communication and cooperation. They take charge of their emotions and responses and work hard to build community and engagement.

What can you observe from the writings, statements, and actions of the leader in this case study that demonstrate the skills of positive relationships?

_____

_____

_____

_____

4. AUTHENTICITY & INTEGRITY. Mindful Leaders are often respected for their authenticity and integrity. Their authenticity is reflected in the truthfulness of their intentions, behaviors, and commitments. Their integrity is reflected in their honesty, their strong moral principles, and their ability to live by those principles. Mindful Leaders are clear on their values and their priorities and make decisions and take actions based upon these values. They are aware of their strengths and look for ways to leverage their strengths in the pursuit of their goals and in the service of others.

What can you observe from the writings, statements, and actions of the leader in this case study that demonstrate the skills of authenticity and integrity?

_____

_____

_____

_____

5. MANAGE STRESS & ENERGY. Mindful Leaders manage their energy and stress in order to maintain high levels of physical, mental, and emotional well-being. They challenge their thoughts to stay in touch with reality, they identify their emotions and emotional triggers and manage their responses, and they consciously monitor and manage their energy.

What can you observe from the writings, statements, and actions of the leader in this case study that demonstrate the skills of manage stress and energy?

_____

_____

_____

_____

6. RESILIENCE. Mindful leaders work to develop resilience—the capacity to recover from difficulties and adversity. They focus on the heroic rather than the debilitating aspects adversity; they let go of perfectionism and shortcomings and focus on the possible and potential; and they practice compassion and self-compassion.

What can you observe from the writings, statements, and actions of the leader in this case study that demonstrate the skills of resilience?

_____

_____

_____

_____

INTRODUCTION: POSITIVE RELATIONSHIPS

Having good relationships with others is crucial to wellbeing. The happiest 10% of people have just one thing in common. It's not that they are on the *Fortune 500* list, live in sunny California, or even that they have more objectively positive events—it's that they report having satisfying close relationships. Even those who tend to be introverted and enjoy solitary pursuits benefit by prioritizing relationships. Most people report relationships as the number one source of happiness and rate love as the most powerful positive emotion. Shame and loneliness are often said to be the most devastating emotions. Most also identify relationships as the biggest source of difficulties, frustration, and emotional pain.

RELATIONSHIP POSITIVITY RATIO (5:1)

John Gottman is a world-renowned expert known for his work on marital stability and divorce prediction. He has authored 190 published academic articles and is the author or co-author of 40 books. In his work at the Relationship Research Institute at University of Washington, John Gottman and colleagues have demonstrated that strong, healthy intimate relationships have a 5:1 ratio of positive to negative emotions. In other words, we need to have five positive interactions for every equally negative interaction.

Trust provides a foundation for managing relationships whether it is resolving conflict or deepening intimacy. Research shows that people with the strongest and most satisfying relationships have the ability to build and maintain trust with others across situations, even during conflict.

RESEARCH—POSITIVE RELATIONSHIPS IN THE WORKPLACE

Establishing Positive Emotional Climates to Advance Organizational Transformation. Sekerka and Fredrickson (cited below) draw upon positive psychology research to demonstrate how positive emotional climates can promote positive change as organizations expand and grow—particularly through what is labeled "transformative cooperation." This involves employees collaborating to develop new ways of relating to one another and their role within the organization.

The study examines how the broadening and building capacities of positive emotions can sustain organizations as they purposively evolve. It reviews the role of strength-based organizational development and change (ODC) processes to evoke positive emotions in support of a particular form of transformation.
Sekerka, L.E. & Fredrickson, B.L. (2008) Establishing positive emotional climates to advance organizational transformation. In Ashkansy, N. & Cooper, C. *Research companion to emotion in organizations* (pp. 531-545) Cheltenham, UK: Edward Elgar.

Charisma, Positive Emotions, and Mood Contagion. This meta-study by Bono and Ilies (cited below) examines the role of positive emotions in the charismatic leadership process. In studies 1 and 2, ratings of charisma in a natural work setting were linked to leaders' positive emotional expressions. In study 3, leaders' positive emotional expressions were linked to mood states of simulated followers. Results suggest that mood contagion may be one of the psychological mechanisms by which charismatic leaders influence followers. In study 4, the authors used a trained actor and manipulated leaders' positive emotional expressions to isolate the effects of positive emotions from the potential effects of non-emotional aspects of effective leadership (e.g., vision, other inspirational influence processes).

A positive link between leader emotions and follower mood was found. Results also indicate that both leaders' positive emotional expressions and follower mood influenced ratings of leader effectiveness and attraction to the leader. Bono, J.E., & Ilies, R. (2006). Charisma, positive emotions and mood contagion. *Leadership Quarterly.* 17(4), 317-344.

WIRED TO CONNECT

Humans are social animals. We have a fundamental need to connect to others and be part of a community. Historically, our survival depended on interdependence. In modern society, much of our success depends upon our ability to effectively navigate relationships. Our survival as a species and as individuals has always and still does depend on our ability to connect with others.

We can read and make snap judgments in milliseconds about others. In a sense, our brains evolved to detect whether another is a friend or a foe, trustworthy or dangerous. It also evolved to build social connection and deepen familial bonds. It as been said that humans are the winners of a bet that the weaker, clawless, social creatures with the capacity to collaborate and use tools would survive. Indeed, we have fundamental capacities and instincts to understand, connect, be altruistic, and build loving bonds with others.

In the past decade, understanding of the underpinnings of social connection has grown enormously. A field called *interpersonal neurobiology* illuminates the importance of relationships and social connections for surviving and thriving. Interpersonal neurobiology examines how brain structures and functioning are built to foster relationships and how these relationships shape its structures and functioning.

RESEARCH—Interpersonal Neurobiology

Below are abstracts from a selection of scientific studies published in major peer reviewed journals. Topics from the field of Interpersonal Neurobiology include Emotional Contagion, Mirror Neurons, and Empathy.

Stress Emotional Contagion. Female participants were exposed to high or low threat in the presence of another person believed to be facing either the same or a different situation. In Study 1, each dyad consisted of 2 actual participants, whereas in Study 2, each dyad consisted of 1 participant and 1 confederate, trained to convey either a calm or a nervous reaction to the situation. In both studies, a participant's felt affiliation towards their partner, defined in terms of the amount of time spent looking at the affiliate, were consistent with Schachter's (1959) "emotional similarity hypothesis;" threat increased affiliation and did so particularly with partners believed to be facing the same situation.

The authors also found evidence of behavioral mimicry, in terms of facial expressions, and emotional contagion, in terms of self-reported anxiety. The behavioral mimicry and emotional contagion results are considered from both primitive emotional contagion and social comparison theory perspectives. Gump, B. and Kulik, J. (1997) Stress, affiliation, and emotional contagion. *Journal of Personality and Social Psychology,* 72(2): 305-319.

Mood Contagion. The current studies aimed to find out whether a non-intentional form of mood contagion exists and which mechanisms can account for it. In these experiments, participants who expected to be tested for text comprehension listened to an affectively neutral speech that was spoken in a slightly sad or happy voice. The authors found that:
- the emotional expression induced a congruent mood state in the listeners,
- inferential accounts to emotional sharing were not easily reconciled with the findings,
- different affective experiences emerged from intentional and non-intentional forms of emotional sharing, and
- findings suggest that a perception–behavior link (T. L. Chartrand & J. A. Bargh, 1999) can account for these findings, because participants who were required to repeat the philosophical speech spontaneously imitated the target person's vocal expression of emotion. Neumann, R., Strack, F. (2000) Mood Contagion: The automatic transfer of mood between persons. *Journal of Personality and Social Psychology* 79(2): 211-223.

Stress Contagion. Previous research on multiple role stress has hypothesized the existence of two types of stress contagion: spillover, in which the stresses experienced in either the work or home domain lead to stresses in the other domain; and crossover, in which the stresses experienced by one's spouse at work lead to stresses for oneself at home. However, empirical evidence of these processes has been largely indirect and qualitative.

This study provides the first direct quantitative evidence on the causal dynamics of stress contagion across work and home domains in married couples. Contrary to previous thinking, results indicate that husbands are more likely than their wives to bring their home stresses into the workplace. Also, stress contagion from work to home was evident for both husbands and wives. Furthermore, the contagion of work stress into the home sets in motion a process of dyadic adjustment, whereby individuals, particularly wives, appear to modify their housework efforts to compensate for the work stresses of their spouses.

Such findings provide important insights into the dynamics of gender differences in role stress and confirm the value of studying chronic stress processes at the level of analysis where such stresses are inevitably manifest—in day-to-day events and activities. Bolger, N., DeLongis, A., Kessler, R., Wethington, E. (1989). The Contagion of Stress Across Multiple Roles. *Journal of Marriage and Family*. 51(1): 175-183

Prewired Neural Basis for Emotional Contagion. Frequently, one individual becomes 'infected' with emotions displayed by his or her partner. Researchers tested the predictions that the automatic, mostly unconscious component of this process, called 'primitive emotional contagion', is repeatable and fast. Stronger facial expressions of the sender evoke stronger emotions in the viewer, and women are more susceptible to emotional contagion than men.

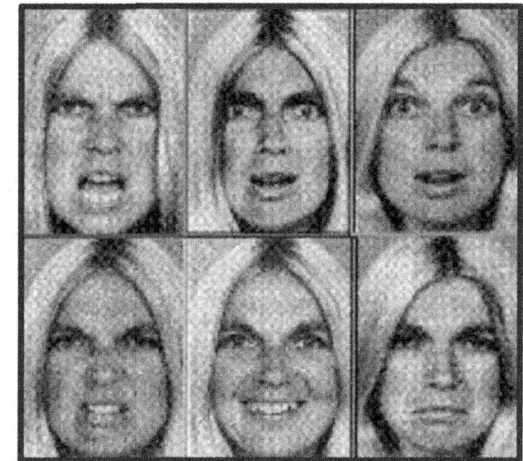

They presented photos on a computer varying the affective content (e.g., happy and sad), the expressive strength, and the duration of presentation. After each photo, subjects rated the strength of experienced happiness, sadness, anger, disgust, surprise, fear and pleasure (image from csupomona.edu). Feelings of happiness or sadness were significantly, specifically and repeatedly evoked in the viewer even with presentations lasting only 500 ms. Stronger expressions evoked more emotion. The gender of the viewer had weak effects.

Researchers posited that this fast and repeatable reaction is likely to have a 'prewired' neural basis. They propose the perception of emotionally expressive faces is related to the detection of emotional states in others and as the basis for one's own reactions. Wild, B., Erbb, M., Bartelsa, M. (2001) Are emotions contagious? Evoked emotions while viewing emotionally expressive faces: quality, quantity, time course and gender differences. *Psychiatry Research*, 102(2): 109-124.

Skill 5. CULTIVATE EMPATHY

How far you go in life depends on your being tender with the young, compassionate with the aged, sympathetic with the striving and tolerant of the weak and strong.
Because someday in your life you will have been all of these.
–George Washington Carver

WHAT IS EMPATHY?

Empathy is the ability to understand another's experience. It is social awareness. This includes understanding their point-of-view, feelings, actions, intentions, values, motivations, and strengths.

The survival of the human species has depended upon the ability to understand others and group dynamics. This has tremendous survival benefit. Even in our modern era, this is crucial. I believe the continued survival of the human race, and certainly thriving as a species, depends upon understanding another's experience. As technology advances, the potential for massive destruction builds exponentially. Just as Thich Nhat Hanh stated, however, when we deeply understand another, no matter how hostile, egregious, or offensive they are, the relationship becomes transformed. Within deep understanding resides the potential for reconciliation, transformation, peace, and love.

Empathy Is Different from Caring. A common misconception about empathy is that it involves caring about the other. Empathy does not imply care. Empathy is independent from emotional valence. It is simply understanding another. Whether you care or not about the other's experience is a separate, independent process. We can know another is suffering but not feel for them or be moved to help. Research shows, for instance, that many psychopaths have a high level of empathy. They can manipulate their victims because they understand.

Our Pledge—To Teach Empathy to Serve the Greater Good. Some of the worst atrocities in history have been masterminded by individuals with high levels of empathy. It is important to know this. For this reason, in our emotional intelligence program, we take a stand. We pledge to always teach empathy coupled with a compassion component. We are a value-driven mission—our aim is to teach these skills in order to have a positive impact on society. Because we recognize their power, we offer these tools to be used in the service of the greater good.

BENEFITS OF EMPATHY

Empathy Is Empowering. Importantly, understanding another does not dictate action, and it is not passive or capitulating. On the contrary, true Social Awareness empowers. It positions us for effective action. That action may be fierce or aggressive. It need not be nice, conciliatory, or foster connection.

For example, some years ago when I was a graduate student in Boston, I was walking home, books in hand, through the Boston Commons. This is a large park in the center of the city. It was about 10pm and I was walking alone across The Common on a dimly lit path. I turned around to see a large male figure walking purposefully toward me. By the aggressive stance and quick pace, I sensed he was following me. I walked faster and he did as well. Fear spiked. There was no one in sight and I was midway through the park. I turned around, squarely faced the figure pacing toward me, and yelled with the loudest, most commanding voice I could muster, "DO NOT FOLLOW ME. GO AWAY!" Surprised, he turned around and dashed into the shadows. In my mind, this confirmed my fears. I believe he was following me, intending to do harm. I could have been mistaken, but had I wrongly accused him, I believe his reaction would have been quite different rather than escaping anonymously into the darkness.

This experience reminds me of the power of Social Awareness. Social Awareness simply refers to *understanding another*. It does not mean agreeing, condoning, or allowing an action to occur. By reading his body language, I sensed malicious intention. This awareness positioned me to take fierce action and protect myself.

OBSTACLES TO EMPATHY

There are several obstacles to accurate and high level empathy. First, true empathy is an aspiration—we can never truly know what another is experiencing. Further, our own experience and point of view distorts clear understanding. We tend to get caught in our own view and intentions—we look but we don't see others. An added challenge is that others may have difficulty communicating their experience, feelings, thoughts, and intentions. They may not even know for themselves, or they actively may attempt to conceal aspects of themselves by intentionally or unintentionally misrepresenting themselves. High-level empathy requires imagination, guess work, self-awareness, and ability to communicate well in order to develop and clarify an understanding of another.

The Root of Empathy. Seeing similarities in others is at the root of empathy. When we notice the internal experiences of others including their motives, fears, hopes and dreams, we can't help but recognize similarities to ourselves. This leads to a natural bonding and care that manifests both in a feeling sense of connection and often action. People who see others as similar, as in the "in group" tend to engage in more altruistic acts and protective gestures. In contrast, the worst atrocities occur when another is out-casted, deemed different, vilified, and at worst dehumanized. Tragically, we have seen this phenomenon repeat itself countless times across human history.

Wired for detecting difference. Our brains are wired to see differences. Just like we are more adept at detecting danger signals than safety signals we more quickly can identify differences than similarities. From an evolutionary perspective this ability has a survival advantage. We might think of difference as a form of change. When things stay the same we know what to expect. We know that if we are safe we will continue to be safe.

When things are different, an element of uncertainty is introduced. Through the lenses of the "caveman and cavewoman brain" differences should be attended to because they may indicate arrival of threat. People within the tribe were safe; people from outside the tribe are more likely to be dangerous.

MIRROR NEURONS

Understanding the Actions of Others. "Mirror" neurons are neurons that discharge both when the monkey makes a particular action and when it observes another individual (monkey or human) making a similar action. Researchers attempted to give a neurophysiological account of the mechanisms underlying behaviors where an individual reproduces, overtly or internally, movements or actions made by another individual.

The basic concept of mirror neurons:

1. Person A performs a physical act.
2. Person B observes.
3. The brain activity in Person A and Person B are similar.

Two types of resonance behavior:

The first type is characterized by imitation, immediate or with delay, of movements made by other individuals. Examples of resonance behavior of this type are the "imitative" behaviors observed in birds, young infants and patients with frontal lesions.

The second type of resonance behavior is characterized by the occurrence, at the observation of an action, of a neural pattern, which, when internally generated, determines the making of the observed action. In this type of resonance behavior the observed action is, typically, not repeated (overtly). We argue that resonance behavior of the second type is at the basis of the understanding of actions made by others. Rizzolatti, G., Fadiga, L., Fogassi, L., Gallese, V. Resonance Behaviors and Mirror Neurons. *Italiennes de Biologie.* 137(2/3).

Performed or Observed Causes Same Neural Response. Many object-related actions can be recognized both by their sound and by their vision. They describe a population of neurons in the ventral premotor cortex of the monkey that discharge both when the animal performs a specific action and when it hears or sees the same action performed by another individual. These 'audiovisual mirror neurons' therefore represent actions independently of whether these actions are performed, heard or seen. The magnitude of auditory and visual responses did not differ significantly in half the neurons. A neurometric analysis revealed that based on the response of these neurons, two actions could be discriminated with 97% accuracy. Keysers, C., Kohler, E., Umilta, M., Nanetti, L., Foggasi, L., Gallese, V. (2003) Audiovisual mirror neurons and action recognition. *Experimental Brain Research,* 153 (4): 628-636.

Inferring Intention through Action. Is it possible to understand the intentions of other people by simply observing their actions? Many believe that this ability is made possible by the brain's mirror neuron system through its direct link between action and observation. However, precisely how intentions can be inferred through action observation has provoked much debate. Researchers suggested that the function of the mirror system can be understood within a predictive coding framework that appeals to the statistical approach known as empirical Bayes. Within this scheme the most likely cause of an observed action can be inferred by minimizing the prediction error at all levels of the cortical hierarchy that are engaged during action observation. This account identifies a precise role for the mirror system in our ability to infer intentions from actions and provides the outline of the underlying computational mechanisms. Kilner, J., Friston, K., Frith, C. (2007) Predictive coding: an account of the mirror neuron system. *Cognitive Processing,* 8(3): 159-166

Brain Structures Involved with Understanding Emotions and Actions. Researchers examined the neural workings behind understanding others. They found that two separate but similar systems provide for the comprehension of the actions and emotions of others. The ability to experientially understand the emotions of others involves the viscero-motor centers. The mirror neuron system supports the ability to understand others' actions. Gallese, V., Keysers, C., Rizzolatti, G. (2004) A unifying view of the basis of social cognition. *Trends in Cognitive Science,* 8(9): 396-403.

High-functioning autistic children and controls were monitored via fMRI as they imitated and observed emotional expression. Performance on the task was similar across both groups but autistic children did not show any mirror neuron activity in the inferior frontal gyrus (pars opercularis), which is tied to the severity of social deficiencies in autism. The research suggests that this area of the brain, in particular this mirror neuron system, plays a vital role in explaining the deficits in social ability in autistic children. Dapretto, M. et al. (2006). Understanding emotions in others: mirror neuron dysfunction in children with autism spectrum disorders. *Nature Neuroscience, 9(1), 28-30.*

Participants completed a social cognition measure ("Visual Discrimination" and the "Static and Dynamic Emotion Recognition" task) while being administered transcranial magnetic stimulation to known mirror neuron areas. Greater neuron activity was observed in the premotor cortex that correlated with performance on the social cognition measure. More specifically, increased MEP amplitude was observed during emotion recognition of static faces; there were no significant correlations between mirror neuron activation and general facial processing, suggesting that mirror neurons do have a role in "variant" expressions (apart from neutral faces), as well as the importance of the mirror neuron system in the premotor cortex in social cognition. Enticott, P.G. et al. (2008). Mirror neuron activation is associated with facial emotion processing. *Neuropsychologia, 46, 2851-2854.*

Participants completed tasks requiring them to observe, discriminate, and imitate facial expressions (i.e. neutral, happy, fearful, and disgust) as well as patterned bodily motion while monitored by fMRI. Passive observation of facial expressions was correlated with increases in the inferior frontal gyrus/insula and the posterior parietal cortex, which is associated with the execution of similar facial expressions. Some regions responded more to specific facial expression than patterned motion (bilateral ventral IFG, bilateral STS/MTG, bilateral amygdala, SMA). Emotional expressions elicited greater activity in the insula and frontal operculum while neutral faces elicited greater activity in the somatosensory cortices. The amygdala showed greater activity in the fear conditions, and the insula for disgust. In the discrimination and imitation tasks, the observed effects were heightened. Van der Gaag, C., Minderaa, R.B., & Keysers, C. (2007). Facial expressions: What the mirror neuron system can and cannot tell us. *Social Neuroscience, 2(3-4), 179-222.*

CONSIDER ANOTHER'S INDIVIDUALITY

This Stranger

This stranger has parents and people who love her, just like me.
This stranger has moments of joy, just like me
This stranger has moments of anguish and suffering, just like me.
This stranger will one day grow old, just like me.
This stranger will go through the cycles of illness and recovery, just like me.
This stranger will one day die, just like me.

–Deepak Chopra

Root of Aggression. Research suggests that the root of aggression resides in the failure to consider the individuality of another person. This provocative line of research shows that at extremes, this failure may facilitate inhumane acts like torture. Members of extreme outgroups that elicit disgust (e.g., homeless people and drug addicts) are differentially processed in the brain.

Common Humanity. This effect, however, can be undone very simply. It only requires considering a member of this group's individuality. In Harris and Fiske's study, they simply asked people if they thought this person (a homeless person) in the photograph would like carrots. This simple question was enough to create a sense of common humanity, and the brain regions associated with disgust became deactivated.

These findings have profound implications for conflict not only between individuals but also for prejudice in society and violence between societies with clashing belief systems.

To love our enemy is impossible. The moment we understand our enemy, we feel compassion towards them, and they are no longer our enemy.
—Thich Nhat Hanh

Look for Similarities. Noticing similarities refers to intentionally considering others' intentions, needs, desires, dreams, fears, or other internal feeling states, perspectives, or objectives. Try looking for similarities when resolving conflict or to deepen connection to enhance empathy and interpersonal problem solving. Consider another's:
- Roles in life
- Goals
- Joys
- Challenges
- Insecurities and concerns

CONSIDER VULNERABILITIES

Considering vulnerabilities can be an especially effective way to transform power differentials and improve one's ability to manage conflict by building empathy. Vulnerabilities are often personal insecurities or areas where people have had difficulty previously. Typically, only close, trusted friends or family know of one's vulnerabilities, and sometimes not even they know. Vulnerabilities often remain hidden, and strong defenses can arise in an attempt to conceal them. Considering another's vulnerabilities can deepen understanding, help us to make sense of unexpected or confusing reactions, and help us feel compassionate during conflict. Awareness of another's vulnerabilities can greatly improve one's ability to deal with a difficult person in a sensitive and effective manner. Common vulnerabilities are:

• Perfectionism	• Fear of failure	• Unrealistic expectations of self or others
• Self-criticism	• Insecurity	• Need for reassurance or approval, or to prove oneself
• Need to be right	• Social anxiety	• Fear of not being good enough or feeling unlovable
• Need to be liked	• Need for predictability	• Excessive need for control

Even in the workplace you might consider another's vulnerabilities or hidden insecurities. Although they may never admit to their insecurities, it can be useful to consider what they might be. This can both increase compassion, empathy, and understanding as well as make others in opposing positions or extreme power positions "more human."

This skill can be invaluable when dealing with a difficult person who is strongly opinionated, stubborn, aggressive, or exhibiting other hard to understand behaviors. It is counterintuitive to see fierceness as a sign of vulnerability, but often fear and vulnerability underlie aggression. Unchecked fear can drive impulsive, strong, and extreme behaviors. Think of how fierce a grizzly bear can become when protecting her young. Aggression often emerges from the perception of threat or insecurity as a defensive or offensive attack to regain safety.

RESEARCH ON EMPATHY

Below are abstracts from a selection of scientific studies published in major peer reviewed journals.

Considering Perspective Increases Empathy. In one study showing that empathy can be increased though a simple practice of considering another's perspective, 92 students were assigned to either a point-of-view writing or a clinical reasoning condition as part of a second year doctoring course. At the end of the year they completed a writing assignment about ER death from cardiac arrest. Results showed that students who were trained in point-of-view writing improved in certain affective dimensions. Shapiro, J. (2006). Point-of-View Writing: A Method for Increasing Medical Students' Empathy, Identification and Expression of Emotion, and Insight. *Education for Health*, 19(1), 96-105.

Empathy through Mindfulness. A pilot project was assessed as a method to teach culturally sensitive, empathic communication skills. It attempted to integrate and communicate the theoretical, conceptual, and experiential understanding of cross-cultural empathy through the practice of mindful attitudes. Students were introduced to materials through a series of exercises, which included mirroring breathing observation, posture, and moving awareness. These exercises fostered a state of openness through the experience of emptying, contemplation, and being-present.

The preliminary findings indicated that the students were able to verbalize new learning experiences, which included: being more attuned with their bodily awareness, sensing the flow of energy with the other, letting go of power struggles, and pre-existing ideas, and experiencing a greater human connectedness with the other. Lu, E., Dane., B., Gellman, A. (2005). The name assigned to the document by the author. This field may also contain sub-titles, series names, and report numbers. An Experiential Model: Teaching Empathy and Cultural Sensitivity. *The entity from which ERIC acquires the content, including journal, organization, and conference names, or by means of online submission from the author. Journal of Teaching in Social Work*, 25(3-4): 89-103

Prejudice and Dehumanization. This study suggests that having prejudice towards out groups that are stereotypically labeled as hostile and incompetent (i.e. homeless people, addicts) can be particularly troublesome and may lead to dehumanizing these extreme out-groups. Functional MRI's were used to examine brain activation in study participants that were shown photographs of social groups and objects. The researchers found increased neural activation to all images of social groups except extreme out-groups, supporting the prediction that extreme out-groups may be seen as less than human. Harris, L. T., & Fiske, S. T. (2006). Dehumanizing the lowest of the low neuroimaging responses to extreme out-groups. *Psychological Science*, 17(10), 847-853.

Recognizing Individuality. Social groups that elicit disgust are differentially processed in mPFC Social neuroscience suggests a decreased activation in the medial pre-frontal cortex (mPFC) to members of extreme outgroups that elicit disgust. Study participants were instructed to either make superficial categorical age estimations (e.g. broad generalizations) or individuating food-preference judgments (i.e. whether the social group member likes carrots) about people as fMRI recorded neural activity.

This study demonstrates that being instructed to see extreme out-groups through an individualistic lens as opposed to making superficial categorical judgments may lead to increased social cognition (demonstrated by increased activation in the mPFC) and help one see extreme out-group members as more similar to oneself - thereby increasing a sense of common humanity. Harris, L. T., & Fiske, S. T. (2007). Social groups that elicit disgust are differentially processed in mPFC. *Social cognitive and affective neuroscience, 2*(1), 45-51.

Consider Others Undoes Dehumanizing Tendencies. The danger in adopting dehumanizing perceptions, research suggests, is a failure to consider the mind of another person, which, in turn, may facilitate inhumane acts like torture. Harris, L. T., & Fiske, S. T. (2011). Dehumanized perception: A psychological means to facilitate atrocities, torture, and genocide?. *Zeitschrift für Psychologie/Journal of Psychology, 219*(3), 175.

Cultivating Compassion and Empathy. Research shows that even when confronted with distressing life events, we can train our compassion "muscle" and reshape our brain to respond with more empathy. Study participants that previously reacted with negative affect before compassion training were found to exhibit increased positive affective experiences, even in response to witnessing others in distress, after compassion training.

This finding further suggests that deliberately cultivating compassion can increase positive affect, affiliation, and common humanity. Klimecki, O. M., Leiberg, S., Lamm, C., & Singer, T. (2012). Functional neural plasticity and associated changes in positive affect after compassion training. *Cerebral Cortex*, bhs142.

Teaching Empathy—An Overview of Two Models. Whether empathy can be "taught" has long been debated. Can we teach an individual to feel for another person, to "walk in someone else's shoes?" Not only is an ability to empathize with others essential for counseling professionals, but empathic individuals fare better in a variety of interpersonal relationships, whether professional, familial, or friendship.

The capacity for empathy serves as a foundation for relationships, has preventative potential in preserving emotional health, and also provides a basis for coping with stress and resolving conflict. Hatcher, S., Nadeau, M., Walsh, L., Reynolds, M., Galea, J., Marz, K. (1994) The teaching of empathy for high school and college students: testing Rogerian methods with the interpersonal reactivity index. *Adolescence Magazine*, winter.

Empathy Prevents Aggression. Current research is establishing the importance of teaching empathy skills to youth in order to prevent aggression and to teach important interpersonal and work skills. The Center for Safe Schools and Communities has developed supplementary Aggression Replacement Training materials (the PEACE Curriculum) that emphasize empathy training with students. Salmon, S. (2003) Teaching Empathy: The PEACE Curriculum. *Reclaiming Children and Youth: The Journal of Strength-based Interventions,* 12(3): 167-173.

Israeli-Palestinian Group Interventions. The workshops of Jewish-Israeli and Palestinian youth conducted in the post-Oslo era with the aim of promoting reconciliation and peace building between the sides. The workshops were organized by an Israeli-Palestinian organization, in the framework of a peace education project. In these workshops, youth from pairs of Israeli and Palestinian high schools met for two days to discuss social, cultural and political topics. Each workshop included approximately 20 youths from each side that were led jointly by a Jewish-Israeli and a Palestinian group facilitator.

The study examined four facets of these dialogue events, using both quantitative and qualitative research methods:
- structure of activities and practices of transformative dialogue used in the encounter events;
- attitudes and mutual stereotypes held by youth from both sides prior to the beginning of the workshops;
- mutual perceptions and attitudes expressed by participants during the encounter;
- effects of participation in the workshops on stereotypes held by the Jewish-Israeli and Palestinian youth (pre-post comparisons).

The study found that the youths initially came to the workshop with negative stereotypes and minimal interactions with each other. However, after participating in the workshops, the youths had more favorable perceptions of each other. They were more likely to view the other group as "tolerant" or "considerate of others." Maoz, I. (2000) An Experiment in Peace: Reconciliation-Aimed Workshops of Jewish-Israeli and Palestinian Youth. *Journal of Peace Research,* 37(6):721-736.

EMPATHY WORKSHEET

Counter the tendency to form the in-group and out-group bias by intentionally looking for similarities in others. This practice is especially helpful when resolving conflict or deepening connection. A fundamental principle in Buddhist philosophy is that all humans share a core need: *All humans are suffering, and all humans seek an end to their suffering.* It can be helpful to keep this in mind when confronted with what may look like inappropriate or irrational behavior. Seeing similarities can be a basis for empathy and interpersonal problem solving.

This application guides you through exploring similarities in others, which can help to deepen connections and/or resolve conflicts.

SITUATION

Consider an individual with whom you have some difficulty and/or a recent situation in which you were in conflict with another. Briefly describe the difficulty you are having with the individual and/or the situation. (Who, What, Where?)

_____

_____

_____

_____

1. LOOK FOR SIMILARITIES

- Roles in life
- Goals
- Joys, Hopes, Dreams
- Challenges

Roles in life. What are his/her roles in life?

_____

_____

Goals. What are his/her possible goals?

_____

_____

Joys, Hopes, & Dreams. What are his/her possible joys, hopes, and dreams?

_____

_____

Challenges. What are his/her possible challenges?

_____

_____

_____

2. CONSIDER VULNERABILITIES

- Perfectionism
- Low self-worth
- Self-criticism
- Social Anxiety
- Fear of failure
- Need to succeed or prove oneself
- Need for reassurance or approval
- Need to be liked, right, or in control

Vulnerabilities. What are some possible vulnerabilities?

_____
_____
_____
_____
_____

Insecurities and Concerns. What are some possible Insecurities and concerns?

_____
_____
_____
_____
_____

3. USE INSIGHTS—To Strengthen Relationship/Resolve Conflict

Explore how you could use the insights from your answers above to:

Strengthen the Relationship.

_____
_____
_____
_____
_____
_____

Resolve Conflict.

_____
_____
_____
_____
_____
_____

EMPATHY TRACKING LOG

DAY	APPLICATION What SIMILARITIES did I notice and with whom? What VULNERABILITIES did I sense and with whom?	IMPACT What was the impact of noticing similarities on me, others, the situation, and/or our relationship?
Day 1		
Day 2		
Day 3		
Day 4		

EMPATHY TRACKING LOG

DAY	APPLICATION What SIMILARITIES did I notice and with whom? What VULNERABILITIES did I sense and with whom?	IMPACT What was the impact of noticing similarities on me, others, the situation, and/or our relationship?
Day 5		
Day 6		
Day 7		

INSIGHTS—What patterns or insights emerged?

_____
_____
_____
_____
_____

JUST LIKE ME MEDITATION

Pausing to look deeper into another's experience often results in the realization that we all share universal human experiences. The purpose of this meditation is to practice taking another's perspective and imagine what it would feel like to be them. This meditation is designed to help you to notice similarities and build empathy.

This meditation guides you through different realms of common experience. It is adapted from Deepak Chopra's compilation of healing affirmations. During all the meditations, try to let go of expectations about how this practice is supposed to feel or what is supposed to happen. Your job is to experience what happens in a nonjudgmental, explorative manner, and each time your mind wanders into thought, turn your attention back.

INSTRUCTIONS
(3-8 MINUTES)

1. FOCUS INWARD: Breathe and Center

- **Center**—Close your eyes and turn your attention inward.

- **Anchor in your Breath**—Feel Your Breath fill and release your body. Breathe deeply with a slower exhale and natural inhale. Place your hand on your abdomen to feel your diaphragm rise and fall. Feel your feet as the rest on the floor. Notice the sensations on the bottom of your feet making contact with the earth. Feel your hands as they rest on your thighs. Open them and notice the sensations and invite them to relax.

- **Set your Intention**—To direct your attention in this time, place, and to the objective of this meditation.

2. DIRECT ATTENTION: *To the way a stranger is Just Like Me.*

- *Make Contact*—Bring to mind a stranger or acquaintance you know. Choose someone who's life story you know little about.

This person has parents and people who love her, just like me.
This person has moments of joy, just like me
This person has moments of anguish and suffering, just like me.
This person will one day grow old, just like me.
This person will go through the cycles of illness and recovery, just like me.
This person will one day die, just like me.

- *Soak in the feelings*—Feel into the experience and sense the energy that runs through your body as you focus on the way that this person is just like you.

3. REFLECT ON INSIGHTS: Breathe and Reflect
- Come back to your breath.
- Reflect on the insights or benefits you gained during this meditation.

4. MAINTAIN YOUR INNER AWARENESS: Soft Gaze and Stay with It
- Slowly open your eyes and keep your gaze soft, directed downward, and settling on a neutral object.
- Stay with the awareness you gained during the meditation.

JUST LIKE ME MEDITATION WORKSHEET

After you have completed the meditation, jot down any observations about what came up during your meditation. Make note of thoughts you had, feelings you experienced, bodily sensations you felt, and/or detours that you took.

1. FOCUS INWARD: Breathe and Center. How well were you able to concentrate inward and turn your attention to your intention in this meditation?

_____
_____
_____

2. DIRECT ATTENTION: *That a stranger is Just Like Me.*

Make Contact. Bring to mind a stranger or acquaintance you know. Choose someone who's life story you know little about.

> This person has parents and people who love her, just like me.
> This person has moments of joy, just like me
> This person has moments of anguish and suffering, just like me.
> This person will one day grow old, just like me.
> This person will go through the cycles of illness and recovery, just like me.
> This person will one day die, just like me.
> This person wants to feel safe and relaxed, just like me.
> This person wants to feel loved, just like me.

Person. What person came up for you?

_____
_____
_____

Images and Feelings. What images or feelings came up?

_____
_____
_____

Soak in the feelings—What was the experience and sense the energy that ran through your body as you focused on the way that this person is just like you?

_____
_____
_____

3. REFLECT ON INSIGHTS: What insights or benefits did you gain?

_____
_____
_____

JUST LIKE ME MEDITATION TRACKING LOG

DAY	APPLICATION Which people or person did I focus on? What internal or external factors helped me successfully complete this meditation?	IMPACT What was the impact of doing this meditation on me, my emotions, thoughts, and/or plan for action in a situation? What insights emerged?
Day 1		
Day 2		
Day 3		
Day 4		

JUST LIKE ME MEDITATION TRACKING LOG

DAY	**APPLICATION** Which people or person did I focus on? What internal or external factors helped me successfully complete this meditation?	**IMPACT** What was the impact of doing this meditation on me, my emotions, thoughts, and/or plan for action in a situation? What Insights emerged?
Day 5		
Day 6		
Day 7		

INSIGHTS - What patterns or benefits emerged?

_____
_____
_____
_____

Skill 6. DEEP DIVE CONVERSATIONS

The only real security is not in owning or possessing, not in demanding or expecting, not in hoping, even. Security in a relationship lies neither in looking back to what it was, nor forward to what it might be, but living in the present and accepting it as it is now.
-Anne Morrow Lindbergh

When things fall apart, people tend to focus on their short-term goals and how and why another person or variable in the situation is blocking their objective. Conversations tend to be about what is right or wrong, on what the other person should have done, what could have been different, etc. Typically, attempts to resolve conflict generally fail when they stay on the level of content. More often, conflict lives at deeper levels of experience. The problem, however, is that we tend to stay on the surface and do not dive deeper into the roots of what people are fighting for. In conflict, whether it is in the workplace or at home, take a step back and consider deeper levels of conflict from each person's perspective.

CRAFT DEEP DIVE CONVERSATIONS

1. **SURFACE.** Identify Target Behavior
    Positive Behavior
    Negative Behavior

2. **UNDER WATERLINE.** Identify the underlying:
    Goal, Intention, Objective
    Needs and Wants

3. **DEEPER NEED.** Identify the deeper needs:
    Trust
    Respect
    Other

---

1. Surface—Target Behavior (Both positive and negative behavior). The behavior that you want to see is the positive target behavior. Also identify the problem behavior, the behavior that is creating an obstacle, or the negative target, that which you want to avoid or get rid of. By focusing on the positive and negative target behavior, you are naturally separating the person from the problem—a crucial component to conflict resolution. Some minor conflicts can be resolved by staying at this surface level, especially if there is a foundation of trust. Oftentimes, however, conflicts live in deeper water, so we need to dive deeper in order to resolve the conflict.

2. Under The Waterline—Underlying Goal, Intention, Or Objective. The underlying goal, intention or objective is the more important or significant issue that underlies the problem behavior. When the underlying goal, intention, or objective is threatened, we tend to act in an extreme manner. Consider what you or the other really wants or needs in the situation, or why you or the other is bothered by the problem behavior. Often this has little to do with the other person; it has more to do with one's perception of their ability to achieve the underlying goal.

"People miss the 'buttons' all the time. I'll be on a conference call with a client and I'll hear a colleague hit a 'button,' something the client really cares about, but then they just pass it by—so often people don't even realize they just came upon a button. They lost an opportunity for an in."
–John Hammond, Sales Manager at a San Francisco SEO company

3. Deeper Need—Trust & Respect. At a deeper level of experience, conflicts with others typically make us feel threatened. Our bodies go into fight or flight mode by increasing attentional vigilance (putting us on high alert for a predator), heart rate, blood pressure, skin conductance (sweating) and other physiological reactions preparing us to fight the attacker. The primitive systems of the body and mind are in "don't get killed mode." Now, in the context of interpersonal conflicts, this primitive circuitry is reacting as if it were a life or death situation. For that reason, at a very primitive level, trust is the foundation of all good relationships.

When in conflict, trust and safety (which translates in modern interactions as respect) are in question. It is often this deeper level that people defend, fight for, and also where the damage occurs if the conflict is not dealt with well. Above all, during conflict, we need to preserve the sense of trust and respect. Otherwise, put simply, the other person will activate this primitive "don't get killed" circuitry and the relationship can slip into doubt, suspicion, self-interest, and defensiveness. Although it feels much more complicated than that in interpersonal dynamics, often the strength of trust and sense of safety (i.e., respect) predicts the potential of relationships.

Decades of research support this proposition. John Gottman, considered the foremost researcher in romantic relationships, identifies trust as the fundamental unit of relationship health. Positive conflict management addresses the problem without threatening the other's sense of trust and feelings of respect in the relationship. This plays out in unspoken, often unconscious assessments of whether the other person is trustworthy and respects you. At an emotional, unconscious level, we may be asking ourselves questions like, "Are you with me or against me?; Do you like me?; Are you on my team?; Can I depend on you?; Are you safe?"

At work these questions often translate into inquiries into issues around competition versus cooperation, deceit and manipulation versus transparency and honesty, criticism versus support, trust and betrayal, etc. Concerns for one's reputation, likeability, acceptance on teams, and other subtle, unspoken insecurities are often examples of one's deeper need for trust and respect. In conflict conversations, it can be useful to consider the degree to which each party feels threatened at a fundamental level and how to preserve or directly address threats to trust and respect.

CRAFT WIN-WIN SOLUTIONS

Creating win-win solutions requires focusing more on the positive alternatives than the obstacles. Of course it is useful to problem solve, but most of us tend to overly focus on the problems rather than the possibilities. Focusing on ways to serve both parties' underlying goals can lead to win-win solutions. The conflicts of interest may not be as large and insurmountable as it initially seemed when viewed from this larger perspective.

DEEP DIVE CONVERSATION WORKSHEET

Conflict is to be expected even in the best relationships. In conflict, rebuilding connection may require you to take a step back and consider the variables at play for each party involved. The purpose of this exercise is to give you an opportunity to analyze a recent conflict and gain a greater level of insight by applying the Deep Dive Conversation approach. Choose a conflict situation you have had with someone, perhaps with a customer/client, colleague, boss, supervisor, manager, or supervisee.

CONFLICT SITUATION

WHO, WHERE, WHEN, & WHAT. Who was involved in the conflict? What happened?

_____

_____

_____

THREE LEVELS OF CONFLICT—YOUR PERSPECTIVE

1. SURFACE—TARGET BEHAVIOR

Negative Target. What is the problem behavior, the behavior that is creating an obstacle (the negative target), that which I want to avoid or get rid of.

_____

_____

_____

Positive Target. What is the behavior do I want to see, the behavior I want them to do instead of the problem behavior (the positive target behavior).

_____

_____

_____

2. UNDER THE WATERLINE—UNDERLYING GOAL, OBJECTIVE, OR INTENTION (situation).
What is MY underlying, more important objective that is threatened by the problem behavior. Consider what I want in this situation.

_____

_____

_____

3. DEEPER NEED—TRUST & RESPECT (personal).
What is my deepest level of need? Consider the degree of trust or respect I feel in the relationship and what I really want and need to feel in this relationship. (e.g., Do they like me as a person? Are they with me or against me?)

_____

_____

_____

THREE LEVELS OF CONFLICT—THE OTHER'S PERSPECTIVE

1. SURFACE—TARGET BEHAVIOR

Negative Target. What is the problem behavior, the behavior that is creating an obstacle (the negative target), that which they want to avoid or get rid of.

_____
_____
_____

Positive Target. What is the positive behavior they want to see, the behavior they want me (or another) to do instead of the problem behavior.

_____
_____
_____

2. UNDER THE WATERLINE—UNDERLYING GOAL, OBJECTIVE, OR INTENTION (situation). What is their underlying, more important objective that is threatened by the problem behavior. Consider what they want in this situation.

_____
_____
_____

3. DEEPER NEED—TRUST & RESPECT (personal). What is their deepest level of need? Consider the degree of trust or respect they feel in the relationship and what they really want and need to feel in this relationship. (e.g., Do they believe I like them as a person? Do they feel I am with them or against them?)

_____
_____
_____

ACTION PLAN

WIN-WIN SOLUTIONS. What are potential win-win solutions or ways to reconnect that address these three levels of conflict?

_____
_____
_____
_____
_____
_____
_____

DEEP DIVE CONVERSATION TRACKING LOG

DAY	APPLICATION Which Deep Dive Conversation did have today? What were my and their 3 levels of conflict? (Target Behaviors, Underlying Goal, Deeper Need for Trust/Respect)	IMPACT What was the impact of this technique on me, others, the situation, and/or the relationship?
Day 1		
Day 2		
Day 3		
Day 4		

DEEP DIVE CONVERSATION TRACKING LOG

DAY	APPLICATION Which Deep Dive Conversation did have today? What were my and their 3 levels of conflict? (Target Behaviors, Underlying Goal, Deeper Need for Trust/Respect)	IMPACT What was the impact of this technique on me, others, the situation, and/or the relationship?
Day 5		
Day 6		
Day 7		

INSIGHTS - What patterns or benefits emerged?

_____

_____

_____

_____

_____

Skill 7. IDENTIFY CONFLICT ESCALATORS

Truth is, I'll never know all there is to know about you just as you will never know all there is to know about me. Humans are by nature too complicated to be understood fully. So, we can choose either to approach our fellow human beings with suspicion or to approach them with an open mind, a dash of optimism and a great deal of candor.
-Tom Hanks

John Gottman has studied over 2,000 married couples over two decades and has identified communication characteristics that cause a breakdown in communication and damage relationships. Based on the degree to which these characteristics are present, Gottman and trained observers can predict with 94% accuracy, which marriages will succeed and which will fail. Gottman's work has been so impressive, that it has been very influential in academic circles as well as in popular media. It has been featured in numerous books, TV interviews, and magazines including the Harvard Business Review.

The four communication characteristics that Gottman posits escalate conflict are Criticism, Defensiveness, Contempt, and Stonewalling. These characteristics are so toxic that he refers to these escalators as the "*Four Horseman of the Apocalypse.*" Each behavior paves the way for the next one.

FOUR HORSEMEN OF THE APOCALYPSE

CONFLICT ESCALATORS—THE FOUR HORSEMEN

1. Criticism. Criticism is attacking another person's personality or character, usually with the intent of making someone right or someone wrong. A critical comment is often preceded by a generalization such as:

> *You always...*
> *You never...*
> *Why are you so...*
> *Why can't you just...*

2. Defensiveness. Defensiveness is trying to position oneself as innocent, not to blame, or as the victim. It is generally an ineffective effort to protect oneself from a perceived attack and is a common reaction to blame and criticism. Often defensiveness feels justified and necessary, so it is typically the most difficult to detect. Healthy alternatives to defensiveness are helping others to understand one's point-of-view, needs, and experience in a situation. Some typical examples of defensiveness are listed below:

- "Yes, but..."—Starting off agreeing but ending up disagreeing.
  I understand your perspective, but I just...

- Making excuses—Attributing external circumstances to being beyond one's control forcing them to act in a certain way.
  It's not my fault...
  I didn't...
  I was just trying to...

- Cross-Complaining. Meeting a partner's complaint or criticism with a different complaint.
  Well, you do that all the time, too...
  My habit is not as bad as your habit of...
  I wouldn't do that if you didn't always...
  That's not true, you're the one who...

- Whining.
  It's not fair...
  It never changes...

3. Stonewalling. Stonewalling is withdrawing from the relationship as a way to avoid conflict. Partners may think they are trying to be neutral, but stonewalling conveys disapproval, icy distance, separation, disconnections, a power play, or smugness. It is a potent Turning Away response that can be very damaging to connection and trust. Some typical expressions of stonewalling are listed below:

- Stony Silence.

- Monosyllabic mutterings.

- Changing the subject.

- Removing yourself physically.

- Ignoring what your partner said.

- Repeating yourself without paying attention to what the other person is saying.

4. Contempt. Contempt is attacking another person's sense of self with the intention to insult or psychologically abuse him or her. Gottman shows that once contempt takes hold in a relationship, it is pretty much doomed. Below are listed some typical expressions of contempt:

- Insults and name calling (ex: jerk, drama-queen, wimp, stupid, lazy, slob)

- Hostile humor, sarcasm, or mockery. (ex: "That extra 40 pounds really looks good on you.")

- Body language and/or tone of voice. (ex: Sneering, eye rolling, curling upper lip.)

CONFLICT ESCALATORS WORKSHEET

Conflict is to be expected even in the best relationships. Conflict escalators can quickly turn a potential problem solving session into a destructive argument.

This application provides an opportunity to deconstruct a conflict situation that you experienced recently, analyze what may have led to the conflict, and what may have increased the intensity of the conflict. Choose a conflict situation you have had with someone, perhaps with a customer/client, a colleague, a family member, significant other, or a close friend.

CONFLICT SITUATION

Identify a recent situation in which a discussion or disagreement escalated beyond the productive stage. (Briefly describe who, what, where, when, how, and why)

WHO. Who was involved in the conflict? _____

WHERE & WHEN DID IT HAPPEN? Did the time, location, or context contribute to the conflict?

_____

_____

WHO DID OR SAID WHAT? What happened?

_____

_____

_____

_____

_____

WHAT WERE THE PRECEDING CIRCUMSTANCES? Were there preceding factors that made it more likely or made me/other more emotionally vulnerable or on edge?

_____

_____

IDENTIFY CONFLICT ESCALATORS

Identify conflict escalators that escalated the situation to the point where it became unproductive.

1. CRITICISM. How was criticism displayed? How might I have brought in criticism?
(Criticism is attacking another person's personality or character, usually with the intent of making someone right or someone wrong. A critical comment is often preceded by a generalization like: *You always...You never...Why are you so....*)

_____

_____

_____

_____

2. DEFENSIVENESS. How was defensiveness displayed? How might I have brought in defensiveness?

Defensiveness is seeing one's self as the victim, and warding off a perceived attack. Often defensiveness feels justified and necessary so it is typically the most difficult to detect. Making excuses—External circumstances beyond my control forced me to act in a certain way. *It's not my fault...I didn't...I was just trying to...*Cross-Complaining. Meeting your partner's complaint or criticism with a complaint of your own. *Well, you do that all the time, too...My habit is not as bad as your habit of... I wouldn't do that if you didn't always...*Disagreeing and then Cross-Complaining. *That's not true, you're the one who...*Yes-butting. Start off agreeing, but end up disagreeing. *I understand your perspective, but I just...* Whining...*It's not fair...It never changes...*)

_____
_____
_____
_____
_____
_____
_____

3. STONEWALLING. If any, how was stonewalling displayed? How might I have stonewalled?

(Stonewalling is withdrawing from the relationship as a way to avoid conflict. Partners may think they are trying to be neutral, but stonewalling conveys disapproval, icy distance, separation, disconnections, and/or smugness. It is a potent turning away response that can be very damaging to connection and trust. Some typical expressions of defensiveness are: Stony Silence; Monosyllabic mutterings; Changing the subject; Removing yourself physically ignoring what your partner said. Repeating yourself without paying attention to what the other person is saying.)

_____
_____
_____
_____
_____
_____
_____

CONTEMPT. Was any contempt displayed? How was it directly or indirectly communicated? How might I have shown contempt?

(Contempt is attacking another person's sense of self with the intention to insult or psychologically hurt them. It might include: insults and name calling (jerk, drama-queen, wimp, stupid, lazy, slob, etc.); hostile humor, sarcasm, or mockery (ex: "That extra 40 pounds really looks good on you."); or body language and/or tone of voice. (Sneering, eye rolling, curling upper lip.)

_____
_____
_____
_____
_____
_____
_____

CONFLICT ESCALATORS TRACKING LOG

DAY	**APPLICATION** Which CONFLICT ESCALATOR did I use? (Criticism, Contempt, Defensiveness, Stonewalling) What were the words, tone, and body language that communicated this Conflict Escalator?	**IMPACT** What was the impact of the conflict escalator on me, others, the situation, and/or the relationship?
Day 1		
Day 2		
Day 3		
Day 4		

CONFLICT ESCALATORS TRACKING LOG

DAY	APPLICATION Which CONFLICT ESCALATOR did I use? (Criticism, Contempt, Defensiveness, Stonewalling) What were the words, tone, and body language that communicated this Conflict Escalator?	IMPACT What was the impact of the conflict escalator on me, others, the situation, and/or the relationship?
Day 5		
Day 6		
Day 7		

INSIGHTS—What patterns or benefits emerged?

_____

_____

_____

_____

Skill 8. POSITIVE CONFLICT

Courage means to keep working a relationship, to continue seeking solutions to difficult problems, and to stay focused during stressful periods.
-Denis Waitley

Skillful communication during conflict has one thing in common—the focus is on moving toward a desirable outcome. We posit that constructive conflict builds more positivity. It is not manipulative, malicious, or one-sidedly advantageous. Instead, it elevates both parties to a higher way of being and is fundamentally a mission to find and create seemingly unavailable possibility and opportunity. It serves the greater good. This process is difficult, sometimes painful, replete with compromise, and all too rare.

Crafting constructive conflict hinges on the ability to communicate clearly and to establish trust and respect no matter how aggressive the message. This requires a commitment to not introducing conflict escalators and attending to the process. These communications typically require a significant amount of effort, planning, and intention—more than most of us presume.

Although positive conflict can lead to innovation, destructive conflict is often extremely wasteful of time and emotional energy. Max Messmer, CEO of Robert Half International, the world's largest staffing firm, conducted a study to assess the percentage of management time spent on resolving personality conflicts. They found that on average 18% of management time is spent managing personality conflicts. Managers waste almost one-fifth of their time as referees.

THE KEY TO CRAFTING POSITIVE CONFLICT

Deliver negative messages without activating "threat sensors"
It is not about "making nice"—it is about being effective.

Constructive conflict is guided by the knowledge that we easily feel attacked. Our primitive emotional circuitry evolved in life or death evolutionary contexts. Therefore, amygdala hijacks easily overwhelm our higher brain centers, and the negativity bias distorts messages.

Amygdala Hijacked Conflict. Most of us fail to realize just how easily the Fight or Flight system gets activated. John Gottman's research suggests that a heart rate of 100 beats per minute indicates an amygdala hijack, shutting down higher brain centers and therefore, effective communication. He suggests that if heart rate exceeds 100 beats per minute during conflict, pause and regain calm before continuing.

FIRST, DO YOUR HOMEWORK

Rewrite Your Victim Story. When we believe someone has wronged us, often we fall into a victim story. Before entering a conflict, challenge and rewrite your "victim story." Challenge thoughts and consider alternative interpretations.

- Consider ways of taking some degree of personal responsibility.
- Challenge thoughts of righteous indignation.
- Make contact with an attitude of emotional generosity and the possibility of forgiveness.
- Let go of your version of things for a moment and listen to the other point of views.
- Claim responsibility for your own well-being.
- Ask yourself what you learn from this conflict.

Digital Communication—Save not Send. Research shows that the emotional distance and lack of cues inherent to email and texts allows for impulsive, reactive actions, and lack of empathy. Without nonverbal indicators, digital communication becomes hard to interpret and requires filling in data points without direct evidence. It also is distancing, becoming impersonal in the absence of nonverbal feedback about the impact on the other person. Thus, proceed cautiously when communicating digitally. Instead of quickly hitting the "reply" button, it can be best to "Save not Send." Consider flagging a heated email correspondence for later response or composing a draft and only sending after calming down or even sleeping on it. All the challenges inherent to face-to-face communication are exponentially larger when communicating in the absence of nonverbal data.

Good Timing. Consider when to begin the conversation. We are much more likely to resolve the issue if we prevent the conflict from escalating in the first place. The best time to begin a difficult conversation is when all parties are well-rested, calm, centered, and have clarity of mind.

HOW TO CRAFT POSITIVE CONFLICT

HOW TO CRAFT POSITIVE CONFLICT
Stage 1. Begin With Connection
Stage 2. Deliver The Negative Message Skillfully
Stage 3. End With Connection

Disarm, Connect, and Orient Toward a Positive Outcome. Structure conflict conversations in a way that is likely to disarm and maintain connection while keeping an eye on reaching a mutually positive outcome. The primary objective in conflict is to be clear, direct, authentic, constructive, maintain trust, communicate respect for the person, and serve a positive outcome. This model provides the structure for incorporating the conflict de-escalators. Consider using the following structure as a guide.

STAGE 1. BEGIN WITH CONNECTION

How it starts is how it will end.

The purpose of beginning with connection is to set a constructive tone. A positive beginning might include a genuine compliment, an acknowledgement, or validation, for example. This approach can still be direct and have transparency, but it skillfully introduces the conflict without putting the other on defense. Setting a positive tone can communicate an intention not to fight but to co-create a solution and respect. John Gottman's research shows that how a conversation starts is generally how it ends: if it starts in conflict, it ends in conflict.

Start Slow. Slow starts refer to easing into the charged part of the conversation. Gottman's research suggests that if it gets of to a bad start, it is best to stop, take a break, and restart the conversation. A slow start:
- Begins with a spirit of kindness and collaboration toward a solution.
- Might include a statement that expresses commonality and understanding.
- Gently introduces the issue that concerns you.

Example of a Slow Start. Marcia is angry that Mike has harshly criticized her publicly at work. She begins the confrontation effectively by starting slowly. She said, "You know I've been really enjoying my first few months here. One thing I really like is that everyone really seems to work well together. It seems like people help each other out and support each other. Even though I am the newest one here, I want to make sure that I find ways to support you and the others on our team. I hope it has seems that way so far."

Mike didn't respond, so Marcia asked directly, "Does it seem that I've been supportive to you and the others?" She goes on to introduce the more charged part of her concern, explaining that she does not feel supported by Mike. Later, she gives examples of his criticism as times when she wonders if he intends to support her.

Harsh Starts. Harsh starts put people on the defensive. Note the implied criticism in the following examples. Although perhaps well-intended, these start-ups would probably cause escalation:

"I don't want to make this a big deal, but..."
"Don't get mad when I say this, but..."
"I'm not being critical, but..."
"You are very sensitive, so I'm going to try to say this very carefully..."

Example of a Harsh Start. Marcia could have started with a statement like: *"Mike, I would like to talk to you. What was going on with you in last week's meeting? I really didn't feel supported by you."*

While some might think this is an effective start because it is direct and to the point, it is likely to immediately put Mike on defense and feel like a criticism. According to research, this would introduce one of the Four Horsemen, escalating the conflict.

Invite an Exploration. Suggest that you work together to explore an issue and find a solution together. This phrasing directly introduces the topic but without introducing criticism, the first of the Four Horseman. Marcia could say something like: *"Mike, I have sensed some tension between us. I'd like to explore with you what this is and understand it better. Would you be willing to chat with me about this?"*

Commit to a Constructive Process. Talk about how to talk about it. Quite often we know from experience that a conversation is likely to be challenging. It can be open helpful to acknowledge it and create "ground rules" or at least an intention to have a constructive, respectful conversation. This is especially helpful in longstanding issues that are common familial and romantic relationships.

"Many times when we discuss your family visiting, I notice we both get tense. It's something I would really like for us to have a constructive conversation about. I am committed to doing my best to keep it constructive. This time, I intend on really hearing your perspective."

Check-In on the Other's Current State. In an effort to gather information and seek understanding, simply ask how the other is doing in that moment. If someone changes his or her behavior for the worse—a daughter begins locking herself in her room, a romantic partner returns phone calls less frequently, or a co-worker's productivity declines dramatically—an initial reaction may be to confront the individual with an accusation or complaint. This will likely put them on defense.

Consider starting with an invitation to share about personal issues, feelings or conflicts that may be influencing their actions. There may be significant contributing factors of which you were unaware. If they are not asked directly with an attitude of support, you may not learn important contributing factors. For example, your teen may be having problems with their friends, a romantic partner may be more stressed than you realize about work, or the co-worker may be dealing with a serious health issue.

Simply, ask: *"Lately, you seem more stressed than usual. How have things been going for you?"*

Inquire about the Other's Perspective. Consider asking the other person to describe what happened. This neutral inquiry avoids the other feeling like you are on a fault-finding mission, and instead, engages them in a neutral fact-finding inquiry.

For example, ask: *"Can you describe what happened?"* or *"Will you walk me through what happened last night?"*

STAGE 2. DELIVER THE NEGATIVE MESSAGE SKILLFULLY

Separate the Person from the Problem. Stay focused on behaviors and actions you'd like to see rather than on abstract issues or personal attacks on character or personality. Communication breaks down when we feel personally insulted, attacks on character, or rejected.

This is sometimes referred to as *issue-focused* conflict rather than *person-focused* conflict. Issue focused conflict more easily fosters win-win negotiation. Person-focused conflict tends to escalate into heated emotional disputes and moral indignation. Issue-focused conflict is likely to stay with actions that are doable and changeable. This also avoids what social psychologists call the "Actor-Observer Error." This is the common tendency to overestimate the role of character traits in problematic situations while underestimating the role of the situational variables.

Make a Neutral Observation. Consider opening a conversation with an observable fact rather than with feelings. It is indisputable and can help direct issue-focused conflict resolution.

Example: "I notice that you left the meeting as soon as Nancy began delegating project roles."

Acknowledge. Acknowledgement does not mean agreeing or making concessions. Instead, it is demonstrating respect for the other and his or her needs and viewpoint. There are several ways show acknowledgement. One way to demonstrate respect is to acknowledge the other's point of view. It is possible to show that you understand another's position without sharing it.

For instance, imagine your employee asked for a raise and you refused. You might say, *"I appreciate that you have been working hard. We feel your contributions are very valuable. We will consider a raise when you hit the next benchmark."*

Or, with a teenager who asks to borrow the car, *"I know you are enjoying the freedom of being able to drive yourself around, and I know you really want to drive tonight. However, I do not feel comfortable with you driving tonight since there will be drinking at the party."*

Validate the Other's Point-of-View. Validating someone's feelings means showing you understand their perspective. If it is true, you might add that you believe their view makes sense given their history, objectives, or values. You do not need to agree or think it is reasonable to understand how they arrived at their point of view. This is simply validating the legitimacy of their viewpoint. This shows the other that you respect their point of view, even if you disagree with it.

For example, *"It makes a lot of sense to me that you are feeling angry that I said 'no'. I know you really wanted that."*

Or, to the employee who was upset about the review, *"It is natural to want your hard work to be recognized."* Or, *"Anyone putting in the number of hours you are is bound to feel overworked."*

Common phrases that express validation:
- *I understand that you are feeling…*
- *I can see your point of view.*
- *It makes sense that you _____, given that you are trying to _____.*
- *I can see that what I said made you feel _____.*
- *I hear you saying that_____.*

Be Specific. Be specific in what you want. Make your requests and/or complaints specific rather than general. For example, if your positive outcome is for someone to be more responsible, requesting "increased accountability," may not be as clear as saying:

"Increased accountability might include doing things like calling me if you are running more than 10 minutes late to a meeting."

Focus on Positive Outcomes. Explicitly describe the positive outcome you want. Describe in actionable, specific behaviors that the person can do. For example—Marcia redirects to a positive outcome that is actionable and specific.

"It is important to me that we collaborate in a timely manner. Could we agree that if a deadline becomes too difficult to meet, then we give at least 48-hour notice by email?"

STAGE 3. END WITH CONNECTION

Focus on a new beginning. Consider positive steps forward and express good will if genuinely felt.

Take Responsibility for Wrongdoings—The Four-Part Apology. Being willing to take responsibility for mistakes or wrongdoings engenders trust. Most people underestimate the power of a well-expressed apology. Referred to as the "Four Part Apology," the following guidelines can help transform an interaction and repair a rupture. The 4 R's are: Responsibility, Remorse, Repair, Recommit. The power of the Four-Part Apology is that it demonstrates responsibility for actions.

THE FOUR PART APOLOGY
1. RESPONSIBILITY
2. REMORSE
3. REPAIR
4. RECOMMIT

(1) RESPONSIBILITY. Take responsibility for what you've done. Use "I statements" to show that you're the one behind the action.

Example:

"I know that I've canceled our plans at the last minute more than once. I can imagine this is frustrating."

(2) REMORSE. Explain your remorse: *"I apologize for hurting you by wasting your time and making you feel disrespected."*

(3) REPAIR. Repair the damage. Right the wrong by going above and beyond what was done.

Ask, *"How can I make it right?"*

Some examples of a repair:

- You show up late for a team meeting, so the next time bring a batch of cookies for everyone.
- Your child was upset that you missed one of his/her events, so you plan a special outing.
- You cancelled for a friend's party last minute, so take that friend out to a nice dinner.
- You lost a borrowed book, and you give a gift card to replace it and buy an additional one.

(4) RECOMMIT: Show commitment to prevent further harm. Perhaps formulate a realistic plan to avoid harm in the future.

Shift To Appreciation. Before ending the conversation, shift to appreciation. Focus on ways to reconnect with the positive in the person and the relationship.

ADDITIONAL RESOURCES

Stone, D., Patton, B., & Heen, S. (1999). *Difficult Conversations: How to discuss what matters most*. New York, NY: Viking.

Gallagher, Richard (2009). *How to Tell Anyone Anything*.

Ury, William (2007). *The Power of a Positive No*.

POSITIVE CONFLICT WORKSHEET

Constructive conversations are a result of the words that are said, they way that they are said, and the conversation strategy that is used by both parties. Your strategy should include techniques that will make the conversation constructive, safe, and outcome oriented. You will also want to use conflict de-escalators to head off conflict before it starts, or to mitigate conflict when it happens. Using conflict de-escalators provides alternatives to the conflict escalators during conflict, and they can foster a sense of connection even when a negative message needs to be delivered. Skillful communication during conflict is having the ability to be firm, direct, have boundaries, and to say "Yes" or "No" without using the *Four Horsemen*. Conflict de-escalators can help to turn a potential problem situation into one in which the problem can be resolve din a reasonable way.

The purpose of this application is to give you an opportunity to practice using some of the techniques for crafting a constructive conversation. First, begin by thinking of a conflict situation that you have experienced recently, and analyze what may have led to the conflict, and what may have increased the intensity of the conflict. Situations might include an interaction with:

- A customer/client.
- A colleague.
- A family member.
- A close friend.

CONFLICT SITUATION

Identify a recent situation in which a discussion or disagreement escalated beyond the productive stage. (Briefly describe who, what, where, when, how, and why)

WHO. Who is/was involved in the conflict?

_____

_____

WHERE & WHEN DID IT HAPPEN? Did the time, location, or context contribute to the conflict?

_____

_____

WHO DID OR SAID WHAT? What happened?

_____

_____

_____

_____

CONSTRUCTIVE CONVERSATION TECHNIQUES

How might constructive conversation techniques might have been used in this conflict situation?

1. CONFLICT DE-ESCALATORS. What conflict de-escalator might have been helpful?

1. Separate Person From Problem.
2. Rewrite Your Victim Story.
3. Validate Other's Viewpoint
4. Start Slow.
5. Be Specific.
6. Positive Outcome Focus.
7. Repair.
8. Shift To Appreciation.

_____

_____

2. CONNECT—DELIVER—CONNECT.

STAGE 1. CONNECT. (Slow Start, Make a Neutral Observation, Acknowledge, or Validate).

_____
_____
_____
_____
_____
_____
_____
_____

STAGE 2. DELIVER MESSAGE SKILLFULLY. (Positive Outcome Focus, Separate the Person from the Problem, Be Specific, Positive Outcome Focus)

_____
_____
_____
_____
_____
_____
_____

STAGE 3. CONNECT. (Take Responsibility for Wrongdoings, Shift to Appreciation.)

_____
_____
_____
_____
_____
_____
_____

3. INSIGHTS. What insights or solutions emerged from doing this process of crafting constructive conflict?

_____
_____
_____
_____
_____

POSITIVE CONFLICT TRACKING LOG

DAY	APPLICATION How and with whom did I craft constructive conflict? Which conflict de-escalators did I use? What worked about what I did?	IMPACT What was the impact on me, others, the situation, and/or our relationship?
Day 1		
Day 2		
Day 3		
Day 4		

POSITIVE CONFLICT TRACKING LOG

DAY	APPLICATION How and with whom did I craft constructive conflict? Which conflict de-escalators did I use? What worked about what I did?	IMPACT What was the impact on me, others, the situation, and/or our relationship?
Day 5		
Day 6		
Day 7		

INSIGHTS—What patterns or benefits emerged?

_____
_____
_____
_____
_____

Mindful Leaders: A Self-Coaching Guide and Toolkit

BEING KINDNESS MEDITATION

This meditation explores the universal desire for an end to distress and for contentment. It will guide you through bringing to mind these universal desires in different kinds of relationships in your life, including yourself. This meditation when practiced regularly has been shown to increase feelings of connection, happiness and lower feelings of loneliness and depression. It does not require that you neglect your own well-being; instead, it allows you to adjust your reaction to unavoidable suffering by assigning a new value to it.

During all the meditations, try to let go of expectations about how this practice is supposed to feel or what is supposed to happen. Your job is to experience what happens in a nonjudgmental, explorative manner, and each time your mind wanders into thought, turn your attention back. After the exercise please jot down observations about your experience.

INSTRUCTIONS
(8-12 minutes)

1. FOCUS INWARD: Breathe and Center

- **Center**—Close your eyes and turn your attention inward.

- **Anchor in your Breath**—Feel Your Breath fill and release your body. Breathe deeply with a slower exhale and natural inhale. Place your hand on your abdomen to feel your diaphragm rise and fall. Feel your feet as the rest on the floor. Notice the sensations on the bottom of your feet making contact with the earth. Feel your hands as they rest on your thighs. Open them and notice the sensations and invite them to relax.

- **Set your Intention**—To direct your attention in this time, place, and to the objective of this meditation.

2. DIRECT ATTENTION: *Send Loving and Kindness toward others and yourself.*

Step 1: Focus on a **positive person** and send vitality. Bring to your mind a positive person in your life. On an exhale, visualize sending them all your happiness vitality, good fortune, health, and goodness. If they are suffering, ill, or having difficulty, imagine they are well or full of joy.

Step 2: Focus on a **neutral person** and send vitality. Bring to your mind a neutral person in your life or someone you do not know well. On an exhale, visualize sending them all your happiness vitality, good fortune, health, and goodness. If they are suffering, ill, or having difficulty, imagine they are well or full of joy.

Step 3: Focus on a **suffering person** and send vitality. Bring to your mind a person in your life who is suffering. On an exhale, visualize sending them all your happiness vitality, good fortune, health, or goodness. If they are suffering, ill, or having difficulty, imagine they are well or full of joy.

Step 4: Focus on **your desire** to be well and receive vitality. Bring to your mind your desire to be well and happy in your life. On an exhale, visualize your distress, suffering and illness leaving your body. On an inhale, visualize filling your body with wellness, happiness vitality, good fortune, health, and goodness.

Step 6: Focus on the **suffering in the universe** and send vitality. Bring to your mind the fact that there is suffering in the universe. On an exhale, visualize sending happiness vitality, health, and goodness to all the suffering and disease. Imagine the universe being filled with goodness. When you inhale, visualize your heart as a bright, luminous sphere. There is no sense that you are burdened.

3. REFLECT ON INSIGHTS: Breathe and Reflect
- Come back to your breath.
- Reflect on the insights or benefits you gained during this meditation.

4. MAINTAIN INNER AWARENESS: Soft Gaze and Stay with Awareness.
- Slowly open your eyes and keep your gaze soft, directed downward, and settling on a neutral object.
- Stay with the awareness you gained during the meditation.

BEING KINDNESS MEDITATION WORKSHEET

After you have completed the meditation, jot down observations about what came up during your meditation. Make note of thoughts you had, feelings you experienced, bodily sensations you felt, and/or detours that you took.

1. FOCUS INWARD: Breathe and Center. How well were you able to concentrate inward and turn your attention to your intention in this meditation?

_____

_____

2. DIRECT ATTENTION: *Send Loving and Kindness toward others and yourself.*

Step 1: Focus on a <u>positive person</u> and send vitality. Who did you bring to your mind? What did you experience when you visualized sending them all your happiness vitality, good fortune, health, and goodness?

_____

_____

Step 2: Focus on a <u>neutral person</u> and send vitality. Who did you bring to your mind? What did you experience when you visualized sending them all your happiness vitality, good fortune, health, and goodness?

_____

_____

Step 3: Focus on a <u>suffering person</u> and send vitality. Who did you bring to your mind? What did you experience when you visualized sending them all your happiness vitality, good fortune, health, and goodness?

_____

_____

Step 4: Focus on <u>your desire</u> to be well and receive vitality. What happened when you brought to your mind your desire to be well and happy in your life? What did you experience when you visualized your distress, suffering and illness leaving your body? What did you experience when you visualized filling your body with wellness, happiness vitality, good fortune, health, and goodness?

_____

_____

Step 6: Focus on the <u>suffering in the universe</u> and send vitality. What did you bring to your mind when you thought about the fact that there is suffering in the universe? What happened when you visualized sending happiness vitality, health, and goodness to all the suffering and disease? What happened when you imagined the universe being filled with goodness? What happened when you visualized your heart as a bright, luminous sphere?

_____

_____

3. Personal Application. How can I use this Mindfulness Practice in developing my Social Awareness?

_____

_____

_____

BEING KINDNESS MEDITATION TRACKING LOG

DAY	APPLICATION When and what did I meditate on?	IMPACT What is the impact of doing a loving-kindness meditation on me, others, and/or the situation?
Day 1		
Day 2		
Day 3		
Day 4		

BEING KINDNESS MEDITATION TRACKING LOG

DAY	APPLICATION When and what did I meditate on?	IMPACT What is the impact of doing a loving-kindness meditation on me, others, and/or the situation?
Day 5		
Day 6		
Day 7		

INSIGHTS - What patterns or benefits emerged?

_____
_____
_____
_____

COACHING GUIDELINES

Use the self-coaching process and coaching tools to create long-term change. For maximum effectiveness, focus on one skill at a time. For each skill, take an *assessment* if one is available, complete a *coaching worksheet*, practice high road and low road techniques, and track your application of the skill over a seven day period using a *Tracking Log*.

Select one skill. Consider which skill would make the greatest difference in your current life circumstances if you used it more frequently and effectively. It is easier to build new habits if you focus on one change at a time. Select the *one skill* in this chapter that is your highest priority:

- Cultivate Empathy
- Deep Dive Conversations
- Identify Conflict Escalators
- Positive Conflict

STEP 1. ASSESS. Assess the need and benefits of practicing this particular skill. Assess your current mastery level of the skill. Use one of the on-line assessment tools if one is available for the skill. The Coaching Worksheet will also help you assess your need and benefits of using the skill.

Assessments—Questionnaires that assess your current skill level and provide data on your progress.

STEP 2. PLAN. To create an action plan, understand how a technique can help you build greater mastery of a skill. Next, consider how you can apply it to your own situations.

Coaching Worksheets—Tools for learning and creating an action plan for practicing the techniques.
- Empathy Worksheet
- Deep Dive Conversations Worksheet
- Conflict Escalators Worksheet
- Positive Conflict Worksheet

STEP 3. PRACTICE. During the following seven days, apply the skill daily. Use both the High Road techniques and the Low Road techniques to practice the skill.

Tracking Logs—Habit forming tools to guide your efforts as you practice the techniques for seven days.

- Empathy Tracking Log
- Deep Dive Conversations Tracking Log
- Conflict Escalators Tracking Log
- Positive Conflict Tracking Log

- Just Like Me Meditation Tracking Log
- Gift of Relationship Meditation Tracking Log

Meditation Guides—Low Road techniques to build the skill at the emotional or non-verbal level.

- Just Like Me Meditation
- Gift of Relationship Meditation

STEP 4. TRACK RESULTS. In addition to systematically helping you to practice the techniques, *Tracking Logs* provide a place to note the impact of the skill on your experience. Tracking Logs help you become more aware of behaviors and patterns in yourself. They are a source of feedback so you can modify a technique to make it more effective.

AUTHENTICITY & INTEGRITY

Living with integrity means:

Not settling for less than what you know you deserve in your relationships.

Asking for what you want and need from others.

Speaking your truth, even though it might create conflict or tension.

Behaving in ways that are in harmony with your personal values.

Making choices based on what you believe, and not what others believe.

~ Barbara De Angelis

AUTHENTICITY & INTEGRITY

The privilege of a lifetime is to become who you truly are. ~ C.G. Jung

Mindful Leaders are often respected for their authenticity and integrity. Their authenticity is reflected in the truthfulness of their intentions, behaviors, and commitments. Their integrity is reflected in their honesty, their strong moral principles, and their ability to live by those principles. Mindful Leaders are clear on their values and their priorities and make decisions and take actions based upon these values. They are aware of their strengths and look for ways to leverage their strengths in the pursuit of their goals and in the service of others.

Mindful leaders inspire others to act in the service of a common goal by reaching into their hearts, by tuning into their purpose, meaning, and reasons why their vision is of highest importance. They communicate this passion to others and touch them so deeply that the leader's reason for action then becomes the reason for others. The leaders' purpose, meaning, reasons and vision becomes their followers'.

AUTHENTICITY & INTEGRITY SKILLS PREVIEW

Introduction: Authenticity & Integrity
  Case Study: Observing Mindful Leadership—John Mackey
    Exercise: Mindful Leadership Case Study Questions
  Finding Flow
    Exercise: A Flow Experience

Skill 9: LEVERAGE STRENGTHS
  A Strengths Perspective
  How to Leverage Your Strengths
    Personal Mentor Journaling Worksheet
    Personal Best Leadership Experience Journaling Worksheet
    Identify Core Strengths & Tracking Log
  Use Strengths in New Ways
    Use Strengths in New Ways Worksheet & Tracking Log
  Leverage Others' Strengths
    Leverage Others' Strengths & Tracking Log
  Moment of Strength Visualization
    Moment of Strength Visualization & Tracking Log

Skill 10: ALIGN ACTIONS WITH VALUES
  Do What Matters to You
  Research—Values in Action
    Values Assessment Worksheet
    Values Alignment Worksheet & Tracking Log
  Life Reflection Visualization
    Life Reflection Visualization & Tracking Log
  Values Journaling
    Values Journaling Worksheet

Skill 11: ALIGN ACTIONS WITH PRIORITIES
  How to Align Activities and Priorities: Life Buckets
    Life Buckets Worksheet
    Priorities Reality Check Tracking Log

Coaching Guidelines

CASE STUDY: OBSERVING MINDFUL LEADERSHIP

JOHN MACKEY
Founder & Co-CEO of Whole Foods

Capitalism is the greatest system for human cooperation and achievement ever conceived, yet so few of us truly appreciate its power and majesty. ~ John Mackey

What do Google, Nordstrom, Patagonia, Starbucks, The Container Store, Southwest Airlines, Tata Sons, and Whole Foods Market have in common? According to John Mackey, they all practice what he calls *conscious capitalism*, "an extraordinary powerful system of value creation, mutually benefitting *all* stakeholders involved, and with the power to elevate humanity upward through continuous improvement."

Wow! That's quite a statement for a hippy-baby-boomer, born in Texas in the 1950's, who majored in philosophy and religion at the University of Texas at Austin and Trinity University in the 1970's, who worked in a vegetarian co-op, was a self-professed democratic socialist, dropped out of college, and whose first health food store was named, "SaferWay," a shot at the corporate behemoth, Safeway. What changed along the way?

Mackey was born on August 15, 1953 in Houston, Texas. He co-founded his first health food store, SaferWay, with his girlfriend Renee Lawson in Austin in 1978. They met while living in a vegetarian housing co-op. They dropped out of college, borrowed $10,000 and raised $35,000 more to start SaferWay. They ran the market on the first floor, a health food restaurant on the second floor, and lived on the third floor. Two years later they merged SaferWay with Clarksville Natural Grocery run by Mark Skiles and Craig Weller and renamed the business *Whole Foods Market*. Since 1980, Mackey has led this natural and organic grocer to a level of success that even his old rival Safeway might be envious of.

Whole Foods Market recent success statistics include:
- A $14 billion, Fortune 500 company.
- More than 410 stores.
- More than 88,000 team members (employees).
- Operates in three countries—USA, Canada, UK.
- For 18 consecutive years included in *Fortune* magazines' *100 Best Companies to Work For*.
- *Fortunes* Most Admired Companies List 2014--Ranked first in the food and drug store industry.

John Mackey has his own impressive list of personal honors:
- Recognized as one of *Fortune's* "World's 50 Greatest Leaders."
- Ernst & Young's "Entrepreneur of the Year Overall Winner for the United States."
- Institutional Investor's "Best CEO in America."
- *Barron's* "World's Best CEO."
- MarketWatch's "CEO of the Year."
- Fortune's "Businessperson of the Year."
- *Esquire's* "Most Inspiring CEO."

The financial press respects Mackey and his results speak for themselves. But, upon closer examination, we see that this is no ordinary CEO, and no ordinary capitalist. In an era where CEO's compensation packages grow with each passing year and CEOs often spend time worrying about their ranking on the "*Forbes Wealthiest*" list, in 2006 Mackey announced that he was reducing his salary to $1 a year, and that he would donate his stock portfolio to charity. He instituted caps on executive pay at the company, caps that limit top executive pay to no more than 19 times the average Team Member pay. While other companies were dropping health care benefits, Mackey expanded Whole Foods health care program, and set up a $100,000 emergency fund for staff facing personal problems.

You can still hear a bit of the idealistic-hippy-baby-boomer in his statement explaining his actions: "I am now 53 years old, and I have reached a place in my life where I no longer want to work for money, but simply for the joy of the work itself and to better answer the call to service that I feel so clearly in my own heart." Where is the selfishness, greed and profit maximization of the stereotypical capitalist? What is this "call to service" that Mackey talks about? It is, in fact, a very clear philosophy and business strategy, that Mackey has used to build Whole Foods Market into an enormously valuable company, and which he has recently articulated in a *New York Times* and *Wall Street Journal* best-selling book entitled *Conscious Capitalism: Liberating the Heroic Spirit of Business*. (Harvard Business Review Press. 2013). He co-authored the book with Rajendra Sisodia, Professor of Marketing at Bentley University.

John Mackey is on a mission to change the negative public stereotype of the successful capitalist and to "change the narrative" about capitalism—one that alleges that all business is based upon greed, selfishness, and exploitation, and its only purpose is money and profits. Mackey says, "This narrative makes people cynical and distrustful about business." He says that "the idea of conscious capitalism currently contradicts most peoples mental model of business, so they reject it."

Instead of the zero-sum game of winners and losers, Mackey points to the win-win solutions that business can provide when human innovation and collaboration creates expanded opportunities. He explains that "business is inherently *good* because it creates value, it is *ethical* because it is based on voluntary exchange, it is *noble* because it can elevate our existence, and it is *heroic* because it lifts people out of poverty and creates prosperity." Mackey points to a few examples of companies that practice conscious capitalism.

- *Whole Foods* focuses on the health and well-being of people, the food system, and the planet.
- *Southwest Airlines* has brought the freedom to fly to ordinary people.
- *The Container Store* endeavors to make people feel more in control and happier by becoming better organized.
- *Google* organizes the world's information and makes it easily accessible and useful.

In his book, John outlines the components of Conscious Capitalism and how he used the principles to build a successful and profitable business while doing a great deal of good for all of the "stakeholders." Mackey deals with four major elements of Conscious Capitalism—Purpose, Stakeholders, Mindful (Conscious) Leaders, and Culture.

Purpose. Mackey advises mindful leaders to begin by asking existential questions like: "Why does our company exist? Why does it need to exist? Why would we be missed if we disappeared?" He says that business has a higher purpose beyond profits and "the real purpose of business is to create value for all stakeholders and thereby improve the lot of humanity."

Mackey gives an example of Whole Foods higher purpose running counter to profits. "When Whole Foods decided it wanted to stop selling overfished species of cod and octopus at its seafood counters, it didn't just abruptly cut off its suppliers. It gave its suppliers three years to come up with a better way of fishing." During that time, the seafood stayed for sale, but with a label of "unsustainable." Mackey explains, "You take a risk when you do that because some of your customers…who don't care about sustainability, they're going to go shop at your competitor's store who has the fish, so you lose some business that way. But it was the right thing to do." In the end, Whole Foods worked with the *Marine Stewardship Council* to find one supplier of sustainable cod.

Stakeholders. Whole Foods is responsible to a long list of stakeholders—customers, team members, suppliers, farmers, the company, investors, communities, governments, and the environment all benefit from their exchanges with Whole Foods. Mackey says "virtually everything that Whole Foods does creates value for all of our stakeholders. Let us take a simple example—selling organic produce. This creates value for our *customers* by providing them high quality foods that help nourish them, enhance their health and well being, and which taste great. This also creates value for our *team members* by helping provide them with jobs, benefits, good working conditions, and purposeful work. Our *suppliers* and *farmers* who sell us the organic produce benefit from their trade with Whole Foods which helps them to flourish."

Mackey continues, "Selling organic produce helps our *company* to succeed financially and this creates value for our *investors*. As our company is financially prosperous we are enabled to be good citizens in our *communities* through philanthropy and voluntary involvement. Part of our profits is also taxed away by various *governments*, some of this money being used in constructive ways to help our larger communities. Finally, selling organic produce uses far less fossil fuels and chemical fertilizers and pesticides, which lessens negative impacts on the *environment*.

Mindful Leadership. Mackey's definition of a conscious leader provides us with his role-model for mindful leadership: "Conscious leaders are usually strong individuals who possess exceptional moral courage and are able to withstand constant scrutiny and criticism from those who view business in a more traditional and narrow manner. Conscious leaders combine analytical intelligence with high levels of emotional, spiritual and systems intelligence. They care deeply about the purpose of the company and lead by example." Mackey's mindful leader avoids traditional carrot and stick motivation and a command and control management style. "They inspire, motivate, mentor, and develop others." His examples of mindful leaders include *Howard Schultz* of Starbucks, *Herb Kelleher* of Southwest Airlines, *Ratan Tata* of Tata Sons, and *Kip Tindell* of The Container Store.

Mackey believes that mindful leaders should be involved in making the world a better place, and he demonstrates this belief by his many undertakings on behalf of this purpose. He was the visionary for:

- *Whole Planet Foundation* to help end poverty in developing nations.
- *Local Producer Loan Program* to help local food producers expand their businesses.
- *Global Animal Partnership's* rating scale for humane farm animal treatment.
- *Health Starts Here initiative* to promote health and wellness.
- *Conscious Capitalism Movement* to encourage doing business grounded in ethical consciousness.

Culture. According to Mackey, a conscious culture is characterized by trust, authenticity and transparency, as well as by accountability and learning. He proposes that people in such cultures are largely self-organizing, self-motivating, and self-managing. This belief is in part demonstrated in the Whole Foods statement of employee benefits found on their Website. The stated goal is "to create a fair and equal work environment that encourages empowerment, creativity, and collaboration. Our Team Members actually have a say in the benefits we offer—we hold a company wide vote every three years. In our last vote, 80 percent of Team Members voted on what benefits they wanted the company to provide.

Healthcare. More than 90 percent of eligible full-time Team Members chose to enroll in the healthcare plan, which was elected through a companywide vote.

Compensation. Whole Foods offers competitive wages based upon position, and salary information, including company's leadership, is available to all inquiring Team Members. Wage transparency helps promote inclusiveness and ensure our compensation system is fair. The salaries of Whole Foods Market executives are limited to 19 times the average full-time Team Member salary. All store Team Members are eligible for *Gainsharing*, a program that rewards team members based on labor productivity. All full-time and part-time Team Members, after 3 years of employment, are eligible to receive stock options through annual leadership grants or service-hour grants.

Career Growth and Retention. In 2014, 8,800 new jobs were created and 90 percent of store leadership positions were filled with internal candidates. Our voluntary turnover rate for full-time Team Members is 11%, low for the retail industry.

Health & Wellness. All Team Members receive a 20 percent discount on Whole Foods products, and are eligible to receive an additional 10 percent (up to 30 percent) through the company's voluntary *Healthy Discount Incentive Program*. In 2014, more than 14,000 members participated in this program, which is based upon meeting certain biometric criteria. The *Total Health Immersion Program* is designed for Team Members who are looking to improve their health and need help in getting started. These comprehensive seven-day programs are presented by experts in the fields of nutrition and preventive medicine and include daily lectures on nutrition and health, exercise, cooking demos, practical skill-building and delicious healthy meals. The company covers all costs. Team Members may use their PTO hours to receive their regular, hourly wage while out of the office. Paid time off which are accrued through service hours can be rolled over from year to year.

John Mackey is a mindful leader with strong values, and he demonstrates his values in his actions. He believes that both for him and his team members, "People are most fulfilled and happiest when their work is aligned with their own inner passions. Personal passion, corporate purpose, and business performance all go together."

Footnote: The information on John Mackey and quotes used in this case study can be found in the following sources:
- *Conscious Capitalism: Liberating the Heroic Spirit of Business*. John Mackey with Bill Georg and Rajendra Sisodia. Harvard Business Review Press, 2013.
- *Be the Solution: How Entrepreneurs and Conscious Capitalists Can Solve all the Worlds Problems*. John Mackey with Michael Strong. John Wiley & Sons, 2009.
- *John Mackey (businessman)* From Wikipedia, the free encyclopedia. (4.12.15).
- *Conversation with John Mackey and Rajendra Sisodia Co-authors of Conscious Capitalism*. http://media.wholefoodsmarket.com
- Co-Chief Executive Officer and Co-Founder, http://media.wholefoodsmarket.com/experts/executives/john-mackey
- *Conscious Capitalism: Liberating the Heroic Spirit of Business*. http://media.wholefoodsmarket.com/news/whole-foods-market-announces-debut-of-conscious-capitalism-liberating-the-h#sthash.A0TwC0aQ.dpuf
- YouTube. *Whole Foods: How Radical CEO Created Grocery Empire* (ABC News)

EXERCISE: MINDFUL LEADERSHIP CASE STUDY QUESTIONS

One of the ways to build a better understanding of the skills of mindful leadership is through role models who demonstrate the skills of mindful leadership in their actions. In the *Observing Mindful Leadership Case Studies*, we examine the accomplishments, the actions, the statements, and sometimes the thoughts and emotions of well-known leaders. The cases can help us to see a diversity of mindful leaders operating in many different types of environments, and help us to see how different leaders and different personalities practice the skills of mindful leadership. Use the following questions to help you to better understand this mindful leader.

---

1. AWARENESS IN THE MOMENT. Mindful Leaders are self-aware of what they are thinking, feeling, and doing, and are aware of what is going on around them. They tune in to the present, to themselves, to their surroundings, and to others. They listen mindfully for information and for emotions and practice global listening. They focus first on determining what is real, before attempting to alter reality.

What can you observe from the writings, statements, and actions of the leader in this case study that demonstrate the skills of awareness in the moment?

_____
_____
_____
_____
_____
_____
_____
_____
_____

2. POSITIVITY & POSSIBILITY. Mindful Leaders are more focused on the positive and the possible than on the negative and impossible. They remain aware of the failures, the risks, the dangers, the realities, and the downsides, but they practice the discipline of thinking in terms of the positives, the opportunities, the probabilities, the options, and the alternatives. Mindful Leaders are aware of the power of positivity to broaden and build positive potential, to encourage novel thoughts and actions, and to inspire productivity and creativity in themselves and others.

What can you observe from the writings, statements, and actions of the leader in this case study that demonstrate the skills of positivity and possibility?

_____
_____
_____
_____
_____
_____
_____
_____
_____

3. POSITIVE RELATIONSHIPS. Mindful Leaders are aware of the power and importance of positive relationships, put conscious time and effort into the development of positive networks, and cultivate empathy, deep dive conversations, and win-win solutions with others. They recognize that some positive conflict can be productive, but go out of their way to avoid negative conflict escalators that thwart communication and cooperation. They take charge of their emotions and responses and work hard to build community and engagement.

What can you observe from the writings, statements, and actions of the leader in this case study that demonstrate the skills of positive relationships?

_____
_____
_____
_____
_____

4. AUTHENTICITY & INTEGRITY. Mindful Leaders are often respected for their authenticity and integrity. Their authenticity is reflected in the truthfulness of their intentions, behaviors, and commitments. Their integrity is reflected in their honesty, their strong moral principles, and their ability to live by those principles. Mindful Leaders are clear on their values and their priorities and make decisions and take actions based upon these values. They are aware of their strengths and look for ways to leverage their strengths in the pursuit of their goals and in the service of others.

What can you observe from the writings, statements, and actions of the leader in this case study that demonstrate the skills of authenticity and integrity?

_____
_____
_____
_____
_____

5. MANAGE STRESS & ENERGY. Mindful Leaders manage their energy and stress in order to maintain high levels of physical, mental, and emotional well-being. They challenge their thoughts to stay in touch with reality, they identify their emotions and emotional triggers and manage their responses, and they consciously monitor and manage their energy.

What can you observe from the writings, statements, and actions of the leader in this case study that demonstrate the skills of manage stress and energy?

_____
_____
_____
_____
_____

6. RESILIENCE. Mindful leaders work to develop resilience—the capacity to recover from difficulties and adversity. They focus on the heroic rather than the debilitating aspects adversity; they let go of perfectionism and shortcomings and focus on the possible and potential; and they practice compassion and self-compassion.

What can you observe from the writings, statements, and actions of the leader in this case study that demonstrate the skills of resilience?

_____
_____
_____
_____

INTRODUCTION: AUTHENTICITY & INTEGRITY

People generally admonish "fakes" but venerate those who show authenticity and integrity. Think of the leaders you admire most. They often have this quality of authenticity. Heroes, entrepreneurs, activists, renaissance thinkers often share defining characteristics—they act from their hearts, have strong principles, and demonstrate an unwavering willingness to live by these principles.

Mindful leaders look for ways to unleash the passion that drives themselves and others. Peak performance emerges when the best self shines through, when passions propel one forward, forging paths where none existed. Vision, passion and purpose fuel innovation, creativity and make people unstoppable. Mindful leaders inspire others to act in the service of a common goal by reaching into their hearts, by tuning into their purpose, meaning, and reasons why their vision is of highest importance. They communicate this passion to others and touch them so deeply that the leader's reason for action then becomes the reason for others. The leaders' purpose, meaning, reasons and vision becomes their followers'.

In this chapter, we ask, "What makes you come alive? What makes you feel like you? Are your actions in line with your purpose, values, and priorities?" We provide techniques for living and working with authenticity, integrity, and inspiration.

Follow your bliss and the universe will open doors for you where there were only walls.
- Joseph Campbell

Living an inspired and inspiring life is much of what most of us imagine when we think of what it means to be thriving. The root of the English word "inspiration" is the Latin word *spiritus*, meaning "breath". What gives you breath? What gives you life? When we are inspired, work is not work—it is something we are drawn to, it's what we can't not do, it flows from meaning and is fueled by passion. In this infectious state, others can't help but be moved by the authentic enthusiasm.

Mindful leaders look for ways to unleash the passion that drives themselves and others. Peak performance emerges when the best self shines through, when passions propel one forward, forging paths where none existed. Vision, passion and purpose fuel innovation, creativity and make people unstoppable. In this chapter, we ask, "What makes you come alive? What makes you feel like you? Are your actions in line with your purpose, values, and priorities?" We provide techniques for living and working from inspiration.

Mindful leaders inspire others to act in the service of a common goal by reaching into their hearts, by tuning into their purpose, meaning, and reasons why their vision is of highest importance. They communicate this passion to others and touch them so deeply that the leader's reason for action then becomes the reason for others. The leaders' purpose, meaning, reasons and vision becomes their followers'.

Mindful Leaders often provide inspiration for others. For example, when Winston Churchill gave his famous "Never Give In" speech to a nation almost overwhelmed by the forces of aggression, he inspired millions of people to take on a seemingly overwhelming challenge:

"Let us therefore brace ourselves to our duties, and so bear ourselves that if the British Empire and its Commonwealth last for a thousand years, men will still say, 'This was their finest hour." (Winston S. Churchill, Never Give In!)

The well-known management consultant Marshall Goldsmith makes the connection between happiness and meaning with his term "Mojo." According to Goldsmith, people with high mojo consistently derive satisfaction and meaning. Goldsmith defines mojo as *that positive spirit towards what we are doing now, that starts from the inside, and radiates to the outside.* It is the moment when we do something that is purposeful, powerful, and positive, and the rest of the world recognizes it. Mojo is at its peak when we experience both happiness and meaning in what we do, and when we verbally or non-verbally communicate this experience to the world around us. A way to find your way to your mojo is to look for your flow activities.

FINDING FLOW—PERSONAL, FOCUS, CHALLENGE, & SKILLS

Flow can be thought of as the state that emerges when completely mindful and present. When you are fully engaged in an activity, you are in a state psychologists refer to as flow. People often refer to flow as being "in the zone." When you are in flow, you are absorbed in a task that challenges you without overwhelming you. Flow is inherently enjoyable. You lose yourself in the moment, and time stops. When you are in the flow, you are doing something that you enjoy. It can produce a natural high stemming from the positive and productive experience. Have you ever been enjoying yourself so much when you suddenly noticed hours had passed though it only felt like minutes? That's flow. Time flies when you are having fun…or when you are in the flow.

Skill Level & Task Difficulty. According to Csikszentmihalyi, the flow experience is related to the challenge involved in the task, and the skill level of the person involved in the task. If the challenge is too high, or the skills of the participant are too low relative to the task, the result may be anxiety. If the challenge is too low, or the skills of the participant are too high relative to the task, the result may be boredom. If the challenge is high enough to engage the skills of the participant at an appropriate level, the result may be FLOW.

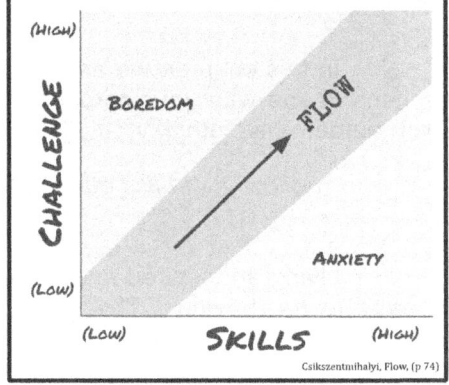

Flow Is Personal. Flow looks different for different people. It is being fully engaged in any activity that challenges you and where you have the skills to succeed. It might be rock climbing, sky diving, ice-skating, chess, bridge, dancing, a great conversation, your favorite hobby, or an exciting work project. Flow is achieved when there is sufficient challenge to be stimulating, along with the adequate skill that is required. Hobbies, sports, work projects, and any other skill-based activities commonly put people in flow, but flow can be experienced during any activity.

Flow Requires Challenge. Do we go with the flow? Can we control the flow? Control is possible in principle. Yet, most likely, in a flow state one is not in complete control. If we were, the balance between challenges and skills would be in favor of the skills – the intensity of the experience would decrease and it wouldn't be flow. Take rock climbing for example: If the challenge isn't there, it's not the flow of rock climbing – it's just walking over rocks. When the challenge is there, the flow is too – concentration is high and so is the probability of success by flow's definition.

Flow Requires Focus. Another way to talk about flow is to recognize that it is the merging of action and awareness. When in the flow, the usual dualism between actor and action disappears. Action becomes spontaneous and without conscious effort. There is also such focus on the present moment that problems and worries of everyday life (the kind that drain us) tend to disappear during flow moments.

Obstacles To Flow. Obstacles to flow include multitasking and self-judgments. Multi-tasking on anything but extremely rote activities is a myth. Our brains can only toggle between tasks. Flow can only happen when fully engaged in a task. Being judgmental and critical takes one out of the task and into observer mode, so these prevent full engagement and therefore flow.

It is virtually impossible to always be in flow, but we do not need to be concerned about having too much flow in life. Flow is simply being engaged in thought or action. Sleep and deep relaxation arguably could be times when one would desire to not be in flow. It is more in line with the concept to consider those times as when flow is irrelevant, rather than an undesirable state. It is the full involvement of flow, rather than happiness, that makes for excellence in life. Rising to a challenge, succeeding, and feeling competent and skilled are at the heart of why flow is part of happiness. Csikszentmihalyi describes what occurs when a person has frequent flow experiences. "When a person's entire being is stretched in the full functioning of body and mind, whatever one does becomes worth doing for its own sake; living becomes its own justification. In the harmonious focusing of physical and psychic energy, life finally comes into its own."

EXERCISE: A FLOW EXPERIENCE

Flow can be thought of as the state that emerges when completely mindful and present. Flow is a state in which you are fully engaged in an activity; when you are "in the zone." When you are in flow, you are absorbed in a task that challenges you without overwhelming you. Flow is inherently enjoyable. Research indicates that people who have more flow experiences in their life experience more joy and a greater sense of satisfaction. Flow is a very personal thing. What creates a sense of flow for one person may create boredom or extreme anxiety in another. The state of flow is initiated by engaging your skills to meet an appropriate challenge. The purpose of this exercise is to make you more aware of the kind of activities that have created a sense of flow for you. You can build on this personal insight as you consider ways to create more personal flow experiences in the future.

WHERE DO I EXPERIENCE FLOW?

1. My Flow Experience. Describe a moment when you experienced a sense of flow, or being in the zone. (Consider work or play, sports, hobbies, dancing, etc. You could have been by yourself or with others.)

_____
_____
_____
_____
_____
_____

2. The Challenge. Describe the nature of the challenge.

_____
_____
_____
_____
_____

3. Personal Skills That I Used. Describe the personal skills that you used during the experience.

_____
_____
_____
_____
_____

4. My Feelings. Describe the feelings that you had during or after the experience.

_____
_____
_____
_____

HOW TO INCREASE FLOW

1. Lack of Flow. What aspects of my life are affected most adversely by lack of flow?

2. Work. What can I do to make my job/daily activities more flow-like?

3. Relationships. What can I do to bring more flow into my relationships?

4. Other Areas. What can I do to have more flow in other areas of my life?

Skill 9. LEVERAGE STRENGTHS

God has given each of us our "marching orders." Our purpose here on Earth is to find those orders and carry them out. Those orders acknowledge our special gifts.
–Soren Kierkegaard

Strengths refer to the talents, skills or inherent characteristics at which you excel and that you feel are personally important. They "make you feel like you" when using them. When we apply our strengths, we naturally feel energized. Some consider strengths as the "backdoor" to happiness, because when we use them, we naturally feel alive, a sense of mastery, and intrigue.

Throughout the centuries, civilizations have recognized and respected certain human qualities as strengths. In recent years there has been a renewed interest in the scientific study of strengths. Most people focus too heavily on their perceived weaknesses and limitations rather than on their strengths. It is often more effective to build strengths rather than fix weaknesses. Strengths are our greatest currency and often go untapped. They pull us out of problems, lead progress and create momentum. Knowing and *leveraging* strengths can have many benefits, including achieving greater potential, feeling more secure during challenges, and having a more positive self-identity.

Signature Strengths. Strengths are reflected in what we like doing and are good at. Leading positive psychologists Chris Peterson and Martin Seligman refer to core strengths as "signature strengths" because they are unique to the individual.

Once you identify your strengths, you can intentionally apply them when pursuing goals and facing challenges. This can improve the ability to navigate situations, increase engagement in activities, and enhance a sense of well-being.

Unrealized Strengths And Learned Behaviors. The Center for Applied Positive Psychology makes a distinction between learned behaviors, realized strengths, unrealized strengths and weaknesses. *Learned behaviors* may be things you do well but don't energize you. *Realized strengths* are things you do well and energize you and you use fairly often. *Unrealized strengths* are strengths that you perform well and find energizing, but don't use often. Both realized and unrealized strengths bring you pleasure or a sense of flow. *Weaknesses* are those things you don't do well.

A STRENGTHS PERSPECTIVE

Build what's strong rather than fix what's wrong.

When we understand and leverage our strengths, we become more engaged, effective, and productive. Some fundamental propositions of a strengths perspective include the following:

- Each person has a unique combination of talents, which embody his or her potential.

- The key to maximum personal achievement is found within a person's greatest talents.

- As individuals learn about their talents, they grow in confidence and become more willing to take on greater challenges, and they become more engaged and persistent.

- To the extent that individuals do not learn how to identify their talents, and to develop and apply strengths, they will have less confidence and motivation to achieve and may become disengaged.

- Individuals may not be aware of their greatest talents, nor how to build upon them to develop and apply strengths for consistent performance.

- Important roles of the individual, the team, and the manager are to:
  - Help individuals identify their greatest talents
  - Help individuals develop strengths
  - Help individuals learn to apply talents and strengths in their personal and professional life

Strengths at Work. The answer to one question predicts the success of an organization: "Do most employees use their strengths on a daily basis?" Using strengths is important to thriving of individuals and of organizations.

A Gallup poll (Buckingham & Clifton, 2001) found that no more than 20% of workers in the United States believe their jobs allow them to do their best on a regular basis. Highly effective work performance and company loyalty, and an overall feeling of self-worth and happiness, comes from playing to what we do well. Rather than focusing on perceived weaknesses or areas that feel like "work," use strengths and natural skills to excel at work and life. Buckingham, M., & Clifton, D. (2001). The strengths revolution. Gallup Management Journal.

Success at Work and the Use of Strengths. Harter and Schmidt report on a study done on 10,855 work units (308,798 employees) in 51 different companies. They state that work units scoring above the median on the statement " At work, I have the opportunity to do what I do best every day" have 44 percent (1.4 times) higher probability of success on customer loyalty and employee retention and 38 percent higher probability of success on productivity measures. Harter, J. K., Schmidt, F.L., & Hayes, T. L. (2002). Business-unit-level relationship between employee satisfaction, employee engagement, and business outcomes: A meta-analysis. *Journal of Applied Psychology,* 87:2.

Harter, J.K., & Schmidt, F. L. (2002). Employee engagement, satisfaction, and business-unit-level outcomes: Meta-analysis. *Gallup Technical Report.*

Productivity and Strengths. Cameron, Dutton, and Quinn state in *Positive Organizational Scholarship* describe how one company benefited by leveraging strengths. In a large automobile manufacturer, two teams were assigned a " study group" and a "control group" (one team considered high performing and another team considered low performing). Individuals were administered the 'Strengths-Finder' assessment (Buckingham & Clifton, 2001) and given feedback, both individually and in group sessions, with follow-up developmental activities related to each individuals dominant talents (Connelly, 2002). Post intervention measurements of employee engagement (via Gallup's '12' instrument; Harter, Schmidt, & Hayes, 2002) and productivity were conducted six months later. Results indicated that the study group (n=48) grew in engagement by significantly more (d=.72) standard score units that the control group (n=297). Additionally, the study group grew in productivity by 50% more than the control group.

Buckingham, M., & Clifton, D.O. (2001). *Now, Discover Your Strengths.* New York: Free Press.

Cameron, K.S., Dutton, J.E., & Quinn, R.E. (2003). *Positive Organizational Scholarship: Foundations of a New Discipline.* San Francisco: Berrett-Koehler.

Connelly, S. (2002). All Together Now. *Gallup Management Journal,* 2:12-18.

Success and Stress. Utilizing personal strengths in goal completion led to higher rates of accomplishment and satisfaction.

Govindji, R., & Linley, P. A. (2007). Strengths use, self-concordance and well-being: Implications for strengths coaching and coaching psychologists. *International Coaching Psychology Review, 2* (2), 143-153.
Utilizing personal strengths in goal completion led to higher rates of accomplishment and satisfaction.

Linley, P. A., Nielsen, K. M., Wood, A. M., Gillett, R., & Biswas-Diener, R., (2010). Using signature strengths in pursuit of goals: Effects on goal progress, need satisfaction, and well-being, and implications for coaching psychologists. *International Coaching Psychology Review, 5* (1), 8-17.

Additional benefits to working with individual strengths are decreased stress levels (Wood et al, 2010) and increased levels of energy.

Wood, A. M., Linley, P. A., Maltby, J., & Hurling, R. (2010). Use of positive psychological strengths leads to less stress and greater self-esteem, vitality, and positive affect over time: A three-wave longitudinal study and validation of the Strengths Use Scale. *Manuscript submitted for publication.*

Signature Strengths and Happiness. Seligman and colleagues (2005) reported that participants who used their signature strengths (e.g., wisdom, creativity) in a new way on a daily basis for one week showed an increase in happiness and a decrease in depression levels. These findings were maintained at 6-month follow-up. Seligman, Steen, Park, & Peterson (2005). Positive psychology progress, *American Psychologist.*

Increased Happiness and Self-Satisfaction. Research shows that using individual strengths increases well-being. Developing and focusing on personal strengths has positive effects on happiness, confidence, and success rates. A 2010 study tracking participants over a four-week period showed that developing personal strengths led to higher levels of happiness and self-satisfaction (Minhas, 2010). Minhas, G. (2010). Developing realised and unrealised strengths: Implications for engagement, self-esteem, life satisfaction and well-being. *Assessment and Development Matters*, in press.

Increased Self Confidence. Proctor, Maltby, and Linley's study of 135 university students found a positive correlation between increased confidence and self-esteem and increased use of personal strengths. Proctor, C., Maltby, J., & Linley, P. A. (2009) Strengths use as a predictor of well-being and health- related quality of life. *Journal of Happiness Studies, 10*, 583-630.

BOOKS ON STRENGTHS

Peterson, C. (2004). *Character Strengths and Virtues : A Handbook and Classification.* New York: Oxford University Press, USA.

Comte-Sponville, A. (2001). *A small treatise on the great virtues* (C. Temerson, Trans.). New York: Metropolitan.

Buckingham, M., & Clifton, D.O. (2001). *Now, Discover Your Strengths.* New York: Free Press.

HOW TO LEVERAGE YOUR STRENGTHS: Identify & Use Strengths

What lies behind us and what lies before us are tiny matters compared to what lies within us.
- Ralph Waldo Emerson

Mindful leaders can become more effective by knowing their own strengths and weaknesses and knowing the strengths and weaknesses of other members of their team. In this section, look at ways to make better use of your own strengths. In a later section, we will discuss ways to make better use of the strengths of you colleagues and/or you team.

Leverage your strengths more by first identifying exactly what your top strengths are. Second, observe how and when you already use them. Note the impact of using them. Last, find ways to use your strengths in new ways.

HOW TO LEVERAGE YOUR STRENGTHS

1. Identify your core strengths.
2. Discover how you already use them.
3. Use your strengths in new ways.

IDENTIFY YOUR CORE STRENGTHS

Identify your core strengths by answering key questions that tend to reveal core strengths another or by taking an empirically developed questionnaire.

Ask Key Questions:

- What did I love to do as a child? What activities that drew me in, activities in which I spent hours engrossed, unique projects or hobbies, activities for which I would have limits imposed upon me because parental figures thought I spent too much time doing them?

- What types of experiences energize me?

- What can't I *not do*? (i.e., what I do in my free time, on vacation, etc.)

- What can I do better than any given 10,000 people?

- What do others admire about me?

Take a Scientifically Developed Questionnaire.

- *VIA Character Strengths Questionnaire.* The VIA Questionnaire is a well-validated test found at www.authentichappiness.org

- *The Realse2 Questionnaire.* This is another well-validated test found at www.CAPPEU.com

- *Clifton Strength Finder*

Use Journaling Worksheets.

- Personal Mentor Journaling Worksheet
- Personal Best Leadership Experience Journaling Worksheet

PERSONAL MENTOR JOURNALING WORKSHEET

In the following worksheet you will have a chance to recall the person or persons who helped you develop into the person that you are today, and to consider who helped you become a whole person—mind, body, spirit, heart. Think about who they are, what they did, how you responded, and what you can learn from their example.

1. Who helped you develop into the person you are now? Describe who this person is and what they saw in you.

_____

_____

_____

_____

_____

_____

_____

_____

_____

2. Who helped you become a whole person (mind, body, spirit, heart)? Describe who this person is and what they saw in you.

_____

_____

_____

_____

_____

_____

_____

_____

_____

_____

_____

_____

3. What specific things did they do? Describe what your mentor(s) did to help you to develop.

_____
_____
_____
_____
_____
_____
_____
_____

4. Strengths. What strengths did they help you to identify? How did they help you to recognize your strengths?

_____
_____
_____
_____
_____
_____
_____
_____

5. What can you learn from their leadership example? What can you learn from their example about inspiring others to reach their potential?

_____
_____
_____
_____
_____
_____
_____
_____
_____
_____
_____
_____

PERSONAL BEST JOURNALING WORKSHEET

In the following worksheet think about yourself in a leadership situation, one in which you feel that you achieved a "personal best." Describe the situation, and then jot down what you were thinking, what you were feeling, what you actually did as a leader, and how others responded to you. Finally, use this personal example to help yourself to better understand your leadership comfort zone and your leadership strengths.

PERSONAL BEST SITUATION

Describe a time when you were at your personal best in a leadership capacity.

_____
_____
_____
_____
_____
_____
_____
_____
_____
_____

1. THOUGHTS. What were your thoughts?

_____
_____
_____
_____
_____
_____
_____
_____
_____
_____

2. BEHAVIORS. What were your behaviors? What did you do?

_____
_____
_____
_____
_____
_____
_____

3. FEELINGS. What were your feelings?

_____
_____
_____
_____
_____
_____
_____

4. RESPONSES FOR OTHERS. How did others respond to you?

_____
_____
_____
_____
_____
_____

5. LEARNING ABOUT YOUR LEADERSHIP COMFORT ZONE & STRENGTHS. What can you learn from this example about your leadership comfort zone and your leadership strengths?

_____
_____
_____
_____
_____
_____
_____
_____

SIGNATURE STRENGTHS

Character Strengths & Virtues

WISDOM & KNOWLEDGE

1. **Curiosity** (Interest)
2. **Love of learning**
3. **Judgment** (Open mindedness)
4. **Creativity** (Ingenuity)
5. **Social intelligence**
6. **Perspective** (Wisdom)

COURAGE

7. **Valor** (Bravery)
8. **Perseverance** (Industriousness)
9. **Integrity** (Authenticity, Honesty)

HUMANITY

10. **Kindness** (Care, Compassion)
11. **Loving**

JUSTICE

12. **Citizenship** (Teamwork, Loyalty)
13. **Fairness** (Equity, Justice)
14. **Leadership** (Motivate, Direct, Coordinate)

TEMPERANCE

15. **Self-control** (Self-Regulation)
16. **Prudence** (Practical, Perspective)
17. **Humility** (Modesty)

TRANSCENDENCE

18. **Appreciation of Beauty and Excellence**
19. **Gratitude** (Appreciation, Thankfulness)
20. **Hope** (Optimism, Future-oriented)
21. **Spirituality** (Purpose, Faith)
22. **Forgiveness** (Mercy)
23. **Humor** (Playfulness)
24. **Zest** (Enthusiasm, Energy, Vitality)

THE 24 SIGNATURE STRENGTHS

WISDOM & KNOWLEDGE
Acquisition and use of knowledge, solving problems.

1. CURIOSITY (Interest, novelty-seeking, openness to experience): Curiosity is taking an interest in all of ongoing experience. It involves actively recognizing and pursuing challenging opportunities and seeking out new knowledge. Curiosity can be broken down into three categories: interest, novelty seeking, and openness to new experience. It is this strength that drives individuals to make discoveries and to explore the boundaries of human knowledge.
   Movies demonstrating curiosity: October Sky (1999) Amélie (2001-French)

2. LOVE OF LEARNING: Love of learning involves enthusiastically studying new skills, topics, and bodies of knowledge. People with this strength enjoy the cognitive engagement of acquiring new skills or satisfying their curiosity, even when the material benefits of learning may not be immediately available. Love of learning allows people to persist in the face of frustrations and obstacles that arise during the course of education, both formal and informal.
   Movies: Billy Elliot (2000), A Beautiful Mind (2001)
   Songs: On the Road to Find Out (Cat Stevens)

3. JUDGMENT (Open-mindedness, critical thinking): Judgment is thinking things through and examining them from all sides. It involves a willingness to consider evidence against one's own beliefs, plans, and goals, and to revise them if necessary. Open-minded people faithfully adhere to the standard of considering evidence fairly. This strength counteracts the pervasive "my-side bias" that prevents many people from considering views other than their own.
   Movies: No Man's Land (2001-Bosnian)

4. CREATIVITY (Originality, Ingenuity): Creativity is the process of using one's originality to devise novel ways to positively contribute to one's own life or the lives of others. Such originality can range from everyday ingenuity to groundbreaking work that becomes highly recognized. Creative people are able to apply their imaginations in new and surprising ways in order to solve the problems that they encounter. Traditional notions of creativity focus on artistic expression and scientific discovery, but this strength can be applied to any area of life in which obstacles can be addressed imaginatively.
   Movies: Shine (1996), Amadeus (1984)

5. SOCIAL INTELLIGENCE (Emotional intelligence, Personal intelligence): Socially intelligent individuals are aware of the emotions and intentions of themselves and others. No matter what the social situation is, they attempt to make everyone involved feel comfortable and valued. Socially intelligent people are perceptive of others' feelings and honest about their own, and are generally adept at fostering healthy relationships.
   Movies: Driving Miss Daisy (1989), Children of a Lesser God (1986), K-Pax (2001) The Five Senses (2001-Canadian)
   Songs: Lean on Me (Al Green), You've Got a Friend (James Taylor or Mariah Carey), Time After Time (Cyndi Lauper or Tuck and Patti), Bridge Over Troubled Water (Simon and Garfunkel or Johnny Cash), I'll Be there for You (The Rembrants)

6. PERSPECTIVE (Wisdom): Perspective, which is often called wisdom, is distinct from intelligence and involves a superior level of knowledge and judgment. This strength involves being able to provide wise counsel to others. It allows its possessor to address important and difficult questions about morality and the meaning of life. People with perspective are aware of broad patterns of meaning in their lives, their own strengths and weaknesses, and the necessity of contributing to their society.
   Movies: The Devil's Advocate (1997), American Beauty (1999)
   Songs: My Way (Frank Sinatra), Strength, Courage, Wisdom, The Miseducation of Lauryn Hill (Lauryn Hill)

COURAGE
Exercising will to accomplish goals in face of opposition.

7. VALOR (Bravery): Bravery is the capacity to take action to aid others in spite of significant risks or dangers. This strength allows people to avoid shrinking from the threats, challenges, or pain associated with attempting to do good works. Brave acts are undertaken voluntarily with full knowledge of the potential adversity involved. Brave individuals place the highest importance on higher purpose and morality, no matter what the consequences might be.
   Movies: Schindler's List (1993), Life as a House (2001)

8. PERSERVERANCE (Persistence, Industriousness): Persistence is the mental strength necessary to continue striving for one's goals in the face of obstacles and setbacks. This sort of perseverance requires dedication, focus, and patience. Persistent individuals finish what they start, persisting in the quest to achieve their goals in spite of any hardships they encounter along the way. The broader and more ambitious one's goals are, the more necessary persistence is in order to achieve them.
   Movies: The Piano (1993), The Legend of Bagger Vance (2000)
   Songs: My Way (Frank Sinatra), On the Road to Find Out (Cat Stevens)

9. INTEGRITY (Authenticity, Honesty): The strength of integrity is manifested speaking the truth and presenting oneself in a genuine way. A person of integrity is open and honest about his or her own thoughts, feelings, and responsibilities, being careful not to mislead through either action or omission. This strength allows one to feel a sense of ownership over one's own internal states, regardless of whether those states are popular or socially comfortable, and to experience a sense of authentic wholeness.
   Movies: *A Few Good Men (1992), Erin Brockovich (2000)*
   Songs: *My Way (Frank Sinatra), Strength, Courage, Wisdom, The Miseducation of Lauryn Hill (Lauryn Hill), The Rose (Bette Midler), On the Road to Find Out (Cat Stevens)*

HUMANITY
Tending to others, building relationships.

10. KINDNESS (Generosity Nurturance, Care, Compassion, Altruistic love): Kindness consists treating others with care and compassion. Generosity often includes doing favors and good deeds for others without the expectation of personal gain. This strength requires respect for others and often includes emotional affection. Kind people find joy in the act of giving and helping other people, regardless of their degree of relatedness or similarity.
   Movies: *As Good as it Gets (1997), The Cider House Rules (1999), Promise (1986)*
   Songs: *Lean on Me (Al Green), You've Got a Friend (James Taylor or Mariah Carey), Time After Time (Cyndi Lauper or Tuck and Patti), Bridge Over Troubled Water (Simon and Garfunkel or Johnny Cash), I'll Be there for You (The Rembrants)*

11. LOVE: Loving individuals value close relationships with others, in particular those in which sharing and caring are reciprocated. Love can be expressed toward those we depend on, toward those who depend on us, and toward those to whom we feel romantic, sexual, and emotional attraction. This strength allows people to put their trust in others and make them a priority in making decisions. They experience a sense of deep contentment from their devotion.
   Movies: *Doctor Zhivago (1965), The English Patient (1996), Sophie's Choice (1982), The Bridges of the Madison County (1995), Iris (2001), My Fair Lady (1964)*
   Songs: *The Rose (Bette Midler), Isn't She Lovely (Stevie Wonder)*

JUSTICE
Social responsibility, fairness, and leadership.

12. CITIZENSHIP (Social Responsibility, Loyalty, Teamwork): Citizenship involves working as a member of a group for the common good. People with this strength are loyal to the organizations of which they are members, ready to make personal sacrifices for their neighbors. The strength of citizenship is manifested through a sense of social belonging and civic responsibility. Good citizens are not blindly obedient, and when necessary they strive to change their groups for the better.
   Movies: *LA Confidential (1997), Finding Forester (2001), Awakenings (1990)*
   Songs: *Lean on Me (Al Green), You've Got a Friend (James Taylor or Mariah Carey), Time After Time (Cyndi Lauper or Tuck and Patti), Bridge Over Troubled Water (Simon and Garfunkel or Johnny Cash), I'll Be there for You (The Rembrants)*

13. FAIRNESS (Equity & Justice): Fairness involves treating everyone according to universal ideals of equality and justice. Fair individuals do not let their personal feelings bias their moral or ethical decisions about others, but instead rely on a broad set of moral values. True fairness incorporates both a respect for moral guidelines and a compassionate approach to caring for others. This strength is applicable at all levels of society, from everyday interactions to international issues of social justice.
   Movies: *The Emperor's Club (2002), Philadelphia (1993)*

14. LEADERSHIP: Leadership is the process of motivating, directing, and coordinating members of a group to achieve a common goal. Leaders assume a dominant role in social interaction, but effective leadership requires listening to the opinions and feelings of other group members as much as it involves active direction. Individuals who possess this strength are able to help their group to achieve goals in a cohesive, efficient, and amiable manner.
   Movies: *Lawrence of Arabia (1962), Dances with Wolves (1990)*

TEMPERANCE
Protecting against excess.

15. SELF-CONTROL (Self-regulation): Self-regulation is the process of exerting control over oneself in order to achieve goals or meet standards. Self-regulating individuals are able to control instinctive responses such as aggression and impulsivity, responding instead according to pre-conceived standards of behavior. This strength can apply both to resisting temptations, such as when a dieter avoids sugary foods, and to initiating actions, such as when someone gets up early to exercise.
   Movies: *Forest Gump (1994)*

16. PRUDENCE (Practical, Perspective): Prudence is a practical orientation toward future goals. It entails being careful about one's choices, not taking undue risks, and keeping long-term goals in mind when making short-term decisions. Prudent individuals monitor and control their impulsive behavior and anticipate the consequences of their actions. This strength is not synonymous with stinginess or timidity, but instead involves an intelligent and efficient perspective towards achieving major goals in life.
Movies: Sense and Sensibility (1995)

17. HUMILITY (Modesty): Humility and modesty involve letting one's strengths and accomplishments speak for themselves. Individuals with this strength do not need to have low self-esteem, but merely avoid seeking the spotlight and regarding themselves as better than others. Humble people are honest with themselves about their own limitations and the fallibility of their own opinions, and are open to advice and assistance from others.
Movies: Gandhi (1982), Little Buddha (1994)

TRANSCENDENCE
Providing meaning, joy, & connection to forces beyond self.

18. APPRECIATION OF BEAUTY AND EXCELLENCE (Awe, wonder, elevation): Individuals with an appreciation for beauty feels a sense of awe at the scenes and patterns around them. They take pleasure in observing physical beauty, the skills and talents of other people, and the beauty inherent to virtue and morality. Beauty can be found in almost every area of life, from nature to arts to mathematics to science to everyday experience. This strength allows people to experience satisfaction and richness in everyday experiences.
Movies: Out of Africa (1985), The Color of Paradise (2000- Iranian)
Songs: Isn't She Lovely (Stevie Wonder), Somewhere Over the Rainbow/What a Wonderful World (Israel Kamakawiwo'ole)

19. GRATITUDE: Gratitude is an awareness of and thankfulness for the good things in one's life. Grateful individuals take time to express thanks and contemplate all that they have been given in life. Gratitude can be directed at a specific person, at a Divinity, or simply expressed outwardly for the mere fact of existence. This strength is a mindset of appreciation and goodwill for the benefits derived from other people.
Movies: Sunshine (2000), Fried Green Tomatoes (1991)
Songs: Strength, Courage, Wisdom, Isn't She Lovely (Stevie Wonder)

20. HOPE (Optimism, future-mindedness, future orientation): Hope is the expectation that good things will happen in the future. Hopeful individuals are confident that their efforts toward future goals will lead to their fruition. This strength leads people to expect the best from themselves and others.
Movies: Gone with the Wind (1939), Life is beautiful (1998-Italian), Good Will Hunting (1997)
Songs: Strength, Courage, Wisdom, The Rose (Bette Midler), Somewhere Over the Rainbow/What a Wonderful World (Israel Kamakawiwo'ole)

21. SPIRITUALITY (Religiousness, faith, purpose): Spirituality is a universal part of human experience involving knowledge of one's place within the larger scheme of things. It can include but is not limited to religious belief and practice. Spirituality affords us an awareness of the sacred in everyday life, a sense of comfort in the face of adversity, and the experience of transcending the ordinary to reach something fundamental.
Movies: Contact (1997), The Apostle (1997), Priest (1994, British)

22. FORGIVENESS (Mercy): This strength involves forgiving those who have wronged or offended us. Forgiveness entails accepting the shortcomings of others, giving people a second chance, and putting aside the temptation to hold a grudge or behave vengefully. Forgiveness allows one to put aside the self-destructive negativity associated with anger and to extend mercy toward a transgressor.
Movies: Pay it Forward (2000), Terms of Endearment (1983), Dead Man Walking (1995), Ordinary People (1980)

23. HUMOR (Playfulness): Humor involves an enjoyment of laughing, friendly teasing, and bringing happiness to others. Individuals with this strength see the light side of life in many situations, finding things to be cheerful about rather than letting adversity get them down. Humor does not necessarily refer just to telling jokes, but rather to a playful and imaginative approach to life.   Movies: Patch Adams (1999)

24. ZEST (Vitality, enthusiasm, vigor, energy): Vitality is an approach to life marked by an appreciation for energy, liveliness, excitement, and energy. A vital person lives life as an adventure to be approached whole-heartedly. A life of vigor allows one to experience the overlap of the mental and physical realms of experience, as stress decreases and health increases. Vitality differs from contentment in that it involves greater psychological and physiological activation and enthusiasm.
Movies: Cinema Paradiso (1988, Italian), My Left Foot (1993), One Flew over the Cuckoo's Nest (1975)
Songs: My Way (Frank Sinatra)

IDENTIFY CORE STRENGTHS WORKSHEET

Core strengths are the abilities, talents, and affinities that you are naturally drawn to and energize you. They are the backdoor to happiness and success. What unique abilities and passions do you have that should be utilized so you can be at your best?

ASK KEY QUESTIONS

1. **Activities.** What did I love to do as a child?
   (Activities that drew me in, activities in which I spent hours engrossed, unique projects or hobbies, activities for which I would have limits imposed upon me because parental figures thought I spent too much time doing them.)

_____

_____

2. **Energize.** What types of experiences or activities energize me?

_____

_____

3. **Can't Not Do.** What types of activities *can't I not do*? (i.e., what I do in my free time, on vacation, etc.)

_____

_____

4. **Excellence.** What can I do better than any given 10,000 people?

_____

_____

5. **Admiration from Others.** What do others admire about me?

_____

_____

REVIEW THE STRENGTHS LIST & DESCRIPTIONS

Identify the top three signature strengths that best describe you, your interests, and/or your talents from the *Signature Strengths List*. Check off all the ones that best fit you, then list the top three below.

_____

_____

TAKE A SCIENTIFICALLY DEVELOPED QUESTIONNARIE

Test yourself using an empirically validated test for core strengths, such as:

    Reaise2 can be found at CAPPEU.com. This is our favorite strengths assessment, because it is well validated by research psychologists, and provides a comprehensive profile of strengths relevant for work.
    VIA Questionnaire is the most rigorously developed and well-validated test. It is found at www.authentichappiness.org
    The Strengths Finder is the most common strengths assessment.

LIST YOUR TOP STRENGTHS

1. STRENGTH ONE: _____

Description. Brief Description of characteristics of this Strength

_____
_____
_____

Current Use. How do I use this strength?

_____
_____
_____

2. STRENGTH TWO: _____

Description. Brief Description of characteristics of this Strength

_____
_____

Current Use. How do I use this strength?

_____
_____
_____

3. STRENGTH THREE: _____

Description. Brief Description of characteristics of this Strength

_____
_____

Current Use. How do I use this strength?

_____
_____
_____

4. UNREALIZED STRENGTHS. These are abilities that you find energizing and are drawn to but do not use often because of circumstances, environment, or lack of awareness. What do you feel energized by and are drawn to, but don't do often?

_____
_____
_____

IDENTIFY CORE STRENGTHS TRACKING LOG

DAY	APPLICATION Which strength did I use? How did I use it?	IMPACT What was the impact of using my strength on me, others, the situation? How did I feel when I was using my strength? Energized?
Day 1		
Day 2		
Day 3		
Day 4		

IDENTIFY CORE STRENGTHS TRACKING LOG

DAY	APPLICATION Which strength did I use? How did I use it?	IMPACT What was the impact of using my strength on me, others, the situation? How did I feel when I was using my strength? Energized?
Day 5		
Day 6		
Day 7		

INSIGHTS - What patterns or benefits emerged?

_____
_____
_____
_____

USE STRENGTHS IN NEW WAYS

Your core strengths are your greatest untapped potential.

When we use our strengths we are usually energized and feel at our best. We find ourselves drawn to using them in different areas of our lives—at work, at home and our during our leisure activities. They are areas where we learn fast and very often others will recognize them in us too. Psychologists have found that people who tried using their strengths in new ways each day for a week were happier and less depressed six months later. Seligman, M. E. P., Steen, T. A., Park, N., & Peterson, C. (2005). Positive psychology progress: Empirical validation of interventions. *American Psychologist*, 60, 410-421.

A study in the UK showed that people who felt they were using their strengths have more positive emotion, greater vitality and self-esteem, compared with people who did not feel they used theirs. [Wood, A.M., Linley, P.A., Maltby, J., Kasden, T.B., & Hurling,R. (2011). Using personal and psychological strengths leads to increases in well-being over time: A longitudinal study and the development of the strengths use questionnaire. *Personality and Individual Differences*, 50 (2011) 15-19

CHALLENGE YOURSELF TO USE YOUR STRENGTHS IN NEW WAYS

Look for ways to use your strengths in new ways. You might want to try using the following approach:

1. Pick one of your top five strengths and ask:
   - How do I use this strength already?
   - In what areas of my life do I use it?
   - What are other areas in my life that I could use it more?
   - What are other ways that I could use it?

2. Everyday for seven days, try to use this strength in a new way or area of your life. For example, if one of your top strengths is *curiosity and interest in the world,* try out simple things to use this strength in new ways:
   - Try out a new breakfast menu.
   - Take a different route to work.
   - Select a different radio channel to listen to on the way to work.
   - Read a different newspaper.
   - Check out a different magazine.
   - Go to lunch with a different person.
   - Visit a "tourist spot" in your town that you haven't been to.
   - Try out a new exercise.
   - Take a short class on a topic you don't know much about.
   - Ask people you know: "What makes you thrive?"

3. At the end of seven days, notice what impact using this strength in a new way had upon you. Then, pick another of your top strengths and repeat the process. Everyday for seven days, try to use this strength in a new way or area of your life.

MINDFULLY USE YOUR STRENGTHS DAILY

Mindful leaders look for opportunities to use their strengths more often and to leverage their strengths to create more impact and joy in their life and the lives of others. Mindful leaders also look for ways to leverage the strengths of their colleagues and the members of their team. When pursuing a goal, reflect on your core strengths and consider how you could leverage them. Leveraging strengths during challenges increases one's sense of control and ability to navigate challenges.

For example:

If you are a natural born *leader*, don't sit at the back of the room in an effort to not shake the boat, assert some direction to the situation. If you have a colleague or member of your team who is a natural born leader, give them an opportunity to lead.

If appreciation of *beauty* or excellence is a core strength, look for role models that can provide guidance for achieving great heights. If you have a colleague or member of your team who has beauty and excellence as a core strength, look for ways to allow them to use this strength to improve the work environment or work processes.

If *wisdom* comes naturally for you, prioritize some alone time to contemplate the meaning of a situation and how it fits in with what you feel is deeply true in life. If you have a colleague or member of your team who is high on wisdom, draw on their wisdom to solve problems.

If *love of learning* is a strength, take some time to reflect on how challenges have taught you important life lessons, or how you can use your learning in this particular situation. If you have a colleague or member of your team who is high on love of learning, help them discover new ways to learn, and new challenges to pursue.

In an interpersonal conflict, reflect on your core strengths and consider how you can leverage them.

Use strengths to build relationships. When building stronger relationships, consider how you can connect with others by engaging in activities that activate your core strengths.

For example,

If *humor* is your talent, find ways to laugh, joke, and play with others. If a member of your team has humor as a talent, draw on this talent to create a better environment.

If *love of learning* feels energizing, invite others to go with you to lectures, have discussions about current news or articles, engage others in conversations about life lessons, organize social events with an educational focus such as documentary movie night, discussion topic dinner, book club, etc.

Unrealized Strengths. Unrealized strengths improve performance, are energizing, and feel enjoyable but by definition, are not used often, perhaps because of circumstances, environment, or lack of awareness.

How could you use your unrealized strengths more often?

USE STRENGTHS IN NEW WAYS WORKSHEET

Playing to strengths, instead of focusing exclusively on shortcomings, is crucial to thriving at work and in life. Research suggests that using strengths in new ways increases happiness levels.

1. WORK

How can I use my top three strengths in new ways and more effectively at work to foster higher levels of energy, satisfaction, and overall sense of thriving?

_____
_____
_____
_____
_____
_____
_____
_____
_____
_____
_____
_____

2. RELATIONSHIPS

How can I use my top three strengths in new ways and more effectively in relationships to foster higher levels of energy, satisfaction, and overall sense of thriving?

_____
_____
_____
_____
_____
_____
_____
_____
_____
_____
_____
_____

3. LEISURE ACTIVITIES

How can I use my top three strengths in new ways and more effectively in leisure activities to foster higher levels of energy, satisfaction, and overall sense of thriving?

_____
_____
_____
_____
_____
_____
_____
_____
_____
_____
_____
_____

4. OTHER REALM OF LIFE

How can I use my top three strengths in new ways and more effectively in another realm of life to foster higher levels of energy, satisfaction, and overall sense of thriving?

_____
_____
_____
_____
_____
_____
_____
_____
_____
_____
_____
_____
_____

USE STRENGTHS IN NEW WAYS TRACKING LOG

DAY	APPLICATION How did I use a core strength in a new way?	IMPACT What was the impact of using this strength on me, others, and/or the situation?
Day 1		
Day 2		
Day 3		
Day 4		

USE STRENGTHS IN NEW WAYS TRACKING LOG

DAY	APPLICATION How did I use a core strength in a new way?	IMPACT What was the impact of using this strength on me, others, and/or the situation?
Day 5		
Day 6		
Day 7		

INSIGHTS - What patterns or benefits emerged?

_____
_____
_____
_____
_____
_____

LEVERAGE OTHERS' STRENGTHS

Mindful Leaders are effective in the use of their own strengths, and they look for ways to maximize the use of the strengths of others. Many organizations encourage their teams to look at the strengths of their individual members and then look for ways to leverage individual strengths for the benefit of the whole team.

In an article in the April, 2007 *Harvard Business Review*, Stephen Miles and Michael Watkins point out the use of complementary strengths in the leadership team. They point out that leveraging the strengths of the various players on a team has a long history. Their article opens with the following example:

> Senior leadership teams whose members play complementary roles have been chronicled as far back as Homer's oral history of the Trojan War. Though the Greeks were led in their quest for retribution against Troy by the powerful King Agamemnon, their victory would not have been possible without Achilles, the mighty warrior; Odysseus, the wily tactician; and Nestor, the wise elder.
>
> Each had a crucial, distinct role to play in the Greek high command. Achilles rallied the troops in the heat of battle. Odysseus provided sound strategic advice during and between engagements. Nestor was a source of cool-headed counsel and diplomacy, mediating between the titanic egos of Agamemnon and Achilles. No one of them could have played all the varied roles necessary to guide the enterprise to victory; collectively they prevailed and won their place in history.
> (*The Leadership Team: Complimentary Strengths or Conflicting Agendas?*, HBR, April, 2007)

Identifying the individual strengths of the members of an organization increases its members' effectiveness by matching their strengths to tasks, and by making use of complimentary strengths. This allows individuals to develop skills more easily, reduces turnover, improves employee morale, and improves the overall performance of the organization.

Core strengths are enduring and unique. When we recognize another's strengths, we are focusing on what is unique about them and honing in on their individuality and the essence of their person. Often we focus on another's actions but not on their enduring character—on content but not substance.

IDENTIFY OTHERS' STRENGTHS

Understanding another's strengths is essential knowledge. It helps us understand them at a deeper level—about what is likely to be important to them, about their values and their potential. This knowledge positions us to relate to them at a deeper level, help them optimize their strengths and leverage their strengths when working toward common objectives. It often makes us feel more connected and can break down barriers when in conflict, because it counters all-or-none, black and white thinking when we are having negative judgments about their character or actions.

Consider what another's core strengths might be. Do this by recalling times when they have demonstrated exceptional aptitude or performance during work situations. These may be small or big occurrences. Look a little deeper than you might during normal social interactions to find the enduring qualities that you admire.

Some specific techniques for assessing another's strengths:

Better than 10,000 people. Ask yourself, "What does this person do better than 10,000 other people?" You might use this knowledge later, or it might simply help you understand who they are and what their unique or admirable qualities are.

Another at their best. When have you seen the other at their best? Think of a time when he/she did something you admired, made a contribution you appreciated, added value, or demonstrated a strong positive character trait. Take note of the character trait or strength behind what they did and why what they did was important to you.

Peak experience. Consider a time when you witnessed another having a peak experience. A peak experience is a moment in time when things were great – they were on top of their game, they felt powerful and strong or were truly thriving.

- It could have occurred at work, home or during leisure activities.
- It can be a point in time (crossing a finish line) or a period in time (i.e., college years).
- It can be when they were an adult or a child.

This is often a period of what Mihalyi Csikszentmihalyi calls "flow" – a state when fully engaged in an activity, sense of self dissolves, and time slips away.

LEVERAGE TEAM MEMBERS' STRENGTHS WORKSHEET

Highly effective work performance and company loyalty, and an overall feeling of self-worth and happiness, comes from working on things we do well and thrive at. Rather than focusing on perceived weaknesses or areas that feel like "work," it is possible to use strengths and natural skills to excel at work and life. Leveraging strengths during challenges increases sense of control and ability to navigate challenges. Using strengths is an important factor in being happy at work and in life. *What unique abilities and passions do others have that should be utilized so they can do their best?*

The purpose of this exercise is to give you practice in the process of assessing another's strengths.

THE PERSON

Identify someone at work who's strengths you wish to leverage. _____

1. IDENTIFY ANOTHER'S STRENGTHS

A. Ask Key Questions.

1. Drawn to. What types of experiences are they drawn to? What can't they *not do*? (Types that activate social intelligence, positivity, fairness, strategic, discipline, analytical, organization, etc.)

_____
_____
_____

2. Energize. What types of activities energize them?

_____
_____
_____

3. Excellence. What do they do better than any given 10,000 people?

_____
_____
_____

4. Admiration from Others. What do others admire about them?

_____
_____
_____

B. Review the Core Strengths List. Identify the top three strengths that seem to best describe them, their interests, and/or values from the Clifton Strengths Finder list.

1. _____
2. _____
3. _____

C. Questionnaires. Suggest that they use a scientifically validated test for core strengths.

VIA Character Strengths Questionnaire found at www.authentichappiness.org
Clifton Strengths Finder
Realise2 found at www.cappeu.com

2. MORE AND BETTER USE OF THEIR STRENGTHS

STRENGTH 1: _____
Current Use. How do they currently use this strength?

_____
_____
_____

More and Better Use. How could they make more and better use of this strength? How could I support these efforts?

_____
_____
_____

STRENGTH 2: _____

Current Use. How do they currently use this strength?

_____
_____
_____

More and Better Use. How could they make more and better use of this strength? How could I support these efforts?

_____
_____
_____

STRENGTH 3: _____

Current Use. How do they currently use this strength?

_____
_____
_____

More and Better Use. How could they make more and better use of this strength? How could I support these efforts?

_____
_____
_____

MOMENT OF STRENGTH VISUALIZATION

The objective of this meditation is to recall and re-experience a moment when you felt a tremendous sense of inner strength. Perhaps recall a moment when you accomplished a goal, received recognition for hard work, felt satisfied after succeeding, made a tough decision you knew was right, courageously acted on your inner wisdom, or successfully employed a core strength.

Choose a moment when you felt strong. Choose one that is fully positive. Avoid choosing a complicated situation or one filled with any negative emotion. Make contact with the memory by recalling details that you heard or saw and then relive the moment in your body, holding that pleasant feeling for 15-30 seconds. This will allow the memory to become more consolidated in long-term memory and strengthen the neural pathways associated with pleasant feelings.

INSTRUCTIONS
(3-8 MINUTES)

1. FOCUS INWARD: Breathe and Center

- **Close Your Eyes**—Close your eyes to better focus your attention inward.

- **Feel Your Breath**—Focus attention by feeling your breath enter and exit your body. Breathe deep into your abdomen. Place your hand on your abdomen to feel your diaphragm rise and fall. Slowly exhale and naturally inhale.

- **Set Your Intention**—To direct your attention in this time, place, and to the objective of this meditation.

2. DIRECT ATTENTION: Relive the Situation

- **Make contact**—Make contact with a memory of a moment of strength.

- **Visualize**—Visualize what you saw, where you were, what others said.

- **Soak in the positive feelings**—Relive the moment feeling the positivity in your body.

- **Expand the feeling**—Invite the feeling to expand into your entire body.

3. REFLECT ON INSIGHTS: Breathe and Reflect

- Come back to your breath.
- Reflect on the insights or benefits you gained during this meditation.

4. MAINTAIN YOUR INNER AWARENESS: Soft Gaze and Stay with It

- Slowly open your eyes and keep your gaze soft, directed downward, and settling on a neutral object.
- Stay with the awareness you gained during the meditation.

MOMENT OF STRENGTH VISUALIZATION WORKSHEET

After you have completed the meditation, jot down any observations about what came up during your meditation. Make note of thoughts you had, feelings you experienced, bodily sensations you felt, and/or detours that you took.

1. FOCUS INWARD: To what extent could you direct attention and turn your mind when it wandered?

_____
_____
_____

2. DIRECT ATTENTION: Relive the situation.

Make contact with a memory of a moment of strength. What was the memory?

_____
_____
_____

Visualize what you saw, where you were, what others said. What did you visualize?

_____
_____
_____

Soak in the positive feelings. Relive the moment, feeling the positivity in your body. What was the feeling?

_____
_____
_____

Expand the feeling. Invite the feeling to expand into your entire body. What did you feel when you expanded the feeling?

_____
_____
_____

3. REFLECT ON INSIGHTS: What insights or benefits did you gain?

_____
_____
_____
_____

Skill 10. ALIGN ACTION WITH VALUES

No one can do all the good that the world needs, but the world needs all the good that you can do.
-Lama Surya Das

DO WHAT MATTERS TO YOU

Does your life on the outside reflect who you are on the inside?

Create a life that is a full expression of you at your best. We all have 24 hours in a day, 7 days in our week. How are you spending them? Do you bring intention to your days, weeks, months, and years? Be the author of your life by intentionally choosing what you do rather than passively reacting to circumstances or obeying the demands of others.

This requires that you turn up the volume of your internal wisdom so that it can guide you. Building activities that are in line with your values and priorities and knowing and employing your signature strengths are powerful steps toward creating a life that reflects who you truly are, your authentic self.

Living a Purposeful Life. The payoff of intentionally choosing activities is living a meaningful, purposeful life. Meaningful activities are powerful contributors to happiness, because they continue to make you feel good when reflected upon. They pay forward. In addition, they contribute to one's self-identity. This enhances self-respect and confidence.

Most people intend to build meaningful activities into their life, but often they pushed into the future, after the more urgent work is finished. This is not surprising since meaningful activities tend to have long term rather than short term benefits. Immediate gratification drives behavior more powerfully unless one intentionally highlights the benefits of long term rewards.

The pay-off is significant, however. Acting inline with values is qualitatively different from actions delivering temporary pleasures, which tend to give temporary highs or relief from boredom, inertia, or negative feelings. Like scratching an itch, with pleasure the need for more returns over and again. A life filled with temporary highs balanced with deeper experiences will have both pleasure and depth of experience. Like happiness, meaning cannot be pursued directly—it emerges under the right conditions.

Authenticity. Acting in accordance with one's core self is considered a basic psychological need. It is living authentically by interacting with the circumstances and people in your life from a place that feels like you. It is being *more yourself.* Do you respect yourself enough to actually be yourself—not posing as someone or something that is not you? Being your "authentic self" refers to having the insight to know what is and is not important to you, having the courage to act on this insight, and allowing others' to get to know you. A benefit of acting authentically is trust. People trust and respond more favorably to people who are coming from a place that is genuine versus contrived and postured.

Being in touch with your inner sense of person is different from being self-centered, selfish, or being self-consumed. Being self-focused commonly results in disregard for others. Instead, being your self emerges from being in touch with what your "*inner guidance system*" is telling you. It is "turning up the volume" on your inner sense of what is right for you or not.

It can require courage to live and express your genuine self. Sometimes others will not respond as positively as they might if you altered yourself to fit their preferences.

Congruency. A critical component of mindful leadership is having congruency between values and actions. When we lack congruence between values and actions internal dissonance produces a range of negative feelings including diminished self-respect, increased depression, and decreased happiness. It is like two boats floating next to each other, one representing values and the other representing actions. Imagine standing with a foot in each boat. When actions drift too far from values, we fall in the water.

Are your activities and actions congruent with what matters most to you? In this next section, you will be guided through developing a deeper understanding of your top values, provided with an opportunity to explore how you put your values and action, and encouraged to choose activities that serve your values.

RESEARCH—VALUES IN ACTION

Studies show that it is important to choose activities and pursue goals that are consistent with your values. Not doing that leads to diminished emotional and physical well-being.

Conflict of values and activities lead to depression. Emmons and King (1988) found that conflict and ambivalence among daily personal strivings (goals behind one's actions) were associated with high levels of negative affect, depression, neuroticism, and psychosomatic complaints. These findings were maintained at a one-year follow-up. When personal strivings were in conflict people felt more ambivalent about these goals, and they spent more time thinking about, and less time engaging in, these strivings.

"Personal strivings, daily life events, and psychological and physical well-being" by Emmons (1991)

"Conflict among personal strivings" by Emmons & King (1988);

"Personal projects, happiness, and meaning" by McGregor & Little (1998)

"Self-determination theory and the facilitation of intrinsic motivation, social development, and well-being" by Ryan & Deci (2000)

"Links between self-discrepancies, rumination, metacognitions, and symptoms of depression in undergraduates." Roelofsa et al. (2006).

VALUES ASESSMENT WORKSHEET

WHO INSPIRES ME?

1. SOMEONE WHO INSPIRES ME IS: _____

Characteristics. Why do they inspire me? What character traits do they exhibit that are inspiring to me?

_____
_____
_____

Examples. What are some examples of them acting on this character trait?

_____
_____
_____

2. SOMEONE WHO INSPIRES ME IS: _____

Characteristics. Why do they inspire me? What character traits do they exhibit that are inspiring to me?

_____
_____
_____

Examples. What are some examples of them acting on this character trait?

_____
_____
_____

3. SOMEONE WHO INSPIRES ME IS: _____

Characteristics. Why do they inspire me? What character traits do they exhibit that are inspiring to me?

_____
_____
_____

Examples. What are some examples of them acting on this character trait?

_____
_____
_____

MY PERSONAL VALUES

Does your life on the outside reflect who you are on the inside?

Review the characteristics of the people who inspire you. Often what inspires us reflects our values. Using these characteristics as a guide or other insights, write down your top values.

1. VALUE: _____

Value in Action. How do I put this value into action (i.e., choices, activities, work projects, development goals, ways that I go about my work day, or other ways that I express it in my work or personal life)?

_____
_____
_____
_____
_____

Out of Alignment. How do I act in ways that is out of alignment with this value? (i.e., choices, activities, work projects, development goals, ways that I go about my work day or personal life)?

_____
_____
_____
_____
_____

2. VALUE: _____

Value in Action. How do I put this value into action (i.e., choices, activities, work projects, development goals, ways that I go about my work day, or other ways that I express it in my work or personal life)?

_____
_____
_____
_____

Out of Alignment. How do I act in ways that is out of alignment with this value? (i.e., choices, activities, work projects, development goals, ways that I go about my work day or personal life)?

_____
_____
_____
_____
_____

MY PERSONAL VALUES

3. VALUE: _____

Value in Action. How do I put this value into action (i.e., choices, activities, work projects, development goals, ways that I go about my work day, or other ways that I express it in my work or personal life)?

_____
_____
_____
_____
_____

Out of Alignment. How do I act in ways that is out of alignment with this value? (i.e., choices, activities, work projects, development goals, ways that I go about my work day or personal life)?

_____
_____
_____
_____
_____

4. VALUE: _____

Value in Action. How do I put this value into action (i.e., choices, activities, work projects, development goals, ways that I go about my work day, or other ways that I express it in my work or personal life)?

_____
_____
_____
_____
_____

Out of Alignment. How do I act in ways that is out of alignment with this value? (i.e., choices, activities, work projects, development goals, ways that I go about my work day or personal life)?

_____
_____
_____
_____
_____

MY PERSONAL VALUES

5. VALUE: _____

Value in Action. How do I put this value into action (i.e., choices, activities, work projects, development goals, ways that I go about my work day, or other ways that I express it in my work or personal life)?

_____
_____
_____
_____
_____

Out of Alignment. How do I act in ways that is out of alignment with this value? (i.e., choices, activities, work projects, development goals, ways that I go about my work day or personal life)?

_____
_____
_____
_____
_____

6. VALUE: _____

Value in Action. How do I put this value into action (i.e., choices, activities, work projects, development goals, ways that I go about my work day, or other ways that I express it in my work or personal life)?

_____
_____
_____
_____

Out of Alignment. How do I act in ways that is out of alignment with this value? (i.e., choices, activities, work projects, development goals, ways that I go about my work day or personal life)?

_____
_____
_____
_____
_____
_____

VALUES ALIGNMENT WORKSHEET

Consider how you could better align your actions with your values. Identify three values you want to target and commit to changing your actions to better align with this value.

HOW COULD I BETTER ALIGN MY ACTIONS WITH MY VALUES?

1. TARGET VALUE: _____

Value Alignment. How could I better align my actions with this value? (i.e., choices, activities, work projects, development goals, how I go about my work day, or other ways in my work or personal life)?

_____

_____

_____

_____

2. TARGET VALUE: _____

Value Alignment. How could I better align my actions with this value? (i.e., choices, activities, work projects, development goals, how I go about my work day, or other ways in my work or personal life)?

_____

_____

_____

_____

3. TARGET VALUE: _____

Value Alignment. How could I better align my actions with this value? (i.e., choices, activities, work projects, development goals, how I go about my work day, or other ways in my work or personal life)?

_____

_____

_____

_____

4. TARGET VALUE: _____

Value Alignment. How could I better align my actions with this value? (i.e., choices, activities, work projects, development goals, how I go about my work day, or other ways in my work or personal life)?

_____

_____

_____

_____

COMMITMENT FOR CHANGE

THIS WEEK I COMMIT TO CHANGE (OR TAKE A STEP TOWARD CHANGE):

_____
_____
_____
_____
_____
_____
_____
_____
_____

OBSTACLES. Consider which competing values, other priorities, or other factors that could hinder change and how you will deal with them.

1. Obstacle One: _____

How will I overcome this obstacle?

_____
_____
_____
_____

2. Obstacle Two: _____

How will I overcome this obstacle?

_____
_____
_____
_____

2. Obstacle Two: _____

How will I overcome this obstacle?

_____
_____
_____
_____

VALUES IN ACTION TRACKING LOG

Each day this week, track how you acted in closer alignment with your values. Consider even very small steps, choices, or activities you did that were inline with your values.

DAY & TIME	APPLICATION Value: What was the Value? What was the choice, activity, or other way that I expressed my value?	IMPACT What was the impact of putting this value in action on me, others, or the situation?
Day & Time		
Day & Time		
Day & Time		
Day & Time		

VALUES IN ACTION TRACKING LOG

Each day this week, track how you acted in better alignment with your values. Consider even very small steps, choices, or activities you did that were inline with your values.

DAY & TIME	APPLICATION Value: What was the Value? What was the choice, activity, or other way that I expressed my value?	IMPACT What was the impact of putting this value in action on me, others, or the situation?
Day & Time		
Day & Time		
Day & Time		

INSIGHTS - What patterns or benefits emerged?

_____
_____
_____
_____
_____

LIFE REFLECTION VISUALIZATION

Life Reflection is a powerful meditation that can help you get in touch with what you value most. In this exercise you will be asked to imagine a major life event where all the important people in your life gather to celebrate and honor you. You might imagine a milestone birthday, (your 50th, 80th, 95th, 105th birthday or whatever), an anniversary, or even your funeral. It is best if you create a scene filled with the meaningful people, currently living or not, that you have had in your life. This is based on Stephen Covey's value exercise in his book *The Seven Habits of Highly Effective People*.

INSTRUCTIONS
(6-8 minutes)

1. FOCUS INWARD: Breathe and Center
- **Center**—Close your eyes and turn your attention inward.
- **Anchor in Your Breath**—Feel your breath fill and release your body.

2. DIRECT ATTENTION: Life Reflection

In your mind's eye, create a scene of a major life gathering, a party or event that honors you. Picture yourself walking inside a room. You see the faces of friends and family in the room. You feel the shared joy of having known you and the love that radiates from the hearts of the people there. All these people have come to honor you, to express feelings of love and appreciation for your life.

Four Speakers

- **Family**. The first is from your family, immediate and also extended—husband, wife, mother, father, children, brothers, sisters, nephews, nieces, aunts, uncles, cousins and grandparents who have come from all over the country to attend. Include anyone who has been significant in your life, even if they are no longer alive.

- **Friends**. The second speaker is one of your friends, someone who can give a sense of what you were as a person.

- **Work**. The third speaker is from your work or profession.

- **Community**. The fourth is from your community, perhaps an organization where you have been involved in service.

What Do They Say? What do each of these speakers say about you and your life?

- What do they remember most about you?
- How do they describe you as a person?
- What contributions and achievements do they remember?
- What difference have you made in their lives?

3. REFLECT ON INSIGHTS: Breathe and Reflect
- Come back to your breath.
- Reflect on the insights or benefits you gained during this meditation.

4. MAINTAIN YOUR INNER AWARENESS: Soft Gaze and Stay with It
- Slowly open your eyes and keep your gaze soft, directed downward, and settling on a neutral object.
- Stay with the awareness you gained during the meditation.

LIFE REFLECTION VISUALIZATION WORKSHEET

After you have completed the meditation, jot down any observations about what came up during your meditation. Make note of thoughts you had, feelings you experienced, bodily sensations you felt, and/or detours that you took.

WHAT DID THE SPEAKERS SAY?

1. FAMILY. The first speaker is from your family, immediate and also extended—husband, wife, mother, father, children, brothers, sisters, nephews, nieces, aunts, uncles, cousins and grandparents who have come from all over the country to attend. Include anyone who has been significant in your life, even if they are no longer alive. **Who was it? What did they say?**

_____

_____

_____

2. FRIENDS. The second speaker is one of your friends, someone who can give a sense of what you were as a person. **Who was it? What did they say?**

_____

_____

_____

3. WORK. The third speaker is from your work or profession. **Who was it? What did they say?**

_____

_____

_____

4. COMMUNITY. The fourth is from your church or some community organization where you've been involved in service. **Who was it? What did they say?**

_____

_____

_____

REFLECT ON INSIGHTS

What comments did you most value?

_____

_____

What wasn't said that you wish they would have said about you?

_____

_____

What could you do to change so that your life is more aligned with what you value most?

_____

_____

VALUES JOURNALING TRACKING LOG

JOURNAL FOR FIVE MINUTES EACH DAY. Every day for one week, journal for five minutes about what you stand for. You might use the following prompts to keep the exploration moving. This is a free flowing, mind dump exercise; therefore, allow the words to just come. Challenge yourself to not lift your pen from the paper and simply write uncensored. You might choose from the below prompts, or choose your own.

OPTIONAL PROMPTS FOR VALUES JOURNALING	
What do I stand for?	When I am at my best in my relationships with my colleagues I …
How do I act on what I stand for?	When I am at my best in my relationships with family/partner/children/friends, I …
If I acted on what I stand for more often, I would	If I lived more aligned with my values, I would do *more* of…
When I am at my best at work I…	If I lived more aligned with my values, I would do *less* of….
I am the kind of person who always….	What I do for other people is…
What I am most proud of in my life is….	What gives my life depth and meaning is…
I find great joy in…	If others knew me well, they would know that I deeply care about…
	My highest purpose in life is…

2. RECORD. In the log below, record when you journaled about, which prompt or topic you explored, and the impact of this journaling.

DAY	APPLICATION When and what did I journal about?	IMPACT What was the impact of journaling (e.g., how did I feel after, level of clarity, insights for my actions or plans)?
Day 1		
Day 2		
Day 3		

VALUES JOURNALING TRACKING LOG

DAY	APPLICATION When and what did I journal about?	IMPACT What was the impact of journaling (e.g., how did I feel after, level of clarity, insights for my actions or plans)?
Day 4		
Day 5		
Day 6		
Day 7		

INSIGHTS - What patterns or benefits emerged?

_____
_____
_____
_____
_____

Skill 10. ALIGN ACTIONS WITH PRIORITIES

Find joy in everything you choose to do. Every job, relationship, home...
it's your responsibility to love it, or change it.
-Chuck Palahniuk

How balanced is your life? Do you live in alignment with your priorities? We have 168 hours in a week. We can't do everything so we must choose. Sometimes our daily, weekly, monthly, and annual activities are consistent with our priorities; sometimes they are not.

HOW TO ALIGN ACTIONS & PRIORITIES: USE THE LIFE BUCKETS PRINCIPLE

One of the powerful ways to get a mental picture of your life is to use the concept of "life buckets." Each bucket can represent an important area and high priority in your life. How full or empty the bucket is represents the amount of resources (time, energy, attention, commitment, money, etc.) that you are expending in that area of your life.

The Life Buckets Exercise. Identify the life buckets, visually fill the buckets up to the point that you feel is representative of what is going on in your life, and then ask yourself questions about the picture that you see. For example, your might label your buckets Health, Work, Spouse/Family & Friends, Finances, and Contribution. Then visually fill each bucket. Ask yourself questions to help yourself to be honest with your self.

- **Health.** Do I eat, drink, exercise and sleep healthy? How much time do I spend on these activities? Do I have annual checkups, know what my healthy numbers are (weight, blood pressure, cholesterol, etc.)? Am I doing all I can to be healthy?

- **Spouse, Family, Friends.** Do I spend quality time with the people that are most important to me? How much time do I actually spend? Am I prioritizing my loved ones appropriately?

- **Work.** Do I enjoy my work? How much time do I spend at work? How much time should I spend? Do I keep work separate from my leisure time? Does my work nurture me? Is my current work helping me to achieve my career and life goals?

- **Finances.** Do I have my finances under control? Do I know where my money goes? Do I have a budget and a plan? Do I know my credit score? How much time do I spend worrying about my finances? How much time do I spend managing my finances?

- **Contribution.** Do I look beyond myself and contribute to a higher cause or to others? Do I take time to give back to my community, my friends and relatives, or to others? How much time do I spend contributing?

The 80% objective. Be aware of filling up any bucket by more than 80%. If we fill any bucket up to the top, there is a danger that we are filling that bucket at the expense of another, equally important bucket. Unfortunately, the business world is filled with "successful" individuals whose Work and Finances buckets are overflowing, but whose Health and Spouse/Family/Friends buckets are running on empty.

Reallocate Your Resources. Once you have a picture of your life buckets, you can begin to challenge your allocation of resources, and begin to reallocate based upon your values, life goals and priorities. Ask your self the questions:
- *Given my values, goals, and priorities, what is the highest and best use of my time?*
- *What buckets do I need to change?*
- *How will I make the change?*

DO A REALITY CHECK: WHERE DO YOU SPEND YOUR TIME?

Periodically take stock of your priorities and get real—are you living your priorities?

SOME COMMON LIFE BUCKETS (PRIORITY AREAS)		
• Fitness/Health	• Romance	• Family
• Career/Job	• Wealth/Finances	• Friends
• Contribution	• Spirituality	• Hobbies/Fun

- Do your activities serve your priorities?
- Are you making tradeoffs that will bring you happiness in life?
- How much time, effort and resources you are allocating to each priority?

For example, you might identify your marriage as your highest priority. Then do a reality check—identify where you actually spend your time, and how much of that time serves this top priority. Identify activities that serve this priority—romantic outings, intimate conversations, time alone together, etc.

Clues from Your Credit Card. It has been said that if you want to know what a person truly values, then look at their bank and credit card statements. Where we spend our money can be a metric for how much we prioritize it. The same can be said about how we invest our time. Does the amount of time you spend on activities that you value reflect their worth to you?

Eliminate Dissonance. Eliminate dissonance by investing your time, energy, attention, and resources where it really matters. Use your inner self as a guide to determine which activities to choose and which to spend less time on. The structure of you life may now dictate what you do, but commit to slowly building a life that feels even more meaningful and authentic.

Build activities and experiences into your life that reflect your priorities. This requires compromising other activities, which are often competing priorities. You must be willing to take the hit, to face the limitation on your time, energy, and resources. Make choices that will give you significant payback. Living your best life takes clarity, determination, and sometimes courage to go against the grain.

LIFE BUCKETS WORKSHEET

If the amount of time, effort, attention, and resources you spent on your top priorities were poured into a bucket, how full would each of your buckets be? Indicate how full each of your priority buckets are currently. A full bucket indicates *your* ideal level of this in your life (not what others' think it *should* be).

INSTRUCTIONS

1. Label Each Priority Bucket. First, label each of the buckets in the space provided as your priorities. You may select labels from the list Common Priority Areas List or come up with your own.

• Fitness/Health	• Romance	• Wealth	• Spirituality	• Friends
• Career/Job	• Contribution	• Finances	• Family	• Hobbies/Fun

2. How Full is the Bucket? Second, draw a horizontal line on the bucket indicating how full that bucket is. The fullness of a bucket represents how much time, effort, and resources you invest in a given priority.

3. How Can I fix the Buckets that are too Empty or Too Full? Where do you want to reallocate resources (time, effort, money) to some buckets (priorities) that appear to be too empty or too full?

BUCKETS—REALLOCATE RESOURCES

1. BUCKET (Priority): _____ ☐ Too Full or ☐ Too Empty

Small, Simple Steps. What are some small, simple steps I can take to change this bucket?

_____
_____

Synergize. How could I synergize with other priorities to change both buckets with one activity/effort/resource?

_____
_____

Obstacles. What blocks my intention to invest more or less time, energy, and resources to empty or fill this bucket? How can I overcome these obstacles?

_____
_____

Choices. What would I have to choose *not* to do in order to invest less or more to change this bucket?

_____
_____
_____

2. BUCKET (Priority): _____ ☐ Too Full or ☐ Too Empty

Small, Simple Steps. What are some small, simple steps I can take to change this bucket?

_____
_____

Synergize. How could I synergize with other priorities to change both buckets with one activity/effort/resource?

_____
_____

Obstacles. What blocks my intention to invest more or less time, energy, and resources to empty or fill this bucket? How can I overcome these obstacles?

_____
_____

Choices. What would I have to choose *not* to do in order to invest less or more to change this bucket?

_____
_____
_____

PRIORITIES REALITY CHECK TRACKING LOG

DAY	APPLICATION Which priority bucket did I <u>under</u> fill today? Which priority bucket did I <u>over</u> fill today?	IMPACT What was the impact of overfilling or under filling my priority bucket on me, others, the situation?
Day 1		
Day 2		
Day 3		
Day 4		

PRIORIITES REALITY CHECK TRACKING LOG

DAY	APPLICATION Which priority bucket did I under fill today? Which priority bucket did I over fill today?	IMPACT What was the impact of overfilling or under filling my priority bucket on me, others, the situation?
Day 5		
Day 6		
Day 7		

INSIGHTS - What patterns or benefits emerged?

_____
_____
_____
_____

COACHING GUIDELINES

Use the self-coaching process and coaching tools to create change in your Target Area. For maximum effectiveness, focus on one skill at a time. For each skill, take an *assessment* if one is available, complete a *coaching worksheet*, practice high road and low road techniques, and track your application of the skill over a seven day period using a *tracking log*.

Select One Skill. Consider which skill would make the greatest difference in your current life circumstances if you used it more frequently and effectively. It is easier to build new habits if you focus on one change at a time. Select the *one skill* in this chapter that is your highest priority:

- Leverage Strengths
- Align Actions with Values
- Align Actions with Priorities

STEP 1. ASSESS. Assess the need and benefits of practicing this particular skill. Identify reasons why this particular skill will improve your Target Area and positivity ratio. Assess your current mastery level of the skill. Use one of the on-line assessment tools if one is available for the skill. The Coaching Worksheets will also help you assess your need and benefits of using the skill.

Assessments—Questionnaires that assess your current skill level and provide data on your progress.
(Available online at www.authentichappiness.org)
- Brief Strengths Test
- VIA Survey of Character Strengths
- VIA Strength Survey for Children

STEP 2. PLAN. To create an action plan, understand how a technique can help you improve your Target Area and build greater mastery of a skill. Next, consider how you can apply it to your own situations.

Coaching Worksheets—Tools for learning and creating an action plan for practicing the techniques.
- *Personal Mentor Journaling Worksheet*
- *Personal Best Leadership Experience Journaling Worksheet*
- *Identify Core Strengths Worksheet*
- *Use Strengths in a New Way Worksheet*
- *Leverage Others' Strengths Worksheet*
- *Values Assessment Worksheet*
- *Values Alignment Worksheet*
- *Values Journaling Worksheet*
- *Life Buckets Worksheet*

STEP 3. PRACTICE. During the following seven days, apply the skill daily. Use both the High Road techniques and the Low Road techniques to practice the skill.

Tracking Logs—Habit forming tools to guide your efforts as you practice the techniques for seven days.
- *Identify Core Strengths Tracking Log*
- *Use Strengths in a New Way Tracking Log*
- *Leverage Others' Strengths Tracking Log*
- *Values-In-Action Tracking Log*
- *Priorities Reality Check Tracking Log*

- *Moment of Strength Visualization Tracking Log*
- *Life Reflection Visualization Tracking Log*

Meditation Guides—Low Road techniques to build the skill at the emotional or non-verbal level.
- *Moment of Strength Visualization Guide*
- *Life Reflection Visualization Guide*

STEP 4. TRACK RESULTS. In addition to systematically helping you to practice the techniques, *Tracking Logs* provide a place to note the impact of the skill on your experience. Tracking Logs help you become more aware of behaviors and patterns in yourself. They are a source of feedback so you can modify a technique to make it more effective.

MANAGE STRESS & ENERGY

*The greatest weapon against stress
is our ability to choose one thought over another.*

-William James

MANAGE STRESS & ENERGY

The energy of the mind is the essence of life. ~ Aristotle

Mindful Leaders manage their energy and stress in order to maintain high levels of physical, mental, and emotional well-being. They challenge their thoughts to stay in touch with reality, they identify their emotions and emotional triggers and manage their responses, and they consciously monitor and manage their energy.

Mindful Leaders not only manage their own stress effectively to maintain peak mental and physical performance, they also monitor the stress levels of their colleagues and team members and help to create an environment that reduces stress and encourages high levels of energy and creativity. The goal is to waste as little energy as possible on reactivity and worry, and to direct emotional and physical energy toward goals, values, relationships, and tasks.

MANAGE STRESS AND ENERGY SKILLS PREVIEW

Introduction—Thoughts and Stress
- Case Study: Observing Mindful Leadership—Arianna Huffington
  - *Exercise: Mindful Leadership Case Study Questions*
- Thoughts are a Source of Stress
- Information Processing Chain

Skill 12: CHALLENGE THOUGHTS
- Benefits of Challenging Thoughts
- Overcoming Mindlessness & Unconscious Bias
- How to Challenge Thoughts: The 3 C's Technique
  - *3C'S Worksheet & Tracking Log*
- Neutralize Thoughts—An Alternate Strategy to Challenging
- Leaves on a Stream Meditation
  - *Leaves on a Stream Meditation & Tracking Log*

Skill 13: IDENTIFY EMOTIONAL TRIGGERS
- Emotional Equations
- Examples—Anxiety, Anger, Sadness
- Triggers & Reactions Chart
  - *Emotional Triggers Worksheet & Tracking Log*
- Take a S.E.A.T. to Overcome Emotional Hijacking
  - *Take a S.E.A.T Meditation & Tracking Log*

Skill 14: MANAGE ENERGY
- Build New Lifestyle Habits
- Sleep Adequately
  - *Sleep Tracking Log Tracking Log*
- Body Scan Meditation
  - *Body Scan Meditation & Tracking Log*
- Eat Mindfully
  - *Eat Mindfully Tracking Log*
- Exercise Regularly—Move
  - *Exercise Regularly Tracking Log*
- Meditate Daily
  - *Meditate Daily Tracking Log*

Coaching Guidelines

CASE STUDY: OBSERVING MINDFUL LEADERSHIP

ARIANNA HUFFINGTON
President & Editor-in-Chief Huffington Post Media Group

We think, mistakenly, that success is the result of the amount of time we put in at work, instead of the quality of time we put in. ~ Arianna Huffington

Arianna Huffington is co-founder and editor-in-chief of the Pulitzer-Prize winning Huffington Post, nationally syndicated columnist, radio host, and best selling author of 14 books. Recently, when asked what is her number one piece of advice on productivity, she said, "*Get more sleep.*"

Get more sleep! What about multiprocessing, time management, more technology, more apps, more personal assistants, more tweets, more projects, more deadlines? Huffington has done all of those things during a varied and accomplished life, but her message now is that they don't work any where near as well as we think they do. More importantly they don't necessarily lead to the life that we might really want to lead.

Arianna Huffington is a *sometimes-mindful-leader* who has needed to be reminded more than once in her life of the importance of mindfulness. She recalls the latest reminder in the opening to her recent book entitled *Thrive: The Third Metric to Redefining Success and Creating a Life of Well-Being, Wisdom, and Wonder*. As she tells it, she was in her home office, lying on the floor in a pool of blood when she got her wake-up call. Her "aha" moment included a broken cheekbone and a nasty gash over her eye as a result of a fall brought on by fatigue.

She writes, "I had collapsed from exhaustion and lack of sleep." While she was in the waiting room of her doctor's office, she found herself asking questions about what kind of life she was leading. As she went from brain MRI to CAT scan to echocardiogram to find out if there was any underlying medical problem beyond exhaustion, she asked herself, "is this really what success feels like?" Those questions led to the writing of her book, *Thrive*, and a commitment to take a more mindful approach to her work and her leadership.

Huffington's list of life accomplishments is impressive. She was born Arianna Stassinopolus in Athens, Greece on July 15, 1950. She moved to Great Britain when she was 16 and graduated from Cambridge University with a masters in economics. She became president of the celebrated debating society, the Cambridge Union, when she was 21. She began writing books, and in 1974, with Random House, she published her first book entitled *The Female Woman*, which brought her into the limelight. She moved to the United States in 1980, and in 1981 she wrote a biography of Maria Callas, *Maria Callas—the Woman Behind the Legend*. In 1989 she wrote a bestselling biography of Pablo Picasso, *Picasso: Creator and Destroyer*. She has published 14 books on a variety of topics ranging from feminism to corporate America to politics.

In 1994, she rose to national prominence during the unsuccessful Senate bid of her oil-millionaire husband, Congressman Michael Huffington, who ran against incumbent, Diane Feinstein. She has continued her involvement in politics and over time has shifted from her previous right-leaning persuasions to the left. She took a brief run at the California governorship in 2003.

In May, 2005, she co-founded *The Huffington Post*, a news and blog site that rapidly became one of the most widely-read, frequently-cited, and linked-to media brands on the Internet. By 2008, *The Observer* ranked The Huffington Post as the most powerful blog in the world. In 2011, Huffington sold the site to AOL for more than $300 million, and she became president and editor-in-chief. The site won a Pulitzer Prize for national reporting in 2012. Huffington serves on the boards of EL PAÍS, PRISA, the Center for Public Integrity, and the Committee to Protect Journalists. She has been recognized in various media outlets for her accomplishments, including: *Time* Magazine's 100 List—A collection of the 100 most influential people in the world; *Forbes'* 100 List—The World's 100 Most Powerful Women.

It is easy to understand how Huffington could lose track of a mindful approach to work. She is a professed workaholic, and has to discipline herself to slow down and take time for other things in life. Her current message is simple, but it contains advice that can be difficult to follow. Her message: "Our relentless pursuit of the two traditional metrics of success—money and power—has led to an epidemic of burnout and stress-related illnesses, and damage to the quality of our relationships, family life, and paradoxically, our careers. We need a new way forward."

In a commencement address that Huffington gave at Smith College, she compared the drive for money and power to two legs of a three-legged stool—they may hold us up temporarily, but at some point we will topple over. And more and more successful people are toppling over. The third leg that is needed, the third metric, includes our well-being, our ability to draw on our intuition and inner wisdom, our sense of wonder, and our capacity for compassion and giving.

She points out, "Our eulogies celebrate our lives very differently from the way society defines success. They don't commemorate our long hours in the office, our promotions, or our sterling PowerPoint presentations as we relentlessly raced to climb up the career ladder. They are not about our resumes—they are about cherished memories, shared adventures, small kindnesses, and acts of generosity, lifelong passions, and the things that made us laugh."

Her message is aimed at all of us, but particularly at people like herself—"entrepreneurs with big ambitions." She advises, "building and looking after our financial capital is not enough. We need to do everything we can to protect and nurture our human capital as well."

Huffington says, "Looking at the Western workplace today, we see two very different and competing worlds.
- In one world, we see a clear manifestation of burnout disorder: a business culture single-mindedly obsessed with quarterly earnings and maximizing short-term profits.
- In the other world, we see an increasing recognition of the effects that workplace stress can have on the well-being of employees—and on a company's bottom line. There is growing evidence that the long-term health of a company's bottom line and the health of its employees are, in fact, very much aligned, and that when we treat them as separate, we pay a heavy price, both personally and collectively."

When asked about the impact of technology on our well-being, wisdom, wonder, and giving, Huffington discusses the paradox of technology. She points out, "Technology, especially when it becomes addictive, makes it harder to connect with ourselves, our wisdom, and our ability to wonder and to give. Our hyper-connectedness is the snake lurking in our digital Garden of Eden. As Kelly McGonigal, a Stanford psychologist, puts it, 'People have a pathological relationship with their devices.'"

She specifies a number of symptoms. "We tend to our Facebook friends more than our real friends. We text while we watch our children. We tie our mental well-being to our inbox. We skimp on sleep to catch up on work."

Continuing on the subject of technology, she goes on to say, "At the same time, paradoxically, one of the biggest growth sectors for tools to help us to deal with technology is...technology. The first stages of the Internet were about data and more data. But now we have plenty of data—indeed, we're drowning in it—and all the distraction we could ever hope for. Technology has been good at giving us what we want, but not always what we need. So now, many in the tech world have realized there's a growth opportunity for applications and tools that help us focus and filter all that data and distraction."

What is her advice to the burned out casualties of work-place stress? She prescribes the following set of activities:
- Meditation
- Mindfulness
- Yoga
- Getting enough sleep
- Unplugging
- Renewing ourselves
- Giving back

Her research has indicated that millennials are the most stressed out generation. Her top three career advice tips to millennials are:

1. Don't be afraid to fail.

2. Don't just go out there and climb the ladder of success. Instead, redefine success, because the world desperately needs it.

3. And finally, remember that while there will be plenty of signposts along your path directing you to make money and climb up the ladder, there will be almost no signposts reminding you to stay connected to the essence of who you are, to take care of yourself along the way, to reach out to others, to pause to wonder, and to connect to that place from which everything is possible.

This is good advice, not just for millennials, but also for anyone at any stage in their career. How well is Huffington taking her own advice? Like many of us who have done our homework on the positive benefits of exercise, or diet, or sleep, or meditation, the challenge continues to be practicing the habits that we know will make our lives better.

Huffington has set up yoga and breathing classes at the office for her company. She has installed two nap rooms in the company offices. She has instituted an Email policy where no one has to return an Email in the evenings after they have left the office—even one that she sends them in the middle of the night. She has shifted her editorial focus to include more stories that relate to thriving. She says that instead of the classic journalistic emphasis on negative news and "If it bleeds, it leads," she has instructed her staff to write more stories about positivity and possibility. Instead of "copy-cat crisis," she is trying to encourage "copy-cat solutions" by featuring stories about problems solved and obstacles overcome.

Huffington has made little adjustments in her own life style. She no longer turns on the TV news the minute she walks into the house. She doesn't charge her phone next to her bed. She tries to meditate, even for a few minutes a day. She sleeps more. But, a lifetime of workaholic habits is hard to change, even for *sometimes-mindful-leaders*. People that work with her say that she still has a tendency to work all the time, and that she still double books flights in case she changes her mind about when exactly she wants to leave. People in the office like the yoga and breathing classes, but often skip them when they have one of her deadlines to meet.

Huffington may not ever embody all of the qualities of the mindful leader that she outlines in her books. She may never take the time to practice all of the disciplines that lead to well-being, the ability to draw on our intuition and inner wisdom, the sense of wonder, and the capacity for compassion and giving. Like all of us, she is human, and as humans, our actions often fall short of our ideal vision.

In this way, she is probably a reasonable role model for many of us who aspire to mindful leadership. Mindful leadership takes mindfulness, and none of us can be totally mindful in all situations at all times. Nor, can most of us be totally disciplined in practicing many of the habits that lead to thriving—Meditation, Mindfulness, Yoga, Getting enough sleep, Unplugging, Renewing ourselves, and Giving back.

We can, however, do our best to build more of these thriving activities into our lives as we continue to strive for higher levels of awareness in the moment, and for higher levels of well-being, wisdom, wonder, and compassion.

Footnote: The information on Arianna Huffington and quotes used in this case study can be found in the following sources:

• *Thrive: The Third Metric to Redefining Success and Creating a Life of Well-Being, Wisdom, and Wonder*, by Arianna Huffington. Harmony Books, 2014.
• *Arianna Huffington, Political Scientist, Journalist.* www.biography.com/people/arianna-huffington-21216537.
• *Arianna Huffington*, Wikipedia, the free encyclopedia. en.wikipedia.org/wiki/Arianna_Huffington. 4/14/15.
• *Maharishi Arianna, Atop AOL, hiring and borrowing freely from the old media, a new age news guru is building her grandest temple yet.* By Vanessa Grigoriadis. New York Magazine. Nov 20, 2011.
• *Arianna Huffington Is Just Like Us.* By Hanna Rosin. Slate. April 25, 2014. www.slate.com
• *Arianna Huffington: Why Entrepreneurs Should Embrace The Third Metric.* By Dan Schawbel. Forbes. March 25, 2014. www.forbes.com
• YouTube. *Arianna Huffington Talks Thrive* (The Ellen Show)

EXERCISE: MINDFUL LEADERSHIP CASE STUDY QUESTIONS

One of the ways to build a better understanding of the skills of mindful leadership is through role models who demonstrate the skills of mindful leadership in their actions. In the *Observing Mindful Leadership Case Studies*, we examine the accomplishments, the actions, the statements, and sometimes the thoughts and emotions of well-known leaders. The cases can help us to see a diversity of mindful leaders operating in many different types of environments, and help us to see how different leaders and different personalities practice the skills of mindful leadership. Use the following questions to help you to better understand this mindful leader.

1. AWARENESS IN THE MOMENT. Mindful Leaders are self-aware of what they are thinking, feeling, and doing, and are aware of what is going on around them. They tune in to the present, to themselves, to their surroundings, and to others. They listen mindfully for information and for emotions and practice global listening. They focus first on determining what is real, before attempting to alter reality.

What can you observe from the writings, statements, and actions of the leader in this case study that demonstrate the skills of awareness in the moment?

_____

_____

_____

_____

_____

_____

_____

_____

_____

2. POSITIVITY & POSSIBILITY. Mindful Leaders are more focused on the positive and the possible than on the negative and impossible. They remain aware of the failures, the risks, the dangers, the realities, and the downsides, but they practice the discipline of thinking in terms of the positives, the opportunities, the probabilities, the options, and the alternatives. Mindful Leaders are aware of the power of positivity to broaden and build positive potential, to encourage novel thoughts and actions, and to inspire productivity and creativity in themselves and others.

What can you observe from the writings, statements, and actions of the leader in this case study that demonstrate the skills of positivity and possibility?

_____

_____

_____

_____

_____

_____

_____

_____

_____

3. POSITIVE RELATIONSHIPS. Mindful Leaders are aware of the power and importance of positive relationships, put conscious time and effort into the development of positive networks, and cultivate empathy, deep dive conversations, and win-win solutions with others. They recognize that some positive conflict can be productive, but go out of their way to avoid negative conflict escalators that thwart communication and cooperation. They take charge of their emotions and responses and work hard to build community and engagement.

What can you observe from the writings, statements, and actions of the leader in this case study that demonstrate the skills of positive relationships?

_____
_____
_____
_____
_____

4. AUTHENTICITY & INTEGRITY. Mindful Leaders are often respected for their authenticity and integrity. Their authenticity is reflected in the truthfulness of their intentions, behaviors, and commitments. Their integrity is reflected in their honesty, their strong moral principles, and their ability to live by those principles. Mindful Leaders are clear on their values and their priorities and make decisions and take actions based upon these values. They are aware of their strengths and look for ways to leverage their strengths in the pursuit of their goals and in the service of others.

What can you observe from the writings, statements, and actions of the leader in this case study that demonstrate the skills of authenticity and integrity?

_____
_____
_____
_____
_____

5. MANAGE STRESS & ENERGY. Mindful Leaders manage their energy and stress in order to maintain high levels of physical, mental, and emotional well-being. They challenge their thoughts to stay in touch with reality, they identify their emotions and emotional triggers and manage their responses, and they consciously monitor and manage their energy.

What can you observe from the writings, statements, and actions of the leader in this case study that demonstrate the skills of manage stress and energy?

_____
_____
_____
_____
_____

6. RESILIENCE. Mindful leaders work to develop resilience—the capacity to recover from difficulties and adversity. They focus on the heroic rather than the debilitating aspects adversity; they let go of perfectionism and shortcomings and focus on the possible and potential; and they practice compassion and self-compassion.

What can you observe from the writings, statements, and actions of the leader in this case study that demonstrate the skills of resilience?

_____
_____
_____
_____

INTRODUCTION: MANAGE STRESS & ENERGY

To achieve excellence, we must first understand the reality of the everyday, with all its demands and potential frustrations.
–Mihalyi Csikszentmihalyi, *Finding Flow*

Stress is estimated to cost American businesses up to $300 billion a year according to a recent report by the World Health Organization. With nearly half of all American workers suffer from moderate to severe stress while on the job, it is referred to as the "health epidemic of the 21st century". It impacts not only health but also productivity. Two-thirds of employees report that they have difficulty focusing on tasks at work because of stress. According employee reports, stress was responsible for errors and/or missed deadlines (21 percent), trouble getting along with co-workers/superiors (15.5 percent), missed days (14.9 percent) and lateness (14.4 percent).

Stress seems to be a fact of modern life and our business environment. A Northwestern Mutual Life Insurance study reported that 7 out of 10 American workers indicated that job stress caused frequent health problems and made workers less productive. In the study, 46% of employees reported that their job was very stressful, 34% thought of quitting their jobs, and 14% actually left because of stress. In California, the number of workers' compensation claims for mental stress increased by almost 700% over eight years.

Leaders need to not only manage stress effectively themselves, but also monitor levels and coach their team members and organization on how to manage stress. Fortunately, effective techniques for stress management are easily learned and when practiced over time, they make a difference.

THOUGHTS ARE A SOURCE OF STRESS

I will use my thoughts wisely. I will respect their power. –Deepak Chopra

In his 1994 book entitled "*Why Zebras Don't Get Ulcers*," Stanford University biologist Robert M. Sapolsky highlights the difference between chronic stress and episodic stress. He points out that unlike humans, animals in the wild experience episodic stress like a zebra fleeing from a lion. Because the stressful event occurs and ends quickly the harmful effects of stress do not build up. For example, zebras don't ruminate over why it happened, what it means to be chased by a lion, and personalizing the experience, asking, "Why me? What does it say about me that the lion chased me and not the other herd members?" Humans on the other hand, carry stressful events and remember, reflect, and predict worrisome outcomes that may or may not happen.

Some estimate that we have at least 30,000 thoughts per day. If that is correct, then calculations suggest we have 210,000 thoughts per week, 10,920,000 thoughts per year, and by the time we are fifty years old we have had approximately 546,000,000 thoughts.

Cognitive psychology research suggests that we tend maintain thought patterns, biases, and mental frameworks, which then produce similar thoughts each day. If we are having essentially the same 210,000 thoughts from week to week, it might be a good idea to monitor the degree to which our thoughts are positive, beneficial, constructive as opposed to negative, counterproductive, and destructive. Indeed, thoughts are the fabric of our day-to-day experience.

When we take a step back from the mind and notice the content of thoughts, what becomes evident is that the mind is constantly creating relationships and attributions, determining patterns, and making snap judgments. Cognitive scientists explain that the mind is designed to make sense of things, to determine cause and effect, to explain why something happened and predict what will happen next. In the evolutionary sense, there was and still is tremendous survival benefit to a mind that can deftly monitor and understand complex environments in order to minimize threat and optimize opportunity. The mind's job is to create stories.

INFORMATION PROCESSING CHAIN

We call the process of formulating these attributions and their subsequent effects on emotional states and actions as the Information Processing Chain. Essentially, all bits of information get processed in this predictable manner.

First, an event occurs and is perceived through the sensory system.

Second, the mind interprets that event.

Third, this interpretation triggers an emotion, and finally the interpretation and emotion are used to formulate a plan and motivate action.

The process happens in milliseconds and is the same in simple as well as highly complex situations.

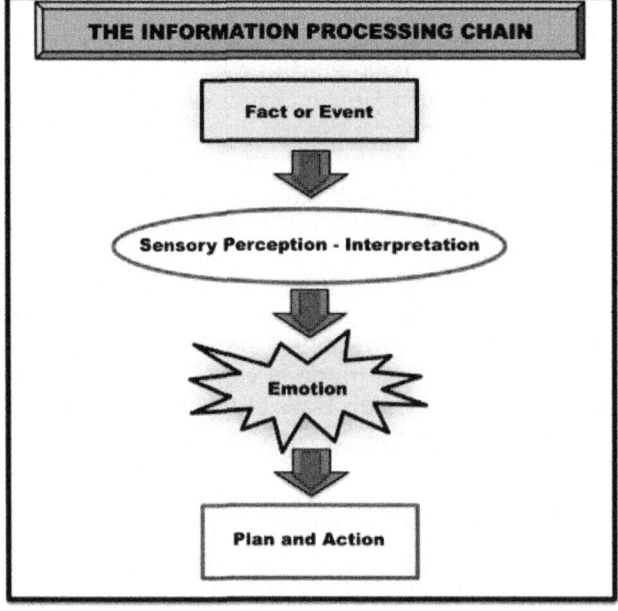

For example:

- **Fact or Event**—*A coiled dark object lies between sticks in the forest where you are hiking.*

- **Perception**—*Your eyes detect something coiled and black on the ground.*

- **Interpretation**—*"It's a snake!"*

- **Emotion**—*Fear.*

- **Action**—*Jump back.*

Another example:

- **Fact or Event**—*An email arrived in your inbox from Lisa. She said she could not make the meeting you arranged. You had asked everyone on the team to attend.*

- **Interpretation**—*"She does not want to meet with me, because she does not respect me. She is not going to cooperate with me and will undermine my ability to do well on this project."*

- **Emotion**—*Frustration, Anxiety, Anger.*

- **Action**—*You write back and tell her firmly that she needs to attend this meeting. You remind her that your boss is very concerned about this project.*

Choice—Consciously Responding Rather Than Reacting. The essential ability in managing stress well is the capacity to monitor the steps in the Information Processing Chain and manage each step. In other words, stress management requires moving from automatic, unconscious reaction to thoughtful, intentional response and management of circumstances. The problem is that often we go on automatic pilot reacting without objectively perceiving events, and without considering the causes and consequences of situations, interpretations, emotional reactions, and actions.

Between a stimulus and a response is a space. In that space is our power to choose our response. In our response, lies our growth and our freedom. –Viktor Frankl

When mindful, we expand that space between the stimulus and response that Frankl points to. When in a mindful state, we are centered and have clarity of mind, thereby promoting a conscious, intentional choice. The techniques are designed to increase mindful thinking so that you can choose a wise response no matter what you face.

The objective of stress management skills is to regain clarity of mind to see causal factors and events themselves objectively, to manage interpretations and emotions, and access to internal wisdom to derive an effective response. Ultimately, the objective is to waste little energy on reactivity and worry and instead, quickly redirect effort toward goals, values, or whatever is meaningful in a moment. The aim is to diminish the interference of pains and problems so that you are free to re-engage with what's important to you or your objectives.

If there's not a problem, no need to worry. If there is a problem, take care of it—there's no need to worry. So don't worry. –The 16th Dalai Lama

RESEARCH ON STRESS MANAGEMENT IN THE WORKPLACE

Organizational Stress. Cooper, Dewe, and O'Driscoll review the sources and outcomes of job-related stress, the methods used to assess levels and consequences of occupational stress, and strategies that might be used by individuals and organizations to confront stress and its associated problems. One chapter is devoted to examining burnout, an extreme form of occupational stress, which has been found to have severe consequences for individuals and their organizations. The book closes with a discussion of scenarios for jobs and work in the new millennium, and the potential sources of stress that these scenarios may generate.

Cooper, C. L., Dewe, P. J., & O'Driscoll, M. P. (2001). Org anizational Stress: A review and critique of theory, research, and applications. *Foundations for Organizational Science*. California: Sage Publications.

Skill 12. CHALLENGE THOUGHTS

*The only thing I know is to question every thought I believe until
every thought ends in a question mark.*
—Byron Katie

When you feel stressed, are challenged by adversity, want to be more effective, innovate, or simply relate more objectively to reality, an essential skill is challenging thoughts. As a result, a measured, thoughtful consideration, objectivity, clarity, and a wise response rather than automatic reactivity becomes more accessible.

Even for the most conscientious, we can easily fail to realize other ways of thinking about a situation, become locked in a mindset, or become limited by our own perspective. Often managing stress and effectiveness hinge on the ability to regain objectivity and reframe a situation.

BENEFITS OF THOUGHT CHALLENGING

Challenging thoughts and beliefs before acting can increase the ability to navigate a situation well. Challenging perspective and beliefs before acting is important, because we all are prone to narrow thinking or biased perspectives. Challenging thoughts is one way to get more accurate and objective in a situation. It results in clarity of mind, better problem solving, and the ability to self-correct problematic reactions.

Challenging thoughts lessens unconscious bias, improves objectivity, diminishes assumptions, and inaccurate conclusions. Implicit biases and mindsets lead to inaccurate understanding and limit possibility for effective action.

OVERCOMING MINDLESSNESS & UNCONSCIOUS BIAS

Challenging thoughts is necessary mainly because we all are prone to mindlessness. As Ellen Langer's research shows, we easily slip into mindlessness, which is characterized by a lack of awareness, limited perspective, judgment, and rigid thinking. We fall into rigid mindsets, fail to question our perspective, and fail to notice changes and subtleties in our environment. Meanwhile, we become certain that we know and understand what's going on.

The Problem with Certainty. The problem is that we often fail to realize our perception and interpretation may be skewed. We fail to recognize that there could be multiple interpretations for any given fact or event. As illustrated with the Information Processing Chain, the interpretation influences the other downstream steps, namely which emotion is triggered, which influences the plan and/or action. If the interpretation is negative, then a negative emotion ensues. If positive, then a positive emotion is triggered. We tend to latch onto one or two interpretations without appreciating that these represent a small sample among the population of logical interpretations. Moreover, once we attach to an interpretation we rarely stop to challenge that interpretation. We tend to relate to thoughts as facts rather than as interpretations.

Don't believe everything you think.

Certainty leads to mindlessness. When we feel certain about something, we stop being interested and inquiring. We lose motivation to notice new developments, changes, or potential. Being certain can be useful in some instances, for example feeling certain about your personal values. More often, however, certainty is problematic and even dangerous. For example, when the stoplight turns green, should you be absolutely certain that it is safe to proceed into the intersection?

Mental Bias. Biases distort perceptions and hamper accuracy. They cause us to lose touch with objective reality and live in a "virtual reality" that we've created in our minds. The problem is that we fail to notice biases and carry on believing we are accurate, logical, and objective. Biases arbitrarily filter details of a situation, magnifying portions and discounting others, independent of objective importance. Thus, when looking through a biased mindset or assumption, misinterpreting events and another's intentions, words, or actions is likely. Becoming aware of and actively challenging common biases can diminish this effect. This helps us to take off the lens that distorts reality.

The more we know, the more blind we become. –Ellen Langer

In complex situations or changing circumstances, the value of maintaining some uncertainty becomes particularly apparent. While you may feel certain that you want to stay married to your spouse for the rest of your life, is it wise to feel certain that it will *just happen*? Clearly, bringing a healthy amount of uncertainty to relationships is wise, because, it motivates us to invest and remain aware that relationships evolve and require effort, intention, and commitment to growth. Research on marriages suggests, for example, that partners who stop being curious about their spouse often become less emotionally connected. Understanding that we naturally fall into inattention, mental passivity, and mindlessness can help us intentionally maintain a more active quality to our attention. A common way this inattention manifests is through unconscious biases.

We aren't there to know we aren't there. –Ellen Langer

Unconscious Bias. The mind has the exquisite ability to make snap judgments. These unconscious determinations provide survival data on what's good or bad, what's safe or unsafe, who is a friend or a threat. Essentially, monitoring the environment for threats, the mind serves its primary evolutionary imperative, "Don't get killed...don't get killed...don't get killed..." These interpretations favor survival function over accuracy. Therefore, perceptions and interpretations are biased toward the threat detection and management. Most of our biases are skewed negative. Psychologists refer to this as the Negativity Bias.

Negativity Bias—Wired to Look for Threats to Well-Being. The emotional circuitry in the brain developed early in human evolution, when ancient ancestors faced predators and other life-or-death threats. It is more advantageous when, as a species that is prey rather than a predator, living in hostile, uncertain environments to have a threat detection system that is more prone to make false positive rather than false negative errors. This is what defines the Negativity Bias.

Numerous laboratory and naturalistic studies show that we detect threat signals much more quickly and accurately than safety signals. Ancestors who assumed the noise in the bush was just the wind did not survive; ancestors who assumed the noise was a saber-tooth tiger fled to safety. Better to be safe than sorry.

No matter how evolved we see ourselves, studies show that we are prone to three errors, referred to as the Negativity Bias:
• Overestimate threats
• Underestimate resources
• Underestimate opportunities

Naturally, this negativity bias continues even in safer environments where collaboration, cooperation, and slower, measured responses are more advantageous. Like a magnet pulling metal filings, problems capture our attention and imagination. Biases are like filters through which we interpret and develop understanding of situations. Information gets filtered through our mindsets, beliefs, expectations, and assumptions

MENTAL BIASES

1. CATASTROPHIZING
- Making a problem much bigger than it actually is.
- Exaggerating the importance of an occurrence.

Example: A mistake is blown out of proportion, thinking that it has ruined all hopes of success in life.

2. "ALL OR NOTHING" THINKING
- Seeing things in black and white categories.
- Example: If performance falls short of perfect, you see yourself as a total failure.

3. SHOULD STATEMENTS
- Thinking that there is a right and a wrong way of doing things, not paying attention to fact that we select certain criteria and disregard others when evaluating a situation.
- "Musts," "should's" and "oughts" signal the presence of this rigid mindset. The problem is that this bias fails to take into account all the relevant facts, causes, and complexity of situations.

Example: "I should have been able to perform better in that meeting." (i.e., perhaps he wished to have performed better, but it was not realistic given his lack of preparation. Therefore, more accurate would be to state that he *should not* have performed better, although he *wanted* to perform well).

4. "PSYCHIC" CONCLUSIONS
Making negative interpretations and conclusion even though there is an absence of evidence.
- **Mind Reading:** Assuming you know what another is thinking without inquiry or considering direct evidence.
- **Fortune Teller Error**: Assuming you know how the future will unfold, as if it were inevitable, a forgone conclusion. Treating the future as *fait accompli*.

5. OVERGENERALIZATION
- Seeing a single negative event as representative of universal patterns.

Example: One failure is evidence of a never-ending pattern of defeat.

6. SELF-FULFILLING PROPHECY
- Expecting the future to be a certain way. The problem is that expectations direct attention, distort interpretations, and shape behavior. In that way, expectations become self-fulfilling and limit possibilities.

HOW TO CHALLENGE THOUGHTS—THE THREE C'S TECHNIQUE

The Three C's Technique is a systematic way to challenge thoughts and widen perspective. This approach can help improve accurate understanding of situations and ability to respond effectively to difficult situations. This technique is adapted from the book *Peaceful Mind* by McQuaid and Carmona.

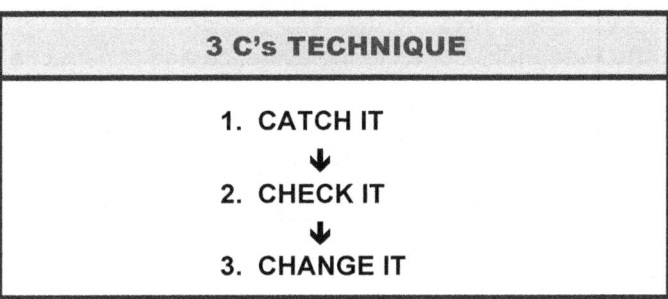

1. CATCH IT: Catch the distressing thought or belief.

Emotions. Notice the presence of distressing emotions and list them. These emotions can provide cues for the presence of negative thoughts and clues about interpretations of situations.

Identify Underlying Negative Belief. Identify the thought or belief that most strongly triggers the distress. You know you have found a core belief if there is emotional charge to the words and/or if it were true it would be truly distressing. Sometimes this step requires identifying a few negative beliefs and then choosing the most distressing one to challenge.

Bias. Look for the presence of unconscious bias. If this belief is an example of a mental bias, identify which type. Biases signal the presence of distorted thinking, alerting the need to challenge thoughts.

2. CHECK IT: Check how true and useful the thought or belief is. This step pulls on logical thinking and analysis.

Absolute Truth. Objectively, how true is this belief? How do you know this belief is absolutely true? Look for direct evidence contrary to your thought or indirect evidence like prior history and other similar situations.

- What evidence do you have in <u>support</u> of this belief?
- What is the evidence that you have <u>against</u> this belief?

Size the Problem. Often when we are in the heat of a moment, we fight for things that are not as important as they seem. When the amygdala cools down, often the seemingly large threats shrink in significance. The mind tends to blow things out of proportion. It can be useful to consider this when triggered. Ask yourself objectively,

- What is the true size of this problem?
- Is this problem actually a big deal?
- In the future, will it seem as big as it does now?

Usefulness.
- How useful is this belief?
- What would you do or how would you think if you didn't have this belief?

3. CHANGE IT: Change the thought or belief to be more consistent with the evidence you gathered.

This is not simply changing it to be more positive. It is changing it to be *more logical* and likely to be more accurate, even if you do not *feel* like it is true or cannot conclude absolute truth.

Balanced Belief Based on the Evidence. Combine the evidence and construct a more balanced belief.

Completely Alternative Explanation. Open your thinking to the possibility of alternative explanations. Considering completely different interpretations is particularly important in situations for which there is little evidence and much uncertainty.

Small Step. Ask yourself what you can do right now to take a step in a positive direction.

3C'S WORKSHEET

Catch It, Check It, Change It—Unlock mindsets and step into possibility.

Challenging negative thoughts in a systematic way can significantly reduce stress in the short term as well as long-term. It is important in the ability to overcome challenges. The purpose of this exercise is to challenge your thoughts relating to an emotionally charged situation. This situation could involve problems with coworkers, disagreements with your children, conflict in your relationships, difficulty dealing with your extended family, worry over your finances, problems with your health, etc.

SITUATION

YOUR SITUATION: Identify "Who, What, and Where" associated with the situation.

_____
_____
_____
_____

1. CATCH IT

EMOTIONS. Notice the presence of distressing emotions. List the emotions:

_____
_____

BELIEF. What is the belief that triggered these emotions? You know you have found a core belief if there is emotional charge to the words and/or if it were true it would be truly distressing.

_____
_____
_____
_____
_____

2. CHECK IT

ABSOLUTE TRUTH. Objectively, how true is this belief? How do I know this belief is absolutely, positively true?

_____
_____
_____

Evidence in Support. What evidence do I have in support of this belief?

_____
_____
_____

Evidence Against. What is the evidence that I have against this belief?

_____
_____
_____

SIZE THE PROBLEM. Objectively, how big is this problem? Will it feel like less of a big deal in the future?

_____
_____
_____

USEFULNESS. How useful is this belief? How would I act or think differently if I didn't have this belief?

_____
_____
_____
_____
_____

3. CHANGE IT

NEW BELIEF:
Balanced Belief. Given the evidence, what is a more balanced belief? If it doesn't check out, change the belief to be truer and/or more useful.

_____
_____
_____
_____

Alternative Belief. If a completely alternative explanation or way of thinking about the situation seems more accurate, what is that new, alternative belief?

_____
_____
_____

SMALL STEP. What can I do today to take one small step in a positive direction?

_____
_____
_____
_____

3C'S TRACKING LOG

SITUATION ONE (When, Where, Who, What?)

1. CATCH IT

DISTRESSING THOUGHT OR BELIEF. IS THERE A MENTAL BIAS?	EMOTIONS & INTENSITY (scale 1-10)

2. CHECK IT

HOW TRUE IS IT?	
Evidence For	Evidence Against

WHAT SIZE IS THE PROBLEM? HOW USEFUL IS IT? HOW WOULD I ACT DIFFERENTLY WITHOUT THIS BELIEF?

3. CHANGE IT

BALANCED AND/OR ALTERNATIVE BELIEF

3C'S TRACKING LOG

SITUATION TWO (When, Where, Who, What?)

1. CATCH IT

DISTRESSING THOUGHT OR BELIEF. IS THERE A MENTAL BIAS?	EMOTIONS & INTENSITY (scale 1-10)

2. CHECK IT

HOW TRUE IS IT?

Evidence For	Evidence Against

WHAT SIZE IS THE PROBLEM? HOW USEFUL IS IT? HOW WOULD I ACT DIFFERENTLY WITHOUT THIS BELIEF?

3. CHANGE IT

BALANCED AND/OR ALTERNATIVE BELIEF

NEUTRALIZE THOUGHTS— AN ALTERNATIVE STRATEGY TO CHALLENGING THOUGHTS

Just like a fish does not realize it is swimming in water, we don't realize we are swimming in thoughts. We go about our days remembering, predicting, interpreting, strategizing, explaining, judging, regretting, and so on typically without considering the content of this mental activity. The mind is essentially a word generating machine. It cannot help itself. Even during sleep, the mind generates thoughts, images, and stories.

Metacognition. The fact that the mind constantly generates thoughts warrants pausing to think about thinking. Psychologists call this "metacognition," which is defined as stepping back from thoughts, monitoring cognitive state, and reflecting on the content and quality of thinking. Monitoring mental content and quality of thinking is an important aspect of self-awareness. Although it is not necessary to monitor mental activity throughout the day, this ability enables cultivating presence, intentional way of being, and effective response. It is especially critical when things go wrong or we want something different.

Strategies for Managing Thoughts. There are two crucial and complimentary strategies for managing thoughts.

1. Challenge The Thought. The first is to challenge the accuracy of the thoughts or beliefs. This is the 3C's technique, which involves analyzing the content of the thought and evaluating the degree to which reality supports this thought.

2. Disengage from the Content. The second, which is an opposite strategy, is to disengage from the content of the thought. In this approach, it does not matter what the content is. If the thought is deemed unhelpful, thoughts are treated simply as mind chatter. They are neutralized so one becomes indifferent to the content of thinking. Thoughts are treated as meaningless mind events.

Both these strategies take into account the usefulness of the thought or belief.

Rumination—Problems stuck in the spin cycle of the mind. Rumination is characterized by repetitive thoughts that focus on a negative event, feeling, or belief. Thoughts are stuck in a spin cycle of the mind, just like a washing machine spinning clothes.

Rumination is characterized by a fixation on problems without taking action. It is associated with poor coping and problems such as pessimism, neediness, hopelessness, self-criticism, and depression.

Moreover, other people tend to respond negatively to rumination, which often makes the ruminating person feel even worse about themselves and their situation.

Mindfulness meditation on thoughts such as the Leaves on a Stream technique provide an experiential realization that thoughts are separate from self, that they are something the mind "does" but they need not define us or our experience.

Thought challenging techniques also assist in separating an individual from their thoughts, challenge the validity of those thoughts, and lead to change in focus.

The *Leaves in a Stream Meditation* practice is a technique for getting distance from thoughts. In this practice, look at your thoughts rather than from your thoughts. Although this practice may sound tedious or overly simplistic, habitually observing thoughts commonly weakens their power. It can be particularly helpful when in an emotional hijack or when chronic thought patterns have a negative effect or undermine presence. The objective is not to think more deeply about the thought, nor to suppress thoughts. The content is inconsequential.

RESEARCH—RUMINATION

Poor Problem Solving. Rumination is not associated with active problem solving. Instead, people who are ruminating remain fixated on the problems and on their feelings about them without taking action, according to Nolen-Hoeksema, Wisco, and Lyubomirsky (2008).

Maladaptive Cognitive Styles. Rumination is correlated with a variety of maladaptive cognitive styles, including negative inferential or attributional styles, dysfunctional attitudes, hopelessness, pessimism, self-criticism, low mastery, dependency, sociotropy, neediness, and neuroticism, as shown by Lyubomirsky and Nolen-Hoeksema, (1995).

LEAVES IN A STREAM MEDITATION

INSTRUCTIONS
(5 to 8 minutes)

1. FOCUS INWARD: Breathe and Center

- **Close Your Eyes**—Close your eyes to better focus your attention inward.

- **Feel Your Breath**—Focus attention by feeling your breath enter and exit your body. Breathe deep into your abdomen. Place your hand on your abdomen to feel your diaphragm rise and fall. Slowly exhale and naturally inhale.

- **Set Your Intention**—To direct your attention in this time, place, and to the objective of this meditation.

2. DIRECT ATTENTION: LEAVES IN A STREAM

- **Visualize**—*Visualize a stream with leaves floating by.* Imagine a slow-moving stream. The water flows over rocks and once in a while a big leaf floats away down the river. Imagine you are sitting beside that stream on a warm sunny day, watching the leaves float by.

- **Observe**—*Observe the leaves as thoughts passing.* Now become conscious of your thoughts. Each time a thought or image pops into your head, place it on a leaf and let it float on by. If you think in words, put them on the leaf as words. If you think in images, put the image on the leaf.

Stay beside the stream and allow the leaves on the stream to keep floating by. No need to try to make the stream go faster or slower, no need to make your thoughts go faster or slower. Just notice the thoughts or images as they arise. As soon as you notice one, just place it on a leaf and watch it float on past you down the river. Watch the leaf float down the stream and out of sight.

If the leaves disappear, if you mentally go somewhere else, or if you find that you are in the stream or on a leaf, just stop and notice that this happened. Gently return your attention to the stream once again, watch a thought come into your mind, place it on a leaf, and let the leaf float away down the stream. Keep doing this for the next few minutes.

3. REFLECT ON INSIGHTS: Breathe and Reflect
- Come back to your breath.
- Reflect on the insights or benefits you gained during this meditation.

4. MAINTAIN YOUR INNER AWARENESS: Soft Gaze and Stay with It
- Slowly open your eyes and keep your gaze soft, directed downward, and settling on a neutral object.
- Stay with the awareness you gained during the meditation.

LEAVES IN A STREAM MEDITATION WORKSHEET

After you have completed the meditation, jot down observations about what came up during your meditation. Make note of thoughts you had, feelings you experienced, bodily sensations you felt, and/or detours that you took.

1. FOCUS INWARD: To what extent could I direct attention and turn my mind when it wandered?

_____
_____

2. DIRECT ATTENTION: Leaves in a Stream. What happened as I watched the leaves on a stream?

_____
_____
_____
_____
_____
_____

3. REFLECT ON INSIGHTS: Breathe and Reflect. What insights or benefits did I gain in the meditation?

_____
_____
_____
_____
_____

4. PERSONAL APPLICATION. How and when could I use this practice to manage my internal state?

_____
_____
_____
_____
_____
_____

LEAVES IN A STREAM MEDITATION TRACKING LOG

DAY	APPLICATION What thoughts did I encounter? How did I observe these thoughts?	IMPACT What was the impact on me, others, and/or the situation?
Day 1		
Day 2		
Day 3		
Day 4		

LEAVES IN A STREAM MEDITATION TRACKING LOG

DAY	APPLICATION What thoughts did I encounter? How did I observe these thoughts?	IMPACT What was the impact on me, others, and/or the situation?
Day 5		
Day 6		
Day 7		

INSIGHTS - What patterns or benefits emerged?

_____
_____
_____

Skill 13. IDENTIFY EMOTIONAL TRIGGERS

Stress Management can be dramatically improved by understanding the origins, consequences, and purpose of emotions. This can help develop a deeper understanding of experience, which is the first step in managing our emotional experience and discovering how to intentionally choose to respond.

EMOTIONAL EQUATIONS

Each emotion has a distinctive biological signature, and each plays a unique role in our emotional repertoire. We can think of every emotion as having a predictable equation that produces it. There are three main causes and effects of each emotion:

    -Triggers   -Action Impulses   -Bodily Reactions

Triggers. A trigger is the event or stimulus that elicits an emotional response. Emotions have predictable origins, which is tied to the interpretation of an event or stimulus. For example, a perception of some form of threat and an injustice results in anger; sadness is triggered when something valued is lost; disappointment is triggered when an expected positive event fails to occur.

EMOTIONAL EQUATIONS

DISTRESSING EMOTIONS

EMOTIONS		TRIGGERS
Anger	←	Injustice/Violation + Threat
Fear / Panic	←	Present Threat
Anxiety	←	Challenge + Doubt
Frustration	←	Effort + Lack of Success
Disappointment	←	Unfulfilled Positive Expectation

PLEASANT EMOTIONS

EMOTIONS		TRIGGERS
Joy	←	Pleasant Experience
Excitement	←	Anticipation of Positive Experience
Love	←	Intimacy + Respect
Contentment	←	Satisfaction with Present
Hopefulness	←	Positive Future Potential

The intensity of the trigger typically parallels the intensity of the emotion. Imagine the minor annoyance of a short traffic jam on your way to work. It is mildly annoying and you wish you were doing something else. The intensity level of those emotions (e.g., annoyance, frustration) is mild. In contrast imagine getting caught in a heavy traffic jam as you are rushing to the hospital with a loved one who has broken their arm and is writhing in pain. The perceived threat is large, and correspondingly, the emotion's intensity will be significantly distressing.

Action impulses. An emotion's action impulse is the urge to react in a certain as a result of an emotion. Every emotion has not only a unique trigger, but it also has an associated action impulse. Emotions ignite an impulse. For example, anger creates an impulse to attack while disappointment evokes an impulse to give up.

Bodily Reactions. The bodily reaction serves the action impulse, readying the body for a particular action. Each emotion has a signature effect on the body's physical and mental systems. Mental effects include the emotion's impact on narrowing or expanding attention, alertness or sluggishness, vigilance or tuning out, and so on. The effect a particular emotion has on the body matches the action impulse.

Examples of Emotional Equations—Anxiety, Anger, & Sadness. Below are descriptions of the triggers, action impulse, and the bodily reactions for three emotions.

Anxiety Trigger: Perception of an imminent threat, anticipation of a negative event, or concern that an unwanted situation will occur in the future. In our evolutionary past, the threat might have been a tiger hiding behind a bush. These days the "threat" may be the possibility of fumbling during a presentation in a board meeting, the expectation of negative response from a loved one, or the arrival of a bill that is larger than the balance of your checking account.

Anxiety Action Impulse: The "Fight or Flight" response is associated with anxiety. This adaptive reaction enhances the ability to overcome a challenge or ward off a threat.

Anxiety Bodily Reaction: The body readies itself to fight or flee with acute and automatic mobilization of resources need for intense attention, physical agility, and burst of strength.
- Increased heart rate, respiration, and blood flow prepare the muscles for action.
- Adrenaline rushes through the body to mobilize for immediate action.
- Attention narrows, vigilance heightens, muscles tighten and perspiration increases.

Anxiety Example: Awaiting the test results from a biopsy, my sister experienced anxiety. The possibility of a malignant tumor was the imminent threat and the lack of control over this unwanted outcome together gave rise to anxiety. In our modern environment, the Fight or Flight response can help us focus on a report that is imminently due or prepare for a difficult meeting. When anxiety is too strong or chronic, however, it becomes maladaptive. Loss of sleep, nervousness, and incessant worry are examples of counterproductive reactions associated with anxiety.

Anger Trigger: A perception of a violation or injustice in addition to a perception of threat.

Anger Action Impulse: To get rid of a threat to well-being and correct the injustice.

Anger Bodily Reaction: Because anger's action impulse is to attack, the body moves into attack mode by shunting blood to the muscles, adrenaline rush to create a surge of energy, narrowing of attention on the perceived threat, and so on. Activates Sympathetic Nervous System (the Flight or Flight reaction), energy spikes, adrenaline excreted, attention narrows, thought takes on an obsessive quality, and vigilance increases..

Anger Example: When I moved across the country I sent several boxes via train. Apparently, there was theft during transit. The items had been insured, but the theft report I filed in the station was never recorded, apparently the result of foul play. Due to an apparent cover-up, I was unable to rectify the damage and my appeals rejected. I had the emotion of anger emerge as a result of the injustice of the theft and of the apparent cover-up.

Sadness Trigger: Losing something that was deemed valuable. This is highly functional, because it facilitates learning from unwanted experiences and/or helps us honor the loss. For example, mourning can be thought of as a way of honoring the deceased.

Sadness Action Impulse: To rest and reflect. Associated with introspection, closing out others, slowing down to reflect.

Sadness Bodily Reaction: A general slowing down of the physiology. Lethargy, tiredness, apathy, and decreased appetite are common. For example: When my ex-boyfriend died suddenly, I experienced sadness and grief for some time. The role of sadness was to get me to slow down and focus on the tragic loss so that I could reflect and, ultimately, honor the love I felt for him. When sadness arose, I would say to myself: *"Sadness is a way of honoring the good times and the positive role that Ron had in my life. Of course I miss him, because I valued him so much. My sadness is a way of honoring all the good that he was to me."*

Triggers Of Emotions And Reactions Chart. The Triggers and Reactions Chart describes primary emotional families and some typical triggers, bodily reactions, and action impulses. On side one of the chart are emotions that help us to survive. Side two outlines emotions that help us thrive.

TRIGGERS & REACTIONS
SURVIVAL EMOTIONS

EMOTION	TRIGGER	BODILY REACTION	ACTION IMPULSE
SURPRISE • Shock • Astonishment • Startle • Bewilderment • Confusion	• **Shock**—Unexpected Negative Event. • **Confusion**—Unclear circumstances, statements, or situations.	• Eye-widening • Increased adrenaline	• Scream. • Step back. • Take in more information.
FEAR • Apprehension • Anxiety • Concern • Edginess • Nervousness • Terror • Consternation • Fright • Panic	• **Fear and/or Panic**—A Present Threat. • **Anxiety**—A Future Threat plus Uncertainty about ability to manage it.	•Spike in adrenaline and heart-rate •Blood to shunted to extremities	• Run, Hide, Attack. • Flight, Freeze, Fight
ANGER • Fury • Resentment • Hostility • Outrage • Frustration • Irritability • Wrath • Indignation • Animosity	• **Anger**—An Injustice or Violation plus Threat. • **Frustration**—Effort plus Lack of Success.	• Seeing red, tightening muscles, quickened breath. •Shut down of non-essential body functions.	• Do something. • Increase aggressiveness. • Physical or verbal outburst.
SADNESS • Grief • Melancholy • Dejection • Sorrow • Gloom • Despair • Loneliness • Depression	• **Grief**—A loss of something or someone valued. • **Loneliness**—Perception of disconnection with others or self.	• Slowing down. • Lethargy, apathy. • Reduced appetite	• Release. • Rest. • Reflect
DISGUST • Contempt • Abhorrence • Distaste • Disdain • Aversion • Revulsion • Scorn • Disappointment	• **Disgust**—Offense to taste or moral sense. • **Disappointment**—Unfulfilled expectations. • **Depression**— Dejection. Helplessness & Hopelessness.	• Gag reflex. • Closing off of senses.	• Limit exposure to stimulus. • Push away.
SHAME • Guilt • Embarrassment • Contrition • Chagrin • Humiliation • Remorse • Regret • Mortification	• **Embarrassment**—Social situation causing self-conscious distress. • **Shame**—Breaking norms of one's culture.	• Blushing. • Lowering of head and gaze.	• Hide/Become invisible. • Not be seen.
BOREDOM • Boredom • Ennui • Complacency	• Lack of Challenge. • Lack of Stimulation.	• Yawning. • Slowing down of system	• Sleep. • Seek stimuli.

TRIGGERS & REACTIONS
THRIVE EMOTIONS

EMOTION	TRIGGER	BODILY REACTION	ACTION IMPULSE
SURPRISE • Wonder • Amazement • Astonishment	• Unexpected Positive Event.	• Eye-widening. • Increased adrenaline	• Grin • Scream in delight
EAGERNESS • Eagerness • Anticipation • Excitement	• Anticipation of Positive experience. • Future opportunities. • Positive futures identified.	Increased adrenaline and dopamine	• Get started. Go after positive stimulus
HOPEFULNESS & OPTIMISM • Hopefulness • Optimism • Anticipation • Confidence • Pride	• Belief in Positive Future. • Belief in oneself. • Belief in one's influence over life events. • Potential for positive Future.	Increased serotonin	• Smile. • Proceed ahead.
CURIOSITY • Curiosity • Interest • Fascination	• Interesting and/or Complex Circumstances. • Interesting and/or Complex People • Interesting and/or Complex Problems	Increased sensitivity to stimuli	• Explore. • Investigate.
CONTENTMENT • Contentment • Satisfaction • Fulfillment	• Fulfilled expectations. • Appreciation for current state of things. • Satisfaction with the Present.	Slowing down of system	• Relax. • Take in surroundings.
ENJOYMENT & PLEASURE • Relief • Amusement • Cheer • Delight • Contentment • Joy • Thrill • Mania • Rapture • Ecstasy	• Reward system • Satisfaction with *past* experience. • Pleasant *current* experience. • Anticipation of positive *future* experience. • Meaning and Fulfillment.	Opening and expansiveness. Often an increase in dopamine, norepinephrine	• Activate. • Approach and pursue.
LOVE • Love • Affection • Gratitude • Compassion	• Feeling of connection • Empathy and desire to relieve pain of another	Opening and expansiveness. Often an increase in dopamine, norepinephrine, oxytocin	• Approach. • Get closer to positive stimulus.

EMOTIONAL TRIGGERS WORKSHEET

Emotions help us navigate a complex world. Describing an emotional state involves articulating its triggers, action impulses, and bodily reactions. A *trigger* is an aspect of experience such as an event or an interaction that elicits an emotional response. An emotion's *action impulse* is the urge to react in a certain way when that emotion is present. The *bodily reaction* serves the action impulse, readying the body for a particular action.

Use this worksheet in conjunction with the *Triggers and Reactions Chart* to identify causes and consequences of emotions.

1. EMOTION. What is the emotion?

"*I am having the emotion of* _____."

Intensity: Rate the intensity level of the emotion (1-10, with 10 being an intolerable level of the emotion):

1   2   3   4   5   6   7   8   9   10

Location: Identify the location in your body where you are feeling the emotion.

_____
_____
_____
_____

2. TRIGGER. What could be the trigger for this emotion?

Emotion Equation. What is the emotion equation (i.e., type of variables that trigger the emotion) for this emotion? (e.g., Loss, Anticipated pleasure, imminent threat, etc.).

_____
_____
_____
_____

My Specific Trigger. What is the *specific trigger* in this situation? (See the *Triggers & Reactions Chart*).

_____
_____
_____
_____
_____

3. ACTION IMPULSE. What action does the emotion tell me to do?

To Approach. Am I being moved to *approach pleasure*, to get more out of something? (Try Harder, Get closer, Connect). What is the action impulse?

_____
_____
_____

To Avoid. Am I being moved to *avoid pain*, to get less out of something? (Fight, Flee, Give Up). What is the action impulse?

_____
_____
_____

4. BODILY REACTIONS. What are the bodily reactions that I am having?

Feelings. How does the emotion make my body feel?

_____
_____
_____

Body State. What is my body state? (e.g., tense, heavy, lethargic, energized, light)?

_____
_____
_____

Verbal & Non-Verbal Clues. What are my non-verbal and verbal expressions of the emotion? (Vocal tone, cadence, body language, facial expressions, emotionally-charged language or word choice, punctuation).

_____
_____
_____

5. INSIGHTS. What does the emotion tell me about what I want or do not want in this situation OR what is it telling me about what's important to me or a need I have?

Want. I want... OR **Don't Want.** I don't want...

_____
_____
_____

Need or What's of Importance to me.

_____
_____
_____

EMOTIONAL TRIGGERS TRACKING LOG

DAY	APPLICATION Which emotion did I observe? What was the trigger for the emotion? What was the bodily reaction? What was the action impulse?	IMPACT What was the impact of identifying triggers & responses on me and my response to the situation?
Day 1		
Day 2		
Day 3		
Day 4		

EMOTIONAL TRIGGERS TRACKING LOG

DAY	APPLICATION Which emotion did I observe? What was the trigger for the emotion? What was the bodily reaction? What was the action impulse?	IMPACT What was the impact of identifying triggers & responses on me and my response to the situation?
Day 5		
Day 6		
Day 7		

INSIGHTS - What patterns or benefits emerged?

_____
_____
_____
_____
_____

TAKE A S.E.A.T.

Work with your emotions, not from your emotions.

"E-motions" do just that—they put us in *motion*. Their job is to alert, inform, motivate, and move us to action. Emotions communicate with us through sensations, through pleasure and pain. This is why it is difficult to not respond to emotions—their job is to make us listen. As the adage says, "pain is the greatest motivator." It goes against our evolutionary instincts to not react to our emotions. Sometimes, however, the effective and wise response depends upon doing just that. This requires the ability to tolerate the discomfort and "ride it out." The challenge is that simply avoiding emotions or trying to will the emotion away make emotions rebound.

Emotions essentially are bodily events. They are physiological responses to stimuli that have evolved to pull us away from danger ("flight or fight") and push us toward rewards. An emotion is basic physiological state characterized by predictable bodily changes (Critchley, 2009). There are emotion-specific autonomic response patterns. Individuals differ in their ability to detect these bodily responses.

EMOTIONAL HIJACKING

When a threat is perceived, the body and mind prepare for fight or flight, shutting down higher order thinking for later, when safer circumstances return. This is what we refer to as "emotional hijacking". In this state, the mind and body go into emotional reactivity, often characterized by impulsivity, highly focused and narrow thinking, and hyperawareness to change. The arousal in the mind and body during an emotional hijack is useful when one must fight off a threat to survival.

Instinctive reactions may be wise in certain circumstances and successfully perform their original survival functions. However, we usually do not have a need to fight or run away from dangers of the kind faced by our prehistoric ancestors. We need to be aware of how the primitive response in the brain's emotional center precedes all rational evaluation and response.

FOUR STEPS TO PROCESSING EMOTIONS: TAKE A SEAT

When emotions are strong and overwhelming or distorting our perceptions it probably is time to pause, step back from the situation, and experience these emotions without reacting. This enables us to respond thoughtfully and intentionally rather than react automatically. When we successfully do this, we improve our ability to productively problem-solve and ultimately reach our objectives.

FOUR STEPS TO PROCESSING EMOTIONS
Stop
Expand
Ask
Take care

Stop: When you notice that you have an emotion welling, stop and take a few deep breaths. This counters the physiological activation that emotions create, and gives space to come back into your center. A common technique for women in labor and childbirth is to breathe through the pain. By breathing deeply, the neuromodulators at the base of the diaphragm, in your lower abdomen, get activated. This ignites the parasympathetic nervous system, which is the relaxation response. Slowing the exhale also ignites the parasympathetic nervous system.

Expand: Experience your emotions are bodily sensations. Fundamentally, that is what emotions are. We experience them as physical sensations, it's just that we tend not to think of them that way. Just like physical pain, emotional pain can be worsened by the way we attend to it. Mindfully experience them as temporary, feeling the effects the emotion has on your body as neutral albeit intense sensations. Feel the physical manifestations of the emotion without judging them as bad or even painful. They are like energy currents that run through the body. Feel the emotion flowing throughout your body, experiencing it with full presence and attention.

Bravely approach and be still with the emotions without resisting them or demanding that they go away. Counter the impulse to get away from pain by going closer to it. Experience the emotion as a bodily sensation and amplify the sensations.

Ask: Emotions have a job to do and they want you to listen. There is usually some wisdom, a legitimate human need under the emotions, even old and tired emotions. Ask yourself what the deeper longing is. Or, what it is that you wish for, deeply desire, or feels threatened in this situation.

Thank your "inner warrior."

Take care: Like gentle (or fierce) warriors, emotions are there to help us. They have an evolutionary benefit. They use pain to wake us up and ensure we pay attention to their message. Honor and essentially thank these emotions—they are trying to help you. Appreciate that they are coming from your survival instinct.

When dealing with emotions it is important to listen to their message and take some type of action. This might simply be offering yourself compassion in a time of emotional pain, soothing your raw nerves, breathing into a weary body or heart. Or it might mean heeding wise action to change a situation, make a direct request, protect or advocate for yourself.

When to Take a SEAT. Take a SEAT with your emotions rather than react to emotions when you recognize that the emotions are:

- *Not useful.* You determine the emotions are not useful or actually getting in your way.

- *Obstructing performance.* You determine that optimal performance or well-being would occur at a lower level of emotional arousal.

- *Creating prolonged negative moods.* You determine that distressing emotions are persistent and driving prolonged negative moods.

- *Persistent.* You have challenged your thoughts or used other coping and yet your emotional state persists. It might be that there is a deeper message that is not attended to or simply that the emotions are a conditioned response and need to be processed through.

TAKE A S.E.A.T. MEDITATION

When distressing emotions show up we usually want to make them go away as soon as possible. They are by their very nature painful. An important step in processing emotions is allowing them space to exist. It is like holding them rather than avoiding them. The very act of allowing them to exist for a moment can be transformative. This is a Low Road practice that is often counterintuitive.

- *Gently approach and be still with the emotions without resisting them or pushing them away.*
- *Counter the impulse to get away from pain by going closer and expanding it.*

Often it is our resistance to the emotion that maintains it. You may have heard the phrase, "If you can't have it, you've got it." By allowing the distress to just be there, you are not adding secondary emotional reactions to it. Then the emotion can naturally fade away. In this meditation, experiment with feeling the effects the emotion has on your body as neutral sensations, noticing only the intensity and characteristics of the sensations. The aim is to feel the emotion flowing throughout your body and experiencing it with full presence and mindful attention.

Choose an emotion that is of moderate distress, not extreme distress. This is probably not the time to process traumatic or overwhelming emotions. As Rick Hanson says, "Make sure that you will be able to swim back from the deep end of the pool." Do not go out so far that you cannot get back on your own. Use your own inner wisdom to decide what to make contact with and how far to go into an emotion.

INSTRUCTIONS
(5 to 10 minutes)

1. FOCUS INWARD: Breathe and Center
- **Close your eyes**— Close your eyes to let your attention turn inward.
- **Feel Your Breath**—Focus attention by feeling your breath enter and exit your body. Breathe deeply with a slower exhale and natural inhale. Place your hand on your abdomen to feel your diaphragm rise and fall.
- **Set your Intention**---To direct your attention in this time, place, and to the objective of this meditation.

2. DIRECT ATTENTION: Make Contact and Take a SEAT with Your Emotion.
Make contact with an emotion you currently feel or recently felt. Words or phrases describing a difficult aspect of a situation might help you generate the emotion. Making a facial expression revealing how you feel can help make greater contact with the emotion.

<u>S</u>TOP—**Breathe into the emotion.** Come into your body. Feel the physical manifestations of the emotion in your body.

<u>E</u>XPAND—**Experience and expand without judgment**—Experience the emotion like an energy current that run through your body. Release the judgment of the emotion as bad or good, pleasant or painful. Take a break from asking yourself whether you like or don't like them. Expand the sensations by breathing into or through them, inviting it to expand throughout your body, filling every cell in your body, from finger tips to toes. Even if uncomfortable, keep going. Expand it even more. Have courageous presence with the emotion.

<u>A</u>SK—**What is the deeper longing?** What is your underlying need or wish?

<u>T</u>AKE CARE: Like gentle (or fierce) warriors, emotions are there to help us. Heed their command and take action. This might mean directing compassion, imagining warm or protection, or figuring out what wise action to take.

3. REFLECT ON INSIGHTS: Breathe and Reflect
- Come back to your breath.
- Reflect on the insights or benefits you gained during this meditation.

4. MAINTAIN INNER AWARENESS: Soft Gaze and Stay with It
- Slowly open your eyes and keep your gaze soft, directed downward, and settling on a neutral object.
- Stay with the awareness you gained during the meditation.

TAKE A S.E.A.T MEDITATION WORKSHEET

After you have completed the meditation, jot down any observations about what came up during your meditation. Make note of thoughts you had, feelings you experienced, bodily sensations you felt, and/or detours that you took.

1. FOCUS INWARD: Breathe and Center. Were you able to concentrate inward and turn your attention back to your intention for this exercise?

_____

_____

2. DIRECT ATTENTION: Take a SEAT.

S̲TOP—Breathe into the emotion. Come into your body. What did impact did stopping and breathing have?

_____

_____

E̲XPAND—Experience and expand without judgment—What was it like to experience the emotion like an energy current that run through your body? How did you attempt to expand it?

_____

_____

Experience without judgment. To what extent did you release your judgment of pleasant or unpleasant? What was the effect?

_____

_____

A̲SK—What is the deeper longing? What was your underlying need or wish?

_____

_____

T̲AKE CARE—How did or will you take care? What was it like when you directed compassion or other self-care method? Is there an action to take?

_____

_____

3. REFLECT ON INSIGHTS: Breathe and Reflect. What did you gain in the meditation?

_____

_____

TAKE A S.E.A.T. TRACKING LOG

DAY	APPLICATION What emotions did I observe? How did I Take a SEAT with these emotions?	IMPACT What was the impact on me, others, or the situation?
Day 1		
Day 2		
Day 3		
Day 4		

TAKE A S.E.A.T. TRACKING LOG

DAY	APPLICATION What emotions did I observe? How did I Take a SEAT with these emotions?	IMPACT What was the impact on me, others, or the situation?
Day 5		
Day 6		
Day 7		

INSIGHTS - What patterns or benefits emerged?

_____
_____
_____
_____
_____

Skill 14. Manage Energy

Manage your energy for a thriving body and mind.

Balance is the ability to equally distribute your time, resources, and emotional energy among the highest value priorities in your life. Sometimes, in the pursuit of our ambitions, we put off the activities that can contribute most to health, happiness, and productivity. Mindful Leaders focus on a more balanced approach.

An important aspect to stress management and sustaining peak performance is managing energy with sleep, nourishment, exercise, and meditation. This takes self-awareness, commitment, and self-discipline. This section provides several tracking records to improve awareness and increase accountability by bringing intention and a sensible plan to energy management.

Therapeutic Lifestyle Changes (TLCs). Roger Walsh of the University of California has written extensively on lifestyle and mental health. In an October 2011 article in the *American Psychologist*, he discusses that TLCs (therapeutic lifestyle changes) are key to mental health and happiness. According to extensive scientific evidence, many of these TLCs are more important in treating mental health than drugs or therapy. Below is a list of his Big Eight TLCs:

- Nutrition and Diet
- Exercise
- Relaxation & Meditation
- Time in Nature
- Recreation
- Relationships
- Service to Others
- Spiritual Involvement

Power of Positive Rituals & Habits. A ritual is a series of actions performed according to a prescribed order to accomplish a specific objective. Rituals become habits. This section provides tools to develop positive rituals around food, sleep, exercise, and meditation.

BUILD NEW LIFESTYLE HABITS

A habit is a regular tendency or practice; therefore, by their very nature habits are hard to change. A structured plan and discipline are necessary to replace old habits with new ones.

Consider using the *Build New Lifestyle Habits* process as you build new or improved habits around managing your exercise, your eating, and your sleeping.

BUILD NEW LIFESTYLE HABITS

1. **Develop Conscious Awareness of Current Rituals**
   - Keep a daily record.
   - Reflect on your experience.

2. **Set a Goal for New Rituals**
   - Decide what specific behavior you want to change.
   - Set a reasonable goal.

3. **Take One Small Step Toward Your Goal**
   - Take a small daily step.
   - Repeat the small step until it becomes a ritual.

4. **Track Your Progress**

SLEEP ADEQUATELY

It can be challenging to find the balance between living actively and vigorously and reserving time for renewal, sleep, and solitude. Many people suffer from a sleep debt resulting in fatigue, diminished alertness, and gloomy moods. While exercise elevates serotonin levels thereby improving mood, lack of sleep has the opposite effect. Not enough sleep actually decreases the levels of serotonin in the body, which can create depressed and irritable moods.

Recently, a study was conducted based on analysis of data from the Centers for Disease Control and Prevention (CDC), the Bureau of Labor Statistics, and the U.S. Census Bureau. This study of over 500,000 Americans found an extremely high correlation between a person's happiness and the amount of sleep or rest they get each day.

Interestingly, sleep ranked higher in relation to a person's happiness than having more money, more education, being fit or thin and staying employed. Having consistent restful sleep is powerfully connected to being and feeling happy.

BENEFITS OF SLEEP

Sleep makes you feel better and enhances your mood. It can also benefit your heart, weight, and mind. Some of the many benefits of sleep were recently outlined by Dr. Rapoport,, associate professor at NYU Langone Medical Center in *Health* (www.health.com).

- **Improve memory**. The mind is busy when you sleep. You strengthen memories or "practice" skills learned while you were awake through a process called consolidation.

- **Live longer.** In a 2010 study of women ages 50 to 79, more deaths occurred in women who got less than five hours or more than six and a half hours of sleep per night.

- **Curb Inflammation.** Inflammation is linked to heart disease, stroke, diabetes, arthritis, and premature aging. Research indicates that people who get less sleep (six or fewer hours per night) have higher blood levels of inflammatory proteins than those who get more.

- **Spur Creativity.** Researchers at Harvard University and Boston College found that people appear to strengthen the emotional components of a memory during sleep which may help encourage the creative process.

- **Increase Physical Performance.** A Stanford University study found that college football players who tried to sleep at least 10 hours a night for seven to eight weeks improved their average sprint time, had more stamina, and less daytime fatigue.

- **Improve Cognitive Function.** Severe and reoccurring sleep deprivation impairs learning and cognitive function. A 2010 study in the journal Sleep indicated that children between the ages of 10 and 16 who have sleep disordered breathing, snoring, or sleep apnea, and other types of interrupted breathing during sleep, are more likely to have problems with attention and learning. In another study, college students who didn't get enough sleep had worse grades than those who did.

- **Have a Healthy Weight.** Researchers at the University of Chicago found that dieters who were well rested lost more fate (56% of their weight loss) than those who were sleep deprived. Dieters in the study also felt more hungry when they got less sleep.

HOW TO SLEEP BETTER

According to Allison Harvey of the University of California, Berkeley, "Accumulated evidence has refuted the idea that sleep is merely an epiphenomenon and supports the view that sleep is an important, but understudied, mechanism" (Harvey, 2008). Below are her recommendations:

- Maintain a standard bedtime and wake time for each day.
- Get regular exercise each day; just not right before you sleep.
- No TV before bed.
- Use curtains or blinds to make your room dark.
- No food or drinks that contain caffeine several hours before bedtime.
- Take a warm bath or shower as part of your bedtime routine.
- Don't drink alcohol 2 hours before bedtime. Alcohol can interfere with your sleep patterns.
- When you go to bed, relax. If you lie awake for more than 30 minutes, get up and do some

other quiet activity away from your bed until you are ready to sleep.

Rest can help recharge our body, and proper amounts of sleep help our memory and can help us learn. We tend to fill our days with activity and have high—often unrealistic—standards for productivity. To get it all done, many people sacrifice sleep time. However, as we sleep less, we become more stressed, experience more sickness, and become more tired and less effective. Efficiency gets compromised and often we accomplish less. Proper amount of rest and sleep is beneficial to being a healthier, happier person.

Sources: National Sleep Foundation, University of Chicago, Harvard University based on a survey of more than 1,000 adults.

SLEEP TRACKING LOG

Collecting sleep records can reveal ways that we can improve sleep. Note the time that you go to bed, actually shut lights out and try to go to sleep, awake, and get out of bed. Also, record any difficulty sleeping such as taking more than five minutes to fall asleep or waking up in the night. Identify sleep conducive and possible sleep interfering actions or factors.

DEVELOP AWARENESS OF CURRENT HABITS—SLEEP TRACKING

Date	Time in bed	Time trying to fall asleep	Time awake	Time out of bed	Total # hours asleep	Difficulty sleeping? Yes/No	How do I feel in the morning?	Sleep-conducive actions or factors	Possible sleep-interfering actions or factors

SLEEP TRACKING LOG (INSIGHTS & ACTION PLAN)

INSIGHTS - What patterns emerged?

Review the *Sleep Tracking Log* results on the previous page. Identify patterns and insights.

_____
_____
_____
_____
_____
_____
_____

ACTION PLAN TO IMPROVE MY SLEEP

Set a Goal for New Rituals.

_____
_____
_____
_____
_____
_____

Small simple steps: What will I change? What is an obstacle to changing it and how will I overcome that obstacle? What is one small simple step I can take to modify this habit?

_____
_____
_____
_____
_____
_____

Personal Balance Action Plan: What will I do to make long-term changes? Where? When? How? Why?

_____
_____
_____
_____
_____
_____

EAT MINDFULLY

Mindful eating refers to choosing the foods that are pleasing to you as well as nourishing to your body. Employing your savoring skills, using all your senses to explore and experience in addition to taste, can enhance it. Mindful eating is another way to further support and stabilize your body and mind, and to make us aware of our own actions, thoughts and feelings. This can help us understand the roots of health and contentment and gain insights into our motivations.

Increased Awareness of the Effect of Food on the Body. Research studies have shown than there is a strong link between food and mood. Foods that are high in tryptophan, an important amino acid found in foods like turkey, avocados, bananas and nuts, are converted into serotonin in the brain. Omega-3 oils, mostly found in oily fish, are also found to create feelings of well-being and diminish mood swings. Avoiding foods that spike glucose levels, such as refined sugar, can also prevent or decrease food-related mood swings.

Mindful Eating Might Include:

- Becoming aware of the positive and nurturing opportunities that are available through food preparation and consumption

- Respecting your own inner wisdom in relation to food

- Acknowledging responses to food (likes, neutral, or dislikes) without judgment

- Learning to be aware of physical hunger and satiety cues to guide your decision to begin eating and to stop eating

- Considering how to achieve specific health goals in relation to food

- Being attuned to the direct experience of eating and feelings of health

- Becoming aware of the interconnection of earth, living beings, and cultural practices and the impact that food choices have on those systems

SOME TIPS TO ENCOURAGE MORE MINDFUL EATING

Dr. Susan Albers is a Cleveland Clinic psychologist and author of *50 Ways to Soothe Yourself Without Food*. Dr. Albers provides a number of suggestions for mindful eating, which include focusing on your food, taking your time, and savoring the experience. You can get many good ideas from her book.

Mindful Eating Reminders. Think about what you can do to encourage yourself to be more mindful of what you eat and how you eat. You might even make up your own list of *Mindful Eating Reminders* and put it on the refrigerator for a few weeks to help you develop the habit of eating mindfully. The list of ideas below can help to get you started with your own list for mindful eating.

1. **Plan for Meals.** Get what you need for your meals so you don't just "eat what's there."

2. **Make Healthy Food Visible.** Place healthy foods where you can see them, and eat these first.

3. **Develop a Taste for Nourishing Foods.** Leave less room for empty calories.

4. **Mindfully Cook.** Try to enjoy the process of cooking and take notice of the food. Be curious and notice the colors, the textures, and the chemistry of cooking.

5. **Make it attractive.** Try to control the surroundings where you eat. Add a flower to the table, or situate yourself where there is a view.

6. **Sit Down.** Try to avoid eating while standing up or walking.

7. Take three deep breaths. Center yourself in the present and think about your meal for a moment.

8. Express Gratitude. Give thanks before you eat.

9. Don't Multitask. Put the computer aside and focus on what you are eating.

10. Pay attention to the Food. Turn off the TV for a few minutes so that you are aware of what you eat.

11. Savor each bite. Use all five senses to heighten the enjoyment of the food.

12. Drink water. Drink water before the meal and during the meal.

13. Be optimistic. Ask yourself *How Can I* eat just enough, and not too much?

14. Don't Battle Cravings. Consciously acknowledge the craving and respond thoughtfully.

15. Be Mindful of Your Dining Colleagues. Set your own eating pace rather than conform to others.

16. Focus on Your Strengths. Healthy habits sometimes change the unhealthy ones with little effort. Ask yourself *What Am I Doing Right* about food?

17. Eat Your Favorite Food Last. Our memories encode the last bite as the best. You are less likely to reach for a treat later if you have a strong memory of enjoying your last bite.

18. Grade Your Experience. At the end of the meal ask yourself on how mindful you were about your meal. Grade yourself high if you were aware, mindful, and savored your experience. You may discover that you enjoy even quick and simple meals more if you take a few moments to be mindful of the food, the surroundings, and the process of eating.

19. Visual Reminders. Put some visual reminders around the kitchen to "Eat Mindfully."

MINDFUL EATING TRACKING LOG

Recording what you eat can be a very effective way to change eating habits. Note all food that you eat and portions. Most importantly, note how the food affected your body and emotions. Did it energize or make you feel sluggish? Did it make you feel better or worse after you finished it?

DEVELOP CONSCIOUS AWARENESS OF CURRENT HABITS & RITUALS

DATE	BREAKFAST WHAT did I eat? WHAT effect on body/emotions?	SNACK WHAT did I eat? WHAT effect on body/emotions?	LUNCH WHAT did I eat? WHAT effect on body/emotions?	SNACK What did I eat? WHAT effect on body/emotions?	DINNER What did I eat? WHAT effect on body/emotions?	SNACK What did I eat? WHAT effect on body/emotions?

MINDFUL EATING TRACKING LOG (INSIGHTS & ACTION PLAN)

INSIGHTS - What patterns emerged?

Review the *Mindful Eating Tracking Log* results on the previous page. Identify patterns and insights.

_____
_____
_____
_____
_____
_____
_____

ACTION PLAN TO IMPROVE MY EATING

Set a Goal for New Rituals.

_____
_____
_____
_____
_____
_____
_____

Small simple steps: What will I change? What is an obstacle to changing it and how will I overcome that obstacle? What is one small simple step I can take to modify this habit?

_____
_____
_____
_____
_____
_____

Personal Balance Action Plan: What will I do to make long-term changes? Where? When? How? Why?

_____
_____
_____
_____
_____
_____

EXERCISE DAILY—MOVE

We are all inundated with research and information touting the benefits of exercise. Physical exercise is not only beneficial to our bodies, but also it promotes strong mental health, including improvement in functioning for the brain and its emotional circuitry.. If you have ever gone for a run, a vigorous walk, or a worked out in the gym after a stressful day, the chances are that you noticed the positive impact of exercise on mood. Research indicates that the effects of physical activity can extend over the long term and can even help alleviate mild depression.

During exercise, chemicals are released in the brain, which are responsible for positive feelings and feeling calm. These naturally occurring neuromodulators are thought to act similar to antidepressant medication. Exercise also plays a major role in controlling the release of cortisol. Cortisol is a hormone that is responsible for increasing blood sugar and elevating blood pressure—two major health concerns. This hormone is released with stress and can cause healthy muscles to break down and compromise the immune system. Exercise reduces stress in part by helping to control levels of cortisol.

Aerobic Exercise. Aerobic, or cardiovascular exercise, improves oxygen consumption by the body. Aerobic means "with oxygen", and refers to the use of oxygen by the body in its metabolic or energy generating process. There are many types of aerobic exercises and by definition are performed at moderate levels of intensity for extended periods of time. Brisk walking, cycling, and distance running are examples. There are many recognized benefits of aerobic exercise including a stronger heart, an increase of the total number of red blood cells, improved breathing, improved muscle health, weight loss, disease reductions, improved immune system, improved mental health, and increased stamina.

Aerobic Exercise as an Antidepressant. Aerobic exercise has been shown to be just as effective as an antidepressant in alleviating mild clinical depression. In one study, men and women age 50 or older completed four months of aerobic exercise, which included cycling, walking or jogging at a moderate pace for 45 minutes three times per week. Those who did the aerobic exercise showed the same mood improvements as those taking a standard antidepressant. Six months later, however, those who exercised were less likely to have a depressive episode relapsed.

Anaerobic Exercise. Anaerobic exercise is the kind of exercise that builds power and muscle mass. Muscles trained under anaerobic conditions develop differently, which leads to greater performance in short duration, high intensity activities, which last up to 2 minutes.

The most common form of anaerobic exercise is strength exercise like weight lifting and resistance exercises. Strength training can increase bone, muscle, tendon, and ligament strength. It can also improve joint function, reduce potential for injury resulting from weak muscles, improve cardiac function, and elevate "good" HDL-cholesterol. It can improve endurance, coordination and balance, and reduce the risk of osteoporosis. It can also help maintain lean body mass, which is important for individuals attempting weigh loss.

RESEARCH ON EXERCISE AND STRESS

Strength training improves mood and confidence. Early in my doctoral studies I was a researcher on a study of the psychological effects of strength training in older adults. Our study demonstrated that participation in 12 weeks of high or low intensity strength training can improve overall physical fitness, mood, and physical self-efficacy in older adults while cognitive functioning remains constant. Favorable psychological changes in the strength-trained subjects included improvements in positive and negative mood, trait anxiety, and perceived confidence for physical capability. The treatment effects of neurocognitive functioning were not significant. Tsutsumi, T., Don, B.M., Zaichkowsky, L.D., & Delizonna L.L. (1997). Physical fitness and psychological benefits of strength training in community dwelling older adults. *Appl Human Sci.* 16(6):257–266.

Workplace Physical Activity Interventions: A Systematic Review. A review of literature reveals that workplace physical activity interventions improve coping behavior in employees. Dugdill, L., Brettle, A., Hulme, C., McCluskey, S., and Long, A.F. (2008). Workplace physical activity interventions: A systematic review. *International Journal of Workplace Health Management,* 1 (20-40).

EXERCISE TRACKING LOG

Studies have shown that keeping an exercise log is a great way to maintain a consistent workout plan. Note what type of exercise you did, the amount of time doing it, how you felt after, what you did or situational factors that helped you successfully meet your exercise goals, and any obstacles that interfered with successfully exercising or made you less successful reaching your exercise goals.

Date & Time	Type of Exercise	How do I feel after? (Rate 1-10)	What helped me follow through or initiate exercise?	Did anything get in the way of my plan?

EXERCISE REGULARLY TRACKING LOG (INSIGHTS & ACTION PLAN)

INSIGHTS - What patterns emerged?

Review the *Exercise Regularly Tracking Log* results on the previous page. Identify patterns and insights.

_____
_____
_____
_____
_____
_____
_____

ACTION PLAN TO IMPROVE MY EXERCISE

Set a Goal for New Rituals.

_____
_____
_____
_____
_____
_____
_____

Small simple steps: What will I change? What is an obstacle to changing it and how will I overcome that obstacle? What is one small simple step I can take to modify this habit?

_____
_____
_____
_____
_____
_____

Personal Balance Action Plan: What will I do to make long-term changes? Where? When? How? Why?

_____
_____
_____
_____
_____
_____

MEDITATION TRACKING LOG

Meditation can be a quiet, reflective exercise to get centered, clear and resilient. Schedule small periods of time when you let go of to do list and breathe. It can be as simple as Focusing on something you care about, taking three deep breaths, or taking a short walk. Keeping a meditation log is a great way to maintain a consistent plan. Note what type of meditation you did, the amount of time doing it, benefits you experienced, and any thoughts you had or external factors that played into encouraging or interfering with completing the meditation.

Date & Time	Meditation completed? Yes/No	Type of Meditation	Benefits that you felt from the Meditation	What helped you do the practice? What interfered?

MEDITATION TRACKING LOG (INSIGHTS & ACTION PLAN)

INSIGHTS - What patterns emerged?

Review the *Meditation Tracking Log* results on the previous page. Identify patterns and insights.

_____
_____
_____
_____
_____
_____
_____

ACTION PLAN TO IMPROVE MY MEDITATION

Set a Goal for New Rituals.

_____
_____
_____
_____
_____
_____
_____

Small simple steps: What will I change? What is an obstacle to changing it and how will I overcome that obstacle? What is one small simple step I can take to modify this habit?

_____
_____
_____
_____
_____
_____

Personal Balance Action Plan: What will I do to make long-term changes? Where? When? How? Why?

_____
_____
_____
_____
_____
_____

BODY SCAN MEDITATION

In the practice of becoming more mindful in general, a key component is recognizing the subtle ways the physical body responds to life experiences. With heightened awareness of how you physically respond to these highs and lows, you will find yourself beginning to navigate these experiences with more balance, more happiness. In this body scan exercise you are drawing awareness to sensations you may not have time to notice through everyday activities. This is a simple practice of observation and awareness using the breath and energy to heighten consciousness.

This exercise promotes relaxation and nurturing the understanding of ourselves. With raised awareness of our bodies we can more readily move energy, which promotes our overall sense of well-being and happiness. This meditation is designed to be done lying down, but you can easily do it in a seated posture.

INSTRUCTIONS
(8-10 minutes)

1. FOCUS INWARD: Breathe and Center

- **Center**—Close your eyes and turn your attention inward.
- **Anchor in your Breath**—Feel your breath fill and release your body. Breathe deeply with a slower exhale and natural inhale. Place your hand on your abdomen to feel your diaphragm rise and fall. Feel your feet as the rest on the floor. Notice the sensations on the bottom of your feet making contact with the earth. Feel your hands as they rest on your thighs. Open them and notice the sensations and invite them to relax.
- **Set your Intention**—To direct your attention in this time, place, and to the objective of this meditation.

2. DIRECT ATTENTION: Observe Presence of Body Sensations

Lower Body. Begin with your feet and toes. Become aware of the sensations you are feeling.

- Foot—The arches of your foot, the backs of your heel and ankles.
- Leg—Moving up the leg, be conscious of the back of your calves and knees.
- Thighs & Hips—Continuing up the legs to the thighs, outer hips and hamstrings.

Mid/Upper Body. Become aware of your stomach and core.

- Hands & Arms—Become aware of your fingertips and move up the forearm, the elbows, your upper arms and shoulders.
- Back & Neck—Pull your awareness through your lower back, upper back, and then up to your neck.
- Neck & Head—Become aware of your neck muscles and jaw. Relax your jaw. Allow the tongue to just rest gently, maybe on the roof of your mouth, and become aware of your cheekbones, your ears, and the sensations behind your eyelids.
- Forehead—Feel the eyebrows, relax the forehead.
- Crown of the head—Be aware of the top of your head.
- Entire Body—Once you've reached the crown of the head take a moment to then become aware of your body as a whole unique being, letting the breath flow in and out.

3. REFLECT ON INSIGHTS: Breathe and Reflect
- Come back to your breath.
- Reflect on the insights or benefits you gained during this meditation.

4. MAINTAIN INNER AWARENESS: Soft Gaze and Stay with Awareness.
- Slowly open your eyes and keep your gaze soft, directed downward, and settling on a neutral object.
- Stay with the awareness you gained during the meditation.

BODY SCAN MEDITATION WORKSHEET

After you have completed the meditation, jot down any observations about what came up during your meditation. Make note of thoughts you had, feelings you experienced, bodily sensations you felt, and/or detours that you took.

1. FOCUS INWARD: To what extent could you direct attention and turn your mind when it wandered?

_____

_____

2. DIRECT ATTENTION: Body Scan

a. Lower Body. Begin with your feet and toes become aware of the sensations you are feeling.
- Foot—The arches of your foot, the backs of your heel and ankles.
- Leg—Moving up the leg, be conscious of the back of your calves and knees.
- Thighs & Hips—Continuing up the legs to the thighs, outer hips and hamstrings.

Describe Your Experience

_____

_____

_____

_____

b. Mid/Upper Body. Become aware of your stomach and core.
- Hands & Arms—Become aware of your fingertips and move up the forearm, the elbows, your upper arms and shoulders.
- Back & Neck—Pull your awareness through your lower back, upper back, and then up to your neck.
- Neck & Head—Become aware of your neck muscles and jaw. Relax your jaw. Allow the tongue to just rest gently, maybe on the roof of your mouth, and become aware of your cheekbones, your ears, and the sensations behind your eyelids.
- Forehead—Feel the eyebrows, relax the forehead.
- Crown of the head—Be aware of the top of your head.
- Entire Body—Once you've reached the crown of the head take a moment to then become aware of your body as a whole unique being, letting the breath flow in and out.

Describe Your Experience

_____

_____

_____

_____

_____

3. REFLECT ON INSIGHTS: What insights or benefits did you gain?

_____

_____

_____

_____

_____

BODY SCAN MEDITATION TRACKING LOG

DAY	APPLICATION What did I meditate on?	IMPACT What was the impact on me, others, and/or the situation?
Day 1		
Day 2		
Day 3		
Day 4		

BODY SCAN MEDITATION TRACKING LOG

DAY	PRACTICE *What did I meditate on?*	IMPACT What was the impact on me, others, and/or the situation?
Day 5		
Day 6		
Day 7		

INSIGHTS - What patterns or benefits emerged?

_____
_____
_____
_____
_____
_____

COACHING GUIDELINES

Use the self-coaching process and coaching tools to create long-term change. For maximum effectiveness, focus on one skill at a time. For each skill, take an *assessment* if one is available, complete a *coaching worksheet*, practice high road and low road techniques, and track your application of the skill over a seven day period using a *Tracking Log*.

Select one skill. Consider which skill would make the greatest difference in your current life circumstances if you used it more frequently and effectively. It is easier to build new habits if you focus on one change at a time. Select the *one skill* in this chapter that is your highest priority:

- Challenge Thoughts
- Identify Emotional Triggers
- Manage Energy

STEP 1. ASSESS. Assess the need and benefits of practicing this particular skill. Assess your current mastery level of the skill. Use one of the on-line assessment tools if one is available for the skill. The Coaching Worksheet will also help you assess your need and benefits of using the skill.

Assessments—Questionnaires that assess your current skill level and provide data on your progress.

STEP 2. PLAN. To create an action plan, understand how a technique can help you build greater mastery of a skill. Next, consider how you can apply it to your own situations.

Coaching Worksheets—Tools for learning and creating an action plan for practicing the techniques.
- 3 C's Worksheet
- Emotional Triggers Worksheet

STEP 3. PRACTICE. During the following seven days, apply the skill daily. Use both the High Road techniques and the Low Road techniques to practice the skill.

Tracking Logs—Habit forming tools to guide your efforts as you practice the techniques for seven days.
- 3 C's Tracking Log
- Emotional Triggers Tracking Log

- Sleep Adequately Tracking Log & Action Plan
- Eat Mindfully Tracking Log & Action Plan
- Move—Exercise Daily Tracking Log & Action Plan
- Meditate Daily Tracking Log & Action Plan

- Leaves in a Stream Meditation Tracking Log
- Take a S.E.A.T. Meditation Tracking Log
- Body Scan Meditation Tracking Log

Meditation Guides—Low Road techniques to build the skill at the emotional or non-verbal level.
- Leaves in a Stream Meditation
- Take a S.E.A.T. Meditation
- Body Scan Meditation

STEP 4. TRACK RESULTS. In addition to systematically helping you to practice the techniques, *Tracking Logs* provide a place to note the impact of the skill on your experience. Tracking Logs help you become more aware of behaviors and patterns in yourself. They are a source of feedback so you can modify a technique to make it more effective.

RESILIENCE

*Success is not final, failure is not fatal:
it is the courage to continue that counts.*

~ Winston Churchill

RESILIENCE

A good half of the art of living is resilience. ~ Alain de Botton

Mindful leaders work to develop resilience—the capacity to recover from difficulties and adversity. They focus on the heroic rather than the debilitating aspects adversity; they let go of perfectionism and shortcomings and focus on the possible and potential; and they practice compassion and self-compassion.

Mindful Leaders develop resilience in themselves and others. Life's infernos leave some people buried in the ashes while others emerge flourishing. The secret is in how one responds. Hardships inevitably arise, so part of being prepared for them is building resilience before they happen. This serves like an emotional bank account that can be drawn upon during the hard times.

Essentially, resilience is having the capacity to acknowledge the difficulty and refocus on the positive and possible. This shift of perspective is profound and paves the way for recovering from adversity, for growth, and ultimately, for developing confidence in one's ability to manage the challenges that will inevitably arise. The goal of resilience is to thrive.

RESILIENCE SKILLS PREVIEW

Introduction—Resilience
Case Study: Observing Mindful Leadership—Arianna Huffington
Exercise: Mindful Leadership Case Study Questions

Skill 15: LET GO OF PERFECT.
Pitfalls of Perfectionism
Roots of Perfectionism
How to Let Go of Perfect: Cultivate Satisfaction
Let Go of Perfect Worksheet & Tracking Log

Skill 16: TELL HERO STORIES
Hero Story Model: The Hero's Journey
How to Tell a Hero Story
Hero Story Worksheet & Heroic Acts Tracking Log
Resilience Meditation
Resilience Meditation & Tracking Log

Skill 17: SELF-COMPASSION
Three Components of Self-Compassion
Research on Self-Compassion
Guided Self Compassion Meditations
Four Steps to Self-Compassion
Self-Compassion Worksheet & Tracking Log
Self-Compassion Meditation
Self-Compassion Meditation & Tracking Log

Coaching Guidelines
Mindful Leadership Self-Assessment

STANFORD SERIES: Positive Psychology and the Keys to Sustainable Happiness

CASE STUDY: OBSERVING MINDFUL LEADERSHIP

DR. RHONDA CORNUM
Brigadier General & Director of Comprehensive Soldier Fitness Program

*I really believe that the glass is half full, but I got tired of that analogy. So, I decided to use this:
At any given time, the world is always half light and half dark,
and it's your choice to concentrate on what is light.*
~ Dr. Rhonda Cornum

When she opened her eyes, the world was half dark. Flight surgeon, Major Rhonda Cornum, could see her breath on that chilly Iraqi morning in February 1991, the fourth day of ground fighting during Operation Desert Storm. She was headed out on a routine flight to shuttle passengers, when her UH-60 Black Hawk crew received a call telling them that their mission had changed. A fighter pilot, Air Force Capt. Bill Andrews, had been shot down behind enemy lines and had a broken leg. They were the closest aircraft, and they needed to rescue him.

On their way to rescue the downed pilot, her Black Hawk and its two escorts came under fire. "Unfortunately, we flew right over a big bunker full of weapons, and they shot the tail off my helicopter...and they shot me," explains Rhonda. She continues, "Focusing on the positive is not the easiest thing to do when faced with certain death. If anyone ever tells you that your whole life flashes before your eyes, they must have started up a lot higher than I did. I do remember thinking, one, that I was going to die, and secondly, at least I was going to die doing something honorable."

Cornum was trapped under the wreckage of the helicopter when it hit the sand. Cornum didn't see any of her other crew members, and struggled to dig herself out of the debris. "I wasn't totally convinced that I was alive, but if I was, there was no way I was going to die in a post-crash fire." Cornum was one of three crewmembers to survive the 140-mile-per-hour-crash. Five others died in the crash. "When I came to, I knew I was either going to be a prisoner, or I was going to be dead. If there is positive spin to being held a prisoner—I do not recommend it. But, it was better than the alternative, so there is no point in dwelling on it. You're in it anyway."

Rhonda survived the crash with two broken arms, a broken finger, a bullet wound to her shoulder, a badly injured knee, and lacerations. She was dirty, bloody, and badly wounded, and she was alive, but the world of darkness had just begun. Five Iraqi soldiers, wielding AK-47s, dragged her from the wreckage. While being transported to the prison, she was sexually molested by an Iraqi Soldier. She received medical treatment only after three days of being roughly shuttled from bunkers to primitive prisons, and was held in a primitive underground jail cell for eight days in what she calls "austere" conditions.

Cornum and her fellow crewmembers were tortured and interrogated by the Iraqi Republican Guard. She was repeatedly questioned about her mission, but never revealed any classified information, not even with a rifle to the back of her head. "I could feel the cold metal barrel poking me in the back of the neck," she recalls. "I waited for the click of metal and the explosion." Fortunately, the click never came, and the Iraqi's finally transferred her to a Baghdad hospital for examination and treatment. She was rescued by the Red Cross and released in an exchange for Iraqi prisoners.

At the time of her capture, Cornum was a major, a wife of an Air Force officer, and mother of a 14-year-old daughter. In reflecting on her experience, Cornum says, "If I had not been an optimistic person, I would have given up." That optimism and resilience has helped her to recover fully from her multiple traumas, to build an impressive career, and to help hundreds of thousands of others to learn to be optimistic and resilient.

Dr. (and Brigadier General) Rhonda L. Cornum was born in Dayton, Ohio. When Cornum's work as a graduate student at Cornell brought her to the attention of the Army, she accepted a commission as an officer in 1978 in order to continue research at the Letterman Army Institute. She decided to go to medical school, but not before qualifying as a parachutist. She completed medical school at the *Uniformed Services University* in 1986, and studied combat field and aerospace medicine. She completed airborne, air assault, and flight surgeon training. In 1991, she became the first U.S. female flight surgeon to enter into combat.

After she returned to the USA, she became the first medical officer to graduate Air Command and Staff College. She published her POW experience in the book, *She Went to War: The Rhonda Cornum Story*, and dedicated the book to her five comrades who gave their lives trying to rescue a fellow aviator. She continued medical training and research in urology, commanded the 28th Combat Support Hospital at Fort Bragg, N.C., and deployed as the Medical Task Force commander to Bosnia. She was the first female commander of Landstuhl Regional Medical Center, Germany, leading medical treatment for over 26,000 injured Iraq and Afghanistan veterans. Her awards include:

- Distinguished Service Medal
- Legion of Merit with two oak leaf clusters
- Distinguished Flying Cross (only 7 women in history have received this award)
- Bronze Star
- Purple Heart
- Air Medal
- POW Medal

She was one of only two women POWs from the Gulf War, and she has become a role model for military women's strength and endurance, and the Army poster child for optimism and resiliency. Although U.S. law prohibited women from serving in combat roles, her experiences and open dialogue as a POW helped pave the way for continued Congressional expansion of military women in combat roles. Not long after Cornum's rescue in 1991, the restriction of women flying aircraft in combat was repealed, and in 1993 Congress rescinded female combat exemption laws, opening up a quarter million jobs previously closed to women.

Building Resilience in Others: Army Comprehensive Soldier and Family Fitness Program (CSF2)

In November of 2008, Martin Seligman, the founder of Positive Psychology, was invited to a lunch at the Pentagon with the chief of staff of the army, George Casey, former commander of the multinational force in Iraq and former Delta Force hero. Casey began, "I want to create an army that is just as psychologically fit as it is physically fit. You are all here to advise me how to go about this cultural transformation. The key to psychological fitness is resilience, and from here on, resilience will be taught and measured throughout the United States Army. Dr. Seligman here is the world's expert on resilience, and he's going to tell us how we are going to do it."

Seligman accepted the challenge. In addition to being the founder of Positive Psychology, he is a world expert on optimism, resiliency, and growth. He suggested that rather than treating PTSD once it has happened, the emphasis should be on training people in better ways to deal with life's adversities as they show up. Using a medical analogy, Seligman recommended that instead of treating the disease of PTSD after it has infected the individual, we should proactively inoculate each person with the psychological tools needed to help ward off or mitigate the disease. Richard Carmona, the surgeon general of the United States, agreed. He said, "If we want health, we should concentrate on building resilience—psychologically and physically."

That meeting was the beginning of the program known as *Comprehensive Soldier and Family Fitness*. It was placed under the command of General Rhonda Cornum, the Army's poster child for optimism and resilience.

The CSF2 program is designed to prevent problems before they occur—to insure that the soldier and the soldier's family can withstand the hardships that are often brought on be life in the military, particularly during times of war. It is a wholistic approch that addresses physical, emotional, social, family, and spiritual aspects of life. Its goal is "to improve soldier performance and readiness and to insure that all soldiers and their families have the skills necessary to grow personally, succeed in their job, thrive in their community, and grow within their family."

Dr. Cornum was the perfect choice for the CSF2 program. She says, "I not only have both a philosophical and a scientifc understanding of the importance of being resilient and of those thinking skills, but I have a personal belief based on my personal experiences that those skills work." The CSF2 program promotes optimism so it becomes second nature. Cornum believes in making the best of every situation and turning disadvantages into advantages, and she believes that this approach to life's adversities can be taught to others.

The CSF2 program defines resilience as, "the mental, physical, emotional, and behavioral ability to face and cope with adversity, adapt to change, recover, learn, and grow from temporary setbacks. Resilience is produced by a combination of knowledge, skills, abilities, and other characteristics found in individuals and groups that are either innate or can be taught and improved through education and training."

The CSF2 program builds on the belief that "people with confidence in their ability to bounce back and recover from adversity, either from training or through experience, are more likely to view challenges as opportunities to grow and succeed. This positive perspective and willingness to overcome obstacles is indicative of the quality of resilience."

The methods of the CSF2 program highlight *mental attitude, activity, nutrition,* and *sleep*. It provides extensive training to soldiers and their families as well as providing resiliency centers. The *Camp Taji Warrior Resiliency Campus* in Iraq is a good example of a resilience center based upon the principles of the CSF2 program. When Brig. Gen. Cornum visited it in 2010, she said, "This resilience center is exactly what CSF was intended for; it is an opportunity to make good people better." It is designed around the five dimensions or strength and resiliency—physical, emotional, social, spiritual, and family. It is designed to allow soldiers to get the relaxation associated with physical fitness or MWR (morale, welfare, and recreation). There is a theater room and a multi-console gaming center. There are privacy booths for phone and video calls to the states. If someone is having a tough day, or has had a difficult conversation with a family member, they can talk to a chaplain or a combat stress counselor. There is a nutritionist on staff.

The Army is doing what many corporations are doing with their wellness and mindfulness programs. They are paying closer attention to the physical, mental, and emotional health of their leaders and their team members and its impact on their productivity and their ability to thrive.

Dr. Cornum is a mindful leader who demonstrated early in her career the power of mindfulness, optimism, and resiliency. The CSF2 program that she has championed has helped many others to build greater resiliency in their own lives. She has had a rich and varied career, which has been enhanced by her optimism and her resiliency. She expressed her core philosophy in a recent presentation:

Adverse things happen to everyone.
The key is figuring out how to find something good about it or make it into something you can use.
My story isn't about how to deploy...it's about how to think when confronted with a challenge,
any challenge. ~ Dr. Rhonda Cornum

Footnote: The information on Rhonda Cornum and quotes used in this case study can be found in the following sources:
- *She Went to War: The Rhonda Cornum Story*. By Rhonda Cornum and Peter Copeland. Presidio Press. June 1, 1993.
- *Flourish: A Visionary New Understanding of Happiness and Well-being*. Martin E.P. Seligman. Free Press, 2011.
- *General Rhonda Cornum Gives Resiliency Chronicle* by Airman Stephan Coleman. Air Force Print News Today. 12/12/2013.
- *Rhonda Cornum*. from Wikipedia, the free encyclopedia. en.wikipedia.org. 4/3/15.
- *Female Prisoners of War* by Alexandra Hemmerly-Brown, Army News Service. March 5, 2012.
- *General's Life Embodies Resiliency, Optimism*. By Spc. Ryan Hallock. www.army.mil/article/67687. Oct 20, 2011.
- YouTube. *Rhonda Cornum's Story* (SAHMRI Wellbeing and Resilience Center).

EXERCISE: MINDFUL LEADERSHIP CASE STUDY QUESTIONS

One of the ways to build a better understanding of the skills of mindful leadership is through role models who demonstrate the skills of mindful leadership in their actions. In the *Observing Mindful Leadership Case Studies*, we examine the accomplishments, the actions, the statements, and sometimes the thoughts and emotions of well-known leaders. The cases can help us to see a diversity of mindful leaders operating in many different types of environments, and help us to see how different leaders and different personalities practice the skills of mindful leadership. Use the following questions to help you to better understand this mindful leader.

---

1. AWARENESS IN THE MOMENT. Mindful Leaders are self-aware of what they are thinking, feeling, and doing, and are aware of what is going on around them. They tune in to the present, to themselves, to their surroundings, and to others. They listen mindfully for information and for emotions and practice global listening. They focus first on determining what is real, before attempting to alter reality.

What can you observe from the writings, statements, and actions of the leader in this case study that demonstrate the skills of awareness in the moment?

_____
_____
_____
_____
_____
_____
_____
_____
_____
_____

2. POSITIVITY & POSSIBILITY. Mindful Leaders are more focused on the positive and the possible than on the negative and impossible. They remain aware of the failures, the risks, the dangers, the realities, and the downsides, but they practice the discipline of thinking in terms of the positives, the opportunities, the probabilities, the options, and the alternatives. Mindful Leaders are aware of the power of positivity to broaden and build positive potential, to encourage novel thoughts and actions, and to inspire productivity and creativity in themselves and others.

What can you observe from the writings, statements, and actions of the leader in this case study that demonstrate the skills of positivity and possibility?

_____
_____
_____
_____
_____
_____
_____
_____
_____
_____

3. POSITIVE RELATIONSHIPS. Mindful Leaders are aware of the power and importance of positive relationships, put conscious time and effort into the development of positive networks, and cultivate empathy, deep dive conversations, and win-win solutions with others. They recognize that some positive conflict can be productive, but go out of their way to avoid negative conflict escalators that thwart communication and cooperation. They take charge of their emotions and responses and work hard to build community and engagement.

What can you observe from the writings, statements, and actions of the leader in this case study that demonstrate the skills of positive relationships?

_____

_____

_____

_____

4. AUTHENTICITY & INTEGRITY. Mindful Leaders are often respected for their authenticity and integrity. Their authenticity is reflected in the truthfulness of their intentions, behaviors, and commitments. Their integrity is reflected in their honesty, their strong moral principles, and their ability to live by those principles. Mindful Leaders are clear on their values and their priorities and make decisions and take actions based upon these values. They are aware of their strengths and look for ways to leverage their strengths in the pursuit of their goals and in the service of others.

What can you observe from the writings, statements, and actions of the leader in this case study that demonstrate the skills of authenticity and integrity?

_____

_____

_____

_____

5. MANAGE STRESS & ENERGY. Mindful Leaders manage their energy and stress in order to maintain high levels of physical, mental, and emotional well-being. They challenge their thoughts to stay in touch with reality, they identify their emotions and emotional triggers and manage their responses, and they consciously monitor and manage their energy.

What can you observe from the writings, statements, and actions of the leader in this case study that demonstrate the skills of manage stress and energy?

_____

_____

_____

_____

6. RESILIENCE. Mindful leaders work to develop resilience—the capacity to recover from difficulties and adversity. They focus on the heroic rather than the debilitating aspects adversity; they let go of perfectionism and shortcomings and focus on the possible and potential; and they practice compassion and self-compassion.

What can you observe from the writings, statements, and actions of the leader in this case study that demonstrate the skills of resilience?

_____

_____

_____

_____

INTRODUCTION: RESILIENCE

The hardest thing to learn is not "how to juggle," but how to let the balls drop.
—Anthony Frost, *Improvisation in Drama*

Mindful Leaders recognize that in order to succeed people need a sense of self-efficacy and an ability to persist in the face of the inevitable obstacles and inequities of life. When individuals learn to face defeat and come back, to tackle difficult obstacles and prevail, and to confront failure and keep on going, they often find the hidden reserves of strength and courage that they did not know they had.

Resilience is having the ability to recover quickly from adversity, to get up from a fall and get back on track. As we stumble through life, this ability to regain balance is essential. The question is not if there are problems, but how do we respond when they occur. Can we regain composure, come back home, brush ourselves off, hold our head high, and carry on?

Having resilience enables us to pursue big dreams because even if they come crashing down, resilience helps us rise up from the ashes after a dream has burned to the ground. Significant challenges can come our way and even if we fail, we are not defeated. This way, we are not tossed around by the ups and downs of life, but we are able to ride the waves to calmer water. This is tremendously empowering and enables a deep sense of confidence and inner stability. No matter what we face, with resiliency, we can still be safe, secure, and happy.

Resilience is like a lifeboat in turbulent waters, but it also plays out in the frequent, seemingly insignificant trials of daily life. When annoyances, frustrations, or disappointments arise, can you maintain emotional balance and positivity, swiftly adapt to changing circumstances, and adjust expectations? Or do daily inconveniences and disruptions send you into an emotional tumble or get a rise out of you? Impatience, harsh comments, critical tone, emotional reactivity, defensiveness, and impulsiveness can indicate a need for greater resiliency.

Grit. A particular type of resilience is grit. The term originated at the height of The Cold War between the United States and the Soviet Union. Osgood formulated a new approach to international relations called "Graduated Reciprocation in Tension-reduction", or GRIT. Studies have shown that those with more 'grit' are more likely to succeed, particularly in adverse circumstances. Researchers believe that 'grit' can be taught and learned.

Singh, K. and S.D. Jha. (2008). Positive and Negative Affect, and Grit as predictors of Happiness and Life Satisfaction. *Journal of the Indian Academy of Applied Psychology.* v34 (Sp) pp 40-45.

Lehrer, J. (03/14/11). Which Traits Predict Success? (The Importance of Grit). In: Wired Science.

Reed, J.; B.L. Pritschet; and D.M. Cutton. (2012). Grit, conscientiousness, and the transtheoretical model of change for exercise behaviour. *Journal of Health Psychology.* 18:5 pp 612-619.

ACCEPTANCE

When failure strikes, how do you pick yourself up and carry on?

Acceptance. Acceptance is key to resilience. Difficult to describe in words, acceptance is an internal state, a feeling sense. It has both a mental process and an emotional state. The mental process is acknowledging the facts of a situation; the emotional state is a releasing of the struggle for what is wished for. Empowerment emerges from the effectiveness behind controlling what you can. Contentment emerges from releasing the struggle and futile attempts to control the uncontrollable. Many describe the feeling of letting go as relief or calm. Others describe it as spaciousness. It is not just changing your thinking. It is a state of mind, heart, and body. It requires having a willingness to participate in the reality of circumstances.

Equanimity. Releasing enables equanimity, a sense of security, and confidence. It requires staying centered and having expectations that are in line with reality; it enables one to remain more unflappable in the face of challenge. With mastery in letting go, you know that no matter what life brings your way you can deal with it. Like a surfer, you do not fight the swells, but instead ride with a wave with courage and clarity.

Grant me the serenity to accept the things I cannot change, the courage to change the things I can, and the wisdom to know the difference. –Reinhold Niebuhr

Three Approaches to Adversity. You can engage with life passionately, knowing you have three options when an unwanted situation arises:
   a) Change it.
   b) Leave it.
   c) Release it (i.e., Change your reaction to it).

The ability to let go of unchangeable situations is what differentiates those who are destroyed by negative events and those who suffer but make it. It is a key component of resilience. Releasing is important for well-being in full range of unwanted experiences. It is necessary when dealing with serious problems, traumas, and extremely negative circumstances (e.g., permanent disability, loss of someone, painful childhood); when faced with life challenges like not getting a job you really wanted, unrequited love, divorce; as well as relatively minor annoyances like traffic jams, workplace stress, or even minor annoyances like long lines at a store.

*If there's a remedy when trouble strikes,
What reason is there for dejection?
And if there is no help for it,
What use is there in being glum?
–Shantideva*

Effectiveness is increased. Research shows that those who can disengage from unattainable goals are much more successful and satisfied than those who continue pursuing unattainable goals. In other words, sometimes it is better to quit when successive attempts have failed. Rather than "hitting your head against the wall," face it, make a new plan and move on.

Pain is minimized. Many describe letting go as being freed from the struggle or as feeling centered. It is not eliminating pain. There may still be a lot of sadness, anger, or disappointment but often there is a feeling that a burden has been lifted. Marsha Linehan, a preeminent researcher in modern psychotherapy, states, "experience the ordinary pain of negative situations, but do not add to it—that is what creates misery."

Linehan describes the relationship between acceptance and pain as:

   Pain + Non-Acceptance   =   Misery

   Pain + Acceptance   =   Ordinary pain

The Need for Compassion. Compassion is crucial for affecting positive change and creating a climate of productivity, high performance, loyalty, and team work. Employees working in companies led by compassion work harder, are more loyal, and innovative because they are *inspired* to bring their best—not because they *need* to. When we feel like someone cares and has our best interest in mind, we will go the extra mile, make sacrifices, and accept even hard circumstances. Leaders that lead from compassion are capable of leaving an indelible trace on the people and organizational structure as a whole. Compassion in the work environment helps colleagues relate to one another as well as to their work environment. If an organization is deemed compassionate by its employees, the employees will also be more likely to think that their colleagues and supervisors are more understanding and kind.

Skill 15. LET GO OF "PERFECT"

*It is not that most people want too much, it is that they don't want enough.
Why not desire complete and utter peace, love, and satisfaction.*
—Nisargadatta Maharaj

Striving for unrealistic, perfectionistic standards undermines our ability to cultivate high levels of peace, love, and satisfaction. *Perfectionism is a belief that perfection can and should be attained in all things at all times.* High achievers are often perfectionists. Perfectionists tend to be chronically dissatisfied even amidst objectively fortunate circumstances.

Positive Perfectionism. At its best, perfectionism can lead to high levels of performance, and can provide the motivation for one to persevere in the face of discouragement and obstacles. Striving for high standards can be engaging during goal achievement and mastery. A healthy perfectionist derives a sense of pleasure from the labors of a painstaking effort and from achieving an end result that meets high standards.

Negative Perfectionism. At its worst, perfectionism can lead to striving compulsively toward impossible goals and chronic dissatisfaction. It often leads to measuring one's worth only in terms of productivity and accomplishment. Perfectionists typically feel highly frustrated, anxious, or unhappy because the individual, others, or outcomes fail to measure up to impossible standards. Sometimes it is more about power and control than accomplishment.

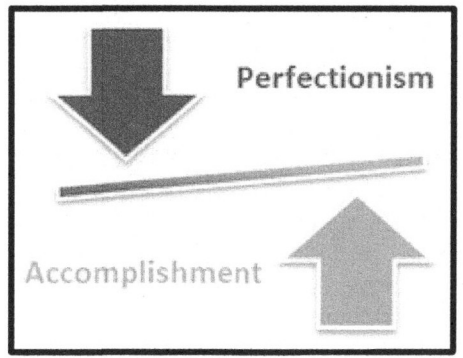

Perfectionists lose sources of satisfaction due to the tendency to feel that they never do things well enough to merit that feeling of satisfaction and any outcome less than perfect is deemed unacceptable.

PITFALLS OF PERFECTIONISM

Maximizers & Satisficers. People differ in the degree to which they routinely try to find the "best" option in situations, as opposed to the "good enough" option. These people are referred to as "*Maximizers*" and "*Satisficers*", respectively.

Maximizers try to find the best possible option and make the ideal decision.

Satisficers seek good enough and do not worry about missing a better option. Learning how and when to satisfice is a crucial skill in one's ability to thrive.

Maximization undermines happiness. Schwartz and colleagues' research show that those with high maximization scores experienced less satisfaction with life, were less happy, were less optimistic, lower self-esteem, feel more regret, and were more depressed than people with low maximization scores. When decision-making, maximizers focus on anticipated regret and perceived opportunity costs, which creates tremendous stress (Schwartz, Ward, Monterosso, Lyubomirsky, White, & Lehman, 2002).

Maximizers achieve more but feel worse. Recent graduates were tracked when searching for jobs. Maximizers were less satisfied than Satisficers with their jobs and experienced more distress during the job selection process. They did, however, obtain higher paying jobs compared to those tending toward "good enough" options (Iyengar, Wells, & Schwartz, 2006).

ROOTS OF PERFECTIONISM

Over 150 years ago Kierkegaard described the love affair humans have with what could be:

"And what wine is so sparkling, what so fragrant, what so intoxicating as possibility?"

The Drive to Thrive. Humans are wired to survive. We previously discussed the many protective psychological mechanisms that help us do this including the negativity bias. In addition, we have an inherent *Drive to Thrive*. We are wired to desire and to feel enormous pleasure when we attain sought after outcomes. The dopamine and opioid systems, for example, ensure that we are sufficiently motivated and rewarded in our efforts to create and improve upon positive circumstances.

This primitive Drive to Thrive has led to tremendous evolutionary success of the species. In modern society it fuels invention and innovation. This Drive to Thrive is responsible for medical and hi-tech advancements in medicine, architectural feats, and explorations in outer space for example. In the social context it motivates efforts to improve relationships with loved ones, to resolve conflict, to create win-win solutions, and innumerable other examples.

The Drive to Thrive is one of our more exquisite instincts. Just like the *Negativity Bias*, however, our greatest strengths as a species can also be among our greatest weaknesses. When experienced in excess, the Drive to Thrive undermines happiness and satisfaction. The Drive to Thrive easily slips into overdrive because another evolutionarily adaptive mechanism called habituation.

HOW TO LET GO OF PERFECT: Cultivate Satisfaction

Satisfaction is the state of being content with what you have. It is feeling that "this is good enough" or "I have enough." Cultivating satisfaction focuses on allowing circumstances or people to be "good enough" rather than trying to maximize every experience, even while seeking improvements. Learn how to do less striving and do more thriving.

The following approaches can be helpful:

1. Know your top priorities or criteria when making a decision. When you know what your "must haves" are versus your "wish list" characteristics, then you are in a better position to pursue what you need and let go of the rest, which could end up being costly to pursue either in time, energy, or effort.

2. Optimize your experience *within* a circumstance, rather than maximize *between* circumstances. As you go about your day, make the best of the moments you experience. Focus on finding the nugget or opportunity for positivity *within* a situation, rather than comparing *between* situations and thereby focusing on how another situation would be preferable.

For example, once you have sat down at a restaurant and ordered dinner, focus on how to enjoy this meal and make the best of your experience at this restaurant rather than mentally noting how you should have chosen another restaurant and much more you would be enjoying yourself if you were there.

3. Consider the cost of maximizing. Every decision has a cost and benefit. Consider what you would have to do or give up if you pursued the best possible option in a situation.

LET GO OF PERFECT WORKSHEET

How often do you catch yourself trying to find the "best" option to situations, rather than going with one that is "good enough" to deal with the situation? People who constantly try to *maximize* every situation often experience higher levels of stress and lower levels of satisfaction. In some situations, less effort is better than more.

The purpose of this worksheet is to help you to learn to let go of striving for perfect in the appropriate circumstances. Think about a recent experience in which you were dissatisfied and consider how you could have increased satisfaction by making the best within the reality of circumstances.

SITUATION

Situation. Describe the situation in which you want to increase satisfaction by making the best within the reality of circumstances.

_____
_____
_____
_____
_____

THREE STEPS TO LETTING GO OF PERFECT

1. Know your top priorities or criteria. What are your "Must Haves" versus "Wish List" factors?

_____
_____
_____
_____
_____
_____
_____

2. Optimize your experience *within* a circumstance. What would it look like to optimize within this experience rather than to try to get the best circumstance compared to other options?

_____
_____
_____
_____
_____

3. Cost of Striving for Perfect. What was the cost to me and others of striving for the perfect situation, performance, or option (i.e., maximizing)?

4. Do Differently. What might I do different in the future?

LET GO OF PERFECT TRACKING LOG

DAY	APPLICATION How did I let go of striving for perfect? What are my Must Have's vs. Wish List criteria?	IMPACT What was the impact of letting go of perfect on me, others, and/or the situation?
Day 1		
Day 2		
Day 3		
Day 4		

LET GO OF PERFECT TRACKING LOG

DAY	APPLICATION How did I let go of striving for perfect? What are my Must Have's vs. Wish List criteria?	IMPACT What was the impact of letting go of perfect on me, others, and/or the situation?
Day 5		
Day 6		
Day 7		

INSIGHTS – What patterns or benefits emerged?

_____
_____
_____
_____

Skill 16. TELL HERO STORIES

The mindful leader is aware of the power of stories. Stories can change the way we think, act, and feel. Early Greek stories like the *Iliad* and the *Odyssey* communicated the values of the Greeks in entertaining action/adventure tales. Today, inspirational stories can form the foundations of an entire workplace culture, and are often used by companies like Disney, Starbucks, Federal Express, etc. to highlight behaviors and values held in high esteem by the culture. They are a quick and powerful way for companies to communicate values and acceptable behaviors.

Stories have the power to break down barriers and turn bad situations around. Stories can capture our imaginations, illustrate our ideas, arouse our passions, and inspire us in a way that cold, hard facts often can't. Stories can be powerful business tools, and successful leaders use them to engage their teams. Mindful leaders are also aware of the negative stories that can drag down an individual or a team, and work hard to help individuals rewrite their negative stories.

The Mind Creates Stories. The mind is wired to make sense of things, to determine cause and effect, to explain why something has happened and predict what will happen next. Our minds are wired to weave stories, predict futures, and explain cause and effect. While this is necessary, we often create disempowering and negative narratives of our experiences without realizing it.

The problem is that we forget that we've constructed just one possible interpretation of reality. We often fail to realize there could be innumerable ways to interpret a situation. We fail to consider where these thoughts came from and whether they are helpful. This is particularly the case in emotionally charged situations.

Recognize Grievance Stories. People who are aware of their thoughts are better able to manage them, which leads to lower levels of anxiety, frustration, and anger, and higher levels of happiness and well-being. When something bad happens, often we first think of other people or external circumstances that made it happen to us. This can lead to feeling victimized, out of control, and powerless. Fred Luskin, a professor at Stanford University and author of *Forgive for Good*, refers to this narrative as the "grievance story." In his research with individuals who have undergone tremendous trauma, rewriting the grievance story as a hero story is a crucial step in healing and resilience.

Being aware of the fact that situations can be seen from different perspectives is beneficial. In a study of mindlessness, Langer and Piper (1988) found that when individuals simply were presented with information in a conditional as opposed to absolute manner (e.g., "this object could be a..." versus "this is a ..."), they generated more creative responses and were more effective in fulfilling the needs presented in the laboratory task.

Heroes. A hero is someone who faces a challenge with courage, determination, bravery, and strength. A hero rises up from the ashes when dreams go down in flames. She or he is a champion, a leader, and is someone who has overcome tremendous adversity.

A hero is an ordinary individual who finds the strength to persevere and endure
in spite of overwhelming obstacles.
-Christopher Reeves

HERO STORY MODEL: HERO'S JOURNEY

The Hero is a character that shows up in most, if not all, of the world's literature. There are heroes in religious stories, in adventure stories, in epics, legends, fables, folklore, etc. Joseph Campbell, a well-known and popular scholar of mythology, suggested that heroes in most stories from traditions all through history and all around the world, share similar characteristics and often perform similar functions. This similar to the idea of Swiss psychiatrist, Carl Jung, who suggested that the hero represents an "archetype" and is an expression of our personal and collective unconscious. Jung believed that everyone is born with a similar, subconscious model of a hero.

Both Joseph Campbell and Carl Jung drew upon early anthropological works including, *The Golden Bough: A Study in Magic and Religion* (1911-15) by the Scottish anthropologist Sir James George Frazer. This work compares the mythic beliefs of cultures all over the world.

A Famous Hero's Journey—*Star Wars*. Star Wars, a movie written and directed by George Lucus, uses many of the elements of the mythological hero on a quest. Lucas was strongly influenced by the work of Joseph Campbell and particularly by his book, *The Hero With a Thousand Faces*. George Lucus rediscovered *The Hero with a Thousand Faces* in 1975 after he had already written two drafts of Star Wars. He used the blueprint of the "Hero's Journey" as an organizing structure to pull his expansive mythology into a coherent story.

The movie *Star Wars* follows the "Hero's Journey" structure. Luke has unusual birth circumstances, and must leave his foster family due to a traumatic event, which leads to adventure and a quest. His light saber is his special weapon, and he has supernatural help in the form of Obi-Wan Kenobi, and in Yoda. Luke must prove himself worthy many times on his road of trials. He takes a long journey to many strange and dangerous places, and gets an un-healable wound when Darth Vader cuts off his hand. He experiences atonement with his father when he converts him back from the Dark Side. Luke is rewarded spiritually by becoming a Jedi Knight and being able to use the power of the Force.

Classic Hero's Journey Structure. A classic structure defines every hero's journey.

    1. Origins—The hero's journey starts with some unique origin, usually adversity, that sets up the need for the hero's journey.

    2. Emotional Wound—The emotional wound that was caused by or related to the unique origins. Healing the wound is part of the hero's journey.

    3. Heroic Acts—*A heroic act* is a response that demonstrates resiliency or strength. Heroic acts might include learning tough lessons, self-growth, or renewed determination.

    4. Weapon (Core Strengths)—The hero has a special weapon only he/she can wield.

    5. Outside Help—The hero is typically gifted with some kind of supernatural power and/or outside help or guidance.

    6. Reward—As a result of the journey, the hero is rewarded with some deeper treasure than the one originally sought.

HOW TO TELL A HERO STORY

How does one move from victim to victor? The following approach can empower you when you feel stuck, victimized, or helpless. When bad things happen it is healthy and crucial to wholeheartedly process the grief, anger, or whatever distressing feelings result. Apply this method only when you feel ready to move into empowerment.

STEP 1. RECOGNIZE YOUR GRIEVANCE STORY.

We shape our experiences of situations by where we focus our attention and how we frame the cause and effect of events. How we tell the story of our experiences can make us the perpetual victim or the victor over adversity. This is not about blame, approval, or letting a perpetrator of aggression off the hook. Instead, it is about regaining dignity, power, and grace.

When you experience a challenge, first become aware of how you explain the reasons behind the negative event. This is an essential step in the process of regaining control.

- Identify the ways that you are identifying as a victim in the story of a challenge or trauma you have experienced.

- Note how you are talking about how things were done to you; how others had all the power; how you had no control.

- Note how you tell your story to others in conversations. Well-intentioned others can collude, solidifying our grievance story.

STEP 2. IDENTIFY YOUR HEROIC ACTS.

Describe how you performed "heroic" acts. A hero is someone who overcomes adversity with courage, valor, bravery, and perseverance. We tend to admire those who face adversity with heroic acts. See yourself as a hero by focusing on ways that you feel good about how you responded, learned from, or grew into a stronger version of yourself in response to the challenge or trauma.

Find your heroic acts as a response to your undesirable situation. Reflect on how you responded to adversity with bravery, courage, or determination to create a more desirable future. Did you learn something from the experience, exercise patience, grapple with difficult conflicts, or try to do your best even in the face of adversity? Ask yourself:
- *How have I faced this adversity with courage and determination?*
- *How did I respond in admirable ways?*

Below are some examples of heroic acts I have seen in close friends.

Cancer. I was talking to a friend who was diagnosed with cancer and given 30-days to live--five years ago. She asked me about another friend's condition with Stage IV cancer (he is also heroic). I explained that he was seeking a new treatment that seems promising. She interrupted me, "No, how is he today?" She stated emphatically, "If he is good today, then he is GOOD. Period."

She is a hero in the face of adversity: She focuses on the gift of today and deals with the challenges of tomorrow, tomorrow. Despite often feeling ill, she is one of the most positive people I know.

Divorce. Another friend reveals his inner hero as he heals from a heartbreaking divorce. Instead of blaming his ex-wife for cheating on him, heroically, he is taking an honest look at how he might have had a part in co-creating the circumstances. In vowing to learn from what went wrong, he rises from the inferno and empowers himself to create a satisfying, lasting future marriage.

I expressed admiration for his willingness to broach a sensitive topic. He exclaimed, "I'm not letting things go unsaid anymore. I've learned that hard discussions just get harder." Breaking old habits, like not speaking up when the little voice inside whispers, takes a Herculean degree of courage and determination. That is a heroic act.

Single Parenting. At age 35, a single friend of mine (I'll call her Carla) found herself peering over the cliff of infertility. When she was diagnosed with waning fertility, instead of falling to her knees in disappointment, she researched her options and elected to become a single-mother-by-choice. Six months of IVF treatment with donated sperm and thirty thousand dollars later, she got pregnant. She loves being a mother and sees herself as closer than ever to meeting the man of her dreams.

She says, "Now the men I meet have to really show-up, so I see their values from the start." Carla's daughter is lucky to have a mom who models extraordinary heroism.

STEP 3. APPLY THE HERO'S JOURNEY STRUCTURE TO YOUR OWN STORY.

Use the *Hero Journey Structure* to help organize your thoughts and make sense of the key elements in your hero story.

Origins—The hero's journey usually starts with some interesting origin that explains how we got to where we are now. It sets up the need for the hero's journey.

Emotional Wound—Acknowledge the emotional wound that may be involved in the situation. Consider the healing of the wound as part of your "hero's quest."

Weapons (Core Strengths)—The hero has a special weapon only he/she can wield. Your core strengths may be your special weapon.

Outside Help—The hero usually has some kind of outside help, support, or guidance.

Reward—As a result of the journey, the hero is rewarded with some deeper treasure than the one originally sought.

RESEARCH ON HEROES

Gender and Heroism. A study conducted on the heroism of men and women in history looked at how heroism should be considered an androgynous trait. Heroism is defined as "actions undertaken to help others, despite the possibility that they may result in the helper's death or injury." The authors reviewed heroism in extremely dangerous situations such as Carnegie heroes (people recognized by the Carnegie Hero Fund for dangerous heroic acts) and people who risked their lives to hide Jews during the Holocaust.

The authors also considered other prosocial and less dangerous acts such as living kidney donation, volunteering for the Peace Corps and volunteering for Doctors of the World. They found that Carnegie heroes who placed their life in serious danger were mostly men. Among Holocaust rescuers, men and women were equally represented. However, if they were unmarried, they were more likely to be women. Women predominated the rest of the situations such as kidney donations and volunteering for Peace Corp and Doctors of the World.

Becker, S W., Eagly, A.H. (2004). The Heroism of Women and Men. *American Psychologist*, 59(3), 163-178.

"What is satisfying about satisfying events? Testing 10 candidate psychological needs" by Sheldon, Elliot, Kim, & Kasser (2001).

HERO STORY WORKSHEET

We shape our experiences of situations by where we focus our attention and how we frame the cause and effect of events. How we tell the story of our experiences can make us the perpetual victim or the victor over adversity. Seeing yourself as a "hero" emerges from focusing on your heroic acts—the admirable ways that you responded, learned from, or discovered deeper truths during a challenge.

The purpose of this worksheet is to help you to identify some of the key components of your grievance story and to transform it into a hero story.

MY GRIEVANCE STORY

1. **My Grievance Story.** What are some components of a current grievance story?
    - What happened?
    - Where and when did it happen?
    - Who was involved?
    - How was I injured and by whom?
    - What were the negative consequences to me?

_____
_____
_____
_____
_____
_____
_____
_____
_____
_____
_____
_____
_____
_____
_____
_____
_____
_____
_____
_____

MY HERO STORY

Rewrite your story with you as the hero. Apply the elements of the *Hero's Journey* to your own life.

1. **Origins**—Your hero's journey starts with some challenging and unique origin that explains how you got initiated into the hero's journey. The unique origin sets up the need for the hero's journey.
    Ask yourself: *What were the circumstances that launched me into this hero's journey?*

_____
_____
_____
_____
_____
_____
_____
_____
_____
_____
_____
_____
_____
_____
_____
_____
_____

2. **Emotional Wound**—Identify the emotional wound that may have resulted from the unique origins. Healing this wound is probably part of your hero journey.
    Ask yourself: *What was my emotional wound or emotional challenge in this situation?*

_____
_____
_____
_____
_____
_____
_____
_____
_____
_____

3. **Weapons (Core Strengths)**—A hero has a special weapon only he/she can wield. Your core strengths may reflect your special weapon.
   Ask yourself: *How did I use my strengths on my journey?*

_____
_____
_____
_____
_____
_____
_____
_____

4. **Outside Help**—A hero usually receives some kind of outside help and/or supernatural power.
   Ask yourself: *Where did I get some outside help, guidance, or support?*

_____
_____
_____
_____
_____
_____
_____
_____

5. **Heroic Acts**—Identify how you took heroic acts or responded in admirable ways in the face of adversity. Ask yourself:
   How have I faced this adversity with courage and determination?
   How did I respond in admirable ways?
   What did I learn or develop in response to this adversity (even though I still may wish I didn't have this experience)?
   How have I grown as a person?
   How have I cultivated greater fortitude, compassion, inner resolve and strength, or wisdom?

_____
_____
_____
_____
_____
_____
_____

6. **Reward**—As a result of the journey, the hero is rewarded with some deeper treasure than the one originally sought.

    Ask yourself: *What is the psychological, emotional, spiritual, or deeper reward or truth that I obtained or developed?*

7. **Insight Into My Situation.** What insight did I get by rewriting my grievance story as a hero story?

HEROIC ACTS TRACKING LOG

DAY	APPLICATION What heroic acts did I do today in response to minor or major challenges?	IMPACT What is the impact of reframing my responses to challenge as heroic acts on me, others, and/or my situation?
Day 1		
Day 2		
Day 3		
Day 4		

HEROIC ACTS TRACKING LOG

DAY	APPLICATION What heroic acts did I do today in response to minor or major challenges?	IMPACT What is the impact of reframing my responses to challenge as heroic acts on me, others, and/or my situation?
Day 5		
Day 6		
Day 7		

INSIGHTS - What patterns or benefits emerged?

_____
_____
_____
_____
_____
_____

RESILIENCE MEDITATION

The purpose of this meditation is to build resiliency. This technique applies the principles of behavioral psychology to create new associations with past difficulty and the principles of neuropsychology to strengthen neural circuitry that is activated during positive feelings. The time to do this meditation is when you are not feeling down, but when you are feeling neutral or positive and want to heal around certain vulnerability. Rick Hanson, author of Buddha's Brain, created this technique. He explains that this can shift the "emotional tones" of memory.

First, make contact with safety and peaceful feelings. Feel these in your body. Second, when you feel grounded, bring to mind a mildly painful issue. Be sure to use your own inner wisdom to guide you in how far to go into difficult feelings. As Rick Hanson says when he teaches this type of meditation, *"Be sure you can swim back from the deep end by yourself."* Continue to experience the positive in the foreground while bringing into awareness the feelings of the difficult experience in the background.

INSTRUCTIONS
(8 MINUTES)

1. FOCUS INWARD: Breathe and Center
- **Close your eyes**—Close your eyes to better focus your attention inward.
- **Feel Your Breath**—Focus attention by feeling your breath enter and exit your body. Breathe deep into your abdomen. Place your hand on your abdomen to feel your diaphragm rise and fall. Slowly exhale and naturally inhale.
- **Set your Intention**—To direct your attention in this time, place, and to the objective of this meditation.

2. DIRECT ATTENTION: Feel the sensations associated with positive emotions while holding a difficult issue.

First, Positive Feelings:
- **Make contact**—Make contact with a moment when you felt positive emotions in your target area.
- **Soak in the positive feelings**—Experience the feeling in your body. Feel the positive sensations and feelings in your body.
- **Expand the feeling**—Invite the feeling to expand and increase in intensity throughout your entire body.

Second, Counter Fear, Anxiety, Vulnerability or Doubt about your self or your life:
- **Make contact**—Make contact with a mildly challenging issue. Keep the positive feelings floating in the foreground.
- **Maintain the positive feelings while holding in the background the challenging issue**—Hold the distress AND feel the positive sensations and feelings in your body.
- **Invite positive feelings to soothe your heart**—Put your hand on your heart and imagine that the positive feelings are radiating into your heart center. Soothing the raw, vulnerable feelings.

Third, Allow the challenging issue to be changed by the positive feelings:
- **Let go**—Allow the challenging issue to drift off taking some of the positive feelings along.
- **Allow the possibility**—Allow the possibility that these feelings can carry forward into your experience in the world, to help the brain register these positive experiences, and become a fundamental and enduring part of yourself.

3. REFLECT ON INSIGHTS: Breathe and Reflect
- Come back to your breath.
- Reflect on the insights or benefits you gained during this meditation.

4. MAINTAIN YOUR INNER AWARENESS: Soft Gaze and Stay with It
- Slowly open your eyes and keep your gaze soft, directed downward, and settling on a neutral object.
- Stay with the awareness you had during the meditation.

RESILIENCE MEDITATION WORKSHEET

After you have completed the meditation, jot down any observations about what came up during your meditation. Make note of thoughts you had, feelings you experienced, bodily sensations you felt, and/or detours that you took.

1. FOCUS INWARD: To what extent could you direct attention and turn your mind when it wandered?

_____

_____

2. DIRECT ATTENTION: Feel yourself experiencing the situation.
MAKE CONTACT WITH FEELINGS OF POSITIVITY

a. **Make contact** with positive feelings. What were the feelings or images?

_____

_____

_____

COUNTER FEAR, ANXIETY, VULNERABILITY OR DOUBT ABOUT YOU OR YOUR LIFE

b. **Make contact**—Make contact with a mildly challenging issue. Bring to mind a challenging issue while you keep the positive feelings floating in the foreground. What was the issue?

_____

_____

c. **Maintain the positive feelings while holding in the background the challenging issue**—What did it feel like to hold the challenging issue in the presence of the positive feelings?

_____

_____

c. **Invite positive feelings to soothe you**— What did it feel like to put your hand on your heart and invite the positive feelings to soothe and calm?

_____

_____

d. **Let go**—Let go of the challenging issue taking some of the positive feelings with it. What did you feel when you let it drift off with some of the positive feelings?

_____

_____

3. REFLECT ON INSIGHTS: What insights or benefits did you gain from your experience and observations?

_____

_____

RESILIENCE MEDITATION TRACKING LOG

DAY	APPLICATION What did I meditate on?	IMPACT What was the impact on me, others, and/or the situation?
Day 1		
Day 2		
Day 3		
Day 4		

RESILIENCE MEDITATION TRACKING LOG

DAY	APPLICATION What did I meditate on?	IMPACT What was the impact on me, others, and/or the situation?
Day 5		
Day 6		
Day 7		

INSIGHTS - What patterns or benefits emerged?

_____
_____
_____
_____
_____
_____

Skill 17. SELF-COMPASSION

*Followers have a very clear picture of what they want and need
from the most influential leaders in their lives: trust, compassion, stability, and hope.*
-Tom Rath

Compassion is crucial for affecting positive change and creating a climate of productivity, high performance, loyalty, and team work. Employees working in companies led by compassion work harder, are more loyal, and innovative because they are *inspired* to bring their best—not because they *need* to. When we feel like someone cares and has our best interest in mind, we will go the extra mile, make sacrifices, and accept even hard circumstances. Leaders that lead from compassion are capable of leaving an indelible trace on the people and organizational structure as a whole. Compassion in the work environment helps colleagues relate to one another as well as to their work environment. If an organization is deemed compassionate by its employees, the employees will also be more likely to think that their colleagues and supervisors are more understanding and kind.

A 2008 study conducted at the Stress Institute in Stockholm by Anna Nyberg found that employees were 60% more likely to have a heart attack or life-threatening heart condition if their believed their managers to be incompetent, secretive, inconsiderate, and uncommunicative. However, employees who had "good" leaders were 40% less likely to suffer heart problems. Many leaders who do not display compassion with their employees are more focused on results. However, how those results are achieved are of little consequence to them. This way of thinking must change so that compassionate leadership becomes the new norm of all organizations.

RESEARCH ON COMPASSION AND LEADERSHIP

Frost, P.J., Dutton, J.E., Maitlis, S., Lilius, J.M., Kanov, J.M., & Worline, M.C. (2005). Seeing organizations differently: Three lenses on compassion. *Handbook of Organizational* Studies, 1-55.

Lilius, J.M., Worline, M.C., Maitlis, S., Kanov, J., Dutton, J.E., & Frost, P. (2008). The contours and consequences of compassion at work. *Journal of Organizational Behavior*, 29, 193-218.

Nyberg, A., Alfredsson, L., Theorell, T., Westerlund, H., Vahtera, J., & Kivimäki. (2008). Managerial leadership and ischaemic heart disease among employees: the Swedish WOLF study. *Journal of Occupational and Environmental Medicine*, 66, 51-55.

Reb, J.M., Narayanan, J., & Chaturvedi, S. (2014). Leading mindfully: Two studies on the influence of supervisor trait mindfulness on employee well-being and performance. *Mindfulness*, 5(1), 36.

SELF-COMPASSION

If your compassion does not include yourself, it is incomplete.
-Jack Kornfield

Self-Compassion is extending compassion to oneself in instances of perceived inadequacy, failure, or general suffering. When in the throws of negative emotion, direct some gentle compassion toward yourself like you would to a child, an animal, friend or loved one if they were in pain. Simply the experiencing of emotional distress warrants compassion—by definition they are difficult to experience and disruptive to our sense of well-being. By having compassion rather than judgment or criticism, the intensity and quality of the negative emotion changes. Many describe a feeling of negativity melting away. Directing compassion towards oneself can be helpful when dealing with intense emotions and situations that cannot be sufficiently managed with other.

THREE COMPONENTS OF SELF-COMPASSION

The pioneer and leading expert on self-compassion, Dr. Kristen Neff, has defined self-compassion as the ability to hold one's feelings of suffering with a sense of warmth, connection, and concern. Neff proposes three main components of self-compassion:

Self-kindness. Being kind and understanding toward oneself in instances of pain or failure rather than being harshly self-critical.

Common humanity. Perceiving one's experiences of suffering and personal failure as part of the larger human experience rather than seeing them as isolating.

Mindfulness. Holding one's present-moment experience in balanced perspective, or "mindful awareness," rather than exaggerating the dramatic story line of one's suffering.

> You will encounter frustrations. Losses will occur, you will make mistakes, bump up against your limitations, fall short of your ideals. This is the human condition, a reality shared by all of us.
>
> —Dr. Kristin Neff

Self-compassion versus Self-esteem. Self-esteem refers to a sense of self-worth, perceived value, or liking oneself. Although psychologists once praised the benefits of self-esteem, recent research has exposed costs associated with the pursuit of high self-esteem, such as narcissism, ego-defensive anger, inaccurate self-perceptions, self-worth contingency, or social comparison. In contrast to self-esteem, self-compassion is not based on self-evaluations. People feel compassion for themselves because all human beings deserve compassion and understanding, not because they possess some particular set of traits.

Unlike self-esteem, self-compassion isn't dependent on external circumstances. It's always available. Research suggests that in comparison to self-esteem, self-compassion is associated with greater emotional resilience, more accurate self-concepts, more caring relationship behavior, as well as less narcissism and reactive anger.

RESEARCH ON SELF-COMPASSION

Below are abstracts from a selection of scientific studies on self-compassion published in major peer reviewed journals.

Compassion is Trainable. Geshe Thupten Jinpa and colleagues set out to determine if compassion is trainable. They studied a sample of 100 adults that were randomly assigned to a 9-week compassion cultivation training (CCT) program and found significant improvements in participants' compassion for others, ability to receive compassion from others, and self-compassion. Their findings suggest that compassion is trainable and is positively correlated to the amount of time one practices formal compassion (metta) meditation. Jazaieri, H., Jinpa, G. T., McGonigal, K., Rosenberg, E. L., Finkelstein, J., Simon-Thomas, E., ...Goldin, P. R. (2013). Enhancing compassion: A randomized controlled trial of a compassion cultivation training program. *Journal of Happiness Studies*, 14(4), 1113-1126.

Meditation Relieves Negative Emotions. Fred Luthans and colleagues examined randomized clinical trials to determine the effectiveness of mindfulness meditation in improving psychological stress. They found that mindfulness meditation had a moderate positive impact on anxiety, depression, and pain and underscore the importance of further studies to explore how meditation may improve the positive aspects of mental health. Luthans, F., Avolio, B. J., Avey, J. B., & Norman, S. M. (2007). Positive psychological capital: Measurement and relationship with performance and satisfaction. Personnel Psychology, 60(3), 541-572.

Self-Compassion Is Associated with Psychological Health and Wellbeing. Most of the research on self-compassion so far has used the *Self-Compassion Scale*, which measures the degree to which individuals display the three elements of self-compassion. Results from the test indicate that self-compassion is significantly correlated with positive mental health outcomes, such as with measures of happiness, optimism, positive affect, wisdom, personal initiative, curiosity and exploration, agreeableness, extroversion, and conscientiousness. It also had a significant negative association with negative affect and neuroticism (Neff, Rude, & Kirkpatrick, 2007).

Self-Compassion Can Be Cultivated. There is a growing body of research that points to self-compassion interventions associated with improved aspects of psychological wellbeing. Baer (2010) asserts that self-compassion is closely related to mindfulness, and like mindfulness, it can be cultivated through meditation practices that originate in the Buddhist tradition and have been adapted for secular use in Western settings. Significant reductions in symptoms of stress and mood disturbance, as well as increases in mindfulness, spirituality and self- compassion were observed after participation in Mindfulness-based stress reduction (MBSR) programs (Birnie, Speca, & Carlson, 2010). Effective methods of teaching self-compassion that aren't based on Buddhist meditation also have been developed, such as Compassionate Mind Training, a form of therapy that emphasizes the development of self-compassion (Gilbert, 2000; Gilbert & Irons, 2004; 2005; Gilbert & Procter, 2006).

Compassion Lowers Stress. A research study suggests that having compassion for others may actually protect us from stress. Fifty-nine study participants took an online questionnaire that measured their levels of compassion. Then these people had to complete a series of stressful tasks while someone else evaluated them; that evaluator either offered supportive, positive feedback or didn't say anything. Participants who showed more compassion on the questionnaire interacted more with the supportive figures than the less compassionate people did, and they reaped the benefits of this support, showing lower blood pressure, heart rate, and levels of cortisol (a hormone released during stress) than their less compassionate counterparts. They also seemed less stressed than the compassionate participants who didn't receive the supportive feedback. The authors suggest compassion for others may open us up to receiving social support, which may lead to more resilience to stress. Cosley, B.J., McCoy, S.K., Saslow, L. R., Epel, E.S. Is Compassion for Others Stress Buffering? Consequences of Compassion and Social Support for Physiological Reactivity to Stress. *Journal of Experimental Social Psychology*, Vol. 46, Issue 5, September 2010, 816-823.

Prejudice and Dehumanization. A research study suggests that having prejudice towards out groups that are stereotypically labeled as hostile and incompetent (i.e. homeless people, addicts) can be particularly troublesome and may lead to dehumanizing these extreme out-groups. Functional MRI's were used to examine brain activation in study participants that were shown photographs of social groups and objects. The researchers found increased neural activation to all images of social groups except extreme out-groups, supporting the prediction that extreme out-groups may be seen as less than human. Harris, L. T., & Fiske, S. T. (2006). Dehumanizing the lowest of the low neuroimaging responses to extreme out-groups. *Psychological Science*, *17*(10), 847-853.

Recognizing Individuality. Social groups that elicit disgust are differentially processed in mPFC Social neuroscience suggests a decreased activation in the medial pre-frontal cortex (mPFC) to members of extreme outgroups that elicit disgust. Study participants were instructed to either make superficial categorical age estimations (e.g. broad generalizations) or individuating food-preference judgments (i.e. whether the social group member likes carrots) about people as fMRI recorded neural activity.

This study demonstrates that being instructed to see extreme out-groups through an individualistic lens as opposed to making superficial categorical judgments may lead to increased social cognition (demonstrated by increased activation in the mPFC) and help one see extreme out-group members as more similar to oneself - thereby increasing a sense of common humanity. Harris, L. T., & Fiske, S. T. (2007). Social groups that elicit disgust are differentially processed in mPFC. *Social cognitive and affective neuroscience*, *2*(1), 45-51.

Consider Others. The danger in adopting dehumanizing perceptions, research suggests, is a failure to consider the mind of another person, which, in turn, may facilitate inhumane acts like torture. Harris, L. T., & Fiske, S. T. (2011). Dehumanized perception: A psychological means to facilitate atrocities, torture, and genocide?. *Zeitschrift für Psychologie/Journal of Psychology*, *219*(3), 175.

GUIDED SELF-COMPASSION MEDITATIONS

Follow this link to Dr. Kristen Neff's website for a series of guided self-compassion meditations: www.self-compassion.org/guided-self-compassion-meditations-mp3

Go to Dr. Kristen Neff's website to test how self-compassionate you are: www.self-compassion.org/test-your-self-compassion-level

FOUR STEPS TO SELF-COMPASSION

The curious paradox is that when I accept myself just as I am, then I can change.
-Carl Rogers

Self-Compassion is the ability to hold one's feelings of suffering with a sense of warmth, connection, and concern. It includes self-kindness, common humanity, and mindfulness directed at oneself. This method can be applied both when dealing with residual distress as well as excruciatingly painful states.

FOUR STEPS TO SELF-COMPASSION

1. Feel into the Emotion.
2. Find the Positive Wish.
3. Replace Self-Critical Self-Talk with Kind Self-Talk.
4. Recognize the Universality of Difficulty.

STEP 1: FEEL INTO THE EMOTION

Bring increased awareness and presence to the physical sensations and emotional pain associated with the emotional experience. Acknowledge to yourself that you are experiencing discomfort or pain. Spend a moment feeling the physical sensations.

STEP 2: FIND YOUR POSITIVE WISH

Identify your unfulfilled desire or positive wish. Listen to what the emotion is telling you about what is important. Under most emotional reactions is an unfulfilled desire or a positive wish for something. Sometimes there is something deeply of value that is being protected or defended. The stronger the emotion the more coveted this underlying wish or desire tends to be. Uncovering the unfulfilled desire or positive wish can both change the intensity of the emotion as well as lead to effective solution finding or problem solving. Ask yourself:

"What is my underlying positive wish or unfulfilled desire in this situation?"

"What is of deep value in this situation that my emotional self is desperately trying to protect?"

Dig deeper to find the source of distressful emotions and strong reactions. Look for a threat that has the power to elicit a significant charge for you. Ask one of the following questions:

- *What am I deeply needing here? Do I need connection, acceptance, reassurance, or respect?*
- *What is it that I deeply cherish and feels threatened?*
- *What part of me or my dreams am I trying to protect?*

For example: In a minor annoyance like being in a long check-out line, the positive wish might be to get your errand done quickly so that you can get home to relax after a long work day. Your positive wish is to relax. The long line interferes with your ability to get home and relax.

For example: In relationship challenges, negative emotions might signal an unfulfilled desire for love, acceptance or companionship.

Honor the Emotion. The emotion is coming from your survival instinct. It has a role and is "trying to do its job." Honor these emotions. Understanding emotions as natural instincts can invite self-forgiveness for feeling unwanted emotions. This stance is less judgmental; therefore, there is less resistance to the emotions.

Thank your "inner warrior."

Your negative emotions are trying to keep you and your dreams safe. They are like "inner warriors" or "silent guardians" that are watching out for you. Negative emotions are trying to help you out. Their job is to alert and help you respond to trouble, imminent danger, and impending problems. They do their job with tough love. Just like a parent drawing a hard line with a wayward teenager, negative emotions remove the kid gloves and get serious. They use pain to wake us up and ensure we pay attention to their message. Paradoxically, this is an act of self-love.

Non-judgment. When you identify the positive wish, essentially you are validating the distressing emotion. In other words, it becomes understandable. This removes the judgment that it is "wrong" or "bad" to be feeling the way you do. It is this judgment that adds fuel to the fire of distressing emotions. There can be a tendency to judge distressing emotions as bad or unacceptable. Judging them as "bad," "wrong" or "weak" is a form of resisting emotions. Underlying judgment is an implicit demand that they go away. It is a variation on struggling with the emotion. This worsens the feeling of the emotion. Essentially it is dog-piling distressing emotions on top of distressing emotions.

STEP 3: REPLACE SELF-CRITICISM WITH KIND SELF-TALK

Catch negative self-talk and replace with less judgmental, more understanding self-talk. Oftentimes we go into harsh self-criticism when we have made mistakes or are in unwanted circumstances. You might imagine what you would say to a good friend or a child undergoing a difficult situation. Often people are more understanding with others than to themselves.

Self-criticism is sometimes a mechanism used in an attempt to motivate oneself to achieve a challenging outcome. Although self-criticism is often well-intended, it generally leads to negative rather than positive consequences, undermining confidence, self-care, and perspective. What's more effective—the carrot or the stick? Consider if critical self-talk is effective. If it's not, replace it with self-compassion.

Ways To Be Kind Rather Than Critical:

- When something painful happens, try to take a balanced view of the situation.

- When you fail at something important to you, try to keep things in perspective.

- Try to be understanding and patient toward those aspects of your personality that you don't like.

- Try to be less judgmental of your own perceived flaws and inadequacies.

- When going through difficult times, give yourself the caring, tenderness, and understanding.

- Do a self-compassion meditation.

STEP 4: RECOGNIZE THE UNIVERSALITY OF DIFFICULTY

Suffering such as disappointment, frustration, and other negative states are universal human experiences. Simply acknowledging that we are not alone can provide relief and normalize the experience.

For example:

- Try to see your failings as part of the human condition.

- When feeling down, bring to mind someone else who may be or has felt in a similar way.

- When feeling inadequate, lonely, or other negative emotions, remind yourself that these feelings are felt by most people.

SELF-COMPASSION WORKSHEET

Compassion powerfully transforms suffering and distress and often giving a moment of relief. When in the throws of negative emotion, direct some gentle compassion toward yourself like you would to a child, an animal, a friend or loved one if they were in pain. Often we are more compassionate to others than we are to ourselves.

DIFFICULT SITUATION

Describe a difficult situation when you felt painful emotions, and you'd like to direct compassion.

_____
_____
_____
_____
_____

DIRECT COMPASSION TOWARDS YOURSELF

STEP 1: FEEL INTO THE EMOTION. What are the physical sensations of this difficulty?

_____
_____
_____
_____
_____
_____

STEP 2: FIND POSITIVE WISH. Ask yourself, "What is my underlying positive wish or unfulfilled desire in this situation?" Or, "What is of deep value in this situation that my being is desperately trying to protect?" Look more deeply your positive wish or unfulfilled desire. Sometimes there is something deeply valuable that we are protecting.

Identify the unfulfilled desire or positive wish. What is my positive wish or unfulfilled desire?

_____
_____
_____
_____
_____
_____

SELF-COMPASSION WORKSHEET

Honor Difficult Emotions. How are these emotions "trying" to protect me?

_____
_____
_____
_____
_____
_____
_____

STEP 3: REPLACE SELF-CRITICISM WITH KIND SELF-TALK. How can I use self-care when dealing with this difficulty? How can I replace self-criticism and negative judgments with gentle, understanding self-talk?

_____
_____
_____
_____
_____
_____
_____
_____
_____
_____
_____

STEP 4: RECOGNIZE THE UNIVERSALITY OF DIFFICULTY. Disappointment, making mistakes, and suffering are universal human experiences. How do I observe others experiencing similar difficulties?

_____
_____
_____
_____
_____
_____
_____

SELF-COMPASSION TRACKING LOG

DAY	APPLICATION What difficult situation did I encounter? How did I direct compassion to myself?	IMPACT What was the impact of directing self-compassion on my bodily state, emotional state, mental state, or actions?
Day 1		
Day 2		
Day 3		
Day 4		

SELF-COMPASSION TRACKING LOG

DAY	APPLICATION What difficult situation did I encounter? How did I direct compassion to myself?	IMPACT What was the impact of directing self-compassion on my bodily state, emotional state, mental state, or actions?
Day 5		
Day 6		
Day 7		

INSIGHTS - What patterns or benefits emerged?

_____
_____
_____
_____
_____

SELF-COMPASSION MEDITATION

Compassion happens at verbal and nonverbal levels. Both are important. Below is a Low Road technique for increasing self-compassion.

INSTRUCTIONS
(2 to 3 minutes)

1. FOCUS INWARD: Breathe and Center

- **Close your eyes**— Close your eyes to let your attention turn inward.

- **Feel Your Breath**—Focus attention by feeling your breath enter and exit your body. Breathe deeply with a slower exhale and natural inhale. Place your hand on your abdomen to feel your diaphragm rise and fall.

- **Set your Intention**---To direct your attention in this time, place, and to the objective of this meditation.

2. DIRECT ATTENTION: Direct compassion to yourself—Validate your pain: distressing emotions are designed to cause suffering.

- Imagine seeing yourself from above sitting here experiencing difficulty.

- Direct warmth and comfort to yourself.

- Say to yourself, *"May I have relief from suffering, be free from pain; may I have peace, contentment, joy."*

- With the in-breath, visualize filling your body with wellness, happiness, vitality, joy, health, and goodness.

3. REFLECT ON INSIGHTS: Breathe and Reflect

- Come back to your breath.

- Reflect on the insights or benefits you gained during this meditation.

4. MAINTAIN YOUR INNER AWARENESS: Soft Gaze and Stay with It

- Slowly open your eyes and keep your gaze soft, directed downward, and settling on a neutral object.

- Stay with the awareness you gained during the meditation.

SELF-COMPASSION MEDITATION WORKSHEET

After you have completed the meditation, jot down observations about what came up during your meditation. Make note of thoughts you had, feelings you experienced, bodily sensations you felt, and/or detours that you took.

1. FOCUS INWARD: Were you able to concentrate inward and turn your attention to the intention you set for this meditation?

_____
_____
_____
_____
_____
_____
_____

2. DIRECT ATTENTION: Direct compassion. What was it like to direct compassion to yourself?

_____
_____
_____
_____
_____
_____
_____

3. REFLECT ON INSIGHTS: What insights or benefits did you gain during the meditation?

_____
_____
_____
_____
_____

4. When to use this meditation. When do you think this meditation would be useful to use?

_____
_____
_____
_____
_____

SELF-COMPASSION MEDITATION TRACKING LOG

DAY	APPLICATION What was the difficult situation or emotion? How did I direct compassion?	IMPACT What was the impact of the meditation on my bodily state, emotional state, mental state, or actions?
Day 1		
Day 2		
Day 3		
Day 4		

SELF-COMPASSION MEDITATION TRACKING LOG

DAY	APPLICATION What was the difficult situation or emotion? How did I direct compassion?	IMPACT What was the impact of the meditation on my bodily state, emotional state, mental state, or actions?
Day 5		
Day 6		
Day 7		

INSIGHTS - What patterns or benefits emerged?

_____
_____
_____
_____
_____

COACHING GUIDELINES

Use the self-coaching process and coaching tools to create long-term change. For maximum effectiveness, focus on one skill at a time. For each skill, take an *assessment* if one is available, complete a *coaching worksheet*, practice high road and low road techniques, and track your application of the skill over a seven day period using a *Tracking Log*.

Select one skill. Consider which skill would make the greatest difference in your current life circumstances if you used it more frequently and effectively. It is easier to build new habits if you focus on one change at a time. Select the *one skill* in this chapter that is your highest priority:

- Let Go of Perfect
- Tell Hero Stories
- Self-Compassion

STEP 1. ASSESS. Assess the need and benefits of practicing this particular skill. Assess your current mastery level of the skill. Use one of the on-line assessment tools if one is available for the skill. The Coaching Worksheet will also help you assess your need and benefits of using the skill.

Assessments—Questionnaires that assess your current skill level and provide data on your progress.

STEP 2. PLAN. To create an action plan, understand how a technique can help you build greater mastery of a skill. Next, consider how you can apply it to your own situations.

Coaching Worksheets—Tools for learning and creating an action plan for practicing the techniques.

- Let Go of Perfect Worksheet
- Hero Story Worksheet
- Self-Compassion Worksheet

STEP 3. PRACTICE. During the following seven days, apply the skill daily. Use both the High Road techniques and the Low Road techniques to practice the skill.

Tracking Logs—Habit forming tools to guide your efforts as you practice the techniques for seven days.

- Let Go of Perfect Tracking Log
- Heroic Acts Tracking Log
- Self-Compassion Tracking Log

- Resilience Meditation Tracking Log
- Self-Compassion Meditation Tracking Log

Meditation Guides—Low Road techniques to build the skill at the emotional or non-verbal level.

- Resilience Meditation
- Self-Compassion Meditation

STEP 4. TRACK RESULTS. In addition to systematically helping you to practice the techniques, *Tracking Logs* provide a place to note the impact of the skill on your experience. Tracking Logs help you become more aware of behaviors and patterns in yourself. They are a source of feedback so you can modify a technique to make it more effective.

MINDFUL LEADERSHIP SELF-ASSESSMENT

NAME: _____ DATE: _____

Mindful Leadership is about being aware in your everyday life and in your work. It is being more self-aware of what you are thinking, feeling and doing; more observant of what is going on around you; more focused on the positive and possible; more intentional about your emotions, feelings, thoughts, and behaviors; more observant of your impact on others; and more thoughtful about your relationship strategies. This informal self-assessment tool is designed to assist you to become more familiar with the qualities of mindful leadership. It can also provide you with a way to measure your progress in developing the qualities of mindful leadership.

Instructions: Below is a collection of statements about your everyday use of mindful leadership skills. Using the 1-7 scale below, please indicate how frequently or infrequently you currently use the skill. Please answer according to what your are really doing rather than what you think you should be doing. This will help you get a more accurate current assessment. Please treat each item separately from every other item.

RATING SCALE

1	2	3	4	5	6	7
Never	Almost Never	Very Infrequently	Somewhat Infrequently	Somewhat Frequently	Very Frequently	Almost Always

AWARENESS IN THE MOMENT

1. I am self-aware of what I am thinking, feeling, and doing.   1 2 3 4 5 6 7
2. I am aware of what is going on around me.   1 2 3 4 5 6 7
3. I tune in to the present, and can eliminate mental chatter.   1 2 3 4 5 6 7
4. I tune in to others without being distracted.   1 2 3 4 5 6 7
5. I take time to savor the moment and my experiences.   1 2 3 4 5 6 7
6. I listen for information and for emotions.   1 2 3 4 5 6 7
7. I practice global listening.   1 2 3 4 5 6 7
6. I find out what are the real facts before I make judgments.   1 2 3 4 5 6 7

POSITIVITY & POSSIBILITY

7. I focus more on the positive than on the negative.   1 2 3 4 5 6 7
8. I focus on the possible rather than the impossible.   1 2 3 4 5 6 7
9. I look for risks, dangers, and downsides, but practice the discipline of thinking in terms of the probabilities, options, and opportunities.   1 2 3 4 5 6 7
10. I use positivity and positive emotions to broaden and build my awareness and to encourage novel thoughts and actions.   1 2 3 4 5 6 7
11. I challenge my fears and stimulate productive planning by asking myself: HOW can I?   1 2 3 4 5 6 7

POSITIVE RELATIONSHIPS

12. I am aware of the power and importance of positive relationships.   1 2 3 4 5 6 7
13. I endeavor to make personal and professional connections with others.   1 2 3 4 5 6 7
14. I put conscious time and effort into development of positive networks.   1 2 3 4 5 6 7
15. I cultivate my ability to understand and share the feelings of another.   1 2 3 4 5 6 7

16.	I engage in deep conversations with others.	1	2	3	4	5	6	7
17.	I look for ways to craft win-win solutions with others.	1	2	3	4	5	6	7
18.	I strive to avoid negative conflict escalators (criticism, defensiveness, stonewalling, contempt) that thwart communication and cooperation.	1	2	3	4	5	6	7
19.	I attempt to direct disagreement and conflict toward positive outcomes that build on the insights gained from the conflict.	1	2	3	4	5	6	7
AUTHENTICITY & INTEGRITY								
20.	My behaviors are consistent with my intentions and my commitments.	1	2	3	4	5	6	7
21.	I have strong moral principles and I live by those principles.	1	2	3	4	5	6	7
22.	I am clear on my values and my behaviors are consistent with my values.	1	2	3	4	5	6	7
23.	I am clear on my priorities and my behaviors are consistent with my priorities.	1	2	3	4	5	6	7
24.	I am aware of my strengths and weaknesses.	1	2	3	4	5	6	7
25.	I deliberately organize my work to leverage my strengths.	1	2	3	4	5	6	7
26.	I am aware of the strengths and weaknesses of my associates and team members.	1	2	3	4	5	6	7
27.	I deliberately look for ways to leverage the strengths of my associates and team members.	1	2	3	4	5	6	7
MANAGE STRESS & ENERGY								
28.	I purposely manage my stress and energy in order to maintain high levels of physical, mental, and emotional well-being.	1	2	3	4	5	6	7
29.	I consciously monitor and manage my stress.	1	2	3	4	5	6	7
30.	I consciously monitor and manage my energy.	1	2	3	4	5	6	7
31.	I use healthy techniques to manage my stress and use them every day.	1	2	3	4	5	6	7
32.	I challenge my thoughts to stay in touch with reality and reduce stress.	1	2	3	4	5	6	7
33.	I identify my emotions and emotional triggers, and intentionally manage my responses.	1	2	3	4	5	6	7
RESILIENCE								
34.	I let go of perfectionism and cultivate satisfaction.	1	2	3	4	5	6	7
35.	I focus on positives and potential rather than shortcomings and failures.	1	2	3	4	5	6	7
36.	I focus on the heroic aspects of dealing with the adversities and setbacks in my life.	1	2	3	4	5	6	7
37.	I practice compassion for others.	1	2	3	4	5	6	7
38.	I practice self-compassion for myself.	1	2	3	4	5	6	7

POSITIVE PSYCHOLOGY AND THE KEYS TO SUSTAINABLE HAPPINESS
Stanford University

Positive psychology research has demonstrated that sustainable happiness is based on a skill set that can be learned. This course sequence assists students to gain mastery in these valuable skills.

• *Choosing Happiness* provides a science-based action plan for enhancing sustainable happiness.

• *Enhancing Emotional Intelligence* focuses on building fundamental personal and interpersonal skills for happiness and success.

• *Thriving at Work: Science-Based Practices To Elevate Success & Fulfillment* applies the skills of positive psychology to the workplace.

• *Mindfulness* focuses on cultivating mindfulness as a way of being, and as a powerful tool in daily life.

CHOOSING HAPPINESS
THRIVE: SELF-COACHING FOR HAPPINESS ® AND SUCCESS

Happy people don't just feel better—they do better than less-happy individuals. Research shows they achieve greater success and wealth, are healthier, are more altruistic, and have more satisfying relationships. The keys to happiness are within everyone's reach—because the keys are actually habits. In this course, students learn happiness-enhancing habits that will help them improve responses to stress and opportunities at work, at home, and in relationships. The tools presented are derived from research in the innovative field of positive psychology, the science of well-being.

The course workbook is focused on *The Habits of Happiness*. The workbook is written for this course and includes case examples, summaries of scientific findings, action plans, and weekly practices. Students apply these principles to their daily personal and professional lives and engage in class discussions, mindfulness practices, and experiential exercises.

This course is part of a series in applied positive psychology, which also includes the courses Enhancing Emotional Intelligence, Thriving at Work, and Mindfulness. The series is designed to help students build a comprehensive skill set in sustainable happiness. While these courses build upon one another, each course can be taken independently as well.

ENHANCING EMOTIONAL INTELLIGENCE
MINDFULNESS BASED STRATEGIES FOR HAPPINESS AND SUCCESS

What is the skill set underlying happiness, success, and overall well-being? Research shows that emotional intelligence, which is defined as being self aware and skillful in managing emotions, leads to benefits in a variety of life domains. Emotionally intelligent people tend to have satisfying relationships, manage stress well, and excel in school and at work. Emotional intelligence predicts professional success more than IQ or experience. It is related to confidence, charisma, optimism, and resiliency. Most important, emotional intelligence can be learned.

The aim of this introductory course is to help students assess and build the skills of emotional intelligence. Students improve their ability to understand and manage emotions, change counterproductive thinking patterns, and leverage strengths. Everyone receives a workbook, written for this course by the instructors, on how to build and apply these skills at work, at home, and in relationships. Activities include self-assessment, experiential exercises, mindfulness practices, and working with personal scenarios.

This course is part of a series in applied positive psychology, which also includes the courses Choosing Happiness, Thriving at Work, and Mindfulness. The series is designed to help students build a comprehensive skill set in sustainable happiness. While these courses build upon one another, each course can be taken independently as well.

THRIVING AT WORK
SCIENCE-BASED PRACTICES TO INCREASE SUCCESS & FULFILLMENT AT WORK

Thirty years of Gallup surveys have found that the most successful companies are ones whose employees believe they get to do what they do best every day. (Only one-third of working people do.) A decade of research suggests that happiness at work—defined as pleasure, engagement, and a sense of meaning—can improve productivity, revenue, profitability, staff retention, customer loyalty, and workplace safety. Many of the studies are preliminary, but they strongly suggest that positive emotions, positive relationships, inspiration, and resilience increase creativity and problem-solving ability and aid in fighting negative stress.

People can take control of certain behaviors and habits of mind that will make them happier and more productive at work. They can focus on positive outcomes, listen mindfully, communicate authentically, leverage their strengths, and live their values. They can add gratitude, hope, and a dose of self-control to each working day. They can challenge their negative perceptions, thoughts, and emotions. They can learn to apply the power of realistic optimism. And it's clear that happy bosses perform measurably better, building productive teams and inspiring loyalty. This course is one in a series in applied positive psychology, which also includes the courses Choosing Happiness, Enhancing Emotional Intelligence, and Mindfulness. While these courses build upon one another, each course can be taken independently as well.

MINDFULNESS
SCIENCE-BASED STRATEGIES TO THRIVE AT WORK AND IN LIFE

Research demonstrates that mindful people enjoy many advantages in wellbeing, vitality, and success. Mindfulness is especially relevant in our fast-paced era with increased demands on attention, productivity, innovation, and energy. This course focuses on cultivating mindfulness as a way of being, and as a powerful tool to use in daily life.

While mindfulness is growing in popularity, its definitions differ significantly. We define mindfulness as a mental state characterized by being present, noticing new information, and revising mindsets. Based on the research of Harvard psychologist Ellen Langer, our approach blends traditional and modern views of mindfulness.

We expand on traditional views of mindfulness and include techniques for challenging mindsets, for considering multiple perspectives, and for systematically applying mindfulness in the workplace, in relationships, and in personal well-being and health.

We also explore mindfulness through a modern lens, and employ skill-building techniques that include but are not limited to meditation. Participants engage in interactive exercises, in-class paired discussions, home practice, meditations, and reflective exercises. The interactive, practical exercises help participants relate differently to experiences, and to see circumstances, themselves, and others more objectively and clearly.

Course Instructors

Laura Delizonna, PhD.
&
Ted Anstedt, CEO

Made in the USA
Coppell, TX
08 June 2021